TOP 10

OF EVERYTHING
2003

TOP 10
OF EVERYTHING
2003
RUSSELL ASH

DK Publishing

Contents

LONDON, NEW YORK, MUNICH, MELBOURNE, DELHI
A PENGUIN COMPANY

Senior Editor Nicki Lampon
Senior Art Editor Kevin Ryan
US Editor Margaret Parrish
DTP Designers Sonia Charbonnier,
Rajen Shah
Production Heather Hughes
Picture Research Anna Grapes

Managing Editor Sharon Lucas
Managing Art Editor
Marianne Markham
Category Publisher Stephanie Jackson

Produced for Dorling Kindersley by
Cooling Brown Ltd.,
9–11 High Street,
Hampton, Middlesex TW12 2SA

Editor Alex Edmonds
Art Editor Elaine Hewson
Designers Elly King, Tessa Sanders-Barwick

Author's Project Manager Aylla Macphail

Published in the United States by
Dorling Kindersley Publishing Inc.
95 Madison Avenue, New York, New York 10016

First American Edition 2002
2 4 6 8 10 9 7 5 3 1

Dorling Kindersley books are available at special discounts for bulk purchases for sales promotions or premiums. Special editions, including personalized covers, excerpts of existing guides, and corporate imprints can be created in large quantities for specific needs. For more information, contact Special Markets Dept./Dorling Kindersley Publishing, Inc./95 Madison Ave./New York, NY 10016/Fax: 800-600-9098.

ISBN 0-7894-8917-1

Reproduction by Colourscan, Singapore
Printed and bound by GGP Media GmbH, Germany

See our complete catalogue at
www.dk.com

Introduction

LIVING WITH LISTS

The heroine of the book, *Bridget Jones's Diary,* concludes her list of New Year's resolutions with "Stop making lists." But who can? Lists have become a method of organizing and understanding our complicated lives. Those in *The Top 10 of Everything* provide a shorthand way of presenting what might otherwise be an impenetrable mass of data and figures.

EVOLUTION

This, the 14th annual edition of *The Top 10 of Everything*, introduces an exciting fresh design and stunning pictures to enhance its many new lists. A year is a long time in the life of a list, and many change dramatically between editions – compare the highest-earning film lists of 2003 with those of previous editions and you'll see how chameleonlike the film industry is.

MADE TO MEASURE

All the Top 10 lists here are strictly quantifiable – there are no "bests" other than bestsellers, as with books and albums, which can be measured by sales. Top 10 film lists, such as those of stars, directors, or studios, or those of a special genre, are based on global box office earnings. Some of this information is confidential, and while we cannot publish the precise figures, we are able to rank entries based on it, thus indicating the relative measure of success.

FIRSTS & LASTS

The innovative First and Last boxes feature such "firsts" as the first public performance by the Beatles, as well as numerous 2003 anniversaries. Centenaries of events of the year 1903 are especially notable. This was a year of major breakthroughs – not simply because it saw such advances as the first electrocardiogram. It was also the year that gave us the first fax, film star, and transatlantic broadcast – and even the first decaffeinated coffee.

A TOP 10 CHALLENGE

As ever, *The Top 10 of Everything* would not be possible without the input of the many experts and specialized organizations that supply information. Their contribution is credited either on the lists or in the acknowledgments on page 286. Some lists remain elusive, however, and any suggestions for other unusual or obscure lists would be welcomed. I try to respond to all the letters and emails from readers, many of which contain helpful suggestions. So if you have any list ideas or comments, please write to me c/o the publishers or email me directly at ash@pavilion.co.uk.

Other recent Dorling Kindersley books by Russell Ash:
The Top 10 of Sports (with Ian Morrison)
The Factastic Book of 1,001 Lists
The Factastic Book of Comparisons
Great Wonders of the World

SPECIAL FEATURES

• More than 800 lists containing comprehensive Top 10 facts on wide-ranging subjects – from art and architecture to zoology.

• New First or Last features reveal surprising facts from 100 years ago and major firsts or lasts in world history.

• Additional text on some lists reveals the stories behind the lists, including background information that brings the list entries to life and explains how they were compiled.

THE UNIVERSE & THE EARTH

TOP 10 | COMETS COMING CLOSEST TO THE EARTH

COMET	DATE*	(AU)#	DISTANCE (MILES)	(KM)
1 Comet of 1491	Feb 20, 1491	0.0094	873,784	1,406,220
2 Lexell	Jul 1, 1770	0.0151	1,403,633	2,258,928
3 Tempel-Tuttle	Oct 26, 1366	0.0229	2,128,688	3,425,791
4 IRAS-Araki-Alcock	May 11, 1983	0.0313	2,909,516	4,682,413
5 Halley	Apr 10, 837	0.0334	3,104,724	4,996,569
6 Biela	Dec 9, 1805	0.0366	3,402,182	5,475,282
7 Grischow	Feb 8, 1743	0.0390	3,625,276	5,834,317
8 Pons-Winnecke	Jun 26, 1927	0.0394	3,662,458	5,894,156
9 Comet of 1014	Feb 24, 1014	0.0407	3,783,301	6,088,633
10 La Hire	Apr 20, 1702	0.0437	4,062,168	6,537,427

* Of closest approach to the Earth

\# Astronomical Units: 1AU = mean distance from the Earth to the Sun (92,955,793 miles/149,597,870 km)

TOP 10 | LARGEST BODIES IN THE SOLAR SYSTEM

BODY	MAXIMUM DIAMETER (MILES)	(KM)
1 Sun	865,036	1,392,140
2 Jupiter	88,846	142,984
3 Saturn	74,898	120,536
4 Uranus	31,763	51,118
5 Neptune	30,778	49,532
6 Earth	7,926	12,756
7 Venus	7,520	12,103
8 Mars	4,222	6,794
9 Ganymede	3,274	5,269
10 Titan	3,200	5,150

Most of the planets are visible to the naked eye and have been studied since ancient times. The exceptions are Uranus, discovered on March 13, 1781, by British astronomer Sir William Herschel; Neptune, found by German astronomer Johann Galle, who announced his discovery on September 23, 1846; and Pluto, found by American astronomer Clyde Tombaugh on March 13, 1930.

DAVIDA FIRST OBSERVED

FIRST OR LAST

THE RATE OF ASTEROID DISCOVERIES increased dramatically after 1890, when Max Wolf of Heidelberg Observatory introduced astronomical photography. This breakthrough made searches for asteroids much faster. Davida was first seen from Heidelberg on May 30, 1903, by American astronomer Raymond Smith Dugan (1878–1940). The seventh largest asteroid to be discovered, it was one of 16 located by Heidelberg between 1902 and 1904. The 511th to be found, Davida was named after David Peck Todd (1855–1939), director of Amhurst College Observatory. Dugan himself has a crater named after him on the Moon.

TOP 10 | LARGEST ASTEROIDS

NAME	YEAR DISCOVERED	DIAMETER (MILES)	(KM)
1 Ceres	1801	582	936
2 Pallas	1802	377	607
3 Vesta	1807	322	519
4 Hygeia	1849	279	450
5 Euphrosyne	1854	229	370
6 Interamnia	1910	217	349
7 Davida	1903	200	322
8 Cybele	1861	192	308
9 Europa	1858	179	288
10 Patientia	1899	171	275

It is thought that, on average, one asteroid larger than ¼ mile (0.4 km) hits the Earth every 50,000 years. A huge asteroid crash-landed on Earth 65 million years ago. Some people believe that this was what destroyed the dinosaurs.

TOP 10 | LARGEST PLANETARY MOONS

MOON	PLANET	DIAMETER (MILES)	(KM)
1 Ganymede	Jupiter	3,274	5,269
2 Titan	Saturn	3,200	5,150
3 Callisto	Jupiter	2,986	4,806
4 Io	Jupiter	2,263	3,642
5 Moon	Earth	2,159	3,475
6 Europa	Jupiter	1,945	3,130
7 Triton	Neptune	1,680	2,704
8 Titania	Uranus	980	1,578
9 Rhea	Saturn	949	1,528
10 Oberon	Uranus	946	1,522

The Largest Moon in the Solar System
One of Jupiter's 16 satellites, Ganymede was discovered by the Italian astronomer Galileo on January 7, 1610, using his newly invented telescope. Named after the Moon's original discoverer, NASA's Galileo probe reached Ganymede in June 1996, after a 7-year journey.

TOP 10 | GALAXIES NEAREST TO THE EARTH

	GALAXY	DISTANCE (LIGHT-YEARS)
1	Large Cloud of Magellan	169,000
2	Small Cloud of Magellan	190,000
3	Ursa Minor dwarf	250,000
4	Draco dwarf	260,000
5	Sculptor dwarf	280,000
6	Fornax dwarf	420,000
7	Leo I dwarf	750,000
=	Leo II dwarf	750,000
9	Barnard's Galaxy	1,700,000
10	Andromeda Spiral	2,200,000

By Jupiter!
The fifth planet from the Sun, Jupiter contains more matter than that of all the other eight planets combined, so is therefore the most massive planet in the solar system.

TOP 10 | LARGEST METEORITES FOUND IN THE US

	SITE	PRESENT LOCATION	ESTIMATED WEIGHT (TONS)
1	Canyon Diablo*, Arizona	Various	33.1
2	Willamette, Oregon	American Museum of Natural History, New York, NY	16.5
3	Old Woman, California	Desert Discovery Center, Barstow, CA	3.0
4	Brenham, Kansas	UCLA/American Meteorite Society	2.6
5	Navajo, Arizona	University of New Mexico, Albuquerque, NM	2.4
6	Quinn Canyon, Nevada	Field Museum, Chicago, IL	1.6
7	Goose Lake, California	American Museum of Natural History, New York, NY	1.3
8	Norton County, Kansas	University of New Mexico, Albuquerque, NM	1.1
9	Tucson, Arizona	Smithsonian Institution, Washington, DC	1.0
10	Sardis#, Georgia	National Museum of Natural History, Washington, DC†	0.9

* Formed meteor crater; fragmented – total in public collections c.12.7 tons

Now badly corroded

† Small pieces also in museums in Chicago, Perth, Moscow, Calcutta, and London

TOP 10 | STARS NEAREST TO THE EARTH*

	STAR	DISTANCE (LIGHT-YEARS)	DISTANCE MILES (MILLIONS)	DISTANCE KM (MILLIONS)
1	Proxima Centauri	4.22	24,792,500	39,923,310
2	Alpha Centauri	4.35	25,556,250	41,153,175
3	Barnard's Star	5.98	35,132,500	56,573,790
4	Wolf 359	7.75	45,531,250	73,318,875
5	Lalande 21185	8.22	48,292,500	77,765,310
6	Luyten 726-8	8.43	49,526,250	79,752,015
7	Sirius	8.65	50,818,750	81,833,325
8	Ross 154	9.45	55,518,750	89,401,725
9	Ross 248	10.40	61,100,000	98,389,200
10	Epsilon Eridani	10.80	63,450,000	102,173,400

* Excluding the Sun

A spaceship traveling at 25,000 mph (40,237 km/h) – which is faster than any human has yet traveled in space – would take more than 113,200 years to reach the Earth's closest star, Proxima Centauri.

Journeys into Space

THE 10 FIRST BODIES TO HAVE BEEN VISITED BY SPACECRAFT

	BODY	SPACECRAFT/COUNTRY	DATE
1	Moon	Luna 1, USSR	Jan 2, 1959
2	Venus	Venera 1, USSR	May 19, 1961
3	Sun	Pioneer 5, US	Aug 10, 1961
4	Mars	Mariner 4, US	Jul 14, 1965
5	Jupiter	Pioneer 10, US	Dec 3, 1973
6	Mercury	Mariner 10, US	Mar 29, 1974
7	Saturn	Pioneer 11, US	Sep 1, 1979
8	Comet Giacobini-Zinner	International Sun-Earth Explorer 3 (International Cometary Explorer), Europe/US	Sep 11, 1985
9	Uranus	Voyager 2, US	Jan 30, 1986
10	Halley's Comet	Vega 1, USSR	Mar 6, 1986

Only the first spacecraft successfully to approach or land on each body is included. Several of the bodies listed have since been visited on subsequent occasions, either by fly-bys, orbiters, or landers. Other bodies also visited since the 10 first include Neptune (by Voyager 2, US, 1989) and asteroids Gaspra (by Galileo, US/Europe, 1991) and Hyakutake (by NEAR, US, 1996).

Moon Machine
The Soviet Luna 9 was the first spacecraft to achieve a soft landing on the Moon and transmit photographs back to the Earth. It sent back striking panoramic views of the lunar landscape.

THE 10 FIRST UNMANNED MOON LANDINGS

	NAME	COUNTRY	DATE (LAUNCH/IMPACT)
1	Lunik 2	USSR	Sep 12/14, 1959
2	Ranger 4*	US	Apr 23/26, 1962
3	Ranger 6	US	Jan 30/Feb 2, 1964
4	Ranger 7	US	Jul 28/31, 1964
5	Ranger 8	US	Feb 17/20, 1965
6	Ranger 9	US	Mar 21/24, 1965
7	Luna 5*	USSR	May 9/12, 1965
8	Luna 7*	USSR	Oct 4/8, 1965
9	Luna 8*	USSR	Dec 3/7, 1965
10	Luna 9	USSR	Jan 31/Feb 3, 1966

* Crash-landed

TOP 10 LONGEST SPACE SHUTTLE FLIGHTS *

	SHUTTLE	DATES	DURATION OF FLIGHT (DAYS)	(HR)	(MIN)	(SEC)
1	STS-80 Columbia	Nov 19–Dec 7, 1996	17	08	53	18
2	STS-78 Columbia	Jun 20–Jul 7, 1996	16	21	48	30
3	STS-67 Endeavor	Mar 2–18, 1995	16	15	09	46
4	STS-73 Columbia	Oct 20–Nov 5, 1995	15	21	53	16
5	STS-90 Columbia	Apr 17–May 3, 1998	15	21	15	58
6	STS-75 Columbia	Feb 22–Mar 9, 1996	15	17	41	25
7	STS-94 Columbia	Jul 1–17, 1997	15	16	46	01
8	STS-87 Atlantis	Sep 25–Oct 6, 1997	15	16	35	01
9	STS-65 Columbia	Jul 8–23, 1994	14	17	55	00
10	STS-58 Columbia	Oct 18–Nov 1, 1993	14	00	12	32

* Up to January 1, 2001

THE 10 FIRST ASTRONOMICAL SATELLITES *

	SATELLITE/COUNTRY/PURPOSE	LAUNCH DATE
1	**Ariel 1,** UK Investigating solar UV and X-radiation.	Apr 26, 1962
2	**Ariel 2I,** UK Radio astronomy.	Mar 27, 1964
3	**Orbiting Astronomical Observatory (OAO) 1,** US Active for only three days.	Apr 8, 1966
4	**Ariel 3,** UK Radio astronomy.	May 5, 1967
5	**Explorer 38,** US Radio astronomy. Discovered the Earth's radio radiation.	Jul 4, 1968
6	**OAO 2,** US 11 UV telescopes, discovered a supernova.	Dec 7, 1968
7	**Explorer 42 (Uhuru),** US First X-ray satellite observatory	.Dec 12, 1970
8	**Ariel 4,** UK Radio astronomy.	Dec 11, 1971
9	**TD-1A,** Europe Equipped with UV, X-ray, and Gamma-ray instruments.	Mar 12, 1972
10	**OAO 3 (Copernicus),** US 31 in (80 cm) UV telescope.	Aug 21, 1972

* Excludes planetary probes and solar research probes

THE 10 | FIRST PLANETARY PROBES

	PROBE	COUNTRY	PLANET	ARRIVAL*
1	Venera 4	USSR	Venus	Oct 18, 1967
2	Venera 5	USSR	Venus	May 16, 1969
3	Venera 6	USSR	Venus	May 17, 1969
4	Venera 7	USSR	Venus	Dec 15, 1970
5	Mariner 9	US	Mars	Nov 13, 1971
6	Mars 2	USSR	Mars	Nov 27, 1971
7	Mars 3	USSR	Mars	Dec 2, 1971
8	Venera 8	USSR	Venus	Jul 22, 1972
9	Venera 9	USSR	Venus	Oct 22, 1975
10	Venera 10	USSR	Venus	Oct 25, 1975

* Successfully entered orbit or landed

This list excludes fly-bys – probes that passed by but did not land on the surface of another planet.

TOP 10 | BODIES MOST VISITED BY SPACECRAFT

	BODY*	SPACECRAFT VISITS
1	Moon	66
2	Mars	32
3	Venus	26
4	Sun	14
5	Jupiter	7
6	Halley's Comet	5
7	Saturn	4
8	=Mercury	1
	=Neptune	1
	=Uranus	1

*Single visits to comets and asteroids are not included

With the exception of some visits to the Moon, all the visiting spacecraft were unmanned space probes known as fly-bys, landers, or orbiters.

THE 10 | FIRST ARTIFICIAL SATELLITES

	SATELLITE	COUNTRY	LAUNCH DATE
1	Sputnik 1	USSR	Oct 4, 1957
2	Sputnik 2	USSR	Nov 3, 1957
3	Explorer 1	US	Feb 1, 1958
4	Vanguard 1	US	Mar 17, 1958
5	Explorer 3	US	Mar 26, 1958
6	Sputnik 3	USSR	May 15, 1958
7	Explorer 4	US	Jul 26, 1958
8	SCORE	US	Dec 18, 1958
9	Vanguard 2	US	Feb 17, 1959
10	Discoverer 1	US	Feb 28, 1959

Sputnik 1, an 184-lb (83.6-kg) metal sphere, transmitted signals back to the Earth for 3 weeks before its batteries failed, although it continued to be tracked until it fell to Earth and burned up on January 4, 1958.

US Space Shuttle
The Space Shuttle STS-78 Columbia lifted off on June 20, 1996, on a 16-day scientific mission. It carried nine astronauts on a journey of 7,000,000 miles (11,265,508 km).

Space Explorers

TOP 10 MOST EXPERIENCED MEN IN SPACE*

	ASTRONAUT/COSMONAUT	MISSIONS	TOTAL DURATION OF MISSIONS (DAYS)	(HRS)	(MINS)	(SECS)
1	Sergei V. Avdeyev	3	747	14	22	47
2	Valeri V. Polyakov	2	678	16	33	18
3	Anatoli Y. Solovyov	5#	651	00	11	25
4	Sergei K. Krikalyov	5#	624	09	16	21
5	Viktor M. Afanasyev	3	545	02	34	41
6	Musa K. Manarov	2	541	00	29	38
7	Alexander S. Viktorenko	4	489	01	35	17
8	Yuri V. Romanenko	3	430	18	21	30
9	Alexander Y. Kaleri	3	415	03	19	16
10	Alexander A. Volkov	3	391	11	52	14

* To January 1, 2002; all Soviet/Russian

\# Including flights aboard US Space Shuttles

Hair-raising Experience

Tamara E. Jernigan – one of the world's most experienced female astronauts – found a novel use for the air-conditioning during the record-breaking STS-80 mission in 1996. She used it as a hairdryer!

TOP 10 MOST EXPERIENCED WOMEN IN SPACE*

	ASTRONAUT/COSMONAUT#	MISSIONS	TOTAL DURATION OF MISSIONS (DAYS)	(HRS)	(MINS)	(SECS)
1	Shannon W. Lucid	5	223	2	52	26
2	Susan J. Helms	5	210	23	06	27
3	Yelena V. Kondakova	2	178	10	41	31
4	Tamara E. Jernigan	5	63	01	25	40
5	Marsha S. Ivins	5	55	21	47	46
6	Bonnie J. Dunbar	5	50	08	24	44
7	Janice E. Voss	5	49	02	49	05
8	Kathryn C. Thornton	4	40	15	15	18
9	Linda M. Godwin	4	38	06	13	49
10	Wendy B. Lawrence	3	37	05	23	20

* To January 1, 2002   \# All US except Kondakova (Soviet)

Shannon Lucid became both the most experienced American astronaut and the world's most experienced female astronaut in 1996. She took off in US Space Shuttle STS-76 Atlantis on March 22, transferred to the Russian Mir space station, and re-boarded the STS-79 Atlantis on September 26, after traveling 75,200,000 miles (121,000,000 km) in 188 days, 4 hours, 0 minutes, 14 seconds.

THE 10 FIRST PEOPLE TO WALK ON THE SURFACE OF THE MOON

	ASTRONAUT	SPACECRAFT	TOTAL EVA* (HRS:MINS)	MISSION DATES
1	Neil A. Armstrong	Apollo 11	2:32	Jul 16–24, 1969
2	Edwin E. ("Buzz") Aldrin	Apollo 11	2:15	Jul 16–24, 1969
3	Charles Conrad Jr.	Apollo 12	7:45	Nov 14–24, 1969
4	Alan L. Bean	Apollo 12	7:45	Nov 14–24, 1969
5	Alan B. Shepard	Apollo 14	9:23	Jan 31–Feb 9, 1971
6	Edgar D. Mitchell	Apollo 14	9:23	Jan 31–Feb 9, 1971
7	David R. Scott	Apollo 15	19:08	Jul 26–Aug 7, 1971
8	James B. Irwin	Apollo 15	18:35	Jul 26–Aug 7, 1971
9	John W. Young	Apollo 16	20:14	Apr 16–27, 1972
10	Charles M. Duke	Apollo 16	20:14	Apr 16–27, 1972

* Extra Vehicular Activity (time spent out of the lunar module on the Moon's surface)

Six US Apollo missions resulted in successful Moon landings (Apollo 13, April 11–17, 1970, was aborted after an oxygen tank exploded). During the last of these (Apollo 17, December 7–19, 1972), Eugene A. Cernan and Harrison H. Schmitt became the only other astronauts to date who have walked on the surface of the Moon. No further Moon landings are planned by the US, and while Russia has declared its intention to revive its unmanned exploration of Mars, its program received a setback with the failure of the November 16, 1996, launch of its Mars 96 mission. However, the US space program has announced that a manned landing on Mars is to be its next goal.

THE 10 FIRST PEOPLE TO WALK IN SPACE

	ASTRONAUT/COSMONAUT	SPACECRAFT	EVA* (HRS:MINS)	DATE
1	Alexei Leonov	Voskhod 2	0.23	Mar 18, 1965
2	Edward H. White	Gemini 4	0:36	Jun 3, 1965
3	Eugene A. Cernan	Gemini 9	2:07	Jun 3, 1966
4	Michael Collins	Gemini 10	0:50	Jul 19, 1966
5	Richard F. Gordon	Gemini 11	0:33	Sep 13, 1966
6	Edwin E. ("Buzz") Aldrin	Gemini 12	2:29	Nov 12, 1966
7	=Yevgeny Khrunov	Soyuz 5	0:37	Jan 16, 1969
	=Alexei Yeleseyev	Soyuz 5	0:37	Jan 16, 1969
9	=Russell L. Schweickart	Apollo 9	0:46	Mar 6, 1969
	=David R. Scott	Apollo 9	0:46	Mar 6, 1969

* Extra Vehicular Activity

Walking in Space

The first American to walk in space, Edward H. White, traveled 6,500 miles (10,460 km) while attached to his Gemini spacecraft by a 25-ft (7.6-m) umbilical cord. Here he carries an HHSMU – a Hand Held Self Maneuvering Unit.

TOP 10 LONGEST SPACEWALKS*

	ASTRONAUTS	SPACECRAFT	DATE	DURATION (HRS:MINS)
1	James Voss, Susan Helma	STS-102/ Space station	Mar 10–11, 2001	8:56
2	Thomas D. Akers, Richard J. Hieb, Pierre J. Thuot	STS-49	May 13, 1992	8:29
3	John M. Grunsfeld, Steven L. Smith	STS-103	Dec 22, 1999	8:15
4	C. Michael Foale, Claude Nicollier	STS-103	Dec 23, 1999	8:10
5	John M. Grunsfeld, Steven L. Smith	STS-103	Dec 24, 1999	8:08
6	Daniel T. Barry, Tamara E. Jernigan	STS-96/ ISS 2A.1	May 29, 1999	7:55
7	Jeffrey A. Hoffman, F. Story Musgrave	STS-61	Dec 4, 1993	7:54
8	Thomas D. Akers, Kathryn C. Thornton	STS-49	May 14, 1992	7:44
9	Takao Doi, Winston E. Scott	STS-87	Nov 24, 1997	7:43
10	Chris Hadfield, Scott Parazynski	STS-100	Apr 24, 2001	7:40

* To January 1, 2002

All these EVAs (Extra Vehicular Activities) were from NASA Space Shuttles – most of them concerned with capture of or repairs to satellites and other equipment, including the Hubble space telescope.

TOP 10 LONGEST SPACE MISSIONS*

	COSMONAUT[#]	MISSION DATES	DURATION (DAYS:HRS:MINS)
1	Valeri V. Polyakov	Jan 8, 1994– Mar 22, 1995	437:17:59
2	Sergei V. Avdeyev	Aug 13, 1998– Aug 28, 1999	379:14:52
3	=Musa K. Manarov	Dec 21, 1987– Dec 21, 1988	365:22:39
	=Vladimir G. Titov	Dec 21, 1987– Dec 21, 1988	365:22:39
5	Yuri V. Romanenko	Feb 5– Dec 5, 1987	326:11:38
6	Sergei K. Krikalyov	May 18, 1991– Mar 25, 1992	311:20:01
7	Valeri V. Polyakov	Aug 31, 1988– Apr 27, 1989	240:22:35
8	=Oleg Y. Atkov	Feb 8– Oct 2, 1984	236:22:50
	=Leonid D. Kizim	Feb 8– Oct 2, 1984	236:22:50
	=Anatoli Y. Solovyov	Feb 8– Oct 2, 1984	236:22:50

* To 1 January 2002   # All Soviet/Russian

Waterworld

TOP 10 DEEPEST OCEANS AND SEAS

	OCEAN/SEA	GREATEST DEPTH (FT)	(M)	AVERAGE DEPTH (FT)	(M)
1	Pacific Ocean	35,837	10,924	13,215	4,028
2	Indian Ocean	24,460	7,455	13,002	3,963
3	Atlantic Ocean	30,246	9,219	12,880	3,926
4	Caribbean Sea	22,788	6,946	8,685	2,647
5	South China Sea	16,456	5,016	5,419	1,652
6	Bering Sea	15,659	4,773	5,075	1,547
7	Gulf of Mexico	12,425	3,787	4,874	1,486
8	Mediterranean Sea	15,197	4,632	4,688	1,429
9	Sea of Japan	12,276	3,742	4,429	1,350
10	Arctic Ocean	18,456	5,625	3,953	1,205

The deepest point in the deepest ocean is the Marianas Trench in the Pacific, at a depth of 35,837 ft (10,924 m) according to a recent survey. The slightly lesser depth of 35,814 ft (10,916 m) was recorded on January 23, 1960, by Jacques Piccard and Donald Walsh during the deepest-ever ocean descent into the trench.

TOP 10 LONGEST RIVERS

	RIVER	LOCATION	LENGTH (MILES)	(KM)
1	Nile	Tanzania/Uganda/Sudan/Egypt	4,145	6,670
2	Amazon	Peru/Brazil	4,007	6,448
3	Yangtze–Kiang	China	3,915	6,300
4	Mississippi–Missouri–Red Rock	US	3,710	5,971
5	Yenisey–Angara–Selenga	Mongolia/Russia	3,442	5,540
6	Huang Ho (Yellow River)	China	3,395	5,464
7	Ob'–Irtysh	Mongolia/Kazakhstan/Russia	3,362	5,410
8	Congo	Angola/Dem. Rep. of Congo	2,920	4,700
9	Lena–Kirenga	Russia	2,734	4,400
10	Mekong	Tibet/China/Myanmar/Laos/Cambodia/Vietnam	2,703	4,350

TOP 10 HIGHEST WATERFALLS

	WATERFALL	RIVER	LOCATION	TOTAL DROP (FT)	(M)
1	Angel	Carrao	Venezuela	3,212	979*
2	Tugela	Tugela	South Africa	3,107	947
3	Utigård	Jostedal Glacier	Nesdale, Norway	2,625	800
4	Mongefossen	Monge	Mongebekk, Norway	2,540	774
5	Yosemite	Yosemite Creek	California	2,425	739
6	Østre Mardøla Foss	Mardals	Eikisdal, Norway	2,152	656
7	Tyssestrengane	Tysso	Hardanger, Norway	2,120	646
8	Cuquenán	Arabopo	Venezuela	2,000	610
9	Sutherland	Arthur	South Island, New Zealand	1,904	580
10	Kjellfossen	Naero	Gudvangen, Norway	1,841	561

* Longest single drop 2,648 ft (807 m)

TOP 10 LARGEST LAKES

	LAKE	LOCATION	APPROX. AREA (SQ MILES)	(SQ KM)
1	Caspian Sea	Azerbaijan/Iran/Kazakhstan/ Russia/Turkmenistan	143,000	371,000
2	Michigan/Huron*	Canada/US	45,300	117,610
3	Superior	Canada/US	31,700	82,100
4	Victoria	Kenya/Tanzania/Uganda	26,828	69,500
5	Aral Sea	Kazakhstan/Uzbekistan	15,444	40,000
6	Tanganyika	Burundi/Tanzania/ Dem. Rep. of Congo/Zambia	12,700	32,900
7	Great Bear	Canada	12,096	31,328
8	Baikal	Russia	11,776	30,500
9	Malawi (Nyasa)	Tanzania/Malawi/Mozambique	11,150	29,600
10	Great Slave	Canada	11,030	28,570

* Now considered 2 lobes of the same lake

TOP 10 COUNTRIES WITH THE LARGEST AREAS OF CORAL REEF

	COUNTRY	REEF AREA (SQ MILES)	PERCENTAGE OF WORLD TOTAL
1	Indonesia	19,700	17.95
2	Australia	18,905	17.22
3	The Philippines	9,676	8.81
4	France – overseas territories	5,514	5.02
5	Papua New Guinea	5,344	4.87
6	Fiji	3,869	3.52
7	Maldives	3,444	3.14
8	Saudi Arabia	2,572	2.34
9	Marshall Islands	2,359	2.15
10	India	2,235	2.04
	World total (including those not in Top 10)	*109,778*	*100.00*

Source: World Atlas of Coral Reefs

Undersea Paradise
Indonesia has a high proportion of the world's coral reefs, the most spectacular of which is preserved off the coast and islands of the Bunaken Manado Tua Marine National Park, in the province of North Sulawesi.

TOP 10 MOST ISOLATED ISLANDS

	ISLAND/LOCATION	ISOLATION INDEX*
1	**Easter Island,** South Pacific	149
2	**Rapa Iti,** Tubuai Islands, South Pacific	130
3	**Kiritimati,** Line Islands, Central Pacific	129
4	**Jarvis Island,** Central Pacific	128
5	**=Kosrae,** Micronesia, Pacific	126
	=Malden, Line Islands, Central Pacific	126
	=Starbuck, Line Islands, Central Pacific	126
	=Vostok, Line Islands, Central Pacific	126
9	**=Bouvet Island,** South Atlantic	125
	=Gough Island, South Atlantic	125
	=Palmyra Island, Central Pacific	125

Source: *United Nations*

* The United Nations' isolation index is calculated by adding together the square roots of the distances to the nearest island, group of islands, and continent.

On Top of the World

TOP 10 HIGHEST ISLANDS

ISLAND/LOCATION	HIGHEST ELEVATION (FT)	(M)
1 **New Guinea,** Papua New Guinea/Indonesia	16,503	5,030
2 **Akutan,** Alaska	14,026	4,275
3 **Hawaii**	13,796	4,205
4 **Borneo,** Indonesia/Malaysia/Brunei	13,698	4,175
5 **Formosa,** China	13,114	3,997
6 **Sumatra,** Indonesia	12,480	3,804
7 **Ross,** Antarctica	12,448	3,794
8 **Honshu,** Japan	12,388	3,776
9 **South Island,** New Zealand	12,349	3,764
10 **Lombok,** Lesser Sunda Islands, Indonesia	12,224	3,726

Source: *United Nations*

TOP 10 LONGEST MOUNTAIN RANGES

RANGE/LOCATION	LENGTH (MILES)	(KM)
1 **Andes,** South America	4,500	7,242
2 **Rocky Mountains,** North America	3,750	6,035
3 **Himalayas/Karakoram/Hindu Kush,** Asia	2,400	3,862
4 **Great Dividing Range,** Australia	2,250	3,621
5 **Trans-Antarctic Mountains,** Antarctica	2,200	3,541
6 **Brazilian East Coast Range,** Brazil	1,900	3,058
7 **Sumatran/Javan Range,** Sumatra/Java	1,800	2,897
8 **Tien Shan,** China	1,400	2,253
9 **Eastern Ghats,** India	1,300	2,092
10 **=Altai,** Asia	1,250	2,012
=Central New Guinean Range, Papua New Guinea	1,250	2,012
=Urals, Russia	1,250	2,012

The Top 10 includes only ranges that are continuous (the Sumatran/Javan Range is divided only by a short interruption between the 2 islands). The Aleutian Range extends for 1,650 miles (2,655 km), but is fragmented across numerous islands of the northwest Pacific. As well as these ranges that lie above the surface of the Earth, there are also several submarine ranges that are even longer.

Peak Performance
The Andes, the world's longest mountain range, stretches the length of South America, from Lago de Maracaibo in the north to Tierra del Fuego in the south.

TOP 10 HIGHEST MOUNTAINS

MOUNTAIN/LOCATION	TEAM NATIONALITY*	FIRST ASCENT	HEIGHT# (FT)	(M)
1 **Everest,** Nepal/China	British/ New Zealander	May 29, 1953	29,035	8,850
2 **K2 (Chogori),** Pakistan/China	Italian	Jul 31, 1954	28,238	8,607
3 **Kangchenjunga,** Nepal/India	British	May 25, 1955	28,208	8,598
4 **Lhotse,** Nepal/China	Swiss	May 18, 1956	27,923	8,511
5 **Makalu I,** Nepal/China	French	May 15, 1955	27,824	8,481
6 **Lhotse Shar II,** Nepal/China	Austrian	May 12, 1970	27,504	8,383
7 **Dhaulagiri I,** Nepal	Swiss/Austrian	May 13, 1960	26,810	8,172
8 **Manaslu I (Kutang I),** Nepal	Japanese	May 9, 1956	26,760	8,156
9 **Cho Oyu,** Nepal	Austrian	Oct 19, 1954	26,750	8,153
10 **Nanga Parbat (Diamir),** Kashmir	German/ Austrian	Jul 3, 1953	26,660	8,126

* Team leaders only

 # Height of principal peak; lower peaks of the same mountain are excluded

The current "official" height of Everest was announced in November 1999 following analysis of data beamed from sensors on Everest's summit to GPS (Global Positioning System) satellites. This superseded the previous "official" measurement of 29,028 ft (8,848 m), recorded on April 20, 1993.

TOP 10 | HIGHEST ACTIVE VOLCANOES

	VOLCANO/LOCATION	LATEST ACTIVITY	HEIGHT (FT)	(M)
1	**San Pedro,** Chile	1960	20,161	6,145
2	**Aracar,** Argentina	1993	19,954	6,082
3	**Guallatiri,** Chile	1985	19,918	6,071
4	**Tupungatito,** Chile	1986	19,685	6,000
5	**Sabancaya,** Peru	1986	19,577	5,967
6	**Cotopaxi,** Ecuador	1942	19,393	5,911
7	**Putana,** Chile	1972	19,324	5,890
8	**San Jose,** Chile	1960	19,212	5,856
9	**El Misti,** Peru	1948	19,101	5,822
10	**Tutupaca,** Peru	1902	19,078	5,815

This list includes only volcanoes that were active at some time during the 20th century. The tallest currently active volcano in Europe is Mt. Etna, Sicily (10,855 ft/3,311 m), which has been responsible for numerous deaths. Etna's last major eruption took place on March 11, 1669, when the lava flow engulfed the town of Catania, killing at least 20,000. Before that, an eruption in 1169 killed more than 15,000 people in Catania cathedral, where they had taken shelter. More people died when a tsunami caused by the same eruption hit the port of Messina, Sicily.

TOP 10 | HIGHEST MOUNTAINS IN SOUTH AMERICA

	MOUNTAIN/LOCATION	HEIGHT (FT)	(M)
1	**Cerro Aconcagua,** Argentina	22,834	6,960
2	**Ojos del Salado,** Argentina/Chile	22,588	6,885
3	**Bonete,** Argentina	22,550	6,873
4	**Pissis,** Argentina/Chile	22,244	6,780
5	**Huascarán,** Peru	22,205	6,768
6	**Llullaillaco,** Argentina/Chile	22,057	6,723
7	**Libertador,** Argentina	22,050	6,721
8	**Mercadario,** Argentina/Chile	21,884	6,670
9	**Yerupajá,** Peru	21,765	6,634
10	**Tres Cruces,** Argentina/Chile	21,720	6,620

TOP 10 | HIGHEST MOUNTAINS IN NORTH AMERICA

	MOUNTAIN/LOCATION	HEIGHT* (FT)	(M)
1	**McKinley,** Alaska	20,320	6,194
2	**Logan,** Canada	19,545	5,959
3	**Citlaltépetl (Orizaba),** Mexico	18,409	5,611
4	**St. Elias,** Alaska/Canada	18,008	5,489
5	**Popocatépetl,** Mexico	17,887	5,452
6	**Foraker,** Alaska	17,400	5,304
7	**Ixtaccihuatl,** Mexico	17,343	5,286
8	**Lucania,** Canada	17,147	5,226
9	**King,** Canada	16,971	5,173
10	**Steele,** Canada	16,644	5,073

* Height of principal peak; lower peaks of the same mountain are excluded

Face of the Earth

Mammoth Cave, Kentucky
The limestone rocks of Kentucky contain a vast network of underground passages and caverns that include the Mammoth, the world's longest cave system.

TOP 10 DEEPEST DEPRESSIONS

	DEPRESSION/LOCATION	MAXIMUM DEPTH BELOW SEA LEVEL (FT)	(M)
1	**Dead Sea**, Israel/Jordan	1,312	400
2	**Lake Assal**, Djibouti	511	156
3	**Turfan Depression**, China	505	154
4	**Qattâra Depression**, Egypt	436	133
5	**Mangyshlak Peninsula**, Kazakhstan	433	132
6	**Danakil Depression**, Ethiopia	383	117
7	**Death Valley**, California/Nevada	282	86
8	**Salton Sink**, California	235	72
9	**Zapadny Chink Ustyurta**, Kazakhstan	230	70
10	**Prikaspiyskaya Nizmennost'**, Kazakhstan/Russia	220	67

Much of Antarctica is below sea level (as much as 8,326 ft/2,538 m), but the land there is covered by an ice cap that averages 6,890 ft (2,100 m) in depth.

TOP 10 DEEPEST CAVES

	CAVE/LOCATION	DEPTH (FT)	(M)
1	**Krubera (Voronja)**, Georgia	5,609	1,710
2	**Lamprechtsofen**, Austria	5,354	1,632
3	**Gouffre Mirolda**, France	5,282	1,610
4	**Réseau Jean Bernard**, France	5,256	1,602
5	**Torca del Cerro**, Spain	5,213	1,589
6	**Shakta Pantjukhina**, Georgia	4,948	1,508
7	**Ceki 2**, Slovenia	4,869	1,484
8	**Sistema Huautla**, Mexico	4,839	1,475
9	**Sistema de la Trave**, Spain	4,738	1,444
10	**Boj Bulok**, Uzbekistan	4,642	1,415

Source: *Tony Waltham, BCRA*

The world's deepest cave was discovered in 2001 by a team of Ukrainian cave explorers. In the Arabikskaja system, in the Caucasus mountains of Georgia, they found a branch of the Voronja cave that was deeper than any cave ever found before.

TOP 10 LONGEST CAVES

	CAVE/LOCATION	TOTAL KNOWN LENGTH (MILES)	(KM)
1	**Mammoth Cave System**, Kentucky	346	557
2	**Optimisticheskaya**, Ukraine	130	208
3	**Wind Cave**, South Dakota	126	203
4	**Jewel Cave**, South Dakota	126	201
5	**Hölloch**, Switzerland	109	175
6	**Lechuguilla Cave**, New Mexico	107	171
7	**Fisher Ridge Cave System**, Kentucky	101	161
8	**Siebenhengstehohle**, Switzerland	87	140
9	**Ozernaya**, Ukraine	69	111
10	**Gua Air Jernih**, Malaysia	68	109

Source: *Tony Waltham, BCRA*

TOP 10 LARGEST DESERTS

DESERT/LOCATION	APPROX. AREA (SQ MILES)	(SQ KM)
1 **Sahara,** North Africa	3,500,000	9,100,000
2 **Australian,** Australia*	1,300,000	3,400,000
3 **Arabian Peninsula,** Southwest Asia#	1,000,000	2,600,000
4 **Turkestan,** Central Asia†	750,000	1,900,000
5 **=Gobi,** Central Asia	500,000	1,300,000
=North American Desert, US/Mexico§	500,000	1,300,000
7 **Patagonia,** Southern Argentina	260,000	670,000
8 **Thar,** Northwest India/Pakistan	230,000	600,000
9 **Kalahari,** Southwest Africa	220,000	570,000
10 **Takla Makan,** Northwest China	185,000	480,000

* Includes Gibson, Great Sandy, Great Victoria, and Simpson

\# Includes an-Nafud and Rub alKhali

† Includes Kara-Kum and Kyzylkum

§ Includes Great Basin, Mojave, Sonorah, and Chihuahuan

TOP 10 COUNTRIES WITH THE LOWEST ELEVATIONS

COUNTRY	HIGHEST POINT	ELEVATION (FT)	(M)
1 **Maldives**	Unnamed	10	3
2 **=Marshall Islands**	Unnamed	20	6
=Tuvalu	Unnamed	20	6
4 **The Gambia**	Unnamed	141	43
5 **Bahamas**	Mount Alvernia	206	63
6 **Nauru**	Unnamed	225	68
7 **Qatar**	Dukhan Heights	240	73
8 **Kiribati**	Banaba	270	81
9 **Bahrain**	Jabal al-Dukhan	440	134
10 **Denmark**	Yding Skovhøj	568	173

These 10 countries are definitely off the agenda if you are planning a hiking trip, since not one of them possesses a single elevation that is taller than a medium-sized skyscraper.

TOP 10 LARGEST METEORITE CRATERS

CRATER/LOCATION	DIAMETER (MILES)	(KM)
1 **Vredefort,** South Africa	186	300
2 **Sudbury,** Canada	155	250
3 **Chicxulub,** Mexico	107	170
4 **=Manicougan,** Canada	62	100
=Popigai, Russia	62	100
6 **Acraman,** Australia	56	90
7 **Chesapeake Bay,** Virginia	53	85
8 **Puchezh-Katunki,** Russia	50	80
9 **Morokweng,** South Africa	43	70
10 **Kara,** Russia	40	65

Source: *Canada Geological Survey, Continental Geoscience Division*

Sahara Desert
The Sahara Desert covers most of North Africa, an area nearly as large as the US. It is said to have been given its name by Ibn-al Hakam in the 9th century.

TOP 10 MOST COMMON ELEMENTS IN THE EARTH'S CRUST

ELEMENT	PARTS PER MILLION
1 Oxygen	474,000
2 Silicon	277,100
3 Aluminum	82,000
4 =Calcium	41,000
=Iron	41,000
6 =Magnesium	23,000
=Sodium	23,000
8 Potassium	21,000
9 Titanium	5,600
10 Hydrogen	1,520

This Top 10 is based on the amounts of elements found in igneous rock.

TOP 10 ELEMENTS WITH THE LOWEST MELTING POINTS*

ELEMENT	MELTING POINT (°F)	(°C)
1 Mercury	37.8	-38.8
2 Francium	80.6	27.0
3 Cesium	83.1	28.4
4 Gallium	85.6	29.8
5 Rubidium	102.7	39.3
6 Phosphorus	111.6	44.2
7 Potassium	146.1	63.4
8 Sodium	207.9	97.7
9 Iodine	236.7	113.7
10 Sulfur	239.4	115.2

Solids only

Among other familiar elements that melt at relatively low temperatures are tin (449.4°F/231.9°C) and lead (621.5°F/327.5°C).

TOP 10 ELEMENTS WITH THE HIGHEST MELTING POINTS

ELEMENT	MELTING POINT (°F)	(°C)
1 Carbon	6,38	5,527
2 Tungsten	6,19	3,422
3 Rhenium	5,76	3,186
4 Osmium	5,49	3,033
5 Tantalum	5,46	3,017
6 Molybdenum	4,75	2,623
7 Niobium	4,49	2,477
8 Iridium	4,47	2,466
9 Ruthenium	4,23	2,334
10 Hafnium	4,05	2,233

Other elements that melt at high temperatures include chromium (3,465°F/1,907°C), iron (2,800°F/1,538°C), and gold (1,947°F/1,064°C). For comparison, the surface of the Sun attains 9,626°F (5,330°C).

TOP 10 MOST COMMON ELEMENTS ON THE MOON

ELEMENT	PERCENTAGE
1 Oxygen	40.0
2 Silicon	19.2
3 Iron	14.3
4 Calcium	8.0
5 Titanium	5.9
6 Aluminum	5.6
7 Magnesium	4.5
8 Sodium	0.33
9 Potassium	0.14
10 Chromium	0.002

This Top 10 is based on the analysis of the 45.8 lb (20.77 kg) of rock samples brought back to Earth by the crew of the 1969 Apollo 11 lunar mission. One of the minerals they discovered was named Armalcolite in honor of the 3 astronauts – Armstrong, Aldrin, and Collins.

ELEMENTARY FIRSTS

ALTHOUGH SOME 30 elements had been discovered up to the end of the 18th century, it was not until then that their unique nature, as the fundamental building blocks of all matter in the universe, was first described. The French chemist Antoine Laurent de Lavoisie defined and then attempted to classify them in a publication dating from 1789. As more elements were discovered, many attempts were made to list them. It was left to Russian scientist Dimitri Mendeleyev to come up with the periodic table of the elements. In 1869, he evolved the notion of a table that would not only list all the known elements in groups but would also leave space for those elements as yet undiscovered.

FIRST OR LAST

TOP 10 PRINCIPAL COMPONENTS OF AIR

COMPONENT	VOLUME PERCENT
1 Nitrogen	78.110
2 Oxygen	20.953
3 Argon	0.934
4 Carbon dioxide	0.01–0.10
5 Neon	0.001818
6 Helium	0.000524
7 Methane	0.0002
8 Krypton	0.000114
9 =Hydrogen	0.00005
=Nitrous oxide	0.00005

Dry air at sea level is composed of this basic 10, plus 1 further component, xenon (0.0000087 percent). In addition to these, water vapor, ozone, and various pollutants, such as carbon monoxide from motor vehicle exhausts, are present in variable amounts.

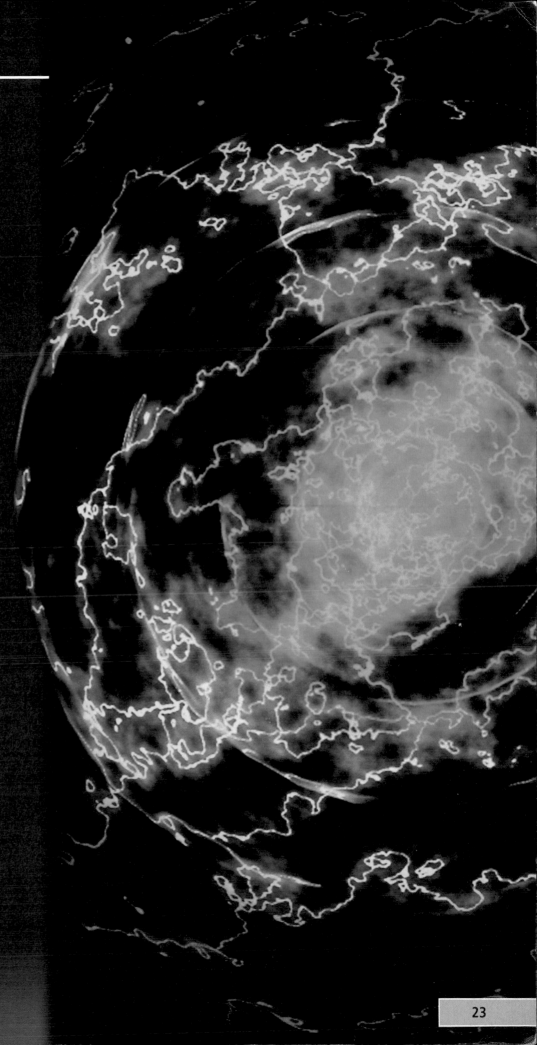

TOP 10 MOST COMMON ELEMENTS IN THE UNIVERSE

ELEMENT	PARTS PER MILLION
1 Hydrogen	739,000
2 Helium	240,000
3 Oxygen	10,700
4 Carbon	4,600
5 Neon	1,340
6 Iron	1,090
7 Nitrogen	970
8 Silicon	650
9 Magnesium	580
10 Sulfur	440

Hydrogen is the simplest atom – a single proton circled by a single electron. The atoms of hydrogen in the universe outnumber those of all the other elements combined.

TOP 10 MOST COMMON ELEMENTS IN THE SUN

ELEMENT	PARTS PER MILLION
1 Hydrogen	745,000
2 Helium	237,000
3 Oxygen	8,990
4 Carbon	3,900
5 Iron	1,321
6 Neon	1,200
7 Nitrogen	870
8 Silicon	830
9 Magnesium	720
10 Sulfur	380

It's a Gas!

A cloud of electrons surround a helium atom. Helium was discovered in the Sun during an eclipse in 1868 and was isolated on Earth in 1895. The name derives from *helios*, the Greek name for the Sun.

World Weather

Cold Comfort
A Yakut cook gazes out of the window of an ice-encrusted restaurant in Verkhoyansk in Siberia, Russia, one of the world's coldest inhabited places.

TOP 10 | COLDEST PLACES – THE EXTREMES

	LOCATION*	LOWEST RECORDED TEMPERATURE (°F)	(°C)
1	**Vostok#**, Antarctica	-138.6	-89.2
2	**Plateau Station#**, Antarctica	-129.2	-84.0
3	**Oymyakon**, Russia	-96.0	-71.1
4	**Verkhoyansk**, Russia	-90.0	-67.7
5	**Northice#**, Greenland	-87.0	-66.0
6	**Eismitte#**, Greenland	-85.0	-64.9
7	**Snag**, Yukon, Canada	-81.4	-63.0
8	**Prospect Creek**, Alaska	-79.8	-62.1
9	**Fort Selkirk**, Yukon, Canada	-74.0	-58.9
10	**Rogers Pass**, Montana	-69.7	-56.5

* Maximum of 2 places per country listed
 # Present or former scientific research base
Source: *Philip Eden*

TOP 10 | HOTTEST PLACES – THE EXTREMES

	LOCATION*	HIGHEST RECORDED TEMPERATURE (°F)	(°C)
1	**Al'Az-īz-īyah**, Libya	136.4	58.0
2	**Greenland Ranch,** Death Valley	134.0	56.7
3	**=Ghudamis**, Libya	131.0	55.0
	=Kebili, Tunisia	131.0	55.0
5	**Tombouctou**, Mali	130.1	54.5
6	**Araouane**, Mali	130.0	54.4
7	**Tirat Tavi**, Israel	129.0	53.9
8	**Ahwāz**, Iran	128.3	53.5
9	**Aghā Jarī**, Iran	128.0	53.3
10	**Wadi Halfa**, Sudan	127.0	52.8

* Maximum of 2 places per country listed
Source: *Philip Eden*

TOP 10 | DRIEST PLACES – AVERAGE

	LOCATION*	AVERAGE ANNUAL RAINFALL# (IN)	(MM)
1	**Arica**, Chile	0.03	0.7
2	**=Al'Kufrah**, Libya	0.03	0.8
	=Aswân, Egypt	0.03	0.8
	=Luxor, Egypt	0.03	0.8
5	**Ica**, Peru	0.09	2.3
6	**Wadi Halfa**, Sudan	0.10	2.6
7	**Iquique**, Chile	0.20	5.0
8	**Pelican Point**, Namibia	0.32	8.0
9	**=Aoulef**, Algeria	0.48	12.0
	=Callao, Peru	0.48	12.0

* Maximum of 2 places per country listed
 # Annual total averaged over a long period of years
Source: *Philip Eden*

TOP 10 | PLACES WITH THE MOST RAINY DAYS

	LOCATION*	RAINY DAYS PER ANNUM#
1	**Waialeale**, Hawaii	335
2	**Marion Island**, South Africa	312
3	**Pohnpei**, Federated States of Micronesia	311
4	**Andagoya**, Colombia	306
5	**Macquarie Island**, Australia	299
6	**Gough Island**, Tristan da Cunha group, South Atlantic	291
7	**Palau**, Federated States of Micronesia	286
8	**Heard Island**, Australia	279
9	**Camp Jacob**, Guadeloupe	274
10	**Atu Nau**, Alaska	268

* Maximum of 2 places per country listed
 # Averaged over a long period of years
Source: *Philip Eden*

TOP 10 | PLACES WITH THE FEWEST RAINY DAYS

	LOCATION*	NUMBER OF RAINY DAYS#
1	**Arica**, Chile	1 day every 6 years
2	**Asyût**, Egypt	1 day every 5 years
3	**Dakhla Oasis**, Egypt	1 day every 4 years
4	**Al'Kufrah**, Libya	1 day every 2 years
5	**=Bender Qaasim**, Somalia	1 day per year
	=Wadi Halfa, Sudan	1 day per year
7	**Iquique**, Chile	2 days per year
8	**=Dongola**, Sudan	3 days per year
	=Faya-Largeau, Chad	3 days per year
	=Masirāh Island, Oman	3 days per year

* Maximum of 2 places per country listed
 # Lowest number of days with rain per year, averaged over a long period of years
Source: *Philip Eden*

TOP 10 | PLACES WITH THE HEAVIEST DAILY DOWNPOURS

	LOCATION*	MOST RAINFALL IN 24 HOURS[#] (IN)	(MM)
1	**Chilaos,** Réunion	73.6	1,870
2	**Baguio,** Philippines	46.0	1,168
3	**Alvin,** Texas	43.0	1,092
4	**Cherrapunji,** India	41.0	1,041
5	**Smithport,** Pennsylvania	39.9	1,013
6	**Crohamhurst,** Australia	35.7	907
7	**Finch-Hatton,** Australia	34.6	879
8	**Suva,** Fiji	26.5	673
9	**Cayenne,** French Guyana	23.5	597
10	**Aitutaki,** Cook Islands	22.5	572

* *Maximum of 2 places per country listed*

Based on limited data

Source: *Philip Eden*

TOP 10 | CLOUDIEST PLACES

	LOCATION*	PERCENTAGE OF MAX. POSSIBLE SUNSHINE	AVERAGE ANNUAL HRS OF SUNSHINE[#]
1	**Ben Nevis,** Scotland	16	736
2	**Hoyvik,** Faeroes, Denmark	19	902
3	**Maam,** Ireland	19	929
4	**Prince Rupert,** British Columbia, Canada	20	955
5	**Riksgransen,** Sweden	20	965
6	**Akureyri,** Iceland	20	973
7	**Raufarhöfn,** Iceland	21	995
8	**Nanortalik,** Greenland	22	1,000
9	**Dalwhinnie,** Scotland	22	1,032
10	**Karasjok,** Norway	23	1,090

* *Maximum of 2 places per country listed*

Lowest annual sunshine total, averaged over a long period of years

Source: *Philip Eden*

TOP 10 | SUNNIEST PLACES

	LOCATION*	PERCENTAGE OF MAX. POSSIBLE SUNSHINE	AVERAGE ANNUAL HRS OF SUNSHINE[#]
1	**Yuma,** Arizona	91	4,127
2	**Phoenix,** Arizona	90	4,041
3	**Wadi Halfa,** Sudan	89	3,964
4	**Bordj Omar Driss,** Algeria	88	3,899
5	**Keetmanshoop,** Namibia	88	3,876
6	**Aoulef,** Algeria	86	3,784
7	**Upington,** South Africa	86	3,766
8	**Atbara,** Sudan	85	3,739
9	**Mariental,** Namibia	84	3,707
10	**Bilma,** Niger	84	3,699

* *Maximum of 2 places per country listed*

Highest yearly sunshine total, averaged over a long period of years

Source: *Philip Eden*

Under the Sun
Death Valley, California, is the lowest, hottest, and driest place in the US. Greenland Ranch weather station recorded an unbelievable all-time high for Death Valley of 134.0°F (56.7°C) on July 10, 1913.

Natural Disasters

THE 10 | WORST EPIDEMICS

	EPIDEMIC	LOCATION	DATE	ESTIMATED NO. KILLED
1	Black Death	Europe/Asia	1347–51	75,000,000
2	AIDS	Worldwide	1981–	21,800,000
3	Influenza	Worldwide	1918–20	21,640,000
4	Bubonic plague	India	1896–1948	12,000,000
5	Typhus	Eastern Europe	1914–15	3,000,000
6	="Plague of Justinian"	Europe/Asia	541–90	millions*
	=Cholera	Worldwide	1846–60	millions*
	=Cholera	Europe	1826–37	millions*
	=Cholera	Worldwide	1893–94	millions*
10	Smallpox	Mexico	1530–45	over 1,000,000

* No precise figures available

Dance of Death
Human mortality and the ever-present threat of natural disaster was portrayed in the medieval period by illustrations of death as a dancing partner, as in this woodcut dating from 1486.

THE 10 | COUNTRIES WITH THE MOST DEATHS DUE TO NATURAL DISASTERS

	COUNTRY	ESTIMATED DEATHS IN 2000
1	India	3,424
2	China	2,448
3	Nigeria	1,989
4	Philippines	869
5	Mozambique	847
6	Indonesia	739
7	Bangladesh	681
8	Vietnam	636
9	Russia	410
10	Pakistan	348
	US	280

Source: *EM-DAT, CRED, University of Louvain, Belgium*

In 2000 an estimated total of 20,045 people died worldwide as a result of natural disasters. A total of 256,415,680 people were affected globally, of whom 229,117,986 were in Asia, 23,043,144 in Africa, 2,906,470 in Europe, 1,341,521 in the Americas, and 6,559 in Oceania.

THE 10 | MOST COSTLY TYPES OF DISASTER*

	TYPE OF DISASTER	ESTIMATED DAMAGE IN 1991–2000 ($)
1	Floods	272,818,900,000
2	Earthquakes	239,601,200,000
3	Wind storms	198,095,800,000
4	Droughts	30,535,700,000
5	Forest/scrub fires	26,292,800,000
6	Non-natural disasters (including industrial and transport accidents)	23,080,300,000
7	Extreme temperatures	16,673,200,000
8	Avalanches/landslides	1,666,500,000
9	Volcanic eruptions	778,100,000
10	Insect infestations and waves/surges	243,300,000
	World total	809,785,800,000

* Includes natural and non-natural disasters

Source: *EM-DAT, CRED, University of Louvain, Belgium*

THE 10 | WORST TSUNAMIS OF THE 20TH CENTURY

	LOCATIONS AFFECTED	DATE	ESTIMATED NO. KILLED
1	Agadir, Morocco*	Feb 29, 1960	12,000
2	Papua New Guinea	Jul 18, 1998	8,000
3	=Philippines	Aug 17, 1976	5,000
	=Chile/Pacific Islands/Japan	May 22, 1960	5,000
5	Japan/Hawaii	Mar 2, 1933	3,000
6	Japan*	Dec 21, 1946	1,088
7	Kii, Japan	Dec 4, 1944	998
8	Lomblem Island, Indonesia	Jul 18, 1979	539
9	Hawaii/Aleutians/California	Apr 1, 1946	173
10	Colombia/Ecuador*	Dec 12, 1979	133

* Combined effect of earthquake and tsunamis

Tsunamis (from the Japanese *tsu*, port, and *nami*, wave) are powerful waves caused by undersea disturbances such as earthquakes or volcanic eruptions. They are often mistakenly called tidal waves, which are a different phenomenon. Tsunamis can be so intense that they frequently cross entire oceans, devastating islands and coastal regions in their paths.

THE 10 | WORST EARTHQUAKES

	LOCATION	DATE	ESTIMATED NO. KILLED
1	**Near East/Mediterranean**	May 20, 1202	1,100,000
2	**Shenshi,** China	Feb 2, 1556	820,000
3	**Calcutta,** India	Oct 11, 1737	300,000
4	**Antioch,** Syria	May 20, 526	250,000
5	**Tang-shan,** China	Jul 28, 1976	242,419
6	**Nan-shan,** China	May 22, 1927	200,000
7	**Yeddo,** Japan	Dec 30, 1703	190,000
8	**Kansu,** China	Dec 16, 1920	180,000
9	**Messina,** Italy	Dec 28, 1908	160,000
10	**Tokyo/Yokohama,** Japan	Sep 1, 1923	142,807

There are some discrepancies between the "official" death tolls in many of the world's worst earthquakes and the estimates of other authorities: a figure of 750,000 is sometimes quoted for the Tang-shan earthquake of 1976, for example, and totals range from 58,000 to 250,000 for the quakes that devastated Messina in 1908. Several other earthquakes in China and Turkey resulted in deaths of 100,000 or more.

THE 10 | WORST FLOODS

	LOCATION	DATE	ESTIMATED NO. KILLED
1	**Huang He River,** China	Aug 1931	3,700,000
2	**Huang He River,** China	Spring 1887	1,500,000
3	**Netherlands**	Nov 1, 1530	400,000
4	**Kaifong,** China	1642	300,000
5	**Henan,** China	Sep–Nov 1939	over 200,000
6	**Bengal,** India	1876	200,000
7	**Yangtze River,** China	Aug–Sep 1931	140,000
8	**Netherlands**	1646	110,000
9	**North Vietnam**	Aug 30, 1971	over 100,000
10	**=Friesland,** Netherlands	1228	100,000
	=Dort, Netherlands	Apr 16, 1421	100,000
	=Canton, China	Jun 12, 1915	100,000
	=Yangtze River, China	Sep 1911	100,000

China's Huang He River has flooded at least 1,500 times since records began.

China's Sorrow
The frequent flooding of the Huang He, or Yellow River, has earned it the nickname "China's Sorrow." Along with other rivers in China, it has caused some of the worst disasters of all time.

LIFE ON
EARTH

Extinct & Endangered Species

TOP 10 COUNTRIES WITH THE MOST CAPTIVE ELEPHANTS

	COUNTRY	ELEPHANTS*
1	US	624
2	Germany	276
3	UK	129
4	Italy	74
5	Japan	68
6	France	59
7	Spain	49
8	Netherlands	48
9	South Africa	46
10	Canada	45

* Total of known elephants in captivity in zoos, circuses, and private collections for the year 2000

Battle of the Dinosaurs
The discovery of dinosaur fossils in the early 19th century provoked controversy when it threw established beliefs about creation into disarray.

THE 10 FIRST DINOSAURS TO BE NAMED

	NAME	MEANING	NAMED BY	YEAR
1	Megalosaurus	Great lizard	William Buckland	1824
2	Iguanodon	Iguana tooth	Gideon Mantell	1825
3	Hylaeosaurus	Woodland lizard	Gideon Mantell	1833
4	Macrodontophion	Large tooth snake	A. Zborzewski	1834
5	=Thecodontosaurus	Socket-toothed lizard	Samuel Stutchbury and Henry Riley	1836
	=Paleosaurus	Ancient lizard	Samuel Stutchbury and Henry Riley	1836
7	Plateosaurus	Flat lizard	Hermann von Meyer	1837
8	=Cladeiodon	Branch tooth	Richard Owen	1841
	=Cetiosaurus	Whale lizard	Richard Owen	1841
10	Pelorosaurus	Monstrous lizard	Gideon Mantell	1850

The 10 First dinosaurs were all identified and named within a quarter of a century – although subsequent research has since cast doubt on the authenticity of certain specimens. Curiously, all the first 7 dinosaurs had been named before the word "dinosaur" had been coined: "Dinosauria," meaning "terrible lizards," was proposed as a name for the group by Richard Owen in July 1841 at the Plymouth meeting of the British Association for the Advancement of Science. Owen himself named a number of dinosaurs and was the driving force behind the creation in 1854 of the life-sized dinosaur models at Crystal Palace, London, UK (which can be seen to this day). After the 1850s, the hunting, identifying, and naming of dinosaurs became highly competitive, with dinosaurologists vying with each other to discover and assign names to every new find.

TOP 10 MOST IMPORTANT ISLANDS FOR CONSERVATION

	ISLAND/LOCATION	ENDEMIC SPECIES	THREATENED SPECIES	CONSERVATION IMPORTANCE INDEX
1	**New Caledonia,** South West Pacific	2,688	172	115
2	**Mauritius,** Indian Ocean	316	223	85
3	**Malta,** Mediterranean Sea	32	230	63
4	**Lord Howe Island,** Australia	130	79	58
5	**St. Helena,** South Atlantic	62	54	50
6	**Rapa Iti,** South West Pacific	225	51	49
7	**Madeira,** Atlantic Ocean	230	136	48
8	**Henderson,** Pitcairn, South Pacific	21	2	47
9	**Viti Levu,** Fiji, South West Pacific	9	4	44
10	**=Jamaica,** Caribbean Sea	1,020	13	42
	=Vanua Levu, Fiji, South West Pacific	2	3	42

Source: *United Nations System-wide Earthwatch*

The United Nations' Conservation Importance Index is a ranking of islands which takes into account terrestrial and marine conservation importance, endemic (native) species, threatened species, level of vulnerability, and special features, such as seabird rookeries and sea turtle nesting areas.

TOP 10 | COUNTRIES WITH THE MOST THREATENED MAMMAL SPECIES

COUNTRY/MOST THREATENED SPECIES*	TOTAL NO. OF THREATENED MAMMALS
1 Indonesia	140
Dwarf gymnure#, Sumatran water shrew#, Flores shrew#, Sumatran rabbit#, Sumatran rhinoceros, Javan rhinoceros, Mentawai macaque monkey#, Javan gibbon#, long-footed water rat, lesser small-toothed rat#, Alpine wooly rat#, lowland brush mouse, Enganno rat#, Sumatran flying squirrel#	
2 India	86
Pygmy hog, Malabar civet#, Wroughton's free-tailed bat#, Salim Ali's fruit bat#, Jenkin's shrew#, Sumatran rhinoceros, Javan rhinoceros, Namdapha flying squirrel#	
3 Brazil	79
Black-faced lion tamarin monkey#, golden-rumped lion tamarin monkey#, golden lion tamarin monkey#, yellow-breasted capuchin monkey#, Brazilian tree mouse#	
4 China	76
Mongolian wild horse (extinct in the wild), Przewalski's gazelle#, Père David's deer#, Chinese lake dolphin#, Gansu shrew#, Kozlov's shrew#, red-toothed shrew#, Helen Shan pika#, Javan rhinoceros, Cheng's jird#	
5 Mexico	69
Gulf porpoise#, Omilteme rabbit# (may be extinct), Oaxacan pocket gopher#, Querétaro pocket gopher#, San Jose kangaroo-rat#, Margarita Island kangaroo-rat#, Nelson's spiny pocket mouse#, false canyon mouse#, Slevin's mouse#, Chiapan climbing rat#, Tumbala climbing rat#	
6 Australia	63
Troughton's sheathtail bat#, Gilbert's potoroo#, Northern hairy-nosed wombat#, Bramble Cay mosaic-tailed rat#, Alice Springs mouse (probably extinct), blue-gray mouse#, Carpentarian rock rat#, Central Rock rat#	

COUNTRY/MOST THREATENED SPECIES*	TOTAL NO. OF THREATENED MAMMALS
7 Papua New Guinea	58
Bulmer's fruit bat#, Bougainville monkey-faced bat, New Guinea big-eared bat#, long-footed water rat, fly river water rat#, lowland brush mouse, Eastern shrew mouse#	
8 Kenya	51
Hunter's antelope, Peters' musk shrew, Macow's shrew#, Mt. Gargues musk shrew#, Jombeni musk shrew#, black rhinoceros, Cosens' gerbil#	
9 =Madagascar	50
Lesser yellow bat, tree shrew-tenrec#, golden-crowned sifaka monkey#, golden bamboo lemur#, broad-nosed gentle lemur#, greater big-footed mouse#, white-tipped tufted-tailed rat#	
=Philippines	50
Visayan warty pig#, Philippines tube-nosed fruit bat#, Negros shrew#, Isarog striped shrew-rat#, Ilin cloud rat# (may be extinct), Luzon swamp rat#	
US	37

* Listed as "Critically Endangered" on the 2000 IUCN (International Union for Conservation of Nature) Red List, except where otherwise indicated

\# Found in no other countries

Source: 2000 IUCN Red List of Threatened Species/UNEP (United Nations Environment Program)/WCMC (World Conservation Monitoring Center) Animals of the World Database

Under Threat
The Sumatran rhinoceros, or hairy rhino, is considered critically endangered, with fewer than 300 species surviving in the wild.

Natural Killers

HEAVIEST OWLS

OWL*	WINGSPAN (IN)	(CM)	WEIGHT (LB)	(OZ)	(KG)
1 Eurasian eagle-owl	29	75	9	4	4.20
2 Verraux's eagle-owl	26	65	6	14	3.11
3 Snowy owl	28	70	6	8	2.95
4 Great horned owl	24	60	5	8	2.50
5 Pel's fishing-owl	25	63	5	2	2.32
6 Pharaoh eagle-owl	20	50	5	1	2.30
7 Cape eagle-owl	23	58	3	15	1.80
8 Great gray owl	27	69	3	12	1.70
9 Powerful owl	24	60	3	5	1.50
10 Ural owl	24	62	2	14	1.30

* Some owls closely related to these species may be of similar size; most measurements are from female owls because they are usually larger

Source: *Chris Mead*

TOP 10 DEADLIEST SPIDERS

SPIDER	RANGE
1 **Banana spider** (*Phonenutria nigriventer*)	Central and South America
2 **Sydney funnel web** (*Atrax robustus*)	Australia
3 **Wolf spider** (*Lycosa raptoria/erythrognatha*)	Central and South America
4 **Black widow** (*Latrodectus* sp.)	Widespread
5 **Violin spider/Recluse spider**	Widespread
6 **Sac spider**	Southern Europe
7 **Tarantula** (*Eurypelma rubropilosum*)	Neotropics
8 **Tarantula** (*Acanthoscurria atrox*)	Neotropics
9 **Tarantula** (*Lasiodora klugi*)	Neotropics
10 **Tarantula** (*Pamphobeteus* sp.)	Neotropics

This list ranks spiders according to their "lethal potential" – their venom yield divided by their venom potency. The banana spider, for example, yields 6 mg of venom, with 1 mg being the estimated lethal dose for humans. However, few spiders are capable of killing humans. There were only 14 recorded deaths caused by black widows in the US in the whole of the 19th century. This is probably because their venom yield is relatively low compared with that of the most dangerous snakes. The tarantula, for example, produces 1.5 mg of venom, but the lethal dose for an adult human is 12 mg. Anecdotal evidence suggests that the black birdeaters from Thailand and Sumatra may be equally dangerous, but insufficient data are available.

TOP 10 HEAVIEST CARNIVORES

CARNIVORE	LENGTH (FT)	(IN)	(M)	WEIGHT (LB)	(KG)
1 **Southern elephant seal**	21	4	6.5	7,716	3,500
2 **Walrus**	12	6	3.8	2,646	1,200
3 **Steller sea lion**	9	8	3	2,425	1,100
4 **Grizzly bear**	9	8	3	1,720	780
5 **Polar bear**	8	6	2.6	1,323	600
6 **Tiger**	9	2	2.8	661	300
7 **Lion**	6	3	1.9	551	250
8 **American black bear**	6	0	1.8	500	227
9 **Giant panda**	5	0	1.5	353	160
10 **Spectacled bear**	6	0	1.8	309	140

Of the 273 mammal species in the order Carnivora, many are omnivorous and around 40 specialize in eating fish or insects. As the Top 10 would otherwise consist exclusively of seals and related marine carnivores, only 3 have been included in order that terrestrial carnivores may appear.

His Lips are Seal's
The southern elephant seal is found in the sub-Antarctic. Male southern elephant seals and males of the northern species (which mainly live off the California coast) are the planet's heaviest carnivores.

DEADLIEST SNAKES

	SNAKE	LETHAL VENOM DOSE (MG)	MAXIMUM VENOM YIELD (MG)	POTENTIAL DEATHS PER BITE	MORTALITY RATE RANGE (%)
1	Black mamba	3.0	800	266	90–100
2	Taipan	2.0	520	260	75
3	Russell's viper	2.0	400	200	40–90
4	Inland taipan	0.7	110	157	Not known
5	Green mamba	7.0	500	71	Not known
6	Jararacussu	25.0	1,500	60	60–80
7	Egyptian cobra	15.0	700	46	50
8	Yellow jawed tommygoff	40.0	1,600	40	Not known
9	Forest cobra	15.0	650	43	70–95
10	Indian cobra	12.0	500	41	30–35

This list represents the results of a comprehensive survey of the factors that determine the relative danger posed by poisonous snakes. These include the strength of the venom (and hence the estimated lethal dose for an adult), and the amount injected per bite: most snakes inject about 15 percent of their venom per bite. This list also takes into account how common the snakes are, whether they live close to humans, how temperamental they are, and whether potential victims can call on prompt medical treatment, especially access to antivenom.

Black Death
The black mamba, which can grow as long as 14 ft (4.3 m), is one of the deadliest snakes. In the absence of tr
has a fatality rate of nearly 100 percent.

LARGEST BIRDS OF PREY*

	BIRD	LENGTH (IN)	(CM)
1	Himalayan Griffon vulture	59	150
2	Californian condor	53	134
3	Andean condor	51	130
4	=Lammergeier	45	115
	=Lappet-faced vulture	45	115
6	Eurasian Griffon vulture	43	110
7	European black vulture	42	107
8	Harpy eagle	41	105
9	Wedge-tailed eagle	41	104
10	Ruppell's griffon	40	101

Diurnal only – hence excluding owls

All these aerial hunters have remarkable eyesight and can spot their victims from great distances, but if they kill animals heavier than themselves, they are generally unable to take wing with them. There are occasional qualified instances where this may have happened – for example when a bird was able to take advantage of a powerful updraft of air.

TYPES OF SHARK THAT HAVE KILLED THE MOST HUMANS

	SHARK SPECIES	UNPROVOKED ATTACKS* (TOTAL)	(FATALITIES#)
1	Great white	254	67
2	Tiger	83	29
3	Bull	69	17
4	Requiem	22	5
5	Blue	15	3
6	Sand tiger	39	2
7	Shortfin mako	13	2
8	=Dusky	3	1
	=Leopard	3	1
10	=Galapagos	1	1
	=Ganges	1	1

1580–2000

Where fatalities are equal, entries are ranked by total attacks

Source: *International Shark Attack File, Florida Museum of Natural History*

PLACES WHERE THE MOST DIVERS ARE ATTACKED BY SHARKS

	COUNTRY	ATTACKS	% OF WORLD TOTAL
1	US*	110	31.8
2	Australia	64	18.2
3	Bahamas	25	7.1
4	South Africa	18	5.1
5	New Zealand	17	4.8
6	New Guinea	15	4.3
7	Fiji Islands	↘14	4.0
8	Italy	9	2.6
9	Mexico	7	2.0
10	=Japan	6	1.7
	=Mascarene Islands	6	1.7

Includes Hawaii, US Marshall Islands, US Virgin Islands, and Puerto Rico

Source: *International Shark Attack File, Florida Museum of Natural History*

Land Animals

TOP 10 LONGEST SNAKES

	SNAKE	MAXIMUM LENGTH (FT)	(M)
1	Reticulated (royal) python	35	10.7
2	Anaconda	28	8.5
3	Indian python	25	7.6
4	Diamond python	21	6.4
5	King cobra	19	5.8
6	Boa constrictor	16	4.9
7	Bushmaster	12	3.7
8	Giant brown snake	11	3.4
9	Diamondback rattlesnake	9	2.7
10	Indigo or gopher snake	8	2.4

The South American anaconda is sometimes claimed to be the longest snake, but this has never been proved. Reports of anacondas up to 120 ft (36.5 m) have been published, but without material evidence.

TOP 10 MAMMALS WITH THE LONGEST GESTATION PERIODS

	MAMMAL	AVERAGE GESTATION (DAYS)
1	African elephant	660
2	Asiatic elephant	600
3	Baird's beaked whale	520
4	White rhinoceros	490
5	Walrus	480
6	Giraffe	460
7	Tapir	400
8	Arabian camel (dromedary)	390
9	Fin whale	370
10	Llama	360

Human gestation ranges from 253 to 303 days. This is exceeded by the mammals above and by others, including the porpoise, horse, and water buffalo.

TOP 10 HEAVIEST PRIMATES

	PRIMATE	LENGTH* (IN)	(CM)	WEIGHT (LB)	(KG)
1	Gorilla	79	200	485	220
2	Human	70	177	170	77
3	Orangutan	54	137	165	75
4	Chimpanzee	36	92	110	50
5	=Baboon	39	100	99	45
	=Mandrill	37	95	99	45
7	Gelada baboon	30	75	55	25
8	Proboscis monkey	30	76	53	24
9	Hanuman langur	42	107	44	20
10	Siamung gibbon	35	90	29	13

Excluding tail

TOP 10 SLEEPIEST MAMMALS

	MAMMAL	AVERAGE HOURS OF SLEEP PER DAY*
1	Koala	22
2	Sloth	20
3	=Armadillo	19
	=Opossum	19
5	Lemur	16
6	=Hamster	14
	=Squirrel	14
8	=Cat	13
	=Pig	13
10	Spiny anteater	12

Excluding periods of hibernation

TOP 10 MOST ABUNDANT CLASSES OF ANIMAL

1	Insects and spiders
2	Crustaceans
3	Worms
4	Fish
5	Molluscs
6	Amphibians
7	Birds
8	Mammals (excluding humans)
9	Humans
10	Reptiles

TOP 10 FASTEST MAMMALS

	MAMMAL	MAXIMUM RECORDED SPEED (MPH)	(KM/H)
1	Cheetah	65	105
2	Pronghorn antelope	55	89
3	=Mongolian gazelle	50	80
	=Springbok	50	80
5	=Grant's gazelle	47	76
	=Thomson's gazelle	47	76
7	Brown hare	45	72
8	Horse	43	69
9	=Greyhound	42	68
	=Red deer	42	68

Shell Out
After insects and spiders, crustaceans, such as crabs, are among the most abundant of all animals – with more than 40,000 known species.

TOP 10 HEAVIEST TERRESTRIAL MAMMALS

MAMMAL	LENGTH (FT)	(M)	WEIGHT (LB)	(KG)
1 African elephant	24	7.3	14,432	7,000
2 White rhinoceros	14	4.2	7,937	3,600
3 Hippopotamus	13	4.0	5,512	2,500
4 Giraffe	19	5.8	3,527	1,600
5 American bison	13	3.9	2,205	1,000
6 Arabian camel (dromedary)	12	3.5	1,521	690
7 Polar bear	8	2.6	1,323	600
8 Moose	10	3.0	1,213	550
9 Siberian tiger	11	3.3	661	300
10 Gorilla	7	2.0	485	220

The list excludes domesticated cattle and horses. It also avoids comparing close kin such as the African and Indian elephants, highlighting instead the sumo stars within distinctive large mammal groups such as bears, deer, big cats, primates, and bovines (oxlike mammals).

Jumbo Sized

Since the demise of dinosaurs, elephants have maintained their status as the heaviest of all land animals, with extreme examples claiming a trunk-to-tail length of as much as 35 ft (10.67 m), and tusks as long as 7 ft 5 in (2.26 m).

TOP 10 ANIMALS WITH THE HEAVIEST BRAINS

ANIMAL*	AVERAGE BRAIN WEIGHT (LB)	(OZ)	(G)
1 Sperm whale	17	3	7,800
2 Elephant	13	4	6,000
3 Bottle-nosed dolphin	3	7	1,550
4 Human	3	0	1,350
5 Walrus	2	7	1,100
6 Camel	1	11	762
7 Giraffe	1	8	680
8 Hippopotamus	1	4	582
9 Leopard seal	1	3	542
10 Horse	1	3	532

* Only the heaviest species of each genus is listed

Aquatic Animals

TOP 10 HEAVIEST TURTLES

TURTLE/TORTOISE	MAX WEIGHT (LB)	(KG)
1 Pacific leatherback turtle*	1,552	704.4
2 Atlantic leatherback turtle*	1,018	463.0
3 Green sea turtle	783	355.3
4 Loggerhead turtle	568	257.8
5 Alligator snapping turtle#	220	100.0
6 Flatback (sea) turtle	171	78.2
7 Hawksbill (sea) turtle	138	62.7
8 Kemps Ridley turtle	133	60.5
9 Olive Ridley turtle	110	49.9
10 Common snapping turtle#	85	38.5

* One species, differing in size according to where they live

\# Freshwater species

Source: Lucy T. Verma

TOP 10 WHALING COUNTRIES

COUNTRY	TOTAL CATCH IN 1999
1 Japan	17,760
2 Norway	591
3 Brazil	501
4 Russia	198
5 France	193
6 Greenland	187
7 St. Lucia	161
8 US	108
9 South Korea	104
10 South Africa	60
World total	19,939

Source: Food and Agriculture Organization of the United Nations

TOP 10 FASTEST FISH

FISH	MAXIMUM RECORDED SPEED (MPH)	(KM/H)
1 Sailfish	69	112
2 Marlin	50	80
3 Wahoo	48	77
4 Bluefin tuna	47	76
5 Yellowfin tuna	46	74
6 Blue shark	43	69
7 =Bonefish	40	64
=Swordfish	40	64
9 Tarpon	35	56
10 Tiger shark	33	53

Source: Lucy T. Verma

Many sharks qualify for the list, but only 2 are included here to prevent the list from becoming shark-infested! But just in case you thought it was safe to go in the water, the great white shark (of *Jaws* fame) can manage 30 mph (48 km/h) with ease. For smaller fish (up to the size of a pike or salmon), a formula for estimating an individual's top swimming speed is just over 10 times its own length in centimeters per second: thus a trout 15-cm (6-in) long swims at 160 cm (63 in) per second or 3.6 mph (5.8 km/h).

TOP 10 LONGEST-LIVED MARINE MAMMALS*

MARINE MAMMAL	LIFESPAN (YEARS)
1 Bowhead whale	200
2 Dugong	60
3 Bottlenose dolphin	48
4 Gray seal	46
5 =Beluga whale	30
=California sea lion	30
=Walrus	30
8 Canadian otter	21
9 Polar bear	20
10 Harbor porpoise	8

* Longest-lived of each genus listed

Source: Lucy T. Verma

Old Man of the Sea

The dugong, the unique member of the family *Dugongidae*, is a large and long-lived marine mammal that – to sailors with vivid imaginations – may have contributed to the mythology of mermaid sightings.

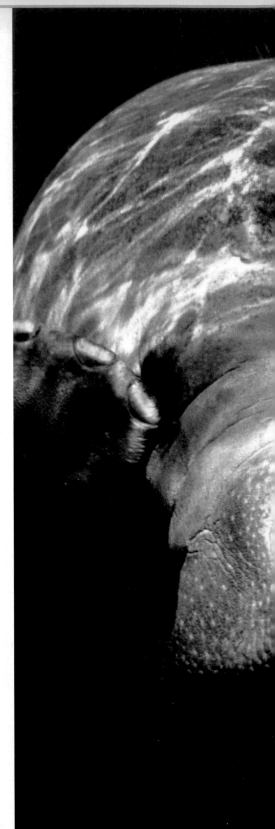

TOP 10 HEAVIEST SPECIES OF SALTWATER FISH CAUGHT

	SPECIES	ANGLER/LOCATION/DATE	WEIGHT (LB)	(OZ)	(KG)
1	Great white shark	Alfred Dean, Ceduna, South Australia, Apr 21, 1959	2,664	0	1,208.4
2	Tiger shark	Walter Maxwell, Cherry Grove, California, Jun 14, 1964	1,780	0	807.4
3	Greenland shark	Terje Nordtvedt, Trondheimsfjord, Norway, Oct 18, 1987	1,708	9	775
4	Black marlin	A. C. Glassell Jr., Cabo Blanco, Peru, Aug 4, 1953	1,560	0	707.6
5	Bluefin tuna	Ken Fraser, Aulds Cove, Nova Scotia, Canada, Oct 26, 1979	1,496	0	679
6	Atlantic blue marlin	Paulo Amorim, Vitoria, Brazil, Feb 29, 1992	1,402	2	636
7	Pacific blue marlin	Jay W. de Beaubien, Kaaiwi Point, Kona, Hawaii, May 31, 1982	1,376	0	624.1
8	Swordfish	L. Marron, Iquique, Chile, May 7, 1953	1,182	0	536.1
9	Mako shark	Patrick Guillanton, Black River, Mauritius, Nov 16, 1988	1,115	0	505.8
10	Sixgilled shark	Jack Reece, Faial, Azores, Oct 18, 1990	1,069	3	485

Source: *International Game Fish Association,* World Record Game Fishes 2000

TOP 10 HEAVIEST MARINE MAMMALS

	MAMMAL	LENGTH (FT)	(M)	WEIGHT (TONS)
1	Blue whale	110.0	33.5	151.0
2	Bowhead whale (Greenland right)	65.0	20.0	95.0
3	Northern right whale (Black right)	60.0	18.6	85.6
4	Fin whale (Common rorqual)	82.0	25.0	69.9
5	Sperm whale	59.0	18.0	48.2
6	Gray whale	46.0	14.0	38.5
7	Humpback whale	49.2	15.0	38.1
8	Sei whale	60.0	18.5	32.4
9	Bryde's whale	47.9	14.6	22.0
10	Baird's whale	18.0	5.5	13.3

Source: *Lucy T. Verma*

Flying Animals

Birds of a Feather
Birds-of-paradise (*Passeriformes*) are among the species found uniquely in New Guinea and its neighbouring islands. These lands are havens for rare birds, many of which are on the endangered list.

TOP 10 BIRDS WITH THE LARGEST WINGSPANS

	BIRD*	MAXIMUM WINGSPAN (IN)	(CM)
1	Great white pelican	141	360
2	Wandering albatross#	138	351
3	Andean condor	126	320
4	Himalayan griffon (vulture)	122	310
5	Black vulture (Old World)	116	295
6	Marabou stork	113	287
7	Lammergeier	111	282
8	Sarus crane	110	280
9	Kori bustard	106	270
10	Steller's sea eagle	104	265

* *By species*

\# *The royal albatross, a close relative, is the same size*

Source: *Chris Mead*

Much bigger wingspans have been claimed for many species, but dead specimens of some species may easily be stretched by 15 to 20 percent. The measurements given are, as far as can be ascertained, for wingtip to wingtip for live birds measured in a natural position.

TOP 10 FURTHEST BIRD MIGRATIONS

	BIRD	APPROXIMATE DISTANCE (MILES)	(KM)
1	Pectoral sandpiper	11,806	19,000*
2	Wheatear	11,184	18,000
3	Slender-billed shearwater	10,874	17,500*
4	Ruff	10,314	16,600
5	Willow warbler	10,128	16,300
6	Arctic tern	10,066	16,200
7	Parasitic jaeger	9,693	15,600
8	Swainson's hawk	9,445	15,200
9	Knot	9,320	15,000
10	Barn swallow	9,258	14,900

* *Thought to be only half of the path taken during a whole year*

Source: *Chris Mead*

This list is of the likely extremes for a normal migrant, not one that has gotten lost and wandered into new territory. All migrant birds fly a lot further than is indicated by the direct route.

TOP 10 ISLANDS WITH THE MOST ENDEMIC BIRD SPECIES*

	ISLAND	SPECIES
1	New Guinea	195
2	Jamaica	26
3	Cuba	23
4	New Caledonia	20
5	Rennell, Solomon Islands	15
6	São Tomé	14
7	=Aldabra, Seychelles	13
	=Grand Cayman, Cayman Islands	13
9	Puerto Rico	12
10	New Britain, Papua New Guinea	11

* *Endemic species are birds that are found uniquely on these islands and nowhere else in the world*

Source: *United Nations*

TOP 10 INCREASINGLY COMMON BIRDS IN THE US

	SPECIES	ANNUAL POPULATION PERCENTAGE INCREASE
1	Wild turkey	11.5
2	Canada goose	9.7
3	=Bald eagle	7.7
	=Brown pelican	7.7
5	Double-crested cormorant	7.0
6	Osprey	6.7
7	Sandhill crane	6.4
8	Black-crowned night heron	6.3
9	Wood duck	5.9
10	European tree sparrow	5.5

Source: North American Breeding Bird Survey/*Chris Mead*

THE FIRST US BIRD RESERVATION

ON MARCH 14, 1903, US PRESIDENT Theodore Roosevelt signed an Executive Order that designated Pelican Island, in Indian River Lagoon near Sebastian, Florida, a "preserve and breeding ground for native birds." This was the first such wildlife refuge in the US. The small island was given this status in order to protect a colony of brown pelicans and herons. Today, 15 federally listed threatened and endangered species live here, including a large population of manatee. Paul Kroegel, a German immigrant, was the first manager of Pelican Island, and a bronze statue of him stands in Sebastian.

FIRST OR LAST

TOP 10 SMALLEST BATS

BAT/HABITAT	LENGTH (IN)	(CM)	WEIGHT (OZ)	(G)
1 **Kitti's hognosed bat,** Thailand	1.10	2.9	0.07	2.0
2 **Proboscis bat,** Central and South America	1.50	3.8	0.09	2.5
3 **=Banana bat,** Africa	1.50	3.8	0.11	3.0
=Smoky bat, Central and South America	1.50	3.8	0.11	3.0
5 **=Little yellow bat,** Central America	1.57	4.0	0.12	3.5
=Lesser bamboo bat, Southeast Asia	1.57	4.0	0.12	3.5
7 **Disc-winged bat,** Central and South America	1.42	3.6	0.14	4.0
8 **Lesser horseshoe bat,** Europe and Western Asia	1.46	3.7	0.18	5.0
9 **California myotis,** North America	1.69	4.3	0.18	5.0
10 **Northern blossom bat,** Southeast Asia to Australia	2.52	6.4	0.53	15.0

This list focuses on the smallest example from 10 different bat families. The weights shown are typical, rather than extreme, and as a bat can eat more than half its own weight, the weights of individual examples may vary considerably. Length includes head and body only, since tail lengths vary.

TOP 10 FASTEST FLYING BIRDS

BIRD	SPEED (MPH)	(KM/H)
1 **Common eider**	47	76
2 **Bewick's swan**	44	72
3 **=Barnacle goose**	42	68
=Common crane	42	68
5 **Mallard**	40	65
6 **=Red-throated diver**	38	61
=Wood pigeon	38	61
8 **Oyster catcher**	36	58
9 **=Pheasant**	33	54
=White-fronted goose	33	54

Source: *Chris Mead*

Recent research reveals that, contrary to popular belief, swifts are not fast fliers, but very efficient, with long, thin wings like gliders. The fastest swimming birds are penguins, who can achieve speeds of 21 mph (35 km/h), and the fastest running bird is the ostrich, which can reach a speed of 44 mph (72 km/h) and maintain it for 20 minutes.

White Lightning
Despite their size, Bewick's swans are among the world's fastest-flying birds. The birds are named after British natural history illustrator Thomas Bewick (1753–1828), who depicted them in woodcuts. Birds such as swans need exceptionally long, strong feathers to power takeoff and sustained flight.

Creepy Crawlies

TOP 10 LARGEST BUTTERFLIES

BUTTERFLY/SCIENTIFIC NAME	WINGSPAN (IN)	(MM)
1 Queen Alexandra's birdwing (*Ornithoptera alexandrae*)	11.0	280
2 African giant swallowtail (*Papilio antimarchus*)	9.1	230
3 Goliath birdwing (*Ornithoptera goliath*)	8.3	210
4 =Buru opalescent birdwing (*Troides prattorum*)	7.9	200
=*Trogonoptera trojana*	7.9	200
=*Troides hypolitus*	7.9	200
7 =Chimaera birdwing (*Ornithoptera chimaera*)	7.5	190
=*Ornithoptera lydius*	7.5	190
=*Troides magellanus*	7.5	190
=*Troides miranda*	7.5	190

TOP 10 LARGEST MOTHS

MOTH/SCIENTIFIC NAME	WINGSPAN (IN)	(MM)
1 Atlas moth (*Attacus atlas*)	11.8	300
2 Owlet moth (*Thysania agrippina*)*	11.4	290
3 *Haematopis grataria*	10.2	260
4 Hercules emperor moth (*Coscinocera hercules*)	8.3	210
5 Malagasy silk moth (*Argema mitraei*)	7.1	180
6 *Eacles imperialis*	6.9	175
7 =Common emperor moth (*Bunaea alcinoe*)	6.3	160
=Giant peacock moth (*Saturnia pyri*)	6.3	160
9 Gray moth (*Brahmaea wallichii*)	6.1	155
10 =Black witch (*Ascalapha odorata*)	5.9	150
=Regal moth (*Citheronia regalis*)	5.9	150
=Polyphemus moth (*Antheraea polyphemus*)	5.9	150

* Exceptional specimen measured at 12.2 in (308 mm)

TOP 10 MOST POPULAR* US STATE INSECTS

INSECT/STATES	NO. OF INSECTS
1 **Honey bee** Arkansas, Georgia, Kansas, Louisiana, Maine, Mississippi, Missouri, Nebraska, New Hampshire, New Jersey, North Carolina, South Dakota, Utah, Vermont, Wisconsin	15
2 **Swallowtail butterfly** Florida (giant/zebra longwing), Georgia (tiger), Mississippi (spicebush), Ohio (tiger), Oklahoma (black), Oregon (Oregon), Virginia (tiger), Wyoming (western)	8
3 **Ladybird beetle/ladybug** Delaware (convergent), Iowa, Massachusetts, New York (nine-spotted), New Hampshire (two-spotted), Ohio, Tennessee (ladybug)	7
4 **Monarch butterfly** Alabama, Idaho, Illinois, Texas, Vermont	5
5 **Firefly** Pennsylvania, Tennessee	2
6 =**Baltimore checkerspot butterfly** Maryland	1
=**California dogface butterfly** California	1
=**Carolina mantis** South Carolina	1
=**Colorado hairstreak butterfly** Colorado	1
=**European praying mantis** Connecticut	1
=**Four-spotted skimmer dragonfly** Alaska	1
=**Green darner dragonfly** Texas	1
=**Karner blue butterfly** New Hampshire	1
=**Tarantula hawk wasp** New Mexico	1
=**Viceroy butterfly** Kentucky	1

* Along with birds, trees, flowers, and other state symbols, most US states have officially adopted an insect or butterfly. These have been nominated by members of the public and are either familiar inhabitants or reflect aspects of the history and culture of the state.

TOP 10 MOST COMMON INSECTS*

SPECIES/SCIENTIFIC NAME	APPROXIMATE NO. OF KNOWN SPECIES
1 **Beetles** (*Coleoptera*)	400,000
2 **Butterflies and moths** (*Lepidoptera*)	165,000
3 **Ants, bees, and wasps** (*Hymenoptera*)	140,000
4 **True flies** (*Diptera*)	120,000
5 **Bugs** (*Hemiptera*)	90,000
6 **Crickets, grasshoppers, and locusts** (*Orthoptera*)	20,000
7 **Caddisflies** (*Trichoptera*)	10,000
8 **Lice** (*Phthiraptera/Psocoptera*)	7,000
9 **Dragonflies and damselflies** (*Odonata*)	5,500
10 **Lacewings** (*Neuroptera*)	4,700

* By number of known species

This list includes only species that have been discovered and named; it is surmised that many thousands of species still await discovery.

TOP 10 MOST COMMON SPIDER FAMILIES

FAMILY/COMMON NAME	KNOWN SPECIES
1 *Salticidae* (jumping spiders)	4,809
2 *Linyphiidae* (sheet-web weavers and dwarf spiders)	4,129
3 *Araneidae* (orb weavers)	2,789
4 *Lycosidae* (wolf spiders)	2,245
5 *Theridiidae* (cobweb weavers or comb-footed spiders)	2,200
6 *Thomisidae* (crab spiders)	2,007
7 *Gnaphosidae* (gnaphosids)	1,926
8 *Tetragnathidae* (long-jawed orb weavers)	979
9 *Sparassidae* (*Heteropodidae*) (huntsman spider)	922
10 *Theraphosidae* (hairy mygalomorphs, "tarantulas" in North America; monkey spiders in South Africa; bird-eating spiders in Australia)	867

Source: *The American Museum of Natural History*

TOP 10 LARGEST MOLLUSCS*

SPECIES/SCIENTIFIC NAME	CLASS	LENGTH (IN)	(MM)
1 Giant squid (*Architeuthis sp.*)	Cephalopod	660#	16,764
2 Giant clam (*Tridacna gigas*)	Marine bivalve	51	1,300
3 Australian trumpet (*Syrinx aruanus*)	Marine snail	30	770
4 *Hexabranchus sanguineus*	Sea slug	20	520
5 *Carinaria cristata*	Heteropod	19	500
6 Steller's Coat of Mail shell (*Cryptochiton stelleri*)	Chiton	18	470
7 Freshwater mussel (*Cristaria plicata*)	Freshwater bivalve	11	300
8 Giant African snail (*Achatina achatina*)	Land snail	7	200
9 Tusk shell (*Dentalium vernedi*)	Scaphopod	5	138
10 Apple snail (*Pila werneri*)	Freshwater snail	4	125

* Largest species within each class   # Estimated; actual length unknown

TOP 10 LARGEST SNAILS

SPECIES/SCIENTIFIC NAME	LENGTH (IN)	(MM)
1 Australian trumpet (*Syrinx aruanus*)	30.3	770
2 Horse conch (*Pleuroploc filamentosa*)	22.8	580
3 =Baler shell (*Voluta amphora*)	18.8	480
=Triton's trumpet (*Charonia tritonis*)	18.8	480
5 Beck's volute (*Voluta becki*)	18.5	470
6 Umbilicate volute (*Voluta umbilicalis*)	16.5	420
7 Madagascar helmet (*Cassis madagascariensis*)	16.1	409
8 Spider conch (*Lambis truncata*)	15.7	400
9 Knobbly trumpet (*Charonia nodifera*)	15.3	390
10 Goliath conch (*Strombus goliath*)	14.9	380

Jumping Spider

The most diverse of all spider groups, jumping spiders (*Salticidae*), can leap over 50 times their own body length, and have remarkable vision – with four large eyes on their faces and four smaller eyes on top of their heads.

Best in Show

TOP 10 PETS IN THE US

PET	ESTIMATED NUMBER
1 Dogs	40,000,000
2 Cats	34,700,000
3 Freshwater fish*	12,200,000
4 Small animal pets†	5,500,000
5 Reptiles	4,000,000
6 Cockatiels	2,600,000
7 Parakeets	2,100,000
8 Saltwater fish	700,000
9 Finches	600,000
10 Parrots	500,000

* *Number of households owning, rather than individual specimens*

† *Includes small rodents – rabbits, ferrets, hamsters, guinea pigs, and gerbils*

Source: *American Pet Products Manufacturers Association*

TOP 10 PET REPTILE POPULATIONS

COUNTRY	ESTIMATED PET REPTILE POPULATION IN 1999
1 US	7,680,000
2 Russia	4,500,000
3 UK	1,730,000
4 =France	1,100,000
=Italy	1,100,000
6 China	612,000
7 Spain	200,000
8 Canada	190,000
9 Thailand	187,000
10 Australia	170,000

Source: *Euromonitor*

TOP 10 PET BIRD POPULATIONS

COUNTRY	ESTIMATED PET BIRD POPULATION IN 2000
1 China	67,765,800
2 Japan	19,362,000
3 US	15,680,000
4 Brazil	15,000,000
5 Indonesia	13,592,000
6 Italy	13,000,000
7 Turkey	8,012,000
8 Spain	7,369,000
9 France	7,000,000
10 Australia	6,900,000

Source: *Euromonitor*

TOP 10 PET FISH POPULATIONS

COUNTRY	ESTIMATED PET FISH POPULATION IN 2000
1 China	111,477,500
2 US	103,400,000
3 Germany	50,000,000
4 Japan	35,200,000
5 Italy	29,000,000
6 France	27,000,000
7 UK	26,600,000
8 Russia	20,500,000
9 Australia	12,400,000
10 Sweden	9,390,000

Source: *Euromonitor*

Fish Fortunes
Perhaps one reason for the huge number of fish kept in China is that the ancient art of Feng Shui tells people that keeping pet fish can bring wealth and progress to their lives.

YEAR	BREED	CHAMPION
2002	Miniature poodle	Surrey Spice Girl
2001	Bichons frises	Special Times Just Right
2000	English springer spaniel	Salilyn 'N Erin's Shameless
1999	Papillon	Loteki Supernatural Being
1998	Norwich terrier	Fairewood Frolic
1997	Standard schnauzer	Parsifal Di Casa Netzer
1996	Clumber spaniel	Clussexx Country Sunrise
1995	Scottish terrier	Gaelforce Post Script
1994	Norwich terrier	Chidley Willum The Conqueror
1993	English springer spaniel	Salilyn's Condor

Source: *Westminster Kennel Club*

Cool for Cats

Ownership of pedigree cats, such as this Siamese, contributes to the substantial feline population of many Western countries. In developing parts of the world, cats continue their traditional role as domestic mouse-catchers.

TOP 10 | PET CAT POPULATIONS

	COUNTRY	ESTIMATED CAT POPULATION IN 2000
1	US	75,075,000
2	China	48,765,600
3	Russia	12,500,000
4	Brazil	11,200,000
5	Italy	9,200,000
6	France	9,000,000
7	UK	8,000,000
8	Japan	7,718,000
9	Ukraine	7,100,000
10	Germany	6,800,000

Source: *Euromonitor*

Estimates of the number of domestic cats in the 20 leading countries reveal a total of 221 million, with the greatest increases experienced in China and other Asian societies.

TOP 10 | PET SMALL MAMMAL POPULATIONS

	COUNTRY	ESTIMATED PET SMALL MAMMAL POPULATION IN 1999
1	US	13,080,000
2	Germany	4,600,000
3	Russia	4,500,000
4	UK	3,670,000
5	Japan	2,830,000
6	France	1,800,000
7	China	1,513,000
8	Italy	1,150,000
9	Canada	1,140,000
10	Spain	1,000,000

Source: *Euromonitor*

TOP 10 | PET DOG POPULATIONS

	COUNTRY	ESTIMATED DOG POPULATION IN 2000
1	US	59,350,000
2	Brazil	27,000,000
3	China	20,387,800
4	Japan	10,054,000
5	Russia	9,500,000
6	South Africa	8,200,000
7	France	8,100,000
8	Poland	7,450,000
9	Italy	7,400,000
10	UK	6,500,000

Source: *Euromonitor*

Trees & Plants

TOP 10 MOST COMMON TREES IN THE US

	TREE
1	Silver maple
2	Black cherry
3	Boxelder
4	Eastern cottonwood
5	Black willow
6	Northern red oak
7	Flowering dogwood
8	Black oak
9	Ponderosa pine
10	Coast douglas fir

Source: *American Forests*

TOP 10 OLDEST BOTANIC GARDENS IN NORTH AMERICA

	GARDEN/LOCATION	FOUNDED
1	**Pierce's Park*,** **Kennett Square,** Pennsylvania	1800
2	**United States** **Botanic Garden,** Washington, DC	1820
3	**Painter's Arboretum#,** Media, Pennsylvania	1830
4	**Missouri Botanical Garden,** St. Louis, Missouri	1859
5	**Arnold Arboretum,** Jamaica Plain, Massachusetts	1872
6	**W. J. Beal Botanical Garden,** East Lansing, Michigan	1873
7	**Dominion Arboretum** **& Botanic Garden,** Ottawa, Ontario, Canada	1886
8	**University of California** **Berkeley Botanic Garden,** Berkeley, California	1890
9	**New York Botanical Garden,** Bronx, New York	1891
10	**Botanic Garden of Smith College,** Northampton, Massachusetts	1893

* *Now Longwood Gardens*   # *Now Tyler Arboretum*

Source: *American Association of Botanical Gardens and Arboreta*

TOP 10 COUNTRIES WITH THE LARGEST AREAS OF FOREST

	COUNTRY	AREA IN YEAR 2000 (SQ MILES)	(SQ KM)
1	Russia	3,287,243	8,513,920
2	Brazil	2,100,359	5,439,905
3	Canada	944,294	2,445,710
4	US	872,564	2,259,930
5	China	631,200	1,634,800
6	Australia	596,678	1,545,390
7	Dem. Rep. of Congo	522,037	1,352,070
8	Indonesia	405,353	1,049,860
9	Angola	269,329	697,560
10	Peru	251,796	652,150
	World total	*14,888,715*	*38,561,590*

Source: *Food and Agriculture Organization of the United Nations*, State of the World's Forests, 2001

THE 10 COUNTRIES WITH THE HIGHEST DEFORESTATION RATE

	COUNTRY	ANNUAL FOREST COVER LOSS, 1990–2000 (SQ MILES)	(SQ KM)
1	Brazil	8,915	23,090
2	Indonesia	5,065	13,120
3	Sudan	3,702	9,590
4	Zambia	3,286	8,510
5	Mexico	2,436	6,310
6	Dem. Rep. of Congo	2,054	5,320
7	Myanmar	1,996	5,170
8	Nigeria	1,537	3,980
9	Zimbabwe	1,235	3,200
10	Argentina	1,100	2,850

Source: *Food and Agriculture Organization of the United Nations*, State of the World's Forests, 2001

Forest Jump
Although the world's forests occupy some 29 percent of the total land area, during the 20th century deforestation has caused a steady decline in the number of trees.

TOP 10 | WILDFLOWERS GROWN FROM SEED IN THE US

1	Texas bluebonnet
2	Indian paintbrush
3	Corn poppy
4	Black-eyed Susan
5	Butterfly weed
6	Cosmos
7	Coreopsis
8	Indian blanket
9	Larkspur
10	Purple cone flower

Source: *Wildseed Farms*

In 1901, after strong lobbying by the Colonial Dames of Texas, the bluebonnet became the official state flower. The Indian paintbrush was adopted by Wyoming in 1917.

TOP 10 | COUNTRIES REGISTERING THE MOST NEW PLANT VARIETIES

	COUNTRY	VARIETIES REGISTERED*
1	Japan	1,017
2	Netherlands	751
3	US	629
4	France	620
5	Germany	309
6	Poland	303
7	Australia	218
8	Russia	216
9	Ecuador	193
10	South Africa	189

* As recorded by World Intellectual Property Organization, 1998

TOP 10 | ANNUAL FLOWERS SOLD IN THE US

1	Sunflower
2	Zinnia
3	Alyssum
4	Marigold
5	Sweet pea
6	Morning glory
7	Nasturtium
8	Cosmos
9	Bachelor's button
10	Portulaca

Source: *NK Lawn & Garden Co.*

TOP 10 | HERBS SOLD IN THE US

1	Basil
2	Parsley
3	Cilantro
4	Dill
5	Chives
6	Mint
7	Oregano
8	Lavender
9	Thyme
10	Sage

Source: *NK Lawn & Garden Co.*

Flower Power
One of US's most popular flowers, the sweet pea was introduced from Europe in the 18th century.

Fruit & Nuts

TOP 10 FRUIT-PRODUCING COUNTRIES

	COUNTRY	PRODUCTION IN 2001 (TONS)
1	China	79,548,281
2	India	48,816,726
3	Brazil	39,775,056
4	US	33,977,833
5	Italy	21,392,208
6	Spain	18,143,245
7	Mexico	15,493,232
8	France	12,395,571
9	Turkey	11,692,049
10	Philippines	11,450,055
	World total	*522,384,554*

Source: *Food and Agriculture Organization of the United Nations*

There are 12 countries in the world (those in the Top 10, plus Iran and Uganda) that each produce more than 10 million tons of fruit annually.

TOP 10 ALMOND-PRODUCING COUNTRIES

	COUNTRY	PRODUCTION IN 2001 (TONS)
1	US	424,876
2	Spain	322,335
3	Italy	131,551
4	Iran	95,874
5	Morocco	71,630
6	Syria	68,641
7	Tunisia	66,120
8	Pakistan	55,210
9	Greece	48,488
10	Turkey	40,774
	World total	*1,558,689*

Source: *Food and Agriculture Organization of the United Nations*

TOP 10 STRAWBERRY-PRODUCING COUNTRIES

	COUNTRY	PRODUCTION IN 2001 (TONS)
1	US	906,725
2	Spain	385,700
3	Poland	262,467
4	Japan	226,240
5	South Korea	192,850
6	Mexico	155,382
7	Italy	152,642
8	Russia	146,566
9	Turkey	121,220
10	Germany	120,331
	World total	*3,425,035*

Source: *Food and Agriculture Organization of the United Nations*

TOP 10 WALNUT-PRODUCING COUNTRIES

	COUNTRY	PRODUCTION IN 2001 (TONS)
1	China	363,660
2	US	247,950
3	Iran	148,770
4	Turkey	134,444
5	Ukraine	57,304
6	India	34,162
7	France	29,754
8	Romania	27,550
9	Yugoslavia	26,201
10	Greece	22,040
	World total	*1,345,962*

Source: *Food and Agriculture Organization of the United Nations*

In a Nutshell
Although China is the world's leading walnut producer, the US remains the foremost exporter, with some 55 percent of the global total coming from US producers.

TOP 10 COCONUT-PRODUCING COUNTRIES

	COUNTRY	PRODUCTION IN 2001 (TONS)
1	Indonesia	18,734,000
2	Philippines	11,130,200
3	India	10,084,953
4	Brazil	2,203,014
5	Sri Lanka	2,148,900
6	Thailand	1,513,224
7	Mexico	1,281,626
8	Vietnam	1,066,736
9	Papua New Guinea	910,252
10	Malaysia	785,726
	World total	*54,837,559*

Source: *Food and Agriculture Organization of the United Nations*

TOP 10 GRAPE-PRODUCING COUNTRIES

	COUNTRY	PRODUCTION IN 2001 (TONS)
1	Italy	10,770,552
2	France	8,595,600
3	Spain	7,364,555
4	US	6,887,500
5	China	3,840,470
6	Turkey	3,746,800
7	Argentina	2,708,274
8	Iran	2,314,200
9	Chile	1,840,340
10	Germany	1,827,777
	World total	*70,846,917*

Source: *Food and Agriculture Organization of the United Nations*

TOP 10 DATE-PRODUCING COUNTRIES

	COUNTRY	PRODUCTION IN 2001 (TONS)
1	Egypt	981,154
2	Saudi Arabia	784,624
3	Pakistan	639,027
4	Iran	440,800
5	Algeria	407,740
6	United Arab Emirates	350,436
7	Oman	286,520
8	Sudan	195,054
9	Libya	146,015
10	China	121,220
	World total	*5,740,681*

Source: *Food and Agriculture Organization of the United Nations*

Date Data
Dates are widely grown throughout the Middle East. They have been an important source of nourishment to desert tribespeople since ancient times.

Crops & Livestock

TOP 10 MOST-PRODUCED CEREAL CROPS

	CROP	PRODUCTION IN 2001 (TONS)
1	Corn	661,171,533
2	Rice (paddy)	645,323,921
3	Wheat	624,660,581
4	Barley	147,445,895
5	Sorghum	64,580,024
6	Millet	30,538,294
7	Oats	28,963,245
8	Rye	25,004,972
9	Triticale	12,403,905
10	Buckwheat	3,565,414
	World total	2,252,658,765

Source: *Food and Agriculture Organization of the United Nations*

Indonesian Rice Bowl
Rice is Indonesia's principal crop, with some 45,174 sq miles (117,000 sq km) of the country devoted to its cultivation.

TOP 10 TYPES OF ANIMALS KEPT AS LIVESTOCK

	ANIMAL	WORLD TOTAL IN 2001
1	Chickens	14,661,643,000
2	Cattle	1,360,136,890
3	Sheep	1,059,107,230
4	Pigs	927,692,033
5	Ducks	915,369,000
6	Goats	693,456,713
7	Rabbits	481,569,000
8	Turkeys	241,377,000
9	Geese	240,627,000
10	Buffaloes	167,611,168

Source: *Food and Agriculture Organization of the United Nations*

Certain countries provide a single figure for all poultry, including chickens, turkeys, and ducks, and data for these countries are shown collectively under "chickens", further boosting a world chicken population that outnumbers that of humans by more than two to one.

TOP 10 CHICKEN PRODUCERS

	COUNTRY	CHICKENS (2001)
1	China	3,771,485,000
2	US	1,728,000,000
3	Brazil	1,006,000,000
4	Indonesia	800,000,000
5	Mexico	480,000,000
6	India	402,000,000
7	Russia	325,000,000
8	Japan	297,000,000
9	Turkey	236,997,000
10	France	230,000,000
	World total	14,661,643,000

Source: *Food and Agriculture Organization of the United Nations*

The Top 10 countries are home to 65 percent of the world's chicken population.

TOP 10 VEGETABLE PRODUCERS

	COUNTRY	PRODUCTION* IN 2001 (TONS)
1	China	316,021,504
2	India	67,080,393
3	US	41,542,975
4	Turkey	24,353,111
5	Italy	16,910,584
6	Egypt	15,055,036
7	Russia	14,087,141
8	Japan	13,954,613
9	South Korea	13,396,139
10	Spain	13,379,397
	World total	745,005,308

* Includes only vegetables grown for human consumption; including watermelons but excluding private garden crops

Source: *Food and Agriculture Organization of the United Nations*

 **GOAT PRODUCERS**

	COUNTRY	GOATS (2001)
1	China	157,361,699
2	India	123,000,000
3	Pakistan	49,100,000
4	Bangladesh	33,800,000
5	Iran	25,200,000
6	Nigeria	24,300,000
7	Ethiopia	16,000,000
8	Indonesia	14,121,000
9	Somalia	12,500,000
10	Tanzania	10,000,000
	World total	693,456,713

Source: *Food and Agriculture Organization of the United Nations*

The goat is one of the most widely distributed of all domesticated animals. It can live in harsh conditions and is fairly disease-resistant, making it well suited to some of the less developed parts of the world – even some of the smaller African countries have one million or more goats.

CABBAGE PRODUCERS

	COUNTRY	PRODUCTION IN 2001 (TONS)
1	China	21,198,000
2	India	4,250,000
3	Russia	3,936,000
4	South Korea	3,200,000
5	Japan	2,600,000
6	US	2,298,700
7	Poland	1,767,280
8	Indonesia	1,750,000
9	Ukraine	1,200,000
10	Romania	1,000,000
	World total	54,432,224

Source: *Food and Agricultural Organization of the United Nations*

Getting the Goat

There are more than 60 countries in the world with one million or more goats. Worldwide goats produce over 13 million tons of milk a year, while more than 300 million are slaughtered annually to provide meat and goatskin.

THE HUMAN
WORLD

The Human Body & Health

TOP 10 MOST COMMON HEALTH DISORDERS

% OF TOTAL*	DISORDERS (MALE)		DISORDERS (FEMALE)	% OF TOTAL*
9.7	Depression	1	Depression	14.0
5.5	Alcohol abuse	2	Iron-deficiency disorders	4.9
5.1	Hearing loss adult onset	3	Hearing loss adult onset	4.2
4.1	Iron-deficiency anemia	4	Osteoarthritis	3.5
3.8	Chronic obstructive pulmonary disease	5	Chronic obstructive pulmonary disease	2.9
3.3	Falls	6	Schizophrenia	2.7
3.0	Schizophrenia	7	Manic depression	2.4
2.7	Traffic accidents	8	Falls	2.3
2.6	Manic depression	9	Alzheimer's and other dementias	2.2
2.2	Osteoarthritus	10	Obstructed labor	2.1

Total includes other disorders not listed above

Source: *World Health Organization*, World Health Report 2001

TOP 10 GLOBAL DISEASES*

	DISEASE	PERCENTAGE OF TOTAL BURDEN OF DISEASE#†
1	Neuropsychiatric disorders	12.3
2	Cardiovascular diseases	10.3
3	Respiratory infections	6.6
4	Perinatal conditions	6.2
5	HIV/AIDS	6.1
6	Malignant neoplasms (cancers)	5.3
7	Respiratory diseases (non-communicable)	4.7
8	Diarrheal diseases	4.2
9	Childhood diseases	3.4
10	Malaria	2.7

* *Those diseases that cause the highest total levels of disability worldwide*

Measured in Disability-Adjusted Life Years (DALYs): a measure of the difference between a population's health and a normative goal of living in full health

† *Total percentage includes injuries at 12.4 percent and nutritional deficiencies at 3.1 percent*

Source: *World Health Organization*, World Health Report 2001

TOP 10 MOST COMMON HOSPITAL ER CASES

	REASON FOR VISIT	VISITS PER 1,000 IN 1999
1	Falls	27.7
2	Open wounds	26.9
3	Sprains and strains	23.2
4	Superficial injuries	22.3
5	Acute upper respiratory infections	19.9
6	Injuries from being struck by/against a stationary object	15.6
7	Motor vehicle crash injuries	15.0
8	Fractures	13.5
9	=Abdominal pain (ill-defined)	12.6
	=Chest pain (ill-defined)	12.6

Source: *National Ambulatory Medical Care Survey/Center for Disease Control/National Center for Health Statistics*

In 1999 there were a total of 102,765,000 emergency room visits. Self-inflicted injuries saw the biggest increase over the 5-year period 1992–99, to 1.6 visits per 1,000 – a rise of 147 percent, followed by diabetes with a rise of 101 percent to 2.2 visits per 1,000.

THE FIRST ELECTROCARDIOGRAM

FIRST OR LAST

Dutch doctor Willem Einthoven (1860–1927) was awarded the Nobel Prize for Physiology or Medicine in 1924 "for his discovery of the mechanism of the electrocardiogram." His work began in 1903 when he invented the "string galvanometer," a machine for measuring the changes in electrical potential resulting from the contractions of the heart and displaying them graphically, thus indicating any defects or heart disease. During subsequent years, the device, the "electrocardiogram," became a vital tool in the medical repertory.

TOP 10 COUNTRIES THAT SPEND THE LEAST ON HEALTH CARE

	COUNTRY	HEALTH SPENDING PER CAPITA IN 1998 ($)
1	Liberia	1
2	Burundi	3
3	Somalia	4
4	=Niger	5
	=Sierra Leone	5
	=Tajikistan	5
7	=Ethiopia	6
	=Madagascar	6
9	=Central African Republic	7
	=Chad	7

Source: *World Health Organization*, World Health Report 2001

TOP 10 COUNTRIES THAT SPEND THE MOST ON HEALTH CARE

	COUNTRY	HEALTH SPENDING PER CAPITA IN 1998 ($)
1	US	4,055
2	Switzerland	3,877
3	Norway	2,848
4	Denmark	2,737
5	Germany	2,697
6	France	2,297
7	Japan	2,244
8	Netherlands	2,166
9	Sweden	2,144
10	Austria	2,097

Source: *World Health Organization*, World Health Report 2001

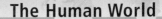
TOP 10 MOST COMMON PHOBIAS

	OBJECT OF PHOBIA	MEDICAL TERM
1	Spiders	Arachnephobia or arachnophobia
2	People and social situations	Anthropophobia or sociophobia
3	Flying	Aerophobia or aviatophobia
4	Open spaces	Agoraphobia, cenophobia, or kenophobia
5	Confined spaces	Claustrophobia, cleisiophobia, cleithrophobia, or clithrophobia
6	=Heights	Acrophobia, altophobia, hypsophobia, or hypsiphobia
	=Vomiting	Emetophobia or emitophobia
8	Cancer	Carcinomaphobia, carcinophobia, carcinomatophobia, cancerphobia, or cancerophobia
9	Thunderstorms	Brontophobia or keraunophobia; related phobias are those associated with lightning (astraphobia), cyclones (anemophobia), and hurricanes and tornadoes (lilapsophobia)
10	=Death	Necrophobia or thanatophobia
	=Heart disease	Cardiophobia

A phobia is a fear that is out of all proportion to the object of the fear. Many people would admit to being uncomfortable about these principal phobias, as well as others such as snakes (ophiophobia), injections (trypanophobia), or ghosts (phasmophobia), but most do not become obsessive about them and allow such fears to rule their lives. True phobias often arise from some incident in childhood when a person has been afraid of some object and has developed an irrational fear that persists into adulthood. Perhaps suprisingly, the Top 10 does not remain static, as "new" phobias become more common: for example, outside the Top 10, "technophobia," the fear of modern technology such as computers, is increasingly reported. Today, as well as the valuable work done by the Phobics Society in Britain and similar organizations in other countries, phobias can be cured by taking special desensitization courses, for example to conquer one's fear of flying.

High Anxiety
Fear of heights is one of the most common of all phobias: devotees of extreme sports such as skydiving achieve thrills by confronting and overcoming this aversion.

The Human Condition

Norwegian Good Life
Ranked by a range of quality-of-life factors, including life expectancy, education, and standard of living, Norway is the best place in the world to live according to the United Nations.

TOP 10 MOST UNDERNOURISHED COUNTRIES

	COUNTRY	APPROXIMATE PERCENTAGE UNDERNOURISHED (1996–98)*
1	Somalia	75
2	Afghanistan	70
3	Burundi	68
4	Eritrea	65
5	Haiti	62
6	Dem. Rep. of Congo	61
7	North Korea	57
8	Ethiopia	49
9	=Liberia	46
	=Niger	46

* Food intake that is insufficient to meet dietary requirements continuously

Source: *United Nations*, Human Development Report

TOP 10 BEST COUNTRIES TO LIVE IN

	COUNTRY	HDI RANK* IN 1999
1	Norway	0.939
2	=Australia	0.936
	=Canada	0.936
	=Sweden	0.936
5	Belgium	0.935
6	US	0.934
7	Iceland	0.932
8	Netherlands	0.931
9	Japan	0.928
10	Finland	0.925

* The UN Human Development Index ranks countries by quality of life. Criteria for the ranking calculations include life expectancy, adult literacy, school enrolment, educational attainment, and per capita GDP

Source: *United Nations*, Human Development Report

TOP 10 FAT CONSUMERS

	COUNTRY	FAT CONSUMPTION PER CAPITA PER DAY (OZ)	(G)
1	France	5.80	164.6
2	Belgium and Luxembourg	5.61	159.1
3	Austria	5.38	152.8
4	Italy	5.37	152.4
5	Greece	5.33	151.3
6	Spain	5.31	150.7
7	US	5.23	148.5
8	Germany	5.18	147.0
9	UK	5.14	145.8
10	Switzerland	5.13	145.7

Source: *Food and Agricultural Organization of the United Nations*

TOP 10 COUNTRIES WITH THE MOST SMOKERS

	COUNTRY	ANNUAL CIGARETTE CONSUMPTION PER ADULT (1992–98)*
1	Greece	3,923
2	Poland	3,143
3	South Korea	2,898
4	Netherlands	2,857
5	Switzerland	2,846
6	Singapore	2,835
7	Bahrain	2,819
8	Croatia	2,632
9	Kuwait	2,525
10	Czech Republic	2,504

* Aged over 15, in those countries for which data available

Source: *United Nations*, Human Development Report

TOP 10 COUNTRIES WITH THE FEWEST DEATHS FROM LUNG CANCER

	COUNTRY	DEATH RATE PER 100,000 FEMALE	MALE*
1	Tanzania	0.00	0.27
2	Nigeria	0.01	0.31
3	Sudan	0.59	0.57
4	Senegal	0.19	0.65
5	Liberia	0.28	0.66
6	Cape Verde	0.22	0.74
7	Benin	0.17	0.90
8	=Ethiopia	1.63	0.94
	=Togo	0.19	0.94
10	Sierra Leone	0.19	0.98

Ranked by incidence in male population

Source: *International Agency for Research on Cancer,* Globocan 2000

THE 10 COUNTRIES WITH THE MOST DEATHS FROM LUNG CANCER

	COUNTRY	DEATH RATE PER 100,000 FEMALE	MALE*
1	Hungary	36.02	123.92
2	Belgium	18.69	119.73
3	Croatia	18.61	105.65
4	Italy	18.60	98.08
5	Greece	15.42	92.69
6	Netherlands	24.70	90.72
7	Luxembourg	19.61	86.66
8	Poland	17.84	86.55
9	Estonia	17.09	85.17
10	UK	44.19	84.58

Ranked by incidence in male population

Source: *International Agency for Research on Cancer,* Globocan 2000

Ashes to Ashes
Greece heads the Top 10 of the world's heaviest smoking populations, leading also to its appearance – though not in first place – among countries with the most deaths from lung cancer.

Cradle to the Grave

TOP 10 | COUNTRIES WITH THE HIGHEST BIRTH RATE

	COUNTRY	ESTIMATED BIRTH RATE (LIVE BIRTHS PER 1,000 IN 2003)
1	Niger	49.3
2	Mali	47.9
3	Chad	47.2
4	Uganda	46.8
5	Somalia	46.4
6	Angola	45.8
7	Liberia	45.4
8	Dem. Rep. of Congo	45.1
9	Marshall Islands	44.9
10	=Ethiopia	44.0
	=Sierra Leone	44.0

Source: *US Census Bureau, International Data Base*

The countries with the highest birth rates are often among the poorest countries in the world.

TOP 10 | COUNTRIES WITH THE LOWEST BIRTH RATE

	COUNTRY	ESTIMATED BIRTH RATE (LIVE BIRTHS PER 1,000 IN 2003)
1	Bulgaria	8.0
2	Latvia	8.6
3	=Germany	8.8
	=Italy	8.8
5	Czech Republic	9.0
6	=Estonia	9.2
	=Slovenia	9.2
8	=Hungary	9.3
	=Spain	9.3
10	Austria	9.4
	US	*14.1*

Source: *US Census Bureau, International Data Base*

Baby Boom
Mali and most of the other countries with high birth rates have rural economies that depend on large families to provide the required labor force.

TOP 10 COUNTRIES WITH THE HIGHEST LIFE EXPECTANCY

	COUNTRY	LIFE EXPECTANCY AT BIRTH YEARS (2000–05)
1	Japan	81.5
2	Sweden	80.1
3	Iceland	79.4
4	=Australia	79.2
	=Israel	79.2
6	=Martinique	79.1
	=Switzerland	79.1
8	=Canada	79.0
	=France	79.0
10	Norway	78.9
	World	66.0
	US	77.5

Source: *United Nations Population Division*

Lease of Life

Japan was the first country to attain an average lifespan of over 80 years – more than double that of many less-developed countries.

THE 10 MOST COMMON CAUSES OF DEATH

	CAUSE	APPROXIMATE DEATHS IN 2000
1	Cancers	6,930,000
2	Ischemic heart disease	6,894,000
3	Cerebrovascular disease (relating to the brain and its blood vessels)	5,101,000
4	Lower respiratory infection	3,866,000
5	HIV/AIDS	2,943,000
6	Chronic obstructive pulmonary disease (relating to the lungs)	2,523,000
7	Perinatal conditions (relating to the time before and after giving birth)	2,439,000
8	Diarrhea, including dysentery	2,124,000
9	Tuberculosis	1,660,000
10	Childhood diseases*	1,385,000

* *Childhood diseases include pertussis (whooping cough), poliomyelitis, diphtheria, measles, and tetanus*

Source: *World Health Organization*, World Health Report 2001

THE 10 COUNTRIES WITH THE LOWEST LIFE EXPECTANCY

	COUNTRY	LIFE EXPECTANCY AT BIRTH YEARS (2000–05)
1	Botswana	36.1
2	Mozambique	38.0
3	Swaziland	38.1
4	Malawi	39.3
5	Lesotho	40.2
6	Sierra Leone	40.5
7	=Burundi	40.6
	=Djibouti	40.6
9	Rwanda	40.9
10	Zambia	42.2

Source: *United Nations Population Division*

THE 10 COUNTRIES WITH THE HIGHEST DEATH RATE

	COUNTRY	ESTIMATED DEATH RATE (DEATHS PER 1,000 IN 2003)
1	Botswana	28.3
2	Mozambique	26.1
3	Zimbabwe	24.9
4	Swaziland	24.6
5	Angola	24.0
6	Namibia	23.7
7	Malawi	23.6
8	=Niger	21.8
	=Zambia	21.8
10	Rwanda	21.7
	US	8.6

Source: *US Census Bureau International Data Base*

TOP 10 COUNTRIES WITH THE LOWEST DEATH RATE

	COUNTRY	ESTIMATED DEATH RATE (DEATHS PER 1,000 IN 2003)
1	Kuwait	2.5
2	Jordan	2.6
3	Brunei	3.4
4	Libya	3.5
5	=Bahrain	4.0
	=Oman	4.0
	=United Arab Emirates	4.0
8	Solomon Islands	4.1
9	=Costa Rica	4.3
	=Guam	4.3
	=Singapore	4.3

Source: *US Census Bureau International Data Base*

For Better or For Worse

COUNTRY	DIVORCE RATE PER 1,000*
1 Colombia	0.11
2 Libya	0.24
3 Mongolia	0.38
4 Georgia	0.42
5 =Mexico	0.43
=Chile	0.43
7 Italy	0.47
8 El Salvador	0.49
9 Macedonia	0.51
10 Turkey	0.52

* In those countries/latest year for which data available

Source: *United Nations*

THE 10 COUNTRIES WITH THE HIGHEST DIVORCE RATES

COUNTRY	DIVORCE RATE PER 1,000*
1 Maldives	10.97
2 Belarus	4.63
3 US	4.34
4 Cuba	3.72
5 Estonia	3.65
6 =Panama	3.61
=Puerto Rico	3.61
8 Ukraine	3.56
9 Russia	3.42
10 Antigua and Barbuda	3.40

* In those countries/latest year for which data available

Source: *United Nations*

TOP 10 COUNTRIES WHERE MOST WOMEN MARRY

COUNTRY	PERCENTAGE OF WOMEN MARRIED BY AGE 50*
1 =Comoros	100.0
=The Gambia	100.0
=Ghana	100.0
=Nauru	100.0
5 Chad	99.9
6 =China	99.8
=Guinea	99.8
=Mali	99.8
=Papua New Guinea	99.8
10 Benin	99.7
US	93.9

* In latest year for which data available

Source: *United Nations*

TOP 10 HONEYMOON DESTINATIONS FOR US COUPLES

	DESTINATION*	PERCENTAGE
1	Hawaii	11.6
2	Mexico	11.0
3	Jamaica	10.8
4	Bahamas	7.6
5	Europe	6.0
6	Virgin Islands	5.8
7	St. Lucia	5.5
8	Aruba	3.6
9	=Canada	3.4
	=Cayman Islands	3.4

Excludes contiguous states

Source: Modern Bride

Brides-to-be
Marriage is part of a deep-rooted tradition in the Comoros Islands, resulting in colorful and extravagant wedding ceremonies that can last for three days.

TOP 10 WEDDING SONGS IN THE US

	TITLE	ARTIST
1	The Power of Love	Celine Dion
2	I Finally Found Someone	Barbara Streisand/ Bryan Adams
3	I Cross My Heart	George Strait
4	Unchained Melody	Righteous Brothers
5	Always	Atlantic Starr
6	Because You Loved Me	Celine Dion
7	Wonderful Tonight	Eric Clapton
8	Always and Forever	Heatwave
9	Keeper of the Stars	Tracy Byrd
10	If You Say My Eyes Are Beautiful	Whitney Houston/ Janet Jackson

Source: *Wedding Zone*

Celine Dion's 1994 platinum single *The Power of Love* was a cover version of Jennifer Rush's 1985 hit single. Along with the rest of the Top 10, it is a middle-of-the-road ballad with lyrics that strike an appropriately sentimental chord with many couples on their wedding day.

Male Grooming
The average age for marriage in most Western countries is in the late 20s, whereas in Nepal, 22 is the norm.

TOP 10 COUNTRIES WHERE WOMEN MARRY THE YOUNGEST

	COUNTRY	AVERAGE AGE AT FIRST MARRIAGE
1	Dem. Rep. of Congo	16.6
2	=Afghanistan	17.8
	=São Tomé and Principe	17.8
4	Niger	17.6
5	=Chad	18.0
	=Mozambique	18.0
7	Bangladesh	18.1
8	Uganda	18.2
9	=Congo	18.4
	=Mali	18.4

Source: *United Nations*

TOP 10 COUNTRIES WHERE MEN MARRY THE YOUNGEST

	COUNTRY	AVERAGE AGE AT FIRST MARRIAGE
1	Nepal	22.0
2	San Marino	22.2
3	Uganda	22.5
4	Mozambique	22.6
5	São Tomé and Principe	23.0
6	Tajikstan	23.1
7	Maldives	23.2
8	Uzbekistan	23.3
9	=Cuba	23.5
	=Malawi	23.5

Source: *United Nations*

What's in a Name?

TOP 10 — FIRST NAMES IN THE US, 2001

GIRLS		BOYS
Emily	1	Jacob
Hannah	2	Michael
Madison	3	Joshua
Samantha	4	Matthew
Ashley	5	Andrew
Sarah	6	Joseph
Elizabeth	7	Nicholas
Kayla	8	Anthony
Alexis	9	Tyler
Abigail	10	Daniel

The Top 10 is based on a 1 percent sample of Social Security applications for the period January to August 2001.

Naming Game

Each new generation of babies receives first names that mirror the fashions of the day, although girls' names are far more volatile than those of boys, whose names tend to be more enduring and traditional.

TOP 10 — LAST NAMES IN THE US

	NAME	PERCENTAGE OF ALL US NAMES
1	Smith	1.006
2	Johnson	0.810
3	Williams	0.699
4	=Brown	0.621
	=Jones	0.621
6	Davis	0.480
7	Miller	0.424
8	Wilson	0.339
9	Moore	0.312
10	=Anderson	0.311
	=Taylor	0.311
	=Thomas	0.311

The Top 10 (or, in view of those in equal 10th place, 12) US last names together make up over 6 percent of the entire US population – in other words, 1 American in every 16 bears one of these names.

TOP 10 — FIRST NAMES IN THE US 100 YEARS AGO

GIRLS		BOYS
Mary	1	John
Margaret	2	William
Helen	3	James
Anna	4	George
Ruth	5	Joseph
Marie	6	Charles
Elizabeth	7	Robert
Florence	8	Frank
Dorothy	9	Walter
Lillian	10	Henry

TOP 10 US PATRONYMS

	NAME/ORIGIN	PERCENTAGE OF ALL US NAMES
1	**Johnson** ("son of John")	0.810
2	**Williams** ("son of William")	0.699
3	**Jones** ("son of John")	0.621
4	**Davis** ("son of Davie/David")	0.480
5	**Wilson** ("son of Will")	0.339
6	=**Anderson** ("son of Andrew")	0.311
	=**Thomas** ("son of Thomas")	0.311
8	**Jackson** ("son of Jack")	0.310
9	**Harris** ("son of Harry")	0.275
10	**Martin** ("son of Martin")	0.273

Patronyms are names recalling a father or other ancestor. Up to one-third of all US surnames may be patronymic in origin. Several US presidents have borne such names, including Andrew Johnson, Lyndon Johnson, Woodrow Wilson, Jackson William Henry and Benjamin Harrison, Thomas Jefferson, and James Madison.

TOP 10 US DESCRIPTIVE LAST NAMES

	NAME/ORIGIN	PERCENTAGE OF ALL US NAMES
1	**Brown** (brown-haired)	0.621
2	**White** (light-skinned, or white-haired)	0.279
3	**Young** (youthful, or a younger brother)	0.193
4	**Gray** (gray-haired)	0.106
5	**Long** (tall)	0.092
6	**Russell** (red-haired)	0.085
7	**Black** (black-haired, or dark-skinned)	0.063
8	=**Little** (small)	0.046
	=**Reid** (red haired)	0.046
10	**Curtis** (courteous, or well-educated)	0.040

This list is headed by the Browns, whose important role as laborers and pioneers was recognized by the 19th-century British author Thomas Hughes in his novel *Tom Brown's Schooldays* (1857). He wrote, "For centuries, in their quiet, dogged, homespun way, they have been subduing the earth in most English counties, and leaving their mark in American forests and Australian uplands."

TOP 10 US LAST NAMES DERIVED FROM OCCUPATIONS

	NAME/ORIGIN	PERCENTAGE OF ALL US NAMES
1	**Smith**	1.006
2	**Miller**	0.424
3	**Taylor** (tailor)	0.311
4	**Clark** (cleric)	0.231
5	**Walker** (cloth worker)	0.219
6	**Wright** (workman)	0.189
7	**Baker**	0.171
8	**Carter** (driver or maker of carts)	0.162
9	**Turner** (woodworker)	0.152
10	**Stewart** (steward)	0.133

It is thought that about 1 in 6 US last names – especially among families of European origin – recalls the occupation of the holder's ancestors. Several US presidents have borne such surnames, including Zachary Taylor and Jimmy Carter. Less obvious is that of the 19th, President Rutherford Hayes: in medieval times, Hayes was the name given to a person in charge of hedges.

Organizations

COUNTRIES WITH THE HIGHEST SCOUT MEMBERSHIP

	COUNTRY	SCOUTING FOUNDED	MEMBERSHIP*
1	Indonesia	1912	9,961,921
2	US	1909	6,253,606
3	Philippines	1923	3,491,911
4	India	1909	1,963,266
5	Bangladesh	1972	1,325,014
6	Thailand	1911	1,237,515
7	UK	1907	542,277
8	Pakistan	1947	508,176
9	South Korea	1922	247,445
10	Canada	1909	238,957

As of Aug 8, 2001

Source: *World Organization of the Scout Movement*

Following a summer camp held in 1907 in Dorset, England, Sir Robert Baden-Powell (1857–1941) launched the Scouting Movement.

COUNTRIES WITH THE HIGHEST GIRL GUIDE AND GIRL SCOUT MEMBERSHIP

	COUNTRY	MEMBERSHIP IN 1998
1	US	3,525,425
2	Philippines	1,177,084
3	India	958,165
4	UK	640,409
5	Canada	215,438
6	Poland	206,476
7	Kenya	110,827
8	South Korea	89,473
9	Italy	88,656
10	Nigeria	82,994

Source: *World Association of Girl Guides and Girl Scouts*

The World Association of Girl Guides and Girl Scouts (WAGGGS) has 136 member organizations, with a total membership of nearly 10 million.

FIRST COUNTRIES TO RATIFY THE UN CHARTER

	COUNTRY	DATE
1	Nicaragua	Jul 6, 1945
2	US	Aug 8, 1945
3	France	Aug 31, 1945
4	Dominican Republic	Sep 4, 1945
5	New Zealand	Sep 19, 1945
6	Brazil	Sep 21, 1945
7	Argentina	Sep 24, 1945
8	China	Sep 28, 1945
9	Denmark	Oct 9, 1945
10	Chile	Oct 11, 1945

Following the June 26, 1945, signing of the World Security Charter, each of the 50 founder member countries progressively ratified the UN Charter.

TOP 10 LABOR UNIONS IN THE US

	UNION	MEMBERS
1	National Education Association	2,500,000
2	International Brotherhood of Teamsters	1,500,000
3	United Food and Commercial Workers' International Union	1,400,000
4	=American Federation of State, County, and Municipal Employees	1,300,000
	=Service Employees International Union	1,300,000
6	Laborers' International Union of North America	775,000
7	United International Union of Automobile, Aerospace, and Agricultural Implement Workers of America	760,000
8	International Association of Machinists and Aerospace Workers	740,000
9	International Brotherhood of Electrical Workers	720,000
10	American Federation of Teachers	685,000

TOP 10 CHARITIES IN THE US

	CHARITY	DONATIONS ($)	INCOME IN 2000 TOTAL ($)
1	Lutheran Services in America	710,263,416	6,909,130,967
2	The National Council of YMCAs	812,098,000	3,987,476,000
3	United Jewish Communities	2,287,585,000	2,881,585,000
4	Salvation Army	1,479,312,917	2,832,633,553
5	American Red Cross	637,664,249	2,492,418,155
6	Catholic Charities USA	358,698,631	2,286,446,586
7	Goodwill Industries International	282,000,000	1,852,900,000
8	Fidelity Investments Charitable Gift Fund	1,087,748,356	1,260,524,937
9	Boys and Girls Club of America	425,125,115	894,914,513
10	American Cancer Society, Inc.	746,391,000	808,883,000

Source: NonProfit Times

Balinese Boy Scouts
Originally established by the Dutch in Indonesia, the country's Scout movement today has the world's highest membership, and engages in many important community projects.

TOP 10 CHILDREN'S CHARITIES IN THE US

	CHARITY	DONATIONS ($)	INCOME IN 2000 TOTAL ($)
1	Boys and Girls Club of America	425,125,115	894,914,513
2	Shriners Hospital for Children	232,911,686	710,072,650
3	Boy Scouts of America	278,911,686	692,600,000
4	Girl Scouts of the USA	121,460,000	665,995,000*
5	ALSCA-St. Jude's Children's Research Hospital	260,397,622	452,867,556
6	Larry Jones International Ministries/ Feed the Children	395,581,981	398,455,754
7	Big Brothers/Big Sisters of America	144,107,884	182,859,319
8	Girls Incorporated	80,499,578	179,485,016
9	US Fund for the United Nations Children's Fund (UNICEF)	150,749,053	158,563,513
10	Young Life	115,867,966	149,127,930

* 1999 financial year data, reporting 1 year behind

Source: NonProfit Times

Politics & Royalty

First Lady
Following her assassinated husband into office, Mrs. Bandaranaike of Ceylon (now Sri Lanka) became the world's first female prime minister on July 21, 1960.

THE 10 FIRST COUNTRIES TO GIVE WOMEN THE VOTE

	COUNTRY	YEAR
1	**New Zealand**	1893
2	**Australia** (South Australia 1894; Western Australia 1898; Australia united in 1901)	1902
3	**Finland** (then a Grand Duchy under the Russian Crown)	1906
4	**Norway** (restricted franchise; all women over 25 in 1913)	1907
5	**Denmark and Iceland** (a Danish dependency until 1918)	1915
6	**=Netherlands**	1917
	=USSR	1917
8	**=Austria**	1918
	=Canada	1918
	=Germany	1918
	=Great Britain and Ireland* (Women over 30 only – lowered to 21 in 1928)	1918
	=Poland	1918

* Ireland was part of the United Kingdom until 1921

THE 10 FIRST FEMALE PRIME MINISTERS AND PRESIDENTS

	PRIME MINISTER/PRESIDENT	COUNTRY	FIRST PERIOD IN OFFICE
1	**Sirimavo Bandaranaike** (PM)	Sri Lanka	Jul 1960–Mar 1965
2	**Indira Gandhi** (PM)	India	Jan 1966–Mar 1977
3	**Golda Meir** (PM)	Israel	Mar 1969–Jun 1974
4	**Maria Estela Perón** (President)	Argentina	Jul 1974–Mar 1976
5	**Elisabeth Domitien** (PM)	Central African Republic	Jan 1975–Apr 1976
6	**Margaret Thatcher** (PM)	UK	May 1979–Nov 1990
7	**Dr. Maria Lurdes Pintasilgo** (PM)	Portugal	Aug 1979–Jan 1980
8	**Vigdís Finnbogadóttir** (President)	Iceland	Jul 1980–Jun 1995
9	**Mary Eugenia Charles** (PM)	Dominica	Jul 1980–Jun 1995
10	**Gro Harlem Brundtland** (PM)	Norway	Feb–Oct 1981

TOP 10 LONGEST-SERVING PRESIDENTS TODAY

	PRESIDENT	COUNTRY	TOOK OFFICE
1	**General Gnassingbé Eyadéma**	Togo	Apr 14, 1967
2	**El Hadj Omar Bongo**	Gabon	Dec 2, 1967
3	**Colonel Mu'ammar Gadhafi**	Libya	*Sep 1, 1969
4	**Zayid ibn Sultan al-Nuhayyan**	United Arab Emirates	Dec 2, 1971
5	**Fidel Castro**	Cuba	Nov 2, 1976
6	**France-Albert René**	Seychelles	Jun 5, 1977
7	**Ali Abdullah Saleh**	Yemen	Jul 17, 1978
8	**Daniel Teroitich arap Moi**	Kenya	Oct 14, 1978
9	**Maumoon Abdul Gayoom**	Maldives	Nov 11, 1978
10	**Saddam Hussein**	Iraq	Jul 16, 1979

* Since a reorganization in 1979, Colonel Gadhafi has held no formal position, but continues to rule under the ceremonial title of "Leader of the Revolution"

All the presidents in this list have been in power for more than 20, and some for over 30 years.

TOP 10 LONGEST-REIGNING QUEENS

	QUEEN*/COUNTRY	REIGN	REIGN IN YEARS
1	Victoria, UK	1837–1901	63
2	Wilhelmina, Netherlands	1890-1948	58
3	=Wu Chao, China	655–705	50
	=Elizabeth II, UK	1952–	50
5	Salote Tubou, Tonga	1918-65	47
6	Elizabeth I, England	1558–1603	44
7	Maria Theresa, Hungary	1740–80	40
8	Maria I, Portugal	1777–1816	39
9	Joanna I, Italy	1343–81	38
10	=Suiko Tenno, Japan	593–628	35
	=Isabella II, Spain	1833–68	35

* Queens and empresses who ruled in their own right, not as consorts of kings or emperors

TOP 10 CURRENT MONARCHIES* WITH MOST RULERS

	COUNTRY	LINE COMMENCED	RULERS#
1	Japan	40BC	125
2	England	802	64
3	Sweden	980	59
4	Denmark	940	55
5	Norway	858	42
6	Brunei	1405	29
7	Monaco	1458	20
8	Spain	1516	18
9	=Netherlands	1572	14
	=Liechtenstein	1699	14

* Including principalities
# Monarchs deposed and later restored counted once only

TOP 10 SHORTEST-SERVING US PRESIDENTS

	PRESIDENT	YEARS	DAYS
1	William H. Harrison*		32
2	James A. Garfield*	—	199
3	Zachary Taylor*	1	127
4	Warren G. Harding*	2	151
5	Gerald R. Ford	2	166
6	Millard Fillmore	2	236
7	John F. Kennedy*	2	306
8	Chester A. Arthur	3	166
9	Andrew Johnson	3	323
10	John Tyler	3	332

* Died in office

Outside of these 10, all other presidents have served either one or 2 full 4-year terms – 3 in the case of Franklin D. Roosevelt.

Royal Riches
In 2002 Queen Elizabeth II became Britain's fourth longest-reigning monarch, and the third longest-reigning queen in world history.

The First to...

THE 10 FIRST PEOPLE TO CROSS NIAGARA FALLS BY TIGHTROPE

	NAME	DATE
1	**Blondin** (Jean François Gravelet)	Jun 30, 1859
2	**Signor Guillermo Antonio Farini** (William Leonard Hunt)	Aug 15, 1860
3	**Harry Leslie**	Jun 15, 1865
4	**J. F. "Professor" Jenkins**	Aug 25, 1869
5	**Signor Henri Belleni**	Aug 25, 1873
6	**Stephen Peer**	Sep 10, 1873
7	**Maria Spelterini**	Jul 8, 1876
8	**Samuel Dixon**	Sep 6, 1890
9	**Clifford Caverley**	Oct 12, 1892
10	**James Hardy**	Jul 1, 1896

Know the Ropes
Tightrope walker Jean-François Gravelet (1824–97), known as Blondin, crossed Niagara Falls on many occasions. On one crossing he even paused to cook and eat an omelette!

THE 10 FIRST MOUNTAINEERS TO CLIMB EVEREST

	MOUNTAINEER/NATIONALITY	DATE
1	**Edmund Hillary,** New Zealander	May 29, 1953
2	**Tenzing Norgay,** Nepalese	May 29, 1953
3	**Jürg Marmet,** Swiss	May 23, 1956
4	**Ernst Schmied,** Swiss	May 23, 1956
5	**Hans-Rudolf von Gunten,** Swiss	May 24, 1956
6	**Adolf Reist,** Swiss	May 24, 1956
7	**Wang Fu-chou,** Chinese	May 25, 1960
8	**Chu Ying-hua,** Chinese	May 25, 1960
9	**Konbu,** Tibetan	May 25, 1960
10	**=Nawang Gombu,** Indian	May 1, 1963
	=James Whittaker, American	May 1, 1963

Nawang Gombu and James Whittaker are 10th equal because, neither wishing to deny the other the privilege of being first, they ascended the last steps to the summit side by side.

THE 10 FIRST SUCCESSFUL HUMAN DESCENTS OVER NIAGARA FALLS

	NAME	METHOD	DATE
1	**Annie Edson Taylor**	Wooden barrel	Oct 24, 1901
2	**Bobby Leach**	Steel barrel	Jul 25, 1911
3	**Jean Lussier**	Steel and rubber ball equipped with oxygen cylinders	Jul 4, 1928
4	**William Fitzgerald** (aka Nathan Boya)	Steel and rubber ball equipped with oxygen cylinders	Jul 15, 1961
5	**Karel Soucek**	Barrel	Jul 3, 1984
6	**Steven Trotter**	Barrel	Aug 18, 1985
7	**Dave Mundy**	Barrel	Oct 5, 1985
8	**=Peter de Bernardi**	Metal container	Sep 28, 1989
	=Jeffrey Petkovich	Metal container	Sep 28, 1989
10	**Dave Mundy**	Diving bell	Sep 26, 1993

Source: *Niagara Falls Museum*

Annie Edson Taylor became the first to survive the drop when she went over the Horseshoe Falls in a 4.5 x 3-ft (1.4 x 0.9-m) barrel. Dave Mundy made a second trip in a diving bell in response to criticism that his original container, a 10-ft (3-m) steel tube, was too sophisticated.

THE 10 FIRST EXPLORERS TO LAND IN THE AMERICAS

	EXPLORER/NATIONALITY	AREA EXPLORED	YEAR
1	**Christopher Columbus,** Italian	West Indies	1492
2	**John Cabot,** Italian/English	Nova Scotia/ Newfoundland	1497
3	**Alonso de Hojeda,** Spanish	Brazil	1499
4	**Vicente Yañez Pinzón,** Spanish	Amazon	1500
5	**Pedro Alvarez Cabral,** Portuguese	Brazil	1500
6	**Gaspar Corte Real,** Portuguese	Labrador	1500
7	**Rodrigo de Bastidas,** Spanish	Central America	1501
8	**Vasco Nuñez de Balboa,** Spanish	Panama	1513
9	**Juan Ponce de León,** Spanish	Florida	1513
10	**Juan Díaz de Solís,** Spanish	Río de la Plata	1515

After his pioneering voyage of 1492, Columbus made 3 subsequent journeys to the West Indies and South America. Following him, several expeditions landed on the same islands of the West Indies (these have not been included as new explorations). Although Hojeda (or Ojeda) was the leader of the 1499 expedition, Amerigo Vespucci, after whom America is named, was also on the voyage.

THE 10 | FIRST PEOPLE TO REACH THE SOUTH POLE

	NAME/NATIONALITY	DATE
1	=Roald Amundsen*, Norwegian	Dec 14, 1911
	=Olav Olavsen Bjaaland, Norwegian	Dec 14, 1911
	=Helmer Julius Hanssen, Norwegian	Dec 14, 1911
	=Helge Sverre Hassel, Norwegian	Dec 14, 1911
	=Oscar Wisting, Norwegian	Dec 14, 1911
6	=Robert Falcon Scott*, British	Jan 17, 1912
	=Henry Robertson Bowers, British	Jan 17, 1912
	=Edgar Evans, British	Jan 17, 1912
	=Lawrence Edward Grace Oates, British	Jan 17, 1912
	=Edward Adrian Wilson, British	Jan 17, 1912

* Expedition leader

THE 10 | FIRST EXPEDITIONS TO REACH THE NORTH POLE OVERLAND

	NAME*/NATIONALITY	DATE
1	Ralph S. Plaisted, American	Apr 19, 1968
2	Wally W. Herbert, British	Apr 5, 1969
3	Naomi Uemura, Japanese	May 1, 1978
4	Dmitri Shparo, Soviet	May 31, 1979
5	Sir Ranulph Fiennes/ Charles Burton, British	Apr 11, 1982
6	Will Steger/Paul Schurke, American	May 1, 1986
7	Jean-Louis Etienne, French	May 11, 1986
8	Fukashi Kazami, Japanese	Apr 20, 1987
9	Helen Thayer, American#	Apr 20, 1988
10	Robert Swan, British	May 14, 1989

* Expedition leader or coleader

 # New Zealand-born

THE 10 | FIRST CROSS-CHANNEL SWIMMERS

	SWIMMER/NATIONALITY	TIME (HR:MIN)	DATE
1	Matthew Webb, British	21:45	Aug 24–25, 1875
2	Thomas Burgess, British	22:35	Sep 5–6, 1911
3	Henry Sullivan, American	26:50	Aug 5–6, 1923
4	Enrico Tiraboschi, Italian	16:33	Aug 12, 1923
5	Charles Toth, American	16:58	Sep 8–9, 1923
6	Gertrude Ederle, American	14:39	Aug 6, 1926
7	Millie Corson, American	15:29	Aug 27–28, 1926
8	Arnst Wierkotter, German	12:40	Aug 30, 1926
9	Edward Temme, British	14:29	Aug 5, 1927
10	Mercedes Gleitze, British	15:15	Oct 7, 1927

The first 3 crossings were from England to France, the rest from France to England. In 1934 Edward Temme also swam from England to France, thus becoming the first person successfully to cross in both directions.

Pole Position
A pioneer in the use of snowmobiles for Arctic exploration, Ralph S. Plaisted became the first confirmed overland conquerer of the North Pole in 1968, after a 43-day journey.

The Nobel Prize

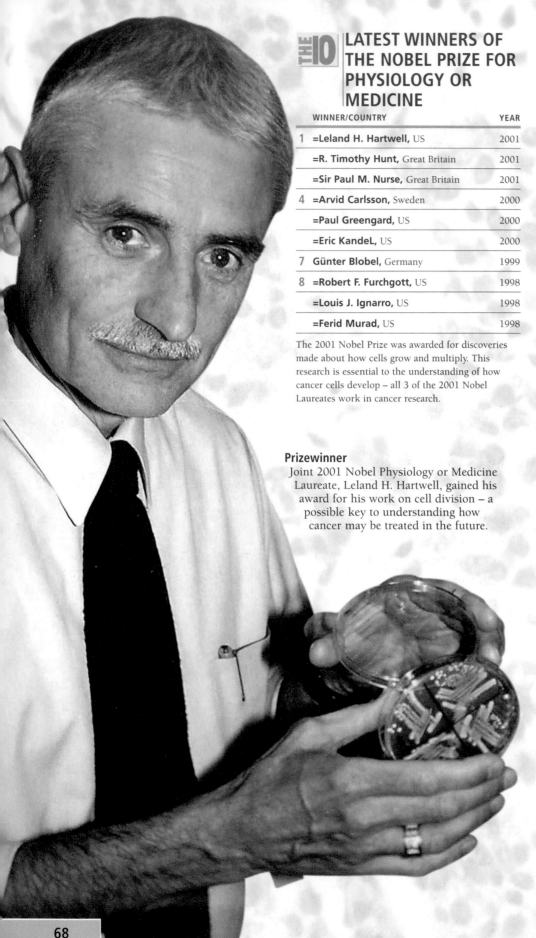

THE 10 LATEST WINNERS OF THE NOBEL PRIZE FOR PHYSIOLOGY OR MEDICINE

	WINNER/COUNTRY	YEAR
1	=Leland H. Hartwell, US	2001
	=R. Timothy Hunt, Great Britain	2001
	=Sir Paul M. Nurse, Great Britain	2001
4	=Arvid Carlsson, Sweden	2000
	=Paul Greengard, US	2000
	=Eric Kandel, US	2000
7	Günter Blobel, Germany	1999
8	=Robert F. Furchgott, US	1998
	=Louis J. Ignarro, US	1998
	=Ferid Murad, US	1998

The 2001 Nobel Prize was awarded for discoveries made about how cells grow and multiply. This research is essential to the understanding of how cancer cells develop – all 3 of the 2001 Nobel Laureates work in cancer research.

Prizewinner

Joint 2001 Nobel Physiology or Medicine Laureate, Leland H. Hartwell, gained his award for his work on cell division – a possible key to understanding how cancer may be treated in the future.

THE 10 LATEST WINNERS OF THE NOBEL PRIZE FOR LITERATURE

	WINNER/COUNTRY	YEAR
1	Sir V. S. Naipaul, Great Britain	2001
2	Gao Xingjian, China	2000
3	Günter Grass, Germany	1999
4	José Saramago, Portugal	1998
5	Dario Fo, Italy	1997
6	Wislawa Szymborska, Poland	1996
7	Seamus Heaney, Ireland	1995
8	Kenzaburo Oe, Japan	1994
9	Toni Morrison, US	1993
10	Derek Walcott, Saint Lucia	1992

The latest winner, British writer Sir V. S. Naipaul, was born in Trinidad. He has written novels set in Trinidad, India, Africa, North and South America, Asia, and England. He was awarded the Nobel Prize for Literature because of his achievements in re-telling histories that have been largely suppressed, through the use of what has been called "perceptive narrative and incorruptible scrutiny."

THE 10 LATEST WINNERS OF THE NOBEL PRIZE FOR ECONOMIC SCIENCES

	WINNER/COUNTRY	YEAR
1	=George A. Akerlof, US	2001
	=A. Michael Spence, US	2001
	=Joseph E. Stiglitz, US	2001
4	=James J. Heckman, US	2000
	=Daniel L. McFadden, US	2000
6	Robert A. Mundell, Canada	1999
7	Amartya Sen, India	1998
8	=Robert C. Merton, US	1997
	=Myron S. Scholes, US	1997
10	=James A. Mirrlees, UK	1996
	=William Vickrey, Canada	1996

During the 1970s, the 2001 Laureates introduced the general theory of markets and "asymmetric information." Many markets are characterized by asymmetric information – when people on one side of the market have much better information than those on the other.

THE 10 LATEST WOMEN TO WIN A NOBEL PRIZE

	WINNER/COUNTRY	PRIZE	YEAR
1	**Jody Williams***, US	Peace	1997
2	**Wislawa Szymborska,** Poland	Literature	1996
3	**Christiane Nüsslein-Volhard#,** Germany	Phys/Med	1995
4	**Toni Morrison,** US	Literature	1993
5	**Rigoberta Menchu Tum,** Guatemala	Peace	1992
6	**Nadine Gordimer,** South Africa	Literature	1991
7	**Aung San Suu Kyi,** Myanmar	Peace	1991
8	**Gertrude B. Elion†,** US	Phys/Med	1988
9	**Rita Levi-Montalcini§,** Italy	Phys/Med	1986
10	**Barbara McClintock,** US	Phys/Med	1983

* *Shared with International Campaign to Ban Landmines*

Shared with Eric F. Wieschaus and Edward B. Lewis

† *Shared with Sir James Black and George H. Hitchings*

§ *Shared with Stanley Cohen*

THE 10 LATEST WINNERS OF THE NOBEL PEACE PRIZE

	WINNER/COUNTRY	YEAR
1	**=United Nations**	2001
	=Kofi Annan, Ghana	2001
2	**Kim Dae Jung,** South Korea	2000
3	**Médecins Sans Frontières,** Belgium	1999
4	**=John Hume,** UK,	1998
	=David Trimble, UK	1998
6	**=International Campaign to Ban Landmines**	1997
	=Jody Williams, US	1997
8	**=Carlos Filipe Ximenes Belo,** East Timor	1996
	=José Ramos-Horta, East Timor	1996
10	**Joseph Rotblat,** UK	1995

Kofi Annan has devoted almost his entire working life to the United Nations, and as Secretary-General has brought an increased emphasis to the United Nations' obligations with regard to human rights.

THE 10 LATEST WINNERS OF THE NOBEL PRIZE FOR PHYSICS

	WINNER/COUNTRY	YEAR
1	**=Eric A. Cornell,** US	2001
	=Wolfgang Ketterie, Germany	2001
	=Carl E. Wieman, US	2001
4	**=Zhores I. Alferov,** Russia	2000
	=Herbert Kroemer, US	2000
	=Jack S. Kilby, US	2000
7	**=Gerardus 't Hooft,** Netherlands	1999
	=Martinus J. G. Veltman, Netherlands	1999
9	**=Robert B. Laughlin,** US	1998
	=Horst L. Störmer, Germany	1998
	=Daniel C. Tsui, US	1998

The 2001 Laureates have discovered a new way of controlling matter. This is going to have huge consequences in such fields as nanotechnology. Nanotechnology deals with the manufacture of objects that are smaller than 100 nanometers. A nanometer is one thousand millionth of a meter.

Jody Williams

The last woman to win a Nobel Prize was Jody Williams, the founding coordinator of the International Campaign to Ban Landmines in 1997.

TOP 10 NOBEL PEACE PRIZE-WINNING COUNTRIES

	COUNTRY	PEACE PRIZES
1	**US**	18
2	**International institutions**	17
3	**UK**	13
4	**France**	9
5	**Sweden**	5
6	**=Belgium**	4
	=Germany	4
	=South Africa	4
9	**=Israel**	3
	=Switzerland	3

Criminal Records

 THE 10 US STATES WITH THE MOST PRISONERS ON DEATH ROW

	STATE	PRISONERS UNDER DEATH SENTENCE*
1	California	607
2	Texas	455
3	Florida	386
4	Pennsylvania	247
5	North Carolina	226
6	Ohio	204
7	Alabama	188
8	Illinois	173
9	Georgia	128
10	Oklahoma	127

* As of January 1, 2002

Source: NAACP Legal Defense Fund

A total of 3,711 prisoners were on death row in January 2002, some having been sentenced in more than 1 state, causing a higher total to be arrived at by adding individual state figures together.

THE 10 COUNTRIES WITH THE HIGHEST PROPORTION OF PRISONERS TO POPULATION

	COUNTRY	TOTAL PRISON POPULATION*	PRISONERS PER 100,000
1	US	1,933,503	700
2	Russia	962,700	665
3	Belarus	56,000	555
4	Kazakhstan	84,000	520
5	Turkmenistan	22,000	490
6	Bahamas	1,401	480
7	Belize	1,097	460
8	=Suriname	1,933	435
	=Ukraine	219,955	435
10	Kyrgyzstan	20,000	425

* Includes pretrial detainees

Source: UK Home Office, World Prison Population List (3rd ed.)

Behind Bars
A prisoner on Rikers Island, Bronx, New York. The US has more prisoners than any other country, and an incarceration rate that has recently overtaken Russia's.

TOP 10 COUNTRIES WITH THE LOWEST REPORTED CRIME RATES

	COUNTRY	RATE*
1	=Burkina Faso	9
	=Nepal	9
3	Mali	10
4	Togo	11
5	Guinea	18
6	Indonesia	60
7	Iran	77
8	=The Gambia	89
	=Syria	89
10	Niger	99

* Reported crime per 100,000 population, in latest year for which data available

There are just 13 countries in the world with reported crime rates of fewer than 100 per 100,000 inhabitants; the other 3 are Burundi (87.0), Syria (89.0), and Ethiopia (94.0). It should be noted, however, that these figures are based on reported crimes. For propaganda purposes, many countries do not publish accurate figures.

THE 10 COUNTRIES WITH THE HIGHEST REPORTED CRIME RATES

	COUNTRY	RATE*
1	Suriname	17,819
2	Iceland	14,727
3	Rwanda	14,550
4	Finland	14,405
5	New Zealand	13,854
6	Sweden	12,982
7	Guam	10,080
8	Norway	10,048
9	UK	9,823
10	Denmark	9,428
	US	5,374

* Reported crime per 100,000 population, in latest year for which data available

An appearance in this list does not necessarily indicate a crime-ridden country, since the rate of crime reporting relates closely to factors such as confidence in local law enforcement authorities. A rate of 1,000 per 100,000 may be considered average.

TOP 10 MOST COMMON REASONS FOR ARREST IN THE US

	OFFENCE	RATE*	ARRESTS IN 2000
1	Drug abuse violations	572.4	1,042,334
2	Driving under the influence	508.6	926,096
3	Larceny theft	429.5	782,082
4	Contravention of liquor laws	239.3	435,672
5	Drunkenness	232.5	423,310
6	Disorderly conduct	231.5	421,542
7	Aggravated assault	173.9	316,630
8	Fraud	117.4	213,828
9	Burglary	104.0	189,343
10	Vandalism	101.3	184,500

* Per 100,000 population

Source: FBI Uniform Crime Reports

TOP 10 LEAST CORRUPT COUNTRIES

	COUNTRY	CPI RATING IN 2001*
1	Finland	9.9
2	Denmark	9.5
3	New Zealand	9.4
4	=Iceland	9.2
	=Singapore	9.2
6	Sweden	9.0
7	Canada	8.9
8	Netherlands	8.8
9	Luxembourg	8.7
10	Norway	8.6
	US	7.6

* Corruption Perceptions Index

Source: Transparency International

THE 10 MOST CORRUPT COUNTRIES

	COUNTRY	CPI RATING IN 2001*
1	Bangladesh	0.4
2	Nigeria	1.0
3	=Indonesia	1.9
	=Uganda	1.9
5	=Azerbaijan	2.0
	=Bolivia	2.0
	=Cameroon	2.0
	=Kenya	2.0
9	Ukraine	2.1
10	Tanzania	2.2

* Corruption Perceptions Index

Source: Transparency International

The Corruption Perceptions Index ranks countries by how likely they are to accept bribes, as perceived by the general public, business people, and risk analysts. The higher the score, the less corrupt. Only 91 countries were covered by the 2001 survey, because of lack of reliable data.

TOP 10 CRIME CITIES IN THE US*

	METROPOLITAN AREA*	CRIMES PER 100,000 PEOPLE
1	Tuscaloosa, Alabama	8,923.9
2	Pine Bluff, Arizona	8,126.5
3	Miami, Florida	8,063.3
4	Albuquerque, New Mexico	7,038.8
5	Gainesville, Florida	7,022.0
6	Greenville, North Carolina	7,018.4
7	Alexandria, Louisiana	6,900.4
8	Monroe, Louisiana	6,887.5
9	Tallahassee, Florida	6,877.3
10	Tucson, Arizona	6,858.1

* Metropolitan Statistical Area

Source: FBI Uniform Crime Reports

MOST COMMON MURDER WEAPONS AND METHODS IN THE US

WEAPON/METHOD	VICTIMS IN 2000
1 Handguns	6,686
2 Knives or cutting instruments	1,743
3 "Personal weapons" (hands, feet, fists, etc.)	900
4 Blunt objects (hammers, clubs, etc.)	604
5 Shotguns	468
6 Rifles	396
7 Strangulation	166
8 Fire	128
9 Asphyxiation	89
10 Narcotics	20
Total	12,943

Source: FBI Uniform Crime Reports

The Bloody Countess
Evil Hungarian Countess Báthory's bloodlust was finally checked in 1610 when she was convicted of murder and walled up alive in her castle at Csejthe.

MOST PROLIFIC SERIAL KILLERS OF ALL TIME*

MURDERER (COUNTRY)	VICTIMS
1 Behram (India)	931

Behram (or Buhram) was the leader of the Thugee cult in India which it is believed was responsible for the deaths of up to 2 million people. At his trial Behram was found guilty of personally committing 931 murders between 1790 and 1830, mostly by ritual strangulation with the cult's traditional cloth, known as a ruhmal.

2 Countess Erszébet Báthory (Hungary) — up to 650

In the period up to 1610 in Hungary, Báthory (1560–1614), known as "Countess Dracula," was alleged to have murdered between 300 and 650 girls (her personal list of 610 victims was described at her trial), in the belief that drinking their blood would prevent her from aging.

3 Dr. Harold Shipman (UK) — up to 400

In January 2000, Manchester doctor Shipman was found guilty of the murder of 15 women patients, but emerging evidence suggests that the total could be as high as 400.

4 Pedro Alonso López (Colombia) — 300

Captured in 1980, López, nicknamed the "Monster of the Andes," led police to 53 graves, but probably murdered at least 300 in Colombia, Ecuador, and Peru. He was sentenced to life imprisonment.

5 Henry Lee Lucas (US) — 200

In 1983, Lucas admitted to 360 murders, many committed with his partner-in-crime Ottis Toole. He remains on Death Row in Huntsville Prison, Texas.

6 Gilles de Rais (France) — up to 200

A fabulously wealthy French aristocrat, Gilles de Laval, Baron de Rais (b.1404), allegedly dabbled in the occult and committed murders as sacrifices during black magic rituals. He was accused of having kidnapped and killed between 60 and 200 children, although this figure – and considerably exaggerated versions of it – may have been fabricated by his political enemies. He was tried, tortured, and found guilty. He was strangled and his body burned at Nantes on October 25, 1440.

7 Hu Wanlin (China) — 196

Posing as a doctor specializing in ancient Chinese medicine, Hu Wanlin was sentenced on October 1, 2000, to 15 years' imprisonment for 3 deaths, but authorities believe he was responsible for considerably more, an estimated 20 in Taiyuan, 146 in Shanxi, and 30 in Shangqui.

8 Luis Alfredo Gavarito (Colombia) — 189

Gavarito confessed in 1999 to a spate of murders. On May 28, 1999, he was sentenced to a total of 835 years' imprisonment.

9 Hermann Webster Mudgett (US) — up to 150

Also known as "H. H. Holmes," Mudgett (b.1860), a former doctor, was believed to have lured over 150 women to his Chicago hotel. It was fully equipped for torturing, murdering, and dissecting his victims and disposing of their bodies in furnaces or an acid bath. Arrested in 1894, he confessed to killing 27 but may have killed on up to 150 occasions (some authorities have calculated that the remains of 200 victims were found at his home). Mudgett was hanged at Moyamensing Prison, Philadelphia, on May 7, 1896.

10 Dr. Jack Kevorkian (US) — 130

In 1999, Kevorkian, who admitted to assisting in 130 suicides since 1990, was convicted of second-degree murder. His appeal against his 10- to 25-year prison sentence was rejected on November 21, 2001.

* Includes only individual murderers

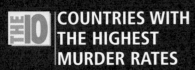

THE 10 COUNTRIES WITH THE HIGHEST MURDER RATES

COUNTRY	RATE*
1 Rwanda	12,500
2 Honduras	154.0
3 Colombia	56.3
4 Namibia	45.2
5 El Salvador	38.8
6 Jamaica	37.2
7 Lesotho	33.9
8 Albania	30.3
9 Bolivia	28.6
10 Guatemala	27.4

* Reported homicides per 100,000 population, in latest year for which data available

Firepower
Some of the most shocking mass murders of all time have been perpetrated by criminals with handguns.

THE 10 WORST GUN MASSACRES*

PERPETRATOR/LOCATION/DATE/CIRCUMSTANCES	KILLED
1 Woo Bum Kong, Sang-Namdo, South Korea, Apr 28, 1982 Off-duty policeman Woo Bum Kong (or Wou Bom-Kon), 27, went on a drunken rampage with rifles and hand grenades, killing 57 and injuring 38, before blowing himself up with a grenade.	57
2 Martin Bryant, Port Arthur, Tasmania, Australia, Apr 28, 1996 Bryant, a 28-year-old Hobart resident, used a rifle in a horrific spree that began in a restaurant and ended with a siege in a guesthouse in which he held hostages and set the building on fire before being captured by police.	35
3 Baruch Goldstein, Hebron, occupied West Bank, Israel, Feb 25, 1994 Goldstein, a 42-year-old US immigrant doctor, carried out a gun massacre of Palestinians at prayer at the Tomb of the Patriarchs before being beaten to death by the crowd.	29
4 Campo Elias Delgado, Bogota, Colombia, Dec 4, 1986 Delgado, a Vietnamese war veteran and electronics engineer, stabbed two and shot a further 26 people before being killed by police.	28
5 =George Jo Hennard, Killeen, Texas, Oct 16, 1991 Hennard drove his pickup truck through the window of Luby's Cafeteria and, in 11 minutes, killed 22 with semiautomatic pistols before shooting himself.	22
=James Oliver Huberty, San Ysidro, California, Jul 18, 1984 Huberty, aged 41, opened fire in a McDonald's restaurant, killing 21 before being shot dead by a SWAT marksman. A further 19 were wounded, including a victim who died the following day.	22

PERPETRATOR/LOCATION/DATE/CIRCUMSTANCES	KILLED
7 =Thomas Hamilton, Dunblane, Stirling, UK, Mar 13, 1996 Hamilton, 43, shot 16 children and a teacher in Dunblane Primary School before killing himself in the UK's worst-ever shooting incident.	17
=Robert Steinhäuser, Erfurt, Germany, April 26, 2002 Former student Steinhäuser returned to Johann Gutenberg secondary school and killed 14 teachers, 2 students, and a police officer with a handgun before shooting himself.	17
8 =Michael Ryan, Hungerford, Berkshire, UK, Aug 19, 1987 Ryan, 26, shot 14 dead and wounded 16 others (2 of whom died later) before shooting himself.	16
=Ronald Gene Simmons, Russellville, Arkansas, Dec 28, 1987 47-year-old Simmons killed 16, including 14 members of his own family, by shooting or strangling. He was caught and, on February 10, 1989, sentenced to death.	16
=Charles Joseph Whitman, Austin, Texas, Jul 31–Aug 1, 1966 25-year-old ex-Marine marksman Whitman killed his mother and wife and the following day took the elevator to the 27th floor of the campus tower and ascended to the observation deck at the University of Texas at Austin, from where he shot 14 and wounded 34 before being shot dead by police officer Romero Martinez.	16

* By individuals, excluding terrorist and military actions; totals exclude perpetrator

Wars & Battles

THE 10 WORST US CIVIL WAR BATTLES

	BATTLE	DATE	CASUALTIES*
1	Gettysburg	Jul 3, 1863	51,116
2	Seven Day Battles	Jun 25–Jul 1, 1862	36,463
3	Chickamauga	Sep 19–20, 1863	34,624
4	Chancellorsville/Fredericksburg	May 1–4, 1863	30,099
5	Wilderness#	May 5–7, 1862	25,416
6	Manassas/Chantilly	Aug 27–Sep 2, 1862	25,340
7	Stone's River	Dec 31, 1862–Jan 1, 1863	24,645
8	Shiloh	Apr 6–7, 1862	23,741
9	Antietam	Sep 17, 1862	22,726
10	Fort Donelson	Dec 13–16, 1862	19,455

Killed, missing, and wounded   # Confederate totals estimated

Source: *Alexis Tregenza*

THE 10 LONGEST WARS OF ALL TIME

	WAR	COMBATANTS	DATE	YEARS
1	Hundred Years War	France vs England	1337–1453	116
2	Greco-Persian Wars	Greece vs Persia	499–448 BC	51
3	=Wars of the Roses	Lancaster vs York, England	1455–85	30
	=Thirty Years War	Catholic vs Protestant	1618–48	30
5	Second Peloponnesian War	Peloponnesian League (Sparta, Corinth, etc.) vs Delian League (Athens, etc.)	432–404 BC	28
6	=First Punic War	Rome vs Carthage	264–241 BC	23
	=Napoleonic Wars	France vs other European countries	1792–1815	23
8	Second Great Northern War	Russia vs Sweden and Baltic states	1700–21	21
9	Vietnam War	South Vietnam (with US support) vs North Vietnam	1957–75	18
10	Second Punic War	Rome vs Carthage	219–202 BC	17

Source: *Alexis Tregenza*

It may be argued that the total period of the Crusades (Christianity vs Islam) constitutes 1 long single conflict spanning a total of 195 years, from 1096 to 1291, rather than a series of 9 short ones, in which case it ranks as the longest war ever. Similarly, if all the Punic Wars between 264 and 146 BC are taken as 1, they would rank second at 118 years. The War of the Spanish Succession (1701–14) is the only other major conflict to have lasted more than 10 years, with the War of the Austrian Succession (1740–48), the American Revolutionary War (1775–83), and the Chinese–Japanese War (1937–45) each lasting 8 years.

THE 10 BATTLES WITH THE MOST CASUALTIES

	BATTLE	WAR/DATE	CASUALTIES*
1	Stalingrad	World War II, 1942–43	2,000,000
2	Somme River I	World War I, 1916	1,073,900
3	Po Valley	World War II, 1945	740,000
4	Moscow	World War II, 1941–42	700,000
5	Verdun	World War I, 1916	595,000
6	Gallipoli	World War I, 1915	500,000
7	Artois-Loos	World War I, 1915	428,000
8	Berezina	War of 1812	400,000
9	38th Parallel	Korean War, 1951	320,000
10	Somme River II	World War I, 1918	300,000

Estimated total of military and civilian dead, wounded, and missing

Source: *Alexis Tregenza*

Total numbers of casualties in the Battle of Stalingrad are best estimates, but it was undoubtedly one of the longest and almost certainly the bloodiest battles of all time. Fought between German (with Hungarian, Romanian, and Italian troops also under German command) and Soviet forces, it continued from August 19, 1942, to February 2, 1943, with huge losses on both sides. Of almost 100,000 German troops captured, only about 5,000 were eventually repatriated.

THE10 | 20TH-CENTURY WARS WITH THE MOST MILITARY FATALITIES

	WAR	YEARS	ESTIMATED MILITARY FATALITIES
1	World War II	1939–45	15,843,000
2	World War I	1914–18	8,545,800
3	Korean War	1950–53	1,893,100
4	=Sino-Japanese War	1937–41	1,200,000
	=Biafra–Nigeria Civil War	1967–70	1,000,000
6	Spanish Civil War	1936–39	611,000
7	Vietnam War	1961–75	546,000
8	French Vietnam War	1945–54	300,000
9	=India–Pakistan War	1947	200,000
	=USSR invasion of Afghanistan	1979–89	200,000
	=Iran–Iraq War	1980–88	200,000

The statistics of warfare have always been an imperfect science. Not only are battle deaths seldom recorded accurately, but figures are often deliberately inflated by both sides in a conflict. For political reasons and to maintain morale, each side is anxious to enhance reports of its military success and low casualty figures, so that often very contradictory reports of the same battle may be issued. These figures thus represent military historians' "best guesses" – and fail to take into account the enormous toll of deaths among civilian populations during the many wars that beset the 20th century.

THE10 | WARS WITH THE MOST US MILITARY FATALITIES

	WAR	YEARS	US MILITARY FATALITIES
1	World War II	1941–45	292,131
2	Civil War	1861–65	140,414*
3	Vietnam War	1961–73	58,193
4	World War I	1917–18	53,513
5	Korean War	1950–53	33,651
6	Revolutionary War	1775–83	4,435
7	War of 1812	1812–15	2,260
8	Mexican War	1846–48	1,733
9	Spanish-American War	1898	385
10	Gulf War	1990–91	148

* Union only; Confederate deaths estimated at 74,524, but data are incomplete and unreliable

Source: Alexis Tregenza

Seige City

Stalingrad was World War II's most prolonged and worst battle. Over one million Soviet soldiers were killed when they encircled the advancing German army within the city.

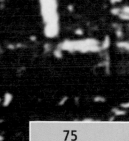

World War II

THE 10 COUNTRIES SUFFERING THE GREATEST CIVILIAN LOSSES IN WORLD WAR II

	COUNTRY	KILLED
1	China	8,000,000
2	USSR	6,500,000
3	Poland	5,300,000
4	Germany	2,350,000
5	Yugoslavia	1,500,000
6	France	470,000
7	Greece	415,000
8	Japan	393,400
9	Romania	340,000
10	Hungary	300,000

Deaths among civilians – many resulting from famine and internal purges, such as those in China and the USSR – were colossal, but they were less well documented than those among fighting forces. These figures are the best available from authoritative sources, but the precise numbers will never be known.

THE 10 COUNTRIES SUFFERING THE GREATEST MILITARY LOSSES IN WORLD WAR II

	COUNTRY	KILLED
1	USSR	13,600,000*
2	Germany	3,300,000
3	China	1,324,516
4	Japan	1,140,429
5	British Empire#	357,116
6	Romania	350,000
7	Poland	320,000
8	Yugoslavia	305,000
9	US	292,131
10	Italy	279,800
	Total	21,268,992

* Total, of which 7.8 million were battlefield deaths, 2.5 million were later deaths from wounds and disease, and 3.3 million were prisoner-of-war deaths

Including Australia, Canada, India, New Zealand, etc.;

TOP 10 LARGEST ARMED FORCES OF WORLD WAR II

	COUNTRY	PERSONNEL*
1	USSR	12,500,000
2	US	12,364,000
3	Germany	10,000,000
4	Japan	6,095,000
5	France	5,700,000
6	UK	4,683,000
7	Italy	4,500,000
8	China	3,800,000
9	India	2,150,000
10	Poland	1,000,000

* At peak strength

Allowing for deaths and casualties, the total forces mobilized during the course of the war is, of course, greater than the peak strength figures: the total for the USSR, for example, has been put as high as 20,000,000; the US 16,354,000, Germany 17,900,000, Japan 9,100,000, and the UK 5,896,000.

TOP 10 LARGEST BATTLESHIPS OF WORLD WAR II

	BATTLESHIP	COUNTRY	STATUS	LENGTH (FT)	(M)	TONNAGE
1	=Musashi	Japan	Sunk Oct 25, 1944	862	263	72,809
	=Yamato	Japan	Sunk Apr 7, 1945	862	263	72,809
3	=Iowa	US	Decommissioned Oct 26, 1990	887	270	55,710
	=Missouri	US	Decommissioned Mar 31, 1992	887	270	55,710
	=New Jersey	US	Decommissioned Feb 8, 1991	887	270	55,710
	=Wisconsin	US	Decommissioned Sep 30, 1991	887	270	55,710
7	=Bismarck	Germany	Sunk May 27, 1941	823	251	50,153
	=Tirpitz	Germany	Sunk Nov 12, 1944	823	251	50,153
9	=Jean Bart	France	Survived the war, later scrapped	812	247	47,500
	=Richelieu	France	Survived the war, later scrapped	812	247	47,500

Massed Ranks

During World War II the US mustered the second largest force ever assembled – the army alone reaching a peak strength of 5,851,000.

TOP 10 FASTEST FIGHTER AIRCRAFT OF WORLD WAR II

	AIRCRAFT	COUNTRY	MAXIMUM SPEED (MPH)	(KM/H)
1	Messerschmitt Me 163	Germany	596	959
2	Messerschmitt Me 262	Germany	560	901
3	Heinkel He 162A	Germany	553	890
4	P-51-H Mustang	US	487	784
5	Lavochkin La11	USSR	460	740
6	Spitfire XIV	UK	448	721
7	Yakolev Yak-3	USSR	447	719
8	P-51-D Mustang	US	440	708
9	Tempest VI	UK	438	705
10	Focke-Wulf Fw190D	Germany	435	700

TOP 10 LUFTWAFFE AIRCRAFT OF WORLD WAR II

	AIRCRAFT	TYPE	NO. PRODUCED
1	Messerschmitt Me 109	Fighter	30,480
2	Focke-Wulf Fw 190	Fighter	20,000
3	Junkers Ju 88	Bomber	15,000
4	Messerschmitt Me 110	Fighter-bomber	5,762
5	Heinkel He 111	Bomber	5,656
6	Junkers Ju 87	Dive bomber	4,881
7	Junkers Ju 52	Transport	2,804
8	Fieseler Fi 156	Communications	2,549
9	Dornier Do 217	Bomber	1,730
10	Heinkel He 177	Bomber	1,446

Modern Military

SPRINGFIELD RIFLE

FEW WEAPONS HAVE SEEN service as long as that of the Springfield 1903 rifle, which remained in use as the US Army standard issue weapon from its introduction on June 20, 1903, up to the Korean War. Developed at the Springfield Armory, Massachusetts (now a National Historic Site), this short-barreled rifle replaced the Krag rifle then in use. President Theodore Roosevelt used a Springfield 1903 for hunting, and personally recommended changes to the design of the bayonet. The rifle derived design features from the German Mauser, and, ironically, the US paid royalties on each rifle bought – even after the US fought Germany in World War I, by which time over a million 1903s had been made.

Sub Power
The US submarine fleet, the world's largest, is principally composed of Los Angeles Class nuclear-powered hunter-killers, named after the first, *USS Los Angeles*, which was commissioned in 1976.

TOP 10 COUNTRIES WITH THE MOST SUBMARINES

COUNTRY	SUBMARINES
1 US	74
2 Russia (and associated states)	67
3 China	65
4 North Korea	26
5 South Korea	19
6 =India	16
=Japan	16
=UK	16
9 =Germany	14
=Turkey	14

TOP 10 COUNTRIES WITH THE SMALLEST DEFENSE BUDGETS

COUNTRY*	BUDGET ($)
1 Antigua and Barbuda	4,000,000
2 Guinea-Bissau	6,000,000
3 =Cape Verde	7,000,000
=Guyana	7,000,000
5 =Belize	8,000,000
=Equatorial Guinea	8,000,000
7 =Seychelles	11,000,000
=Sierra Leone	11,000,000
=Suriname	11,000,000
10 Barbados	12,000,000

* Includes only those countries that declare defense budgets

The defense budget for a whole year in Antigua and Barbuda is equivalent to just 7 minutes-worth of the US defense budget.

TOP 10 COUNTRIES WITH THE LARGEST DEFENSE BUDGETS

COUNTRY	BUDGET ($)
1 US	291,200,000,000
2 Japan	45,600,000,000
3 UK	34,500,000,000
4 Russia	29,000,000,000
5 France	27,000,000,000
6 Germany	23,300,000,000
7 Saudi Arabia	18,700,000,000
8 Italy	16,000,000,000
9 India	15,900,000,000
10 China	14,500,000,000

The so-called "peace dividend" – the savings made as a consequence of the ending of the Cold War between the West and the former Soviet Union – means that both the numbers of personnel and the defense budgets of many countries have been cut.

TOP 10 SMALLEST ARMED FORCES *

	COUNTRY	ESTIMATED TOTAL ACTIVE FORCES
1	Antigua and Barbuda	150
2	Seychelles	450
3	Barbados	610
4	Gambia	800
5	Bahamas	860
6	Luxembourg	899
7	Belize	1,050
8	Cape Verde	1,150
9	Equatorial Guinea	1,320
10	Guyana	1,600

* Includes only those countries that declare a defense budget

TOP 10 LARGEST ARMED FORCES

	COUNTRY	ESTIMATED ACTIVE FORCES			
		ARMY	NAVY	AIR	TOTAL
1	China	1,700,000	220,000	420,000	2,340,000
2	US	471,700	370,700	353,600	1,365,800*
3	India	1,100,000	53,000	150,000	1,303,000
4	North Korea	950,000	46,000	86,000	1,082,000
5	Russia	348,000	171,500	184,600	1,004,100#
6	South Korea	560,000	60,000	63,000	683,000
7	Pakistan	550,000	22,000	40,000	612,000
8	Turkey	495,000	54,600	60,100	609,700
9	Iran	325,000	18,000	45,000	513,000†
10	Vietnam	412,000	42,000	30,000	484,000

* Includes 169,800 Marine Corps

Includes Strategic Deterrent Forces, Paramilitary, National Guard, etc.

† Includes 125,000 Revolutionary Guards

Crouching Tiger
Officially, all males in China are drafted at 18, but in practice conscription is selective. Despite this, China's military manpower dwarfs that of the other world nations.

World Religions

TOP 10 LARGEST BUDDHIST POPULATIONS

	COUNTRY	BUDDHIST POPULATION IN 2000
1	China	107,000,000
2	Japan	88,400,000
3	Thailand	59,180,000
4	Vietnam	52,510,000
5	Myanmar	37,300,000
6	Sri Lanka	13,340,000
7	Cambodia	11,750,000
8	South Korea	10,950,000
9	India	8,000,000
10	Taiwan	5,060,000
	World total	*359,981,000*

Buddhist Monks
Buddhism's espousal of peaceful living and tolerant coexistence has ensured its steady spread throughout Asia and beyond.

TOP 10 LARGEST CHRISTIAN POPULATIONS

	COUNTRY	CHRISTIAN POPULATION IN 2000
1	US	235,742,000
2	Brazil	155,545,000
3	Mexico	95,169,000
4	China	89,056,000
5	Philippines	68,151,000
6	Germany	62,326,000
7	Nigeria	51,123,000
8	Dem. Rep. of Congo	49,256,000
9	Italy	47,010,000
10	France	41,786,000

Source: World Christian Encyclopedia/*Christian Research*

Christian communities are found in most countries in the world. The Christian populations of the countries in this list make up 45 percent of the world total.

TOP 10 RELIGIONS IN THE US

	RELIGION	ESTIMATED NO. OF FOLLOWERS IN MID-2001
1	Christianity	159,030,000
2	Judaism	2,831,000
3	Islam	1,104,000
4	Buddhism	1,082,000
5	Hinduism	766,000
6	Unitarian/Universalism	629,000
7	Paganism	140,000
8	Wiccan	134,000
9	Spiritualist	116,000
10	Native American	103,000

Source: American Religious Identity Survey 2001

The disparities between this and the US figures included in the global lists of Christianity and Jewish populations make clear the difficulties involved in the collection of these types of statistical data.

TOP 10 LARGEST JEWISH POPULATIONS

	COUNTRY	JEWISH POPULATION IN 2000
1	US	5,700,000
2	Israel	4,882,000
3	France	521,000
4	Canada	362,000
5	Russia	290,000
6	UK	276,000
7	Argentina	200,000
8	Ukraine	100,000
9	Brazil	98,000
10	Australia	97,000
	World total	*13,191,500*

Source: American Jewish Year Book, Vol. 100

A result of the Diaspora, or scattering of Jewish people, is that Jewish communities are found in virtually every country in the world.

TOP 10 LARGEST HINDU POPULATIONS

	COUNTRY	HINDU POPULATION IN 2000
1	India	824,000,000
2	Nepal	21,370,000
3	Bangladesh	12,000,000
4	Indonesia	3,830,000
5	Sri Lanka	2,980,000
6	Pakistan	2,550,000
7	Malaysia	1,630,000
8	US	1,032,000
9	Mauritius	600,000
10	South Africa	440,000
	World total	*811,337,000*

TOP 10 LARGEST MUSLIM POPULATIONS

	COUNTRY	MUSLIM POPULATION IN 2000
1	Indonesia	182,570,000
2	Pakistan	134,480,000
3	India	121,000,000
4	Bangladesh	114,080,000
5	Turkey	65,510,000
6	Iran	62,430,000
7	Egypt	58,630,000
8	Nigeria	53,000,000
9	Algeria	30,530,000
10	Morocco	28,780,000
	World total	*1,188,242,000*

There are at least 15 countries where the population is 95 percent Muslim, which include Bahrain, Kuwait, Somalia, and Yemen. Historically, Islam spread as a result of both missionary activity and through contacts with Muslim traders. In such countries as Indonesia, where Islam was introduced as early as the 14th century, its appeal lay in part to its opposition to Western colonial influences. This appeal, along with the concept of the Islamic community and other tenets, has attracted followers worldwide. In the 1980s, the global Muslim population was said to be under 600 million; now the estimated total of 1,188,242,000 is equal to 1 in 5 of the world's population.

Holi Festival
Held throughout India, the Hindu Holi spring festival features brightly colored powders (*gulal*) and colored water, which are thrown and smeared over everyone.

TOWN & COUNTRY

Countries of the World

TOP 10 SMALLEST ISLAND COUNTRIES

	COUNTRY/LOCATION	AREA (SQ MILES)	(SQ KM)
1	**Nauru,** Pacific Ocean	8	21
2	**Tuvalu,** Pacific Ocean	10	26
3	**Marshall Islands,** Pacific Ocean	70	181
4	**Maldives,** Indian Ocean	116	300
5	**Malta,** Mediterranean Sea	124	321
6	**=Grenada,** Caribbean Sea	131	339
	=St. Vincent and the Grenadines, Caribbean Sea	131	339
8	**St. Kitts and Nevis,** Caribbean Sea	139	360
9	**Barbados,** Caribbean Sea	166	430
10	**Antigua and Barbuda,** Caribbean Sea	170	440

Source: *US Census Bureau, International Database*

TOP 10 LARGEST ISLAND COUNTRIES

	COUNTRY	AREA (SQ MILES)	(SQ KM)
1	**Indonesia**	705,192	1,826,440
2	**Madagascar**	224,534	581,540
3	**Papua New Guinea**	174,406	451,709
4	**Japan**	152,411	394,744
5	**Malaysia**	126,853	328,549
6	**Philippines**	115,124	298,171
7	**New Zealand**	103,734	268,671
8	**Cuba**	42,803	110,860
9	**Iceland**	38,707	100,251
10	**Sri Lanka**	24,996	64,740

Ireland and Northern Ireland share an island, so the UK and Ireland are both excluded from this list.

Mother Russia
The USSR was once the world's largest country (8,649,461 sq miles/22,402,000 sq km), a rank now occupied by its principal component, Russia.

TOP 10 COUNTRIES WITH THE LONGEST COASTLINES

	COUNTRY	TOTAL COASTLINE LENGTH (MILES)	(KM)
1	**Canada**	151,485	243,791
2	**Indonesia**	33,999	54,716
3	**Russia**	23,396	37,653
4	**Philippines**	22,559	36,289
5	**Japan**	18,486	29,751
6	**Australia**	16,007	25,760
7	**Norway**	13,624	21,925
8	**US**	12,380	19,924
9	**New Zealand**	9,404	15,134
10	**China**	9,010	14,500
	World	*221,208*	*356,000*

Were it included as a country, Greenland (27,394 miles/44,087 km) would be in third place. However, although Greenland has had home rule since 1979, it remains part of Denmark and is not an independent country.

TOP 10 LARGEST COUNTRIES

	COUNTRY	PERCENTAGE OF WORLD TOTAL AREA	AREA (SQ MILES)	(SQ KM)
1	**Russia**	13.0	6,592,850	17,075,400
2	**China**	7.1	3,600,948	9,326,411
3	**Canada**	7.0	3,560,237	9,220,970
4	**US**	6.9	3,539,245	9,166,601
5	**Brazil**	6.4	3,265,077	8,456,511
6	**Australia**	5.8	2,941,300	7,617,931
7	**India**	2.2	1,148,148	2,973,190
8	**Argentina**	2.1	1,056,642	2,736,690
9	**Kazakhstan**	2.1	1,049,155	2,717,300
10	**Algeria**	1.8	919,595	2,381,741
	World total	*100.0*	*50,580,568*	*131,003,055*

Source: *US Census Bureau, International Database*

The list of the world's largest countries has undergone substantial revision of late: the breakup of the former Soviet Union has effectively introduced 2 new countries, with Russia taking pre-eminent position.

Coast to Coast
Vancouver harbor, British Columbia, represents a fraction of Canada's vast coastline – that of the Northwest Territories alone is almost as long as the distance around the Earth at the Equator.

TOP 10 SMALLEST LANDLOCKED COUNTRIES

	COUNTRY/NEIGHBORS	AREA (SQ MILES)	(SQ KM)
1	**Vatican City,** Italy	0.2	0.44
2	**San Marino,** Italy	23	60
3	**Liechtenstein,** Austria, Switzerland	62	161
4	**Andorra,** France, Spain	174	451
5	**Luxembourg,** Belgium, France, Germany	998	2,585
6	**Swaziland,** Mozambique, South Africa	6,641	17,200
7	**Rwanda,** Burundi, Dem. Rep. of Congo, Tanzania, Uganda	9,633	24,949
8	**Burundi,** Dem. Rep. of Congo, Rwanda, Tanzania	9,903	25,649
9	**Macedonia,** Albania, Bulgaria, Greece, Yugoslavia	9,928	25,713
10	**Armenia,** Azerbaijan, Georgia, Iran, Turkey	11,506	29,800

Source: *US Census Bureau, International Database*

TOP 10 LARGEST LANDLOCKED COUNTRIES

	COUNTRY/NEIGHBORS	AREA (SQ MILES)	(SQ KM)
1	**Kazakhstan,** China, Kyrgyzstan, Russia, Turkmenistan, Uzbekistan	1,049,156	2,717,300
2	**Mongolia,** China, Russia	604,250	1,565,000
3	**Niger,** Algeria, Benin, Burkina Faso, Chad, Libya, Mali, Nigeria	489,075	1,266,699
4	**Chad,** Cameroon, Central African Republic, Libya, Niger, Nigeria, Sudan	486,180	1,259,201
5	**Mali,** Algeria, Burkina Faso, Côte d'Ivoire, Guinea, Mauritania, Niger, Senegal	471,044	1,219,999
6	**Ethiopia,** Djibouti, Eritrea, Kenya, Somalia, Sudan	432,312	1,119,683
7	**Bolivia,** Argentina, Brazil, Chile, Paraguay, Peru	418,685	1,084,389
8	**Zambia,** Angola, Dem. Rep. of Congo, Malawi, Mozambique, Namibia, Tanzania, Zimbabwe	285,993	740,719
9	**Afghanistan,** China, Iran, Pakistan, Tajikistan, Turkmenistan, Uzbekistan	250,001	647,500
10	**Central African Republic,** Cameroon, Chad, Congo, Dem. Rep. of Congo, Sudan	240,534	622,980

World & Country Populations

TOP 10 COUNTRIES WITH THE YOUNGEST POPULATIONS

COUNTRY	EST. PERCENTAGE UNDER 15 IN 2003
1 Uganda	50.8
2 Marshall Islands	48.9
3 Dem. Rep. of Congo	48.2
4 =Chad	47.8
=Niger	47.8
6 São Tomé and Príncipe	47.7
7 Ethiopia	47.3
8 Burkina Faso	47.2
9 Mali	47.1
10 Benin	47.0
World total	28.8
US	20.8

Source: *US Census Bureau, International Data Base*

Countries with high proportions of their population under the age of 15 are usually characterized by high birth rates and high death rates.

TOP 10 COUNTRIES WITH THE OLDEST POPULATIONS

COUNTRY	EST. PERCENTAGE OVER 65 IN 2003
1 Monaco	22.4
2 Italy	18.9
3 Japan	18.5
4 Greece	18.3
5 Spain	17.5
6 =Germany	17.4
=Sweden	17.4
8 Belgium	17.2
9 Bulgaria	17.0
10 San Marino	16.6
World total	7.2
US	12.6

Source: *US Census Bureau, International Data Base*

On average, 1 in every 6.6 people in Europe is over the age of 65 (15.2 percent). The lowest percentages of old people are found in Africa, where the average is only 1 in every 31 people (3.2 percent).

TOP 10 LEAST POPULATED COUNTRIES

COUNTRY	EST. POPULATION IN 2003
1 Tuvalu	11,305
2 Nauru	12,570
3 Palau	19,717
4 San Marino	28,119
5 Monaco	32,130
6 Liechtenstein	33,145
7 St. Kitts and Nevis	38,763
8 Antigua and Barbuda	67,897
9 Andorra	69,150
10 Dominica	69,655

Source: *US Census Bureau, International Data Base*

TOP 10 MOST POPULATED COUNTRIES

COUNTRY	EST. POPULATION IN 2003
1 China	1,295,225,929
2 India	1,061,557,965
3 US	283,054,745
4 Indonesia	235,682,179
5 Brazil	177,541,001
6 Pakistan	150,694,740
7 Russia	144,526,278
8 Bangladesh	135,507,062
9 Nigeria	133,230,617
10 Japan	127,150,434

Source: *US Census Bureau, International Data Base*

Young Ones
Uganda has the most youthful population in the world, with over half its inhabitants aged under 15.

TOP 10 LEAST DENSELY POPULATED COUNTRIES

	COUNTRY	AREA (SQ KM)	EST. MID-YEAR POPULATION IN 2003	POPULATION PER SQ KM
1	Mongolia	1,565,000	2,734,681	1.7
2	Namibia	823,291	1,840,926	2.2
3	Australia	7,617,931	19,731,984	2.6
4	=Botswana	585,371	1,591,774	2.7
	=Suriname	161,471	438,781	2.7
6	=Iceland	100,251	280,798	2.8
	=Mauritania	1,030,400	2,912,584	2.8
8	Libya	1,759,540	5,499,074	3.1
9	Canada	9,220,970	32,207,113	3.5
10	Guyana	196,850	700,375	3.6

Source: *US Census Bureau, International Data Base*

TOP 10 MOST DENSELY POPULATED COUNTRIES

	COUNTRY	AREA (SQ KM)	EST. MID-YEAR POPULATION IN 2003	POPULATION PER SQ KM
1	Monaco	1.95	32,130	16,476.9
2	Singapore	624	4,608,595	7,457.3
3	Malta	321	400,420	1,267.2
4	Maldives	300	329,684	1,106.3
5	Bahrain	619	667,238	961.4
6	Bangladesh	133,911	135,507,062	941.0
7	Taiwan	32,261	22,723,934	635.8
8	Mauritius	1,849	1,210,447	654.6
9	Barbados	430	277,884	646.2
10	Nauru	21	12,570	598.6
	World total	*131,003,055*	*6,310,549,597*	*48.2*
	US	*241,590*	*283,054,745*	*30.9*

Source: *US Census Bureau, International Data Base*

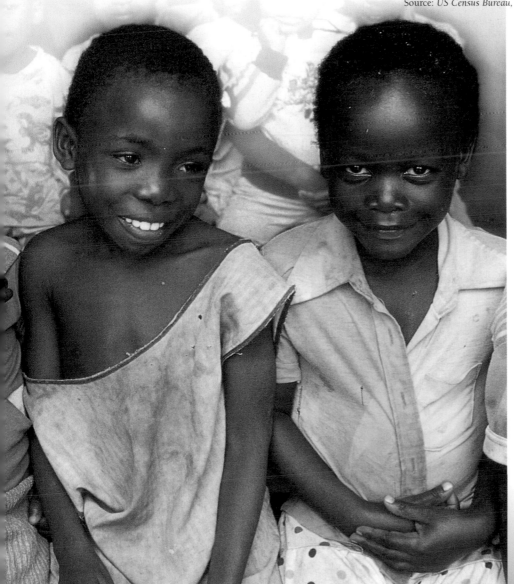

TOP 10 MOST HIGHLY POPULATED ISLAND COUNTRIES

	COUNTRY	EST. POPULATION IN 2003
1	Indonesia	235,682,179
2	Japan	127,150,434
3	Philippines	86,209,634
4	Malaysia	23,092,940
5	Taiwan	22,723,934
6	Sri Lanka	19,742,439
7	Madagascar	16,979,744
8	Cuba	11,263,429
9	Dominican Republic	8,862,875
10	Haiti	7,165,557

Source: *US Census Bureau, International Data Base*

There are 17 island countries in the world with populations of over 1 million. Australia is regarded as a continental land mass rather than an island, but if it were included, its 19,546,792 population would put it in sixth place. The UK (59,778,002) is also excluded, as it shares its land mass with Ireland and is not a self-contained island state.

People on the Move

EMIGRATION COUNTRIES

COUNTRY	EST. NET NO. OF MIGRANTS PER 1,000 POPULATION IN 2003
1 Dominica	-16.1
2 Grenada	-14.6
3 Cape Verde	-12.2
4 Samoa	-11.7
5 Liberia	-10.6
6 Trinidad and Tobago	-10.1
7 Suriname	-8.8
8 St. Kitts and Nevis	-8.3
9 St. Vincent and the Grenadines	-7.7
10 Antigua and Barbuda	-6.2

Source: *US Census Bureau, International Data Base*

Far From Home
Even before the War Against Terrorism focused on it toward the end of 2001, more refugees fled Afghanistan than any other country in the world.

IMMIGRATION COUNTRIES

COUNTRY	EST. NET NO. OF MIGRANTS PER 1,000 POPULATION IN 2003
1 Singapore	25.8
2 Qatar	17.5
3 Kuwait	14.0
4 San Marino	11.1
5 Afghanistan	10.3
6 Luxembourg	9.1
7 Monaco	7.8
8 Eritrea	7.3
9 Jordan	6.8
10 Andorra	6.7
US	3.3

Source: *US Census Bureau, International Data Base*

COUNTRIES OF ORIGIN OF US IMMIGRANTS

COUNTRY OF LAST RESIDENCE	IMMIGRANTS IN 2000
1 Mexico	173,919
2 China	45,652
3 Philippines	42,474
4 India	42,046
5 Vietnam	26,747
6 Nicaragua	24,029
7 El Salvador	22,578
8 Haiti	22,364
9 Cuba	20,831
10 Dominican Republic	17,537

Source: *US Immigration and Naturalization Service*

COUNTRIES TAKING IN THE MOST REFUGEES AND ASYLUM SEEKERS

	COUNTRY/TERRITORY	REFUGEES/ASYLUM SEEKERS*
1	Pakistan	2,019,000
2	Iran	1,900,000
3	Jordan	1,580,000
4	Gaza Strip	824,600
5	West Bank	583,000
6	Tanzania	540,000
7	Yugoslavia	483,800
8	US	481,500
9	Sudan	400,000
10	Guinea	390,000

As of January 1, 2001

Source: *US Committee for Refugees*

COUNTRIES OF ORIGIN FOR REFUGEES AND ASYLUM SEEKERS

	COUNTRY	REFUGEES/ASYLUM SEEKERS*
1	Afghanistan	3,600,000
2	Sudan	460,000
3	Iraq	450,000
4	Burundi	420,000
5	=Angola	400,000
	=Sierra Leone	400,000
7	=Myanmar	380,000
	=Eritrea	380,000
9	Somalia	370,000
10	Dem. Rep. of Congo	350,000

As of January 1, 2001

Source: *US Committee for Refugees*

In addition to these refugees, there are, according to some estimates, as many as 4 million Palestinian refugees in Middle Eastern, African, and other countries. They do not, however, have a country affiliation, since their homeland lies within Israel.

COUNTRIES OF ORIGIN OF REFUGEES ADMITTED TO THE US

	COUNTRY OF ORIGIN	REFUGEES (1988–2001)	IN 2001*
1	Former Soviet Union	464,771	14,888
2	Bosnia	139,565	14,594
3	Iran	39,995	6,582
4	Sudan	17,600	5,958
5	Somalia	40,292	4,939
6	Liberia	12,558	3,415
7	Vietnam	343,301	3,109
8	Afghanistan	14,837	2,964
9	Cuba	39,064	2,944
10	Iraq	31,767	2,473
	Total (including countries not in the Top 10)	1,322,754	68,426

Financial year

Source: *US Committee for Refugees*

LARGEST VOLUNTARY REPATRIATIONS

	COUNTRY RETURNED TO	COUNTRIES OF ASYLUM	NO. OF PEOPLE REPATRIATED IN 2000
1	Afghanistan	Iran, Pakistan	292,500
2	Yugoslavia	Switzerland, Macedonia, Bosnia-Herzegovina	124,700
3	Eritrea	Sudan	68,000
4	East Timor	Indonesia	48,500
5	Somalia	Ethiopia	45,900
6	Liberia	Ivory Coast, Guinea	42,400
7	Sierra Leone	Guinea, Liberia	40,900
8	Rwanda	Dem. Rep. of Congo	26,300
9	Croatia	Former Yugoslavia, Bosnia-Herzegovina	20,700
10	Bosnia-Herzegovina	Former Yugoslavia, Croatia	18,700

Source: *United Nations High Commission for Refugees*, Refugees by Numbers *2001 edition*

Most refugees prefer to return to their own countries, and as soon as circumstances make this possible, such as the end of a conflict, many people will make their way back home. They often need help to do this and organizations such as the UNHCR provide support, which may include transportation, cash, and practical help in the rebuilding of homes, schools, clinics, and roads.

World Cities

TOP 10 MOST URBANIZED COUNTRIES

	COUNTRY	PERCENTAGE OF POPULATION LIVING IN URBAN AREAS IN 1999	EST. IN 2015
1	Singapore	100.0	100.0
2	Kuwait	97.4	98.2
3	Belgium	97.3	98.0
4	=Bahrain	91.8	95.0
	=Luxembourg	91.0	95.0
6	Iceland	92.4	94.6
7	Qatar	92.3	94.3
8	Uruguay	91.0	93.6
9	Oman	82.2	92.7
10	=Argentina	89.6	92.6
	=Lebanon	89.3	92.6
	=Malta	90.3	92.6

Source: *United Nations*, Human Development Report 2001

The last few decades have seen a far more urbanized world, with a much higher proportion of the population living in metropolitan areas. There are also millions of "rural-urban dwellers," who may live in settlements defined by censuses and surveys as rural but who travel to work in urban areas.

TOP 10 HIGHEST CITIES

	CITY/COUNTRY	HEIGHT (FT)	(M)
1	Wenchuan, China	16,730	5,099
2	Potosí, Bolivia	13,045	3,976
3	Oruro, Bolivia	12,146	3,702
4	Lhasa, Tibet	12,087	3,684
5	La Paz, Bolivia	11,916	3,632
6	Cuzco, Peru	11,152	3,399
7	Huancayo, Peru	10,660	3,249
8	Sucre, Bolivia	9,301	2,835
9	Tunja, Colombia	9,252	2,820
10	Quito, Ecuador	9,249	2,819

Lhasa was formerly the highest capital city in the world, a role now occupied by La Paz, the capital of Bolivia. Wenchuan is situated at more than half the elevation of Everest, and even the towns and cities at the bottom of this list are more than one-third as high.

TOP 10 LARGEST US CITIES

	CITY/COUNTRY	ESTIMATED POPULATION IN 2001*
1	New York including Newark and Paterson, New York	21,500,000
2	Los Angeles including Riverside and Anaheim, California	16,700,000
3	Chicago, Illinois	9,300,000
4	Washington including Baltimore, DC	7,750,000
5	San Francisco including Oakland and San Jose, California	7,200,000
6	Philadelphia, Pennsylvania	6,250,000
7	Boston, Massachusetts	5,900,000
8	Detroit including Windsor, Canada, Michigan	5,800,000
9	Dallas including Fort Worth, Texas	5,450,000
10	Houston, Texas	4,850,000

* Of urban agglomeration

Source: *Th. Brinkhoff: The Principal Agglomerations of the World*, http://www.citypopulation.de, 14.10.2001

City and State
Singapore City and the state are synonymous, as a result of which Singapore is considered a totally urbanized country.

TOP 10 LEAST URBANIZED COUNTRIES

	COUNTRY	PERCENTAGE OF POPULATION LIVING IN URBAN AREAS IN 1999	EST. IN 2015
1	Rwanda	6.1	8.9
2	Bhutan	6.9	11.6
3	Burundi	8.7	14.5
4	Nepal	11.6	18.8
5	Uganda	13.8	20.7
6	Cambodia	15.6	22.8
7	Papua New Guinea	17.1	23.7
8	Vietnam	19.7	24.3
9	Ethiopia	17.2	25.8
10	Eritrea	18.4	26.2

Source: *United Nations*, Human Development Report 2001

TOP 10 COUNTRIES WITH THE MOST PEOPLE LIVING IN LARGE CITIES

	COUNTRY	% POPULATION IN CITIES OF OVER 1 MILLION* IN 2000
1	Singapore	100
2	=Dominican Republic	60
	=Kuwait	60
4	Portugal	57
5	Australia	56
6	=Lebanon	47
	=South Korea	47
8	Congo	42
9	=Argentina	41
	=Germany	41

* In those countries for which data are available

Source: *World Bank*, World Development Indicators 2001

TOP 10 LARGEST CITIES

	CITY/COUNTRY	EST. POPULATION IN 2001*
1	Tokyo, Japan	34,700,000
2	New York, New York	21,500,000
3	Seoul, South Korea	20,400,000
4	Mexico City, Mexico	19,450,000
5	São Paulo, Brazil	18,600,000
6	Osaka, Japan	17,950,000
7	Los Angeles, California	16,700,000
8	Bombay, India	16,650,000
9	Cairo, Egypt	14,850,000
10	Jakarta, Indonesia	13,500,000

* Of urban agglomeration

Source: *Th. Brinkhoff: The Principal Agglomerations of the World,* http://www.citypopulation.de, 14/10/2001

TOP 10 OLDEST CITIES IN THE US

	CITY	FOUNDED
1	St. Augustine, Florida	1565
2	Santa Fe, New Mexico	1609
3	Hampton, Virginia	1610
4	Newport News, Virginia	1621
5	=Albany, New York	1624
	=New York, New York	1624
7	Quincy, Massachusetts	1625
8	Salem, Massachusetts	1626
9	=Jersey City, New Jersey	1629
	=Lynn, Massachusetts	1629

The oldest permanently inhabited settlements in what is now the United States are the subject of much debate, but the founding years listed are those from which these cities are generally presumed to date.

Future Shock

TOP 10 MOST DENSELY POPULATED COUNTRIES, 2050

	COUNTRY	AREA (SQ KM)	EST. POPULATION IN 2050	POPULATION (PER SQ KM)
1	Singapore	624	10,790,779	17,292.9
2	Monaco	1.95	32,964	16,482.0
3	Maldives	300	815,031	2,716.8
4	Marshall Islands	181	347,893	1,922.1
5	Bahrain	619	973,412	1,572.6
6	Bangladesh	133,911	205,093,861	1,531.6
7	Malta	321	431,633	1,344.7
8	Nauru	21	22,696	1,080.8
9	Comoros	2,170	1,835,099	845.7
10	Mauritius	1,849	1,451,156	784.8
	World total	131,003,055	9,104,205,830	69.5

Source: *US Census Bureau, International Data Base*

TOP 10 LEAST DENSELY POPULATED COUNTRIES, 2050

	COUNTRY	AREA (SQ KM)	EST. POPULATION IN 2050	POPULATION (PER SQ KM)
1	Botswana	585,371	1,167,054	2.0
2	Suriname	161,47	388,061	2.4
3	Mongolia	1,565,000	4,181,249	2.7
4	Iceland	100,251	4,181,242	2.9
5	Namibia	823,291	2,464,890	3.0
6	Australia	7,617,931	24,175,783	3.2
7	Guyana	196,850	786,846	4.0
8	Canada	9,220,970	41,429,579	4.5
9	Libya	1,759,540	10,817,176	6.1
10	Russia	17,075,400	118,233,243	6.9

Source: *US Census Bureau, International Data Base*

There are still countries where the global population explosion has had little impact, although they include some whose terrain and climate are inhospitable to human settlement.

TOP 10 LARGEST WORLD CITIES, 2015

	CITY/COUNTRY	GROWTH PERCENTAGE (2000–2015)	EST. POPULATION IN 2015
1	Tokyo, Japan	0.0	26,400,000
2	Mumbai, India	2.4	26,100,000
3	Lagos, Nigeria	3.7	23,200,000
4	Dhaka, Bangladesh	3.6	21,100,000
5	São Paulo, Brazil	0.9	20,400,000
6	=Karachi, Pakistan	3.2	19,200,000
	=Mexico City, Mexico	0.4	19,200,000
8	New York, New York	0.3	17,400,000
9	=Calcutta, India	1.9	17,300,000
	=Jakarta, Indonesia	3.0	17,300,000

Source: *United Nations*, World Urbanization Prospects: The 1999 Revision

Despite a growth rate of zero, it is predicted that in 2015 Tokyo will remain the world's most populous city, but high rates elsewhere mean that several cities are destined to overtake it in the future.

TOP 10 LARGEST US STATES, 2015

	STATE	EST. POPULATION IN 2015
1	California	41,373,000
2	Texas	24,280,000
3	New York	18,916,000
4	Florida	18,497,000
5	Illinois	12,808,000
6	Pennsylvania	12,449,000
7	Ohio	11,588,000
8	Michigan	9,917,000
9	Georgia	9,200,000
10	New Jersey	8,924,000

Source: *US Census Bureau*

Between now and 2015, the greatest population increases will occur in 3 states – California, Texas, and Florida, which together will gain more than 16 million persons. California, which in 1900 had only 1,485,000 inhabitants, will contain over 13 percent of the nation's total population.

TOP 10 MOST POPULATED COUNTRIES, 2050

	COUNTRY	EST. POPULATION. IN 2050
1	India	1,619,582,271
2	China	1,470,468,924
3	US	403,943,147
4	Indonesia	337,807,011
5	Nigeria	303,586,770
6	Pakistan	267,813,495
7	Brazil	206,751,477
8	Bangladesh	205,093,861
9	Ethiopia	187,892,174
10	Dem. Rep. of Congo	181,922,656

Source: *US Census Bureau, International Data Base*

Estimates of national populations in 2050 present a striking change, as long-time world leader China is eclipsed by India, a reversal that is projected to take place around the year 2036. New entrants Ethiopia (in 16th place in 2005) and the Democratic Republic of Congo (up from 21st place in 2005) evict Russia and Mexico from the Top 10.

TOP 10 | FASTEST-GROWING CITIES, 1995–2010*

CITY/COUNTRY	INCREASE PERCENTAGE (1975–95)	EST. INCREASE PERCENTAGE (1995–2010)
1 Hangzhou, China	283.5	171.1
2 Addis Ababa, Ethiopia	161.6	170.7
3 Kabul, Afghanistan	200.9	156.3
4 Handan, China	245.9	141.6
5 Isfahan, Iran	150.9	141.3
6 Maputo, Mozambique	318.6	139.9
7 Lagos, Nigeria	211.7	139.5
8 Luanda, Angola	210.9	138.8
9 Nairobi, Kenya	167.4	133.6
10 Qingdao, China	183.8	132.4

* Urban agglomerations of over 1 million only

Source: *United Nations Center for Human Settlements (HABITAT)*

TOP 10 | FASTEST-GROWING COUNTRIES, 2050

COUNTRY*	EST. ANNUAL GROWTH RATE PERCENTAGE (2045–50)
1 Yemen	2.45
2 Niger	2.38
3 Somalia	2.19
4 Angola	2.11
5 Uganda	1.92
6 Liberia	1.89
7 Burkina Faso	1.86
8 Mali	1.76
9 Ethiopia	1.63
10 Dem. Rep. of Congo	1.60

* Countries with one million persons or more in 2000

Source: *United Nations Population Division*

Market Share

A bustling market in Yemen, in the Middle East, forecast to become the world's fastest growing country within the next 50 years.

Place Names

TOP 10 LONGEST PLACE NAMES IN THE WORLD*

NAME	LETTERS
1 Krung thep mahanakhon bovorn ratanakosin mahintharayutthaya mahadilok pop noparatratchathani burirom udomratchanivetmahasathan amornpiman avatarnsathit sakkathattiyavisnukarmprasit	167
When the poetic name of Bangkok, capital of Thailand, is used, it is usually abbreviated to "Krung Thep" (City of Angels).	
2 Taumatawhakatangihangakoauauotamateaturipukakapikimaungahoronukupokaiwhenuakitanatahu	85
This is the longer version (the other has a mere 83 letters) of the Maori name of a hill in New Zealand. It translates as "The place where Tamatea, the man with the big knees, who slid, climbed, and swallowed mountains, known as Land-eater, played on the flute to his loved one."	
3 Gorsafawddachaidraigddanheddogleddollônpenrhynareurdraethceredigion	67
A name contrived by the Fairbourne Steam Railway, Gwynedd, North Wales, for publicity purposes and in order to outdo its rival, No. 4. It means "The Mawddach station and its dragon teeth at the Northern Penrhyn Road on the golden beach of Cardigan Bay."	
4 Llanfairpwllgwyngyllgogerychwyrndrobwllllantysiliogogogoch	58
This is the place in Gwynedd, North Wales, famed especially for the length of its railway tickets. It means "St. Mary's Church in the hollow of the white hazel near to the rapid whirlpool of the church of St. Tysilo near the Red Cave." Questions have been raised about its authenticity, since its official name comprises only the first 20 letters, and the full name appears to have been invented as a hoax in the 19th century by a local tailor.	
5 El Pueblo de Nuestra Señora la Reina de los Ángeles de la Porciúncula	57
The site of a Franciscan mission and the full Spanish name of Los Angeles; it means "The town of Our Lady the Queen of the Angels of the Little Portion." Nowadays it is customarily known by its initial letters, "LA," making it also one of the shortest-named cities in the world.	
6 Chargoggagoggmanchaugagoggchaubunagungamaug	43
America's longest single place name – a lake near Webster, Massachusetts. Its Indian name means "You fish on your side, I'll fish on mine, and no one fishes in the middle." It is said to be pronounced "Char-gogg-a-gogg (pause) man-chaugg-a-gog (pause) chau-bun-a-gung-a-maug."	
7 =Lower North Branch Little Southwest Miramichi	40
Canada's longest place name – a short river in New Brunswick.	
=Villa Real de la Santa Fé de San Francisco de Asis	40
The full Spanish name of Santa Fe, New Mexico, translates as "Royal city of the holy faith of St. Francis of Assisi."	
9 Te Whakatakanga-o-te-ngarehu-o-te-ahi-a-Tamatea	38
The Maori name of Hammer Springs, New Zealand. Like the second name in this list, it refers to a legend of Tamatea, explaining how the springs were warmed by "the falling of the cinders of the fire of Tamatea."	
10 Meallan Liath Coire Mhic Dhubhghaill	32
The longest multiple name in Scotland, a place near Aultanrynie, Highland, alternatively spelled Meallan Liath Coire Mhic Dhughaill (30 letters).	

* Including single-word, hyphenated, and multiple names

TOP 10 COUNTRIES WITH THE LONGEST OFFICIAL NAMES

OFFICIAL NAME*	COMMON ENGLISH NAME	LETTERS
1 al-Jamahiriyah al-'Arabiyah al-Lībīyah ash-Sha'biyah al-Ishtirākiyah	Libya	59
2 al-Jumhuriyah al-Jaza'iriyah ad-Dimuqrātiyah ash-Sha'biyah	Algeria	51
3 United Kingdom of Great Britain and Northern Ireland	United Kingdom	45
4 =Srī Lankā Prajātāntrika Samājavādī Janarajaya	Sri Lanka	41
=Jumhurīyat al-Qumur al-Ittihādīyah al-Islāmīyah	The Comoros	41
6 República Democrática de São Tomé e Príncipe	São Tomé and Príncipe	38
7 al-Jūmhurīyah al-Islāmīyah al-Mūritānīyah	Mauritania	36
8 =al-Mamlakah al-Urdunnīyah al-Hāshimīyah	Jordan	34
=Sathalanalat Paxathipatai Paxaxôn Lao	Laos	34
10 Federation of St. Christopher and Nevis	St. Kitts and Nevis	33

* Some official names have been transliterated from languages that do not use the Roman alphabet; their length may vary according to the method used

TOP 10 LONGEST PLACE NAMES IN THE US*

NAME/STATE	LETTERS
1 Chargoggagoggmanchauggagoggchaubunagungamaugg	45
(See Top 10 Longest Place Names in the World, No. 6)	
2 Nunathloogagamiutbingoi Dunes, Alaska	23
3 Winchester-on-the-Severn, Maryland	21
4 Scraper-Moechereville, Illinois	20
5 Linstead-on-the-Severn, Maryland	19
6 =Kentwood-in-the-Pines, California	18
=Lauderdale-by-the-Sea, Florida	18
=Vermilion-on-the-Lake, Ohio	18
9 =Chippewa-on-the-Lake, Ohio	17
=Fairhaven-on-the-Bay, Maryland	17
=Highland-on-the-Lake, New York	17
=Kleinfeltersville, Pennsylvania	17
=Mooselookmeguntic, Maine	17
=Palermo-by-the-Lakes, Ohio	17
=Saybrook-on-the-Lake, Ohio	17

* Including single-word and hyphenated names (not counting hyphens as characters)
Source: *US Geological Survey*

Christopher Columbus
Columbus is believed to have landed on the coast of Colombia in 1502. The country was named after him over 400 years later.

TOP 10 — MOST COMMON PLACE NAMES IN THE US

	NAME	OCCURRENCES
1	Fairview	287
2	Midway	252
3	Riverside	180
4	Oak Grove	179
5	Five Points	155
6	Oakland	149
7	Greenwood	145
8	=Bethel	141
	=Franklin	141
10	Pleasant Hill	140

Source: *US Geological Survey*

TOP 10 — LARGEST COUNTRIES AND ISLANDS NAMED AFTER REAL PEOPLE

	COUNTRY	NAMED AFTER	AREA (SQ MILES)	(SQ KM)
1	United States of America	Amerigo Vespucci (Italy; 1451–1512)	3,539,245	9,166,601
2	Saudi Arabia	Abdul Aziz ibn-Saud (Nejd; 1882–1953)	830,000	2,149,690
3	Bolivia	Simon Bolivar (Venezuela; 1783–1830)	418,685	1,084,389
4	Colombia	Christopher Columbus (Italy; 1451–1506)	401,044	1,038,699
5	Philippines	Philip II (Spain; 1527–98)	115,124	298,171
6	Falkland Islands	Lucius Cary, 2nd Viscount Falkland (UK; *c.*1610–43)	4,700	12,173
7	Northern Mariana	Maria Theresa (Austria; 1717–80)	184	477
8	Wallis & Futuna	Samuel Wallis (UK; 1728–95)	105	274
9	Cook Islands	Capt. James Cook (UK; 1728–79)	93	241
10	Marshall Islands	Capt. John Marshall (UK; 1748–after 1818)	70	181

Many countries were named after mythical characters, or saints of dubious authenticity – often because they were discovered on the saint's day – but these are all named after real people. It is questionable whether China is named after the Emperor Chin, but if so it would rank first. Some countries have lost their former names – for example Rhodesia, named after Cecil Rhodes, was renamed Zambia and Zimbabwe in 1980.

Great Buildings

TOP 10 HIGHEST HOTELS

	HOTEL/LOCATION	YEAR COMPLETED	STORIES	HEIGHT (FT)	(M)
1	**Jin Mao Tower*#**, Shanghai, China	1998	88	1,214	370
2	**Baiyoke II Tower†#**, Bangkok, Thailand	1997	89	1,013	309
3	**Burj Al Arab#**, Dubai, United Arab Emirates	1999	60	885	270
4	**Emirates Tower 2#**, Dubai, United Arab Emirates	1999	50	858	262
5	**Thai Wah Tower II§**, Bangkok, Thailand	1996	60	853	260
6	**Four Seasons**, Miami, Florida	2002	54	788	241
7	**JR Central Towers**, Nagoya, Japan	1999	53	787	240
8	**Westin Stamford**, Singapore	1986	73	742	226
9	**Westin Peachtree**, Atlanta, Georgia	1973	71	723	220
10	**Marriott Renaissance**, Detroit, Michigan	1973	71	720	219

* *Grand Hyatt Hotel occupies floors 53–87*   # *Excluding spire*
† *Baiyoke Sky Hotel occupies floors 22–74*   § *Westin Banyan Tree Hotel occupies floors 33–60*

High Life
The striking, sail-like Burj Al Arab hotel, Dubai, is the world's tallest all-hotel building. The structure stands on a manmade island and contains a record-breaking 590-ft (180-m) atrium.

NEW YORK'S FIRST SKYSCRAPER

BECAUSE OF ITS TRIANGULAR SHAPE, soon after opening, in 1903, the Fuller Building acquired the name by which it is known today – the Flatiron Building. Designed by Chicago architect Daniel Hudson Burnham (1846–1912), the Flatiron, a 285-ft (87-m), 22-floor office building, was New York's first true skyscraper, and stands today as one of the city's oldest. It was also the first to attract popular imagination, and has been depicted by many leading artists and photographers.

TOP 10 TALLEST CATHEDRALS AND CHURCHES

	CATHEDRAL OR CHURCH/LOCATION	YEAR COMPLETED	HEIGHT (FT)	(M)
1	**Chicago Methodist Temple***, Chicago, Illinois	1924	568	173
2	**Ulm Cathedral**, Ulm, Germany	1890	528	161
3	**Notre Dame de la Paix**, Yamoussoukro, Ivory Coast	1989	519	158
4	**Cologne Cathedral**, Cologne, Germany	1880	513	156
5	**Rouen Cathedral**, Rouen, France	1876	485	148
6	**St. Nicholas**, Hamburg, Germany	1847	475	145
7	**Notre Dame**, Strasbourg, France	1439	465	142
8	**St. Peter's**, Rome, Italy	1612	448	136
9	**St. Stephen's Cathedral**, Vienna, Austria	1433	446	135
10	**St. Martin's Cathedral**, Landshut, Germany	1500	440	134

* *Sited on top of a 25-story, 328-ft (100-m) building*

TOP 10 | OLDEST CHURCHES IN THE US

	CHURCH/LOCATION	BUILT
1	**Convento de Porta Coeli,** San Germán, Puerto Rico*	1609
2	**San Estevan del Rey Mission,** Valencia County, New Mexico	1629
3	**St. Luke's Church,** Isle of Wight County, Virginia	1632
4	**First Church of Christ and the Ancient Burying Ground,** Hartford County, Connecticut	1640
5	**St. Ignatius Catholic Church,** St. Mary's County, Maryland	1641
6	**Merchant's Hope Church,** Prince George County, Virginia	1657
7	**Flatlands Dutch Reformed Church,** King's County, New York	1660
8	**=Church San Blas de Illesces of Coamo,** Ponce, Puerto Rico*	1661
	=Claflin-Richards House, Essex County, Maryland	1661
	=St. Mary's Whitechapel, Lancaster County, Virginia	1661

* Not US territory when built, but now US National Historic Site

Source: *US Department of the Interior,* National Register of Historic Places

TOP 10 | TALLEST LIGHTHOUSES IN THE US

	LIGHTHOUSE/LOCATOIN	HEIGHT* (FT)	(M)
1	**Cape Hatteras,** North Carolina	196	59.7
2	**Cape Charles,** Virginia	191	58.2
3	**Pensacola,** Florida	171	52.1
4	**=Absecon,** New Jersey	170	51.8
	=Cape May, New Jersey	170	51.8
6	**Lookout,** North Carolina	169	51.5
7	**Ponce de Leon Inlet,** Florida	168	51.2
8	**Fire Island,** New York	167	50.9
9	**"New" Cape Henry,** North Carolina	165	50.3
10	**=Bodie Island,** North Carolina	163	49.7
	=Currituck, North Carolina	163	49.7

* Measurement taken from ground level to the top of the lantern

Source: *US Lighthouse Society*

Tall Temple
The Chicago Methodist Temple was completed in 1924 at a cost of $3 million. It was the tallest building in the city until the Chicago Board of Trade was completed in 1930, but it remains the world's tallest church.

CULTURE & LEARNING

Mind Your Language

TOP 10 MOST WIDELY SPOKEN LANGUAGES

	COUNTRY	APPROX. NO. OF SPEAKERS
1	Chinese (Mandarin)	874,000,000
2	Hindustani*	426,000,000
3	Spanish	358,000,000
4	English	341,000,000
5	Bengali	207,000,000
6	Arabic#	206,000,000
7	Portuguese	176,000,000
8	Russian	167,000,000
9	Japanese	125,000,000
10	German (standard)	100,000,000

Hindi and Urdu are essentially the same language – Hindustani. As the official language of Pakistan it is written in modified Arabic script and called Urdu. As the official language of India it is written in the Devanagari script and called Hindi.

 # Includes 16 variants of the Arabic language

In addition to those languages appearing in the Top 10, there are 11 further languages that are spoken by between 50 and 100 million people: Korean (78 million), French (77 million), Chinese (Wu) (77 million), Javanese (75 million), Chinese (Yue) (71 million), Telugu (69 million), Marathi (68 million), Vietnamese (68 million), Tamil (66 million), Italian (62 million), and Turkish (61 million).

TOP 10 LANGUAGES IN THE WORLD 50 YEARS AGO

	COUNTRY	APPROX. NO. OF SPEAKERS*
1	=English	200,000,000
	=Mandarin	200,000,000
3	Russian	120,000,000
4	=German	100,000,000
	=Spanish	100,000,000
6	Japanese	80,000,000
7	French	75,000,000
8	Western Hindi	72,000,000
9	=Bengali	60,000,000
	=Cantonese	60,000,000

People for whom the language is their mother tongue

TOP 10 ONLINE LANGUAGES

	LANGUAGE	INTERNET ACCESS*
1	English	270,000,000
2	Chinese	160,000,000
3	Japanese	75,000,000
4	Spanish	60,000,000
5	German	46,000,000
6	Korean	35,000,000
7	French	30,000,000
8	Portuguese	26,000,000
9	Italian	25,000,000
10	Russian	15,000,000
	World total	793,000,000

Online population estimate for 2003

Source: *Global Reach*

TOP 10 LANGUAGES OFFICIALLY SPOKEN IN THE MOST COUNTRIES

	LANGUAGE	COUNTRIES
1	English	57
2	French	33
3	Arabic	23
4	Spanish	21
5	Portuguese	7
6	=Dutch	5
	=German	5
8	=Chinese (Mandarin)	3
	=Danish	3
	=Italian	3
	=Malay	3

Many countries have more than 1 official language – in Canada, for instance, both English and French are recognized officially. English is used in numerous countries as the lingua franca, a common language that enables people to communicate with each other.

Talking Our Language

Mandarin is the Beijing dialect of Chinese, and is the most-spoken and, since 1917, the official language of China. It is used by more than two-thirds of its population.

TOP 10 COUNTRIES WITH THE MOST ARABIC-LANGUAGE SPEAKERS

	COUNTRY	APPROX. NO. OF SPEAKERS*
1	Egypt	65,080,000
2	Algeria	26,280,000
3	Saudi Arabia	20,920,000
4	Morocco	18,730,000
5	Iraq	17,490,000
6	Yemen	17,400,000
7	Sudan	17,320,000
8	Syria	14,680,000
9	Tunisia#	6,710,000
10	Libya	4,910,000

People for whom Arabic is their mother tongue

 # Another 2,520,000 people speak Arabic-French and 300,000 speak Arabic-English

TOP 10 COUNTRIES WITH THE MOST GERMAN-LANGUAGE SPEAKERS

COUNTRY	APPROX. NO. OF SPEAKERS*
1 Germany	75,060,000
2 Austria	7,444,000
3 Switzerland	4,570,000
4 US	1,850,000
5 Brazil	910,000
6 Poland	500,000
7 Canada	486,000
8 Kazakhstan	460,000
9 Russia	350,000
10 Italy	310,000

People for whom German is their mother tongue

TOP 10 COUNTRIES WITH THE MOST SPANISH-LANGUAGE SPEAKERS

COUNTRY	APPROX. NO. OF SPEAKERS*
1 Mexico	91,080,000
2 Colombia	41,880,000
3 Argentina	35,860,000
4 Spain#	29,860,000
5 Venezuela	23,310,000
6 US	20,720,000
7 Peru	20,470,000
8 Chile	13,640,000
9 Ecuador	11,760,000
10 Dominican Republic	8,270,000

People for whom Spanish is their mother tongue
 # Castilian Spanish

TOP 10 COUNTRIES WITH THE MOST ENGLISH-LANGUAGE SPEAKERS

COUNTRY	APPROX. NO. OF SPEAKERS*
1 US	237,320,000
2 UK	58,090,000
3 Canada	18,218,000
4 Australia	15,561,000
5 Ireland	3,720,000
6 South Africa	3,700,000
7 New Zealand	3,338,000
8 Jamaica#	2,460,000
9 Trinidad and Tobago#†	1,245,000
10 Guyana#	764,000

People for whom English is their mother tongue
 # Includes English Creole
† Trinidad English

After the 10th entry, the figures dive to around or under 260,000 in the case of The Bahamas, Barbados, and Zimbabwe. There are also perhaps as many as one billion who speak English as a second language: a large proportion of the population of the Philippines, for example. In countries such as India, Nigeria, and other former British colonies in Africa, English is either an official language or is widely understood, and used in government and business.

Children at School

STATES WITH THE FEWEST STUDENTS PER TEACHER

	STATE	STUDENTS PER TEACHER IN 1999
1	Vermont	12.3
2	=Maine	12.8
	=Massachusetts	12.8
4	Wyoming	13.3
5	New Jersey	13.4
6	=North Dakota	13.8
	=West Virginia	13.8
8	=Connecticut	13.9
	=Nebraska	13.9
10	=South Dakota	14.0
	=Virginia	14.0

Source: *National Center for Education Statistics*

A Class Apart
Primary school class sizes in countries such as Bangladesh are exceptionally large – the average of 63 pupils per teacher is often exceeded.

COUNTRIES WITH HIGHEST NUMBER OF PRIMARY SCHOOL PUPILS PER TEACHER

	COUNTRY	PUPIL/TEACHER RATIO IN PRIMARY SCHOOLS*
1	Central African Republic	77
2	Congo	70
3	Chad	67
4	Bangladesh	63
5	Malawi	59
6	=Afghanistan	58
	=Mozambique	58
	=Rwanda	58
9	=Benin	56
	=Senegal	56

* In latest year for which figures available
Source: *UNESCO*

BEST COUNTRIES FOR EDUCATION

	COUNTRY	EDUCATION INDEX*
1	=Australia	0.99
	=Belgium	0.99
	=Finland	0.99
	=Netherlands	0.99
	=New Zealand	0.99
	=Sweden	0.99
	=UK	0.99
8	=Norway	0.98
	=Canada	0.98
	=US	0.98
	=Denmark	0.98

* The education index takes into account adult literacy and school enrollment rates

Source: *United Nations*, Human Development Report 2001

WORST COUNTRIES FOR EDUCATION

	COUNTRY	EDUCATION INDEX*
1	Niger	0.15
2	Burkina Faso	0.23
3	Sierra Leone	0.30
4	Guinea	0.33
5	Ethiopia	0.34
6	=Angola	0.36
	=Mali	0.36
	=Mozambique	0.36
	=Senegal	0.36
10	=Burundi	0.37
	=Guinea-Bissau	0.37

* The education index takes into account adult literacy and school enrollment rates

Source: *United Nations*, Human Development Report 2001

TOP 10 COUNTRIES WITH THE LONGEST SCHOOL YEARS

	COUNTRY	SCHOOL YEAR (DAYS)
1	China	251
2	Japan	243
3	Korea	220
4	Israel	215
5	=Germany	210
	=Russia	210
7	Switzerland	207
8	=Netherlands	200
	=Scotland	200
	=Thailand	200
	US	180

THE 10 COUNTRIES WITH THE HIGHEST ILLITERACY

	COUNTRY	FEMALE ILLITERACY RATE (%)	MALE ILLITERACY RATE (%)*
1	Niger	91.7	76.5
2	Burkina Faso	86.9	66.8
3	The Gambia	70.4	56.2
4	Ethiopia	66.6	56.1
5	Senegal	72.4	52.8
6	Mali	66.8	52.1
7	Mauritania	70.5	49.4
8	Sierra Leone	77.4	49.3
9	=Afghanistan	79.2	49.0
	=Haiti	53.5	49.0

*Age over 15 (figures estimated where no recent data available)

Source: UNESCO

TOP 10 PRIVATE EDUCATION COUNTRIES (SECONDARY EDUCATION)

	COUNTRY	% ENROLLMENT IN PRIVATE SECONDARY SCHOOLS*
1	=Mauritius	79
	=Netherlands	79
3	Botswana	78
4	Kiribati	77
5	Zimbabwe	71
6	Belgium	69
7	Lebanon	60
8	Tanzania	51
9	Chile	45
10	Samoa	43

*In latest year and for those countries for which data available

TOP 10 COUNTRIES SPENDING MOST ON EDUCATION

	COUNTRY	EXPENDITURE AS PERCENTAGE OF GNP*
1	Kiribati	11.4
2	Moldova	10.3
3	Namibia	8.5
4	Denmark	7.7
5	Sweden	7.6
6	=South Africa	7.5
	=Zimbabwe	7.5
8	Uzbekistan	7.4
9	Barbados	7.3
10	Saudi Arabia	7.2

*Gross National Product in latest year for which data available

Source: UNESCO

Valuable Education
Education spending in Namibia represents a greater proportion of its Gross National Product than that of any other country in Africa.

Higher Education

TOP 10 COUNTRIES WITH MOST UNIVERSITIES

	COUNTRY	UNIVERSITIES*
1	India	8,407
2	US	5,758
3	Argentina	1,831
4	Indonesia	1,667
5	Spain	1,415
6	Mexico	1,341
7	Bangladesh	1,268
8	Japan	1,243
9	France	1,062
10	China	1,020

* Includes all further educational establishments

TOP 10 OLDEST UNIVERSITIES AND COLLEGES IN THE US

	UNIVERSITY/LOCATION	YEAR CHARTERED
1	Harvard University, Massachusetts	1636
2	College of William & Mary, Virginia	1692
3	Yale University, Connecticut	1701
4	University of Pennsylvania, Pennsylvania	1740
5	Moravian College, Pennsylvania	1742
6	Princeton University, New Jersey	1746
7	Washington & Lee University, Virginia	1749
8	Columbia University, New York	1754
9	Brown University, Rhode Island	1764
10	Rutgers, the State University of New Jersey	1766

Source: National Center for Educational Statistics

TOP 10 LARGEST UNIVERSITIES

	UNIVERSITY/COUNTRY	STUDENTS
1	Kameshwar Singh Darbhanga Sanskrit, India	515,000
2	Paris, France	309,663
3	Calcutta, India	300,000
4	Mexico, Mexico	271,574
5	Bombay, India	262,350
6	Kanpur, India	220,000
7	Guadalajara, Mexico	214,986
8	Utkal, India	200,000
9	Rome, Italy	189,000
10	Buenos Aires, Argentina	183,397

TOP 10 COUNTRIES WITH THE HIGHEST PERCENTAGE OF FEMALE UNIVERSITY STUDENTS

	COUNTRY	PERCENTAGE OF FEMALE STUDENTS*
1	Cyprus	75
2	US Virgin Islands	74
3	Qatar	73
4	=St. Lucia	72
	=United Arab Emirates	72
6	Kuwait	67
7	Myanmar	64
8	Barbados	62
9	Namibia	61
10	=Bulgaria	60
	=Cuba	60
	=Latvia	60
	=Lesotho	60
	=Mongolia	60
	=Panama	60
	US	56

* In latest year and in those countries for which data available

Source: UNESCO

TOP 10 COUNTRIES WITH THE MOST STUDENTS IN HIGHER EDUCATION

	COUNTRY	HIGHER EDUCATION STUDENTS*
1	US	14,350,000
2	India	5,007,000
3	Russia	3,597,900
4	China	3,174,000
5	Japan	3,136,834
6	Indonesia	2,703,886
7	France	2,083,129
8	Philippines	2,022,106
9	Brazil	1,948,200
10	UK	1,820,849

In latest year for which data available

Source: *UNESCO*

TOP 10 COUNTRIES WITH THE MOST UNIVERSITY STUDENTS PER TEACHER

	COUNTRY	HIGHER EDUCATION STUDENTS PER TEACHER*
1	France	39.6
2	Italy	32.6
3	Mauritania	31.5
4	Pakistan	30.9
5	Cameroon	30.5
6	Bangladesh	28.7
7	Fiji	28.5
8	South Korea	27.6
9	Morocco	27.5
10	Togo	26.3

In latest year and for those countries for which data available

Source: *UNESCO*

TOP 10 COUNTRIES WITH THE FEWEST UNIVERSITY STUDENTS PER TEACHER

	COUNTRY	HIGHER EDUCATION STUDENTS PER TEACHER*
1	Antigua and Barbuda	2.9
2	Rwanda	5.2
3	Cuba	5.3
4	Brunei	5.6
5	Bulgaria	6.0
6	=Georgia	6.4
	=Lithuania	6.4
8	Azerbaijan	6.6
9	Zambia	7.0
10	Mozambique	7.5

In latest year and for those countries for which data available

Source: *UNESCO*

TOP 10 BACHELOR'S DEGREES IN THE US (MALE)

	DEGREE	NO. CONFERRED ON MEN IN 1998
1	Engineering	48,582
2	Business administration and management	44,510
3	General biology	20,536
4	Communications	19,631
5	Psychology	17,867
6	Accounting	16,192
7	Teacher education, academic, and vocational programs	15,978
8	History	15,666
9	Political science and government	15,609
10	Criminal justice and corrections	14,624
	All subjects	519,956

Source: *National Center for Educational Statistics*

TOP 10 BACHELOR'S DEGREES IN THE US (FEMALE)

	DEGREE	NO. CONFERRED ON WOMEN IN 1998
1	Psychology	51,507
2	General teacher education	50,289
3	Business administration and management	42,426
4	Nursing	38,894
5	Communications	29,754
6	General biology	26,518
7	English language and literature	25,379
8	Accounting	21,726
9	Teacher education academic and vocational programs	17,925
10	Sociology	17,067
	All subjects	664,450

Source: *National Center for Educational Statistics*

French Lessons
University education has a long history in France: Paris University was founded in 1200 and today is Europe's largest.

Libraries of the World

TOP 10 LARGEST LIBRARIES

	LIBRARY	LOCATION	FOUNDED	BOOKS
1	Library of Congress	Washington, DC	1800	24,616,867
2	=National Library of China	Beijing, China	1909	20,000,000
	=Russian Academy of Sciences Library	St. Petersburg, Russia	1714	20,000,000
4	Deutsche Bibliothek*	Frankfurt, Germany	1990	16,593,000
5	National Library of Canada	Ottawa, Canada	1953	16,000,000
6	British Library#	London, UK	1753	15,000,000
7	Harvard University Library	Cambridge, Massachusetts	1638	13,982,000
8	Institute for Scientific Information on the Social Sciences of Russian Academy of Science	St. Petersburg, Russia	1969	13,500,000
9	Vernadsky Central Scientific Library of the National Academy of Sciences	Kiev, Ukraine	1919	13,000,000
10	Bibliothèque National de France	Paris, France	1400	11,000,000

Formed in 1990 through the unification of the Deutsche Bibliothek, Frankfurt, (founded 1947) and the Deutsche Bucherei, Leipzig

Founded as part of the British Museum, 1753; became an independent body in 1973

TOP 10 COUNTRIES WITH THE MOST PUBLIC LIBRARIES

	COUNTRY	PUBLIC LIBRARIES
1	Russia	33,200
2	UK	23,678
3	Germany	20,448
4	US	9,097
5	Czech Republic	8,398
6	Romania	7,181
7	Bulgaria	5,591
8	Hungary	4,765
9	Brazil	3,600
10	China	2,406

National literary traditions play a major role in determining the ratio of libraries to population. The people of Japan, for example, do not customarily borrow books, and consequently the country has only 1,107 public libraries, whereas Finland, which has a population of little over 4 percent of that of Japan, has 461 libraries.

Shelf Life
The founding of the National Library of Austria dates from 1368, when Archduke Albrecht III established it in the Imperial Castle, Vienna.

THE 10 FIRST PUBLIC LIBRARIES IN THE US

	LIBRARY	FOUNDED
1	**Peterboro Public Library,** Peterboro, NH	1833
2	**New Orleans Public Library,** New Orleans, LA	1843
3	**Boston Public Library,** Boston, MA	1852
4	**Cincinnati & Hamilton County Public Library,** Cincinnati, OH	1853
5	**Springfield City Library,** Springfield, MA	1857
6	**Worcester Public Library,** Worcester, MA	1859
7	**Multnomah County Library,** Portland, OR	1864
8	**=Detroit Public Library,** Detroit, MI	1865
	=St. Louis Public Library, St. Louis, MO	1865
10	**Atlanta-Fulton Public Library,** Atlanta, GA	1867

Source: *Public Library Association*

TOP 10 LARGEST LIBRARIES IN THE US

	LIBRARY	HOLDINGS
1	**Library of Congress**	24,616,867
2	**Harvard University**	13,982,000
3	**New York Public Library**	10,421,691
4	**Yale University Library**	10,108,000
5	**Cincinnati & Hamilton County Public Library**	9,608,333
6	**Chicago Public Library**	9,238,328
7	**University of Illinois-Urbana Library**	9,171,000
8	**Queen's Borough Public Library**	9,143,760
9	**Free Library of Philadelphia**	8,144,478
10	**University of Texas–Austin Library**	7,649,000

Source: *American Library Association/National Center for Education Statistics*

Reading Room
The New York Public Library is the world's largest public library. In addition to its holdings of books, it houses over 30 million catalogued items.

TOP 10 OLDEST NATIONAL LIBRARIES

	LIBRARY/LOCATION	FOUNDED
1	**Národní Knihovně České Republiky,** National Library of the Czech Republic, Prague, Czech Republic	1366
2	**Österreichische Nationalbibliothek,** National Library of Austria, Vienna, Austria	1368
3	**Biblioteca Nazionale Marciana,** Venice, Italy	1468
4	**Bibliothèque Nationale de France,** National Library of France, Paris, France	1480
5	**National Library of Malta,** Valletta, Malta	1555
6	**Bayerische Staatsbibliothek,** Munich, Germany	1558
7	**Bibliothèque Royale Albert 1er,** National Library of Belgium, Brussels, Belgium	1559
8	**Nacionalna i Sveučilišna Knjiznica Zagreb,** National and University Library, Zagreb, Croatia	1606
9	**Helsingin Yliopiston Kirjasto,** National Library of Finland, Helsinki, Finland	1640
10	**Kongeligie Bibliotek,** National Library of Denmark, Copenhagen, Denmark	1653

TOP 10 LARGEST PUBLIC LIBRARIES

	LIBRARY/NO. OF BRANCHES	LOCATION	FOUNDED	BOOKS
1	**New York Public Library** (The Branch Libraries) (85)	New York, NY	1895*	10,421,691#
2	**Public Library of Cincinnati and Hamilton County** (41)	Cincinnati, OH	1853	9,608,333
3	**Chicago Public Library** (79)	Chicago, IL	1872	9,238,328
4	**Queens Borough Public Library** (62)	Jamaica, NY	1896	9,143,760
5	**Shanghai Public Library**	Shanghai, China	1952†	8,200,000
6	**Free Library of Philadelphia** (52)	Philadelphia, PA	1891	8,144,478
7	**Boston Public Library** (25)	Boston, MA	1852	7,438,880
8	**County of Los Angeles Public Library** (85)	Los Angeles, CA	1872	7,289,562
9	**Brooklyn Public Library** (58)	Brooklyn, NY	1896	6,809,959
10	**Carnegie Library of Pittsburgh** (19)	Pittsburgh, PA	1895	6,303,408

* Astor Library founded 1848; consolidated with Lenox Library and Tilden Trust to form New York Public Library, 1895

\# Lending library and reference library holdings available for loan

† Opened to the public in 1996

Source: *American Library Association*

Bestsellers

TOP 10 BEST-SELLING BOOKS OF ALL TIME

#	BOOK/AUTHOR/FIRST PUBLISHED	APPROX. SALES
1	**The Bible,** *c.*1451–55	more than 6,000,000,000
2	**Quotations from the Works of Mao Tse-tung,** 1966	900,000,000
3	**The Lord of the Rings,** J. R. R. Tolkien, 1954–55	more than 100,000,000
4	**American Spelling Book,** Noah Webster, 1783	up to 100,000,000
5	**The Guinness Book of Records** (now Guinness World Records), 1955	more than 90,000,000*
6	**World Almanac,** 1868	75,000,000*
7	**The McGuffey Readers,** William Holmes McGuffey, 1836	60,000,000
8	**The Common Sense Book of Baby and Child Care,** Benjamin Spock, 1946	more than 50,000,000
9	**A Message to Garcia,** Elbert Hubbard, 1899	up to 40,000,000
10	**=In His Steps: "What Would Jesus Do?,"** Rev. Charles Monroe Sheldon, 1896	more than 30,000,000
	=Valley of the Dolls, Jacqueline Susann, 1966	more than 30,000,000

* Aggregate sales of annual publication

It is extremely difficult to establish precise sales even of contemporary books, and virtually impossible to do so with books published long ago. How many copies of the *Complete Works of Shakespeare* have been sold in countless editions? The publication of variant editions, translations, and pirated copies all affect the global picture. As a result, this Top 10 list offers no more than the "best guess" at the great bestsellers of the past, and it may be that there are other books with a valid claim to a place in it.

"NONFICTION" USED

ALTHOUGH NONFICTION has been published as long as there have been books, it is surprising to discover that this entire category went unnamed until barely a century ago. The British journal *Library World* of March 1903 refers to the advertising of "non-fictional wares," while the *Westminster Gazette* of June 2, 1909, contained the first-ever printed reference to "nonfiction." In the US, the trade magazine *Publishers Weekly* began listing nonfiction bestsellers for the first time in 1912, making the category permanent only in 1917, in response to the proliferation of books about World War I.

FIRST OR LAST

TOP 10 BOOK BUYERS

#	COUNTRY	BOOK SALES PER CAPITA IN 2002* ($)
1	Japan	187.70
2	Norway	123.70
3	Germany	105.60
4	Singapore	100.40
5	US	98.10
6	Finland	88.70
7	Belgium	86.20
8	Switzerland	84.70
9	UK	75.50
10	Sweden	73.70

* Estimate based on 2000 prices

Source: *Euromonitor*

Book sales in these economically advanced countries contrast markedly with those in less-developed countries and those with failing economies: per capita book sales in Russia are estimated at $1.00 and in India at 80 cents.

TOP 10 HARDBACK FICTION TITLES OF 2001 IN THE US

#	TITLE/AUTHOR	SALES
1	**Desecration,** Jerry B. Jenkins and Tim LaHaye	2,969,458
2	**Skipping Christmas,** John Grisham	2,093,880
3	**A Painted House,** John Grisham	1,729,115
4	**Dreamcatcher,** Stephen King	1,287,000
5	**The Corrections,** Jonathan Franzen	930,000
6	**Black House,** Stephen King and Peter Straub	928,077
7	**The Kiss,** Danielle Steel	750,000
8	**Valhalla Rising,** Clive Cussler	736,670
9	**A Day Late and a Dollar Short,** Terry McMillan	718,600
10	**Violets Are Blue,** Danielle Steel	718,203

Source: Publishers Weekly

TOP 10 HARDBACK NON-FICTION TITLES OF 2001 IN THE US

#	BOOK/AUTHOR	SALES
1	**The Prayer of Jabez,** Bruce Wilkinson	8,439,540
2	**Secrets of the Vine,** Bruce Wilkinson	3,023,197
3	**Who Moved My Cheese?,** Spencer Johnson	1,778,075
4	**John Adams,** David McCullough	1,452,943
5	**Guinness World Records 2002**	1,300,000
6	**Prayer of Jabez Devotional,** Bruce Wilkinson	898,989
7	**The No Spin Zone: Confrontations with the Powerful and Famous in America,** Bill O'Reilly	866,000
8	**Body for Life: 12 Weeks to Mental and Physical Strength,** Bill Phillips	820,000
9	**How I Play Golf,** Tiger Woods	770,286
10	**Jack,** Jack Welch	724,345

Source: Publishers Weekly

TOP 10 CHILDREN'S HARDBACK TITLES OF ALL TIME IN THE US

	TITLE/AUTHOR/PUBLISHED	SALES
1	**The Poky Little Puppy,** Janette Sebring Lowrey, 1942	14,898,341
2	**The Tale of Peter Rabbit,** Beatrix Potter, 1902	9,380,341
3	**Tootle,** Gertrude Crampton, 1945	8,560,277
4	**Green Eggs and Ham,** Dr. Seuss, 1960	8,143,088
5	**Harry Potter and the Goblet of Fire,** J. K. Rowling, 2000	7,913,765
6	**Pat the Bunny,** Dorothy Kunhardt, 1940	7,562,710
7	**Saggy Baggy Elephant,** Kathryn and Byron Jackson, 1947	7,476,395
8	**Scuffy the Tugboat,** Gertrude Crampton, 1955	7,366,073
9	**The Cat in the Hat,** Dr. Seuss, 1957	7,220,982
10	**Harry Potter and the Chamber of Secrets,** J. K. Rowling, 1999	6,314,391

Source: Publishers Weekly, "All-Time Bestselling Children's Books", *17 December 2001*

TOP 10 MASS MARKET PAPERBACKS OF 2001 IN THE US

	BOOK/AUTHOR	SALES
1	**A Painted House,** John Grisham	3,000,000
2	**Hannibal,** Thomas Harris	2,900,000
3	**Dance upon Air,** Nora Roberts	2,500,000
4	**Heaven and Earth,** Nora Roberts	2,300,000
5	**Bear and Dragon,** Tom Clancy	2,200,000
6	**Carolina,** Nora Roberts	2,100,000
7	**The Lord of the Rings: The Fellowship of the Ring** J. R. R. Tolkien	2,042,826
8	**Last Precinct,** Patricia Cornwell,	2,000,000
9	**Before I Say,** Mary Higgins Clark	1,870,000
10	**Time and Again,** Nora Roberts	1,760,000

Source: Publishers Weekly

J. K., OBE

Harry Potter author J. K. (Joanne Kathleen) Rowling received her OBE (Order of the British Empire) for services to children's literature from the Prince of Wales on March 2, 2001.

Literary Awards

THE 10 LATEST CARNEGIE MEDAL WINNERS

YEAR	AUTHOR	TITLE
2000	Beverley Naidoo	The Other Side of Truth
1999	Aidan Chambers	Postcards from No Man's Land
1998	David Almond	Skellig
1997	Tom Bowler	River Boy
1996	Melvyn Burgess	Junk
1995	Philip Pullman	Northern Lights
1994	Theresa Breslin	Whispers in the Graveyard
1993	Robert Swindells	Stone Cold
1992	Anne Fine	Flour Babies
1991	Berlie Doherty	Dear Nobody

Established in 1937, the Carnegie Medal is awarded annually by the Library Association for an outstanding English-language children's book published during the previous year. It is named in honor of Scots-born millionaire Andrew Carnegie, who was a notable library benefactor.

THE 10 LATEST WINNERS OF HUGO AWARDS FOR THE BEST SCIENCE FICTION NOVEL

YEAR	AUTHOR	TITLE
2001	J. K. Rowling	Harry Potter and the Goblet of Fire
2000	Vernor Vinge	A Deepness in the Sky
1999	Connie Willis	To Say Nothing of the Dog
1998	Joe Haldeman	Forever Peace
1997	Kim Stanley Robinson	Blue Mars
1996	Neal Stephenson	The Diamond Age
1995	Lois McMaster Bujold	Mirror Dance
1994	Kim Stanley Robinson	Green Mars
1993	=Vernor Vinge	A Fire upon the Deep
	=Connie Willis	Doomsday Book

Hugo Awards, named in honor of Hugo Gernsback, the "father of magazine science fiction," were established in 1953 as "Science Fiction Achievement Awards for the best science fiction writing."

THE 10 LATEST WINNERS OF THE PULITZER PRIZE FOR FICTION

YEAR	AUTHOR	TITLE
2002	Richard Russo	Empire Falls
2001	Michael Chabon	The Amazing Adventures of Kavalier & Clay
2000	Jhumpa Lhiri	Interpreter of Maladies
1999	Michael Cunningham	The Hours
1998	Philip Roth	American Pastoral
1997	Steven Millhauser	Martin Dressler: The Tale of an American Dreamer
1996	Richard Ford	Independence Day
1995	Carol Shields	The Stone Diaries
1994	E. Annie Proulx	The Shipping News
1993	Robert Olen Butler	A Good Scent from a Strange Mountain: Stories

THE 10 LATEST WINNERS OF THE JOHN NEWBERY MEDAL

YEAR	AUTHOR	TITLE
2002	Linda Sue Park	A Single Shard
2001	Richard Peck	A Year Down Yonder
2000	Christopher Paul Curtis	Bud, Not Buddy
1999	Louis Sachar	Holes
1998	Karen Hesse	Out of the Dust
1997	E. L. Konigsburg	The View from Saturday
1996	Karen Cushman	The Midwife's Apprentice
1995	Sharon Creech	Walk Two Moons
1994	Lois Lowry	The Giver
1993	Cynthia Rylant	Missing May

The John Newbery Medal is awarded annually for "the most distinguished contribution to American literature for children." The medal is named after John Newbery (1713–67), a London bookseller and publisher who specialized in children's books, one of which, *A Little Pretty Pocket-Book*, issued in 1744, contained the first printed reference to and illustration of the game of "Base-Ball" – a century before the game was played in the US.

THE 10 LATEST WINNERS OF THE NATIONAL BOOK CRITICS CIRCLE AWARD FOR FICTION

YEAR	AUTHOR	TITLE
2001	Winfried Georg Sebald	Austerlitz
2000	Jim Crace	Being Dead
1999	Jonathan Lethem	Motherless Brooklyn
1998	Alice Munro	The Love of a Good Woman
1997	Penelope Fitzgerald	The Blue Flower
1996	Gina Berriault	Women in Their Beds
1995	Stanley Elkin	Mrs. Ted Bliss
1994	Carol Shields	The Stone Diaries
1993	Ernest J. Gaines	A Lesson Before Dying
1992	Cormac McCarthy	All the Pretty Horses

The National Book Critics Circle was founded in 1974 and consists of almost 700 active reviewers. The Circle presents annual awards in five categories: fiction, general nonfiction, biography and autobiography, poetry, and criticism. Awards are made every year in March, and winners receive a scroll and citation. The first fiction award was won in 1975 by E. L. Doctorow for his novel *Ragtime*.

THE 10 LATEST WINNERS OF THE EDGAR ALLAN POE AWARD FOR BEST NOVEL

YEAR	AUTHOR	TITLE
2001	Joe R. Lansdale	The Bottoms
2000	Jan Burke	Bones
1999	Robert Clark	Mr. White's Confession
1998	James Lee Burke	Cimmaron Rose
1997	Thomas A. Cook	The Chatham School Affair
1996	Dick Francis	Come to Grief
1995	Mary Willis Walker	The Red Scream
1994	Minette Walters	The Sculptress
1993	Margaret Maron	Bootlegger's Daughter
1992	Lawrence Block	A Dance at the Slaughterhouse

Popularly called the "Edgar," this award has been presented by the Mystery Writers of America since 1954 for novels in the genres of suspense, detective, and spy fiction. It is named after the great American mystery writer Edgar Allan Poe, a ceramic bust of whom is presented to the winner.

True Fiction
Australian author Peter Carey's *True History of the Kelly Gang* won the Booker Prize in 2001. His book *Oscar and Lucinda* was the 1988 winner. Only he and J. M. Coetzee have won the prestigious prize twice.

THE 10 | LATEST WINNERS OF THE BOOKER PRIZE

YEAR	AUTHOR	TITLE
2001	Peter Carey	True History of the Kelly Gang
2000	Margaret Atwood	The Blind Assassin
1999	J. M. Coetzee	Disgrace
1998	Ian McEwan	Amsterdam
1997	Arundhati Roy	The God of Small Things
1996	Graham Swift	Last Orders
1995	Pat Barker	The Ghost Road
1994	James Kelman	How Late It Was, How Late
1993	Roddy Doyle	Paddy Clarke Ha Ha Ha
1992	=Michael Ondaatje	The English Patient
	=Barry Unsworth	Sacred Hunger

The Booker Prize, awarded for a novel in English by a citizen of Britain, the Commonwealth, Ireland, or South Africa, has been awarded annually since 1969.

THE 10 | LATEST WINNERS OF THE PEN/FAULKNER AWARD FOR FICTION

YEAR	AUTHOR	TITLE
2002	Ann Patchett	Bel Canto
2001	Philip Roth	The Human Stain
2000	Ha Jin	Waiting
1999	Michael Cunningham	The Hours
1998	Rafi Zabor	The Bear Comes Home
1997	Gina Berriault	Women in Their Beds
1996	Richard Ford	Independence Day
1995	David Guterson	Snow Falling on Cedars
1994	Philip Roth	Operation Shylock
1993	E. Annie Proulx	Postcards

Established in 1980, the PEN (Poets, Playwrights, Editors, Essayists, and Novelists) Faulkner Award is presented annually to an American fiction writer.

THE 10 | LATEST WINNERS OF THE NATIONAL BOOK AWARD FOR FICTION

YEAR	AUTHOR	TITLE
2001	Jonathan Franzen	The Corrections
2000	Susan Sontag	In America
1999	Ha Jin	Waiting
1998	Alice McDermott	Charming Billy
1997	Charles Frazier	Cold Mountain
1996	Andrea Barrett	Ship Fever and Other Stories
1995	Philip Roth	Sabbath's Theater
1994	William Gaddis	A Frolic of His Own
1993	E. Annie Proulx	The Shipping News
1992	Cormac McCarthy	All the Pretty Horses

The National Book Award is presented by the National Book Foundation as part of its program to foster reading in the US. Winners receive $10,000.

Poetry Please

TOP 10 MOST POPULAR POEMS BY EMILY DICKINSON

	POEM
1	There's a Certain Slant of Light
2	Because I Could Not Stop for Death
3	I Heard a Fly Buzz When I Died
4	Safe in Alabaster Chambers
5	This is My Letter to the World
6	My Life Closed Twice Before its Close
7	Success Is Counted Sweetest
8	I Died for Beauty – But Was Scarce
9	I Dwell in Possibility
10	She Dealt Her Pretty Words Like Blades

Source: *The Poetry Poll*

American poet Emily Elizabeth Dickinson (1830–86) lived a reclusive life in her hometown of Amherst, Massachusetts. She wrote nearly 1,800 poems, only 10 of which were published during her lifetime, and was not "discovered" until after her death, since when she has been hailed as a genius whose works figure in poetry popularity polls on both sides of the Atlantic.

Popular Poetess
Emily Dickinson has achieved cult status through both her powerful and highly personal poetry and the secrecy surrounding her private life.

THE 10 LATEST US POETS LAUREATE

TERM	POET
2001–2002	Billy Collins
2000–2001	Stanley Kunitz
1997–2000	Robert Pinsky
1995–1997	Robert Hass
1993–1995	Rita Dove
1992–1993	Mona Van Duyn
1991–1992	Joseph Brodsky
1990–1991	Mark Strand
1988–1990	Howard Nemerov
1987–1988	Richard Wilbur

These are the 10 most recent appointees of the role of Poet Laureate Consultant in Poetry to the Library of Congress. The position was established in 1937, and was originally called "Consultant in Poetry to the Library of Congress," but received its present name by a 1985 act of Congress. The Laureate, who is appointed annually (serving from October to May), receives a stipend of $35,000 and bears responsibility for raising national consciousness to a greater appreciation of the reading and writing of poetry.

TOP 10 BEST-SELLING POETRY BOOKS IN THE US

	BOOK/AUTHOR OR EDITOR/DATE	ESTIMATED SALES
1	**The Prophet,** Kahil Gilbran, 1923	6,000,000
2	**101 Famous Poems,** R. J. Cook (ed.), 1916	up to 6,000,000
3	**The Pocket Book of Verse,** M. E. Speare (ed.), 1940	2,719,600
4	**Listen to the Warm,** Rod McKuen, 1967	2,025,000
5	**Stanyan Street and Other Sorrows,** Rod McKuen, 1967	1,500,000
6	**Pocket Book of Ogden Nash,** Ogden Nash, 1955	1,121,000
7	**Anthology of Robert Frost's Poems,** Robert Frost (ed. Louis Untermeyer), 1949	1,054,910
8	**Immortal Poems of the English Language,** Oscar Williams (ed.), 1952	1,054,500
9	**A Heap O' Livin',** Edgar Guest, 1916	1,000,000
10	**John Brown's Body,** Stephen Vincent Bénet, 1928	755,630

Based on a survey of bestsellers during the period 1895–1975, this list reflects the poetry-reading public's taste during a period when a select few books sold in substantial numbers. Only Rod McKuen's collections have matched these earlier triumphs, and, since the million-selling poetry book is such a rarity, it is unlikely that any of these works have been overtaken in more recent years.

TOP 10 MOST ANTHOLOGIZED ENGLISH POEMS

	POEM/POET	APPEARANCES
1	**The Tyger,** William Blake (British; 1757–1827)	170
2	**How Do I Love Thee?** (Sonnet 42), Elizabeth Barrett Browning (British; 1806–61)	136
3	**London,** William Blake (British; 1757–1827)	122
4	**With How Sad Steps, O Moon, Thou Climb'st the Skies** (Sonnet 31), Sir Philip Sidney (British; 1554–86)	98
5	**She Dwelt Among the Untrodden Ways** ("Lucy"), William Wordsworth (British; 1770–1850)	97
6	**Kubla Khan,** Samuel Taylor Coleridge (British; 1722–1834)	95
7	**La Belle Dame sans Merci,** John Keats (British; 1795–1821)	92
8	**To His Coy Mistress,** Andrew Marvell (British; 1621–78)	87
9	**Stopping by Woods on a Snowy Evening,** Robert Frost (American; 1874–1963)	85
10	**Love ("Love Bade Me Welcome But My Soul Drew Back"),** George Herbert (British; 1593–1633)	84

"Appearances" refers to the number of anthologies in which the poem is found, out of a total of more than 400 listed in *The Columbia Granger's Index to Poetry in Anthologies* (12th edition, Columbia University Press, 2002).

TOP 10 MOST POPULAR POEMS IN THE WORLD

	POEM	POET
1	Do Not Go Gentle into That Good Night	Dylan Thomas
2	The Tyger	William Blake
3	The Raven	Edgar Allan Poe
4	Stopping by Woods on a Snowy Evening	Robert Frost
5	Jabberwocky	Lewis Carroll
6	How Do I Love Thee?	Elizabeth Barrett Browning
7	There's a Certain Slant of Light	Emily Dickinson
8	Shall I Compare Thee to a Summer's Day	William Shakespeare
9	Because I Could Not Stop for Death	Emily Dickinson
10	Mending Wall	Robert Frost

Source: *The Poetry Poll*

These are the Top 10 poems voted for in an international poll to discover the most popular poetry in the world. The poll, in which some 50,000 people participated, was conducted on the Internet over the 6-year period 1992–98.

THE 10 LATEST WINNERS OF THE PULITZER PRIZE FOR POETRY

YEAR	POET/POEM
2002	Carl Dennis, *Practical Gods*
2001	Stephen Dunn, *Different Hours*
2000	C. K. Williams, *Repair*
1999	Mark Strand, *Blizzard of One*
1998	Charles Wright, *Black Zodiac*
1997	Lisel Mueller, *Alive Together: New and Selected Poems*
1996	Jorie Graham, *The Dream of the Unified Field*
1995	Philip Levine, *The Simple Truth*
1994	Yusef Komunyakaa, *Neon Vernacular: New and Selected Poems*
1993	Louise Gluck, *The Wild Iris*

Dylan's Number 1

Half a century after Welsh poet Dylan Thomas (1914–53) penned *Do Not Go Gentle into That Good Night*, it topped an international poll of favorite poems.

TOP 10 MOST POPULAR POEMS BY T. S. ELIOT

	POEM
1	The Waste Land
2	The Love Song of J. Alfred Prufrock
3	The Hollow Men: commentary
4	Sweeney Among the Nightingales
5	Preludes
6	Portrait of a Lady
7	La Figlia Che Piange (The Weeping Girl)
8	Journey of the Magi
9	Macavity: The Mystery Cat
10	Rhapsody on a Windy Night

Source: *The Poetry Poll*

The Press

TOP 10 ENGLISH-LANGUAGE DAILY NEWSPAPERS

	NEWSPAPER	COUNTRY	AVERAGE DAILY CIRCULATION
1	The Sun	UK	3,472,841
2	Daily Mail	UK	2,476,625
3	The Mirror	UK	2,187,960
4	USA Today	USA	2,140,933
5	Wall Street Journal	USA	1,780,605
6	Times of India	India	1,687,000
7	New York Times	USA	1,109,371
8	The Daily Telegraph	UK	1,020,889
9	Daily Express	UK	957,574
10	Los Angeles Times	USA	944,303

Source: *World Association of Newspapers/Audit Bureau of Circulations*

Launched on September 15, 1964 with a printrun of 3.5 million, *The Sun* was a revamp of the *Daily Herald*, which had been published since 1911 and had been the first newspaper to sell 2 million copies. *The Sun* was relaunched as a tabloid on November 17, 1969.

TOP 10 COUNTRIES WITH THE HIGHEST NEWSPAPER CIRCULATIONS

	COUNTRY	AVERAGE DAILY CIRCULATION
1	Japan	71,896,000
2	US	55,945,000
3	China	50,000,000
4	India	30,772,000
5	Germany	23,946,000
6	Russia	23,800,000
7	UK	19,052,000
8	France	8,799,000
9	Brazil	7,883,000
10	Italy	6,024,000

Source: *World Association of Newspapers*

Newspaper circulation varies enormously around the world. The countries featuring in the Top 10 tend to be those with relatively small numbers of very high-circulation national and regional papers. Japan, for example, has 2 newspapers that have achieved daily sales in excess of 10 million.

TOP 10 COUNTRIES WITH THE MOST NEWSPAPER TITLES PER CAPITA

	COUNTRY	DAILY TITLES PER 1,000,000 PEOPLE
1	Uruguay	26.89
2	Norway	22.89
3	Russia	22.04
4	Switzerland	17.70
5	Cyprus	16.28
6	Luxembourg	14.18
7	Sweden	13.60
8	Finland	13.01
9	Estonia	11.78
10	Latvia	10.75
	US	5.36

Source: *World Association of Newspapers*

Not only do these countries publish the most newspapers in relation to their populations, but several of them record the highest readership: in Norway 720 people out of every 1,000 buy a daily paper, contrasting with 409 in the UK, and just 264 in the US.

FIRST NEWSPAPER WITH PHOTOGRAPHS

ALFRED HARMSWORTH, who in 1896 founded Britain's first tabloid (small format newspaper), the *Daily Mail*, launched the world's first paper illustrated exclusively with photographs, the London *Daily Mirror*, on November 2, 1903. On its first day it sold 276,000 copies, but by January 1904, circulation had dropped to below 25,000, and it was losing money. By broadening its appeal beyond its original target audience of "gentlewomen," sales increased.

FIRST OR LAST

TOP 10 DAILY NEWSPAPERS IN THE US

	NEWSPAPER	AVERAGE DAILY CIRCULATION*
1	USA Today	2,140,933
2	Wall Street Journal	1,780,605
3	New York Times	1,109,371
4	Los Angeles Times	944,303
5	Washington Post	759,864
6	New York Daily News	734,473
7	Chicago Tribune	675,847
8	Long Island Newsday	577,354
9	Houston Chronicle	551,854
10	New York Post	533,860

* *Through September 30, 2001*

Source: *Audit Bureau of Circulations*

Apart from the *Wall Street Journal*, which focusses on financial news, *USA Today* remains the US's only true national daily newspaper. Historically, America's press has been regionally based, and so the Top 4 listed are the only newspapers with million-plus circulations.

TOP 10 SUNDAY NEWSPAPERS IN THE US

	NEWSPAPER	AVERAGE SUNDAY CIRCULATION*
1	New York Times	1,568,650
2	Los Angeles Times	1,368,066
3	Washington Post	1,059,646
4	Chicago Tribune	1,010,704
5	New York Sunday News	802,215
6	Denver Post/ Rocky Mountain News	801,315
7	Dallas Morning News	766,367
8	Detroit News & Free Press	749,113
9	Houston Chronicle	744,884
10	Philadelphia Enquirer	732,412

* *Through September 30, 2001*

Source: *Audit Bureau of Circulations*

The *New York Times* was first published in 1851, issuing its first Sunday edition on April 21, 1861. By 1921, circulation of the daily *Times* had reached 330,000 and that of the Sunday paper 500,000.

Read All About It
Despite the proliferation of television and online news media, traditional newspapers have preserved their popularity as sources of information and entertainment.

TOP 10 MAGAZINE GENRES IN THE US

	GENRE	PUBLICATIONS
1	Medicine	962
2	Religion and theological	908
3	Sports and sporting goods	864
4	Regional interest	821
5	Business and industry	708
6	Travel	706
7	Computers and animation	699
8	Education	541
9	Music and music trades	521
10	Health	505

Source: National Directory of Magazines

An estimated 31,390 magazines are published in the US – more than double the total in 1988 (14,654).

TOP 10 NEWSSTAND MAGAZINES IN THE US

	MAGAZINE/ISSUES PER YEAR	AVERAGE SINGLE COPY CIRCULATION, 2001
1	Cosmopolitan (12)	1,875,735
2	Family Circle (17)	1,630,000
3	National Enquirer (52)	1,589,916
4	Woman's World (52)	1,573,764
5	Woman's Day (17)	1,555,059
6	People (52)	1,468,413
7	Star (52)	1,253,778
8	TV Guide (54)	1,163,379
9	First For Women (17)	1,145,056
10	Good Housekeeping (12)	1,037,995

Source: *Audit Bureau of Circulations/Magazine Publishers of America*

TOP 10 SUBSCRIPTION MAGAZINES IN THE US

	MAGAZINE/ISSUES PER YEAR	AVERAGE SUBSCRIPTION CIRCULATION, 2001
1	NRTA/AARP Bulletin (10)	21,465,126
2	Modern Maturity (36)	18,363,840
3	Reader's Digest (12)	11,841,776
4	TV Guide (52)	8,096,076
5	National Geographic Magazine (12)	7,477,732
6	Better Homes and Gardens (12)	7,243,173
7	Time (54)	3,908,323
8	Ladies' Home Journal (12)	3,722,970
9	Good Housekeeping (12)	3,493,087
10	Home & Away (6)	3,310,934

Source: *Audit Bureau of Circulations/Magazine Publishers of America*

Art at Auction

TOP 10 — MOST EXPENSIVE WORKS OF ART BY LIVING ARTISTS

WORK/ARTIST/SALE	PRICE ($)
1 **False Start,** Jasper Johns (American; 1930–), Sotheby's, New York, November 10, 1988	15,500,000
2 **Two Flags,** Jasper Johns, Sotheby's, New York, November 8, 1989	11,000,000
3 **Henry Moore Bound to Fail, Back View,** Bruce Nauman (American; 1941–), Christie's Rockefeller, New York, May 17, 2001	9,000,000
4 **Corpse and Mirror,** Jasper Johns, Christie's, New York, November 10, 1997	7,600,000
5 **White Numbers,** Jasper Johns, Christie's, New York, November 10, 1997	7,200,000
6 **Rebus,** Robert Rauschenberg (American; 1925-), Sotheby's, New York, April 30, 1991	6,600,000
7 **Two Flags,** Jasper Johns, Christie's Rockefeller, New York, May 13, 1999	6,500,000
8 **White Flag,** Jasper Johns, Christie's, New York, November 9, 1988	6,400,000
9 **Red Interior 1954–55,** Robert Rauschenberg, Christie's, New York, November 10, 1997	5,800,000
10 **Rebus,** Robert Rauschenberg, Sotheby's, New York, November 10, 1998	5,750,000

Art Master
Thirty years after his death, Pablo Picasso's highly prized works continue to dominate the global art market.

TOP 10 — MOST EXPENSIVE OLD MASTER PAINTINGS

PAINTING/ARTIST/SALE	PRICE ($)
1 **Portrait of Duke Cosimo I de Medici,** Jacopo da Carucci (Pontormo) (Italian; 1493–1558), Christie's, New York, May 31, 1989	32,000,000
2 **Portrait of Lady aged 62, perhaps Aeltje Pietersdr, Uylenburgh, wife of Johannes Cornelisz,** Rembrandt (Dutch; 1606–69), Christie's, London, December 13, 2000	26,460,000 (£18,000,000)
3 **The Old Horse Guards, London, from St. James's Park,** Canaletto (Italian; 1697–1768), Christie's, London, April 15, 1992	16,008,000 (£9,200,000)
4 **Vue de la Giudecca et du Zattere à Venice,** Francesco Guardi (Italian; 1712–93), Sotheby's, Monaco, December 1, 1989	13,943,218 (F.Fr. 85,000,000)
5 **Portrait of Omai, Standing in a Landscape, Wearing Robes and a Head-dress,** Sir Joshua Reynolds (British; 1723–92), Sotheby's, London, November 29, 2001	13,348,000 (£9,400,000)
6 **Venus and Adonis,** Titian (Italian; c.1488–1576), Christie's, London, December 13, 1991	12,376,000 (£6,800,000)
7 **Tieleman Roosterman in Black Doublet, White Ruff,** Frans Hals the elder (Dutch; c.1580–1666), Christie's, London, July 8, 1999	11,625,001 (£7,500,000)
8 **Portrait of a Bearded Man in a Red Doublet,** Rembrandt, Christie's Rockefeller, New York, January 26, 2001	11,500,000
9 **Le Retour du Bucentaure le Jour de l'Ascension,** Canaletto, Ader Tajan, Paris, December 15, 1993	11,316,457 (F.Fr.66,000,000)
10 **The Risen Christ,** Michelangelo (Italian; 1475–1564), Christie's, London, July 4, 2000	11,174,001 (£7,400,000)

TOP 10 — ARTISTS WITH THE MOST WORKS SOLD FOR MORE THAN ONE MILLION DOLLARS

ARTIST	TOTAL VALUE OF SALES ($)	WORKS SOLD
1 **Pablo Picasso** (Spanish, 1881–1973)	1,399,203,108	298
2 **Claude Monet** (French, 1888–1926)	1,016,435,017	229
3 **Pierre Auguste Renoir** (French, 1841–1919)	664,578,714	206
4 **Edgar Degas** (French, 1834–1917)	354,635,303	108
5 **Henri Matisse** (French, 1869–1954)	350,639,390	91
6 **Paul Cézanne** (French, 1839–1906)	486,000,573	85
7 **Camille Pissaro** (French, 1830–1903)	152,898,994	81
8 **Marc Chagall** (Russian, 1887–1985)	168,593,200	76
9 **Amedeo Modigliani** (Italian, 1884–1920)	289,213,301	65
10 **Vincent van Gogh** (Dutch, 1853–90)	551,850,639	60

TOP 10 MOST EXPENSIVE PAINTINGS

PAINTING/ARTIST/SALE	PRICE ($)
1 **Portrait of Dr. Gachet,** Vincent van Gogh (Dutch; 1853–90), Christie's, New York, May 15, 1990. Both this painting and the one in No. 2 position were bought by Ryoei Saito, chairman of the Japanese firm Daishowa Paper Manufacturing.	75,000,000
2 **Au Moulin de la Galette,** Pierre-Auguste Renoir (French; 1841–1919), Sotheby's, New York, May 17, 1990	71,000,000
3 **Portrait de l'Artiste Sans Barbe,** Vincent van Gogh, Christie's, New York, November 19, 1998	65,000,000
4 **Rideau, Cruchon et Compotier,** Paul Cézanne (French; 1839–1906), Sotheby's, New York, May 10, 1999	55,000,000
5 **Les Noces de Pierrette, 1905,** Pablo Picasso (Spanish; 1881–1973), Binoche et Godeau, Paris, November 30, 1989. This painting was sold by Swedish financier Fredrik Roos and bought by Tomonori Tsurumaki, a Japanese property developer, bidding from Tokyo by telephone.	51,671,920 (F.Fr. 315,000,000)
6 **Femme aux Bras Croisés,** Pablo Picasso, Christie's Rockefeller, New York, November 8, 2000	50,000,000
7 **Irises,** Vincent van Gogh, Sotheby's, New York, November 11, 1987. After much speculation, its mystery purchaser was eventually confirmed as Australian businessman Alan Bond. However, as he was unable to pay for it in full, its former status as the world's most expensive work of art has been disputed.	49,000,000
8 **Femme Assise dans un Jardin,** Pablo Picasso, Sotheby's, New York, November 10, 1999	45,000,000
9 **Le Rêve,** Pablo Picasso, Christie's, New York, November 10, 1997. Victor and Sally Ganz had paid $7,000 for this painting in 1941.	44,000,000
10 **Self Portrait; Yo Picasso,** Pablo Picasso, Sotheby's, New York, May 9, 1989. The purchaser has remained anonymous but unconfirmed reports have identified him as Stavros Niarchos, the Greek shipping magnate.	43,500,000

Georgian Art
Three of the 10 highest prices ever paid for works by women artists have been for paintings by the celebrated American artist Georgia O'Keeffe.

TOP 10 MOST EXPENSIVE PAINTINGS BY WOMEN ARTISTS

PAINTING/ARTIST/SALE	PRICE ($)
1 **Calla Lilies with Red Anemone,** Georgia O'Keeffe (American; 1887–1986), Christie's Rockefeller, New York, May 23, 2001	5,600,000
2 **The Conversation,** Mary Cassatt (American; 1844–1926), Christie's, New York, May 11, 1988	4,100,000
3 **Cache-cache,** Berthe Morisot (French; 1841–95), Sotheby's, New York, November 9, 2000	4,000,000
4 **=Black Cross with Stars and Blue,** Georgia O'Keeffe, Christie's Rockefeller, New York, May 23, 2001	3,700,000
=In the Box, Mary Cassatt, Christie's, New York, May 23, 1996	3,700,000

PAINTING/ARTIST/SALE	PRICE ($)
6 **=Cache-cache,** Berthe Morisot, Sotheby's, New York, May 10, 1999	3,500,000
=Mother, Sara and the Baby, Mary Cassatt, Christie's, New York, May 10, 1989	3,500,000
8 **From the Plains,** Georgia O'Keeffe, Sotheby's, New York, December 3, 1997	3,300,000
9 **Après le Déjeuner,** Berthe Morisot, Christie's, New York, May 14, 1997	3,250,000
10 **Autoretrato con Chango y Loro,** Frida Kahlo (Mexican; 1907–54), Sotheby's, New York, May 17, 1995	2,900,000

Sculptures & Statues

TOP 10 MOST EXPENSIVE SCULPTURES BY AUGUSTE RODIN

SCULPTURE/SALE	PRICE ($)
1 **Eve,** Christie's Rockefeller, New York, November 8, 1999	4,400,000
2 **Les Bourgeois de Calais Grands Modeles – Pierre de Wiessant Vetu,** Sotheby's, New York, May 17, 1990	3,900,000
3 **Balzac,** Sotheby's, New York, May 13, 1998	3,200,000
4 **Le Baiser,** Christie's Rockefeller, New York, May 8, 2000	2,500,000
5 **Le Baiser,** Sotheby's, New York, November 7, 2001	2,200,000
6 **Psyche Regardant l'Amour,** Sotheby's, New York, November 8, 1995	1,800,000
7 **=L'Age d'Airain,** Sotheby's, New York, May 8, 2001	1,600,000
=L'Eternel Printemps, Premier Etat, Christie's Rockefeller, New York, May 8, 2000	1,600,000
9 **Le Grande Ombre,** Christie's Rockefeller, New York, May 12, 1999	1,500,000
10 **Eve aprés le Pêche – La Pudeur,** Christie's, London, June 24, 1998	1,245,000 (£750,000)

Auguste Rodin (1840–1917) was the foremost French sculptor of his day. He achieved international fame through such creations as *The Thinker* and *The Kiss*. Bronze casts of Rodin's works mean that multiple copies exist of a number of them, including *The Burghers of Calais*, one of his most celebrated sculptures.

TOP 10 MOST EXPENSIVE SCULPTURES BY PABLO PICASSO

SCULPTURE/SALE	PRICE ($)
1 **Tête de Femme – Fernande,** Christie's Rockefeller, New York, November 6, 2001	4,500,000
2 **Tête de Femme – Fernande,** Sotheby's, New York, November 15, 1989	2,500,000
3 **Verre d'Absinthe,** Sotheby's, New York, November 12, 1990	2,300,000
4 **Tête de Femme – Fernande,** Sotheby's, London, June 27, 2000	2,265,000 (£1,500,000)
5 **Jacqueline au Ruban Vert,** Christie's, New York, May 15, 1990	1,600,000
6 **Sylvette,** Sotheby's, New York, November 12, 1996	975,000
7 **Tête de Fou,** Christie's, New York, May 15, 1990	550,000
8 **Tête de Fou,** Piasa Commissaires-Priseurs, Paris, December 9, 1998	549,785 (F.Fr.3,050,000)
9 **Le Fou – Arlequin,** Kornfeld, Bern, June 23, 2000	520,161 (S.Fr.860,000)
10 **Tête de Fou,** Christie's, New York, November 13, 1996	520,000

TOP 10 TALLEST FREE-STANDING STATUES

STATUE/LOCATION	HEIGHT (FT)	(M)
1 **Chief Crazy Horse,** Thunderhead Mountain, South Dakota Started in 1948 by Polish-American sculptor Korczak Ziolkowski and continued after his death in 1982 by his widow and 8 of his children, this gigantic equestrian statue, even longer than it is high (641 ft/195 m), is not expected to be completed for several years.	563	172
2 **Buddha,** Tokyo, Japan This Japanese-Taiwanese project, unveiled in 1993, took 7 years to complete and weighs 1,100 tons.	394	120
3 **The Indian Rope Trick,** Riddersberg Säteri, Jönköping, Sweden Sculptor Calle Örnemark's 159-ton wooden sculpture depicts a long strand of "rope" held by a fakir, while another figure ascends.	337	103
4 **Motherland,** 1967, Volgograd, Russia This concrete statue of a woman with a raised sword, designed by Yevgeniy Vuchetich, commemorates the Soviet victory at the Battle of Stalingrad (1942–43).	270	82
5 **Kannon,** Otsubo-yama, near Tokyo, Japan The immense statue of the goddess of mercy was unveiled in 1961 in honor of the dead of World War II.	170	52
6 **Statue of Liberty,** New York Designed by Auguste Bartholdi and presented to the US by the people of France, the statue was shipped in sections to Liberty (formerly Bedloes) Island where it was assembled, before being unveiled on October 28, 1886.	151	46
7 **Christ,** Rio de Janeiro, Brazil The work of sculptor Paul Landowski and engineer Heitor da Silva Costa, the figure of Christ was unveiled in 1931.	125	38
8 **Tian Tan (Temple of Heaven) Buddha,** Po Lin Monastery, Lantau Island, Hong Kong, China This was completed after 20 years' work and unveiled on December 29, 1993.	112	34
9 **Quantum Cloud,** Greenwich, London, UK A gigantic steel human figure surrounded by a matrix of steel struts, this statue was created in 1999 by Antony Gormley, the sculptor of the similarly gigantic 66-ft (20-m) *Angel of the North* in Gateshead, UK.	95	29
10 **Kim Il-Sung,** Pyongyang, North Korea Claimed to be the world's largest one-piece bronze statue, it was erected to celebrate the leader's 60th birthday in 1972.	75	23

Two of the Seven Wonders of the World were giant free-standing statues: the *Colossus of Rhodes*, a 106-ft (32-m) bronze of the sun-god Helios or Apollo by the sculptor Chares of Lindus, which fell in an earthquake in 226 BC, and the 43-ft (13-m) statue of Zeus in the temple at Olympia, created by Phidias in 433 BC. Former entrants in this list, 2 Buddha statues at Bamian, Afghanistan, measuring 174 ft (53 m) and 125 ft (38 m), were destroyed by Taliban fundamentalists in March 2001. The world's largest Buddha statue, the *Buddha Maitreya*, is being constructed at Bodhgaya, India, and is scheduled for completion in 2005. Made of 3,000 bronze panels on a steel framework, it will soar to a stunning 500 ft (152.4 m).

TOP 10 MOST EXPENSIVE PIECES OF SCULPTURE

SCULPTURE/ARTIST/SALE	PRICE ($)
1 **Danaïde,** Constantin Brancusi (Romanian; 1876–1956), Christie's Rockefeller, New York, May 7, 2002	16,500,000
2 **Grande Femme Debout I,** Alberto Giacometti (Swiss; 1901–66), Christie's Rockefeller, New York, November 8, 2000	13,000,000
3 **La Serpentine Femme à la Stele – l'Araignée,** Henri Matisse (French; 1869–1954), Sotheby's, New York, May 10, 2000	12,750,000
4 **La Forêt,** Alberto Giacometti Christie's Rockefeller, New York, May 7, 2002	12,000,000
5 **Figure Decorative,** Henri Matisse Sotheby's, New York, May 10, 2001	11,500,000
6 **Petite Danseuse de Quatorze Ans,** Edgar Degas (French; 1834–1917), Sotheby's, New York, November 11, 1999	11,250,000
7 **Petite Danseuse de Quatorze Ans,** Edgar Degas Sotheby's, New York, November 12, 1996	10,800,000
8 **Petite Danseuse de Quatorze Ans,** Edgar Degas Sotheby's, New York, June 27, 2000	10,570,000 (£7,000,000)
9 **The Dancing Faun,** Adriaen de Vries (Dutch; c.1550–1626) Sotheby's, London, December 7, 1989	9,796,000 (£6,200,000)
10 **Nu Couche, Aurore,** Henri Matisse Phillips, New York, May 7, 2001	9,500,000

TOP 10 MOST EXPENSIVE WORKS BY ALEXANDER CALDER

MOBILE OR SCULPTURE/SALE	PRICE ($)
1 **Stegosaurus,** Sotheby's, New York, November 14, 2000	3,800,000
2 **Brazilian Fish,** Sotheby's, New York, November 17, 1999	3,550,000
3 **The Tree,** Selkirks, St. Louis, May 22, 1989	1,900,000
4 **Constellation,** Sotheby's, New York, May 18, 1999	1,800,000
5 **Constellation,** Sotheby's, New York, November 10, 1993	1,650,000
6 **Janey Waney,** Sotheby's, New York, November 14, 2001	1,600,000
7 **Trepied,** Sotheby's, New York, May 18, 1999	1,400,000
8 **Eighteen Numbered Black,** Sotheby's, New York, November 17, 1998	1,150,000
9 **Mobile au Plomb,** Christie's, London, June 28, 2000	1,087,200
10 **Untitled,** Sotheby's, New York, November 14, 2000	1,050,000

Although best known for his large mobiles, a record price was gained in 2000 for an Alexander Calder stabile (a stationary sculpture), with the auction of his gigantic red metal *Stegosaurus*.

Little Dancer
Produced in multiple versions from 1881 onward, Degas' popular *Petite Danseuse de Quatorze Ans* combines bronze and wax with real hair and clothes.

Art on Show

TOP 10 BEST-ATTENDED ART EXHIBITIONS IN NEW YORK, 2001

EXHIBITION/VENUE	ATTENDANCE
1 **Jacqueline Kennedy: White House Years,** Metropolitan Museum	559,902
2 **Vermeer and the Delft School,** Metropolitan Museum	554,287
3 **Modern Starts: Open Ends,** Museum of Modern Art	442,500
4 **Frank Gehry,** Guggenheim Museum	397,032
5 **Giorgio Armani,** Guggenheim Museum	319,486
6 **Van Gogh's Postman,** Museum of Modern Art	312,387
7 **Mies in Berlin,** Museum of Modern Art	283,407
8 **Joel Shapiro,** Metropolitan Museum	264,197
9 **William Blake,** Metropolitan Museum	227,631
10 **Gursky,** Museum of Modern Art	224,129

Source: The Art Newspaper

TOP 10 BEST-ATTENDED EXHIBITIONS AT THE FINE ARTS MUSEUM, BOSTON

EXHIBITION/YEAR(S)	ATTENDANCE
1 **Monet in the 20th Century,** 1998	565,992
2 **Monet in the Nineties,** 1990	537,502
3 **Renoir,** 1985–86	515,795
4 **John Singer Sargent,** 1999	318,707
5 **Van Gogh: Face to Face,** 2000	316,049
6 **Picasso: The Early Years, 1892–1906,** 1997–98	283,423
7 **Winslow Homer,** 1996	276,922
8 **A New World: Masterpieces of American Painting 1760–1910,** 1983	264,640
9 **Herb Ritts: Work,** 1996–97	253,649
10 **Mary Cassatt Modern Woman,** 1999	230,750

Source: *Museum of Fine Arts, Boston*

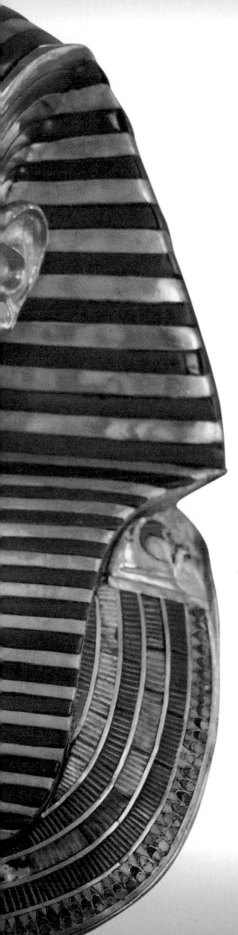

TOP 10 | BEST-ATTENDED EXHIBITIONS AT THE METROPOLITAN MUSEUM OF ART, NEW YORK

	EXHIBITION/YEAR(S)	ATTENDANCE
1	The Treasures of Tutankhamun, 1978–79	1,226,467
2	Mona Lisa, 1963	1,007,521
3	The Vatican Collection: The Papacy and Art, 1983	896,743
4	Glory of Russian Costume, 1976–77	835,862
5	Origins of Impressionism, 1994–95	794,108
6	Romantic and Glamorous Hollywood, 1974–75	788,665
7	The Horses of San Marco, 1980	742,221
8	Man and the Horse, 1984–85	726,523
9	Masterpiece of Fifty Centuries, 1979–81	690,471
10	Seurat, 1991–92	642,408

Source: *Metropolitan Museum of Art*

TOP 10 | BEST-ATTENDED EXHIBITIONS AT THE NATIONAL GALLERY, WASHINGTON, D.C.

	EXHIBITION/YEAR(S)	ATTENDANCE
1	Rodin Rediscovered, 1981–82	1,053,223
2	Treasure Houses of Britain, 1985–86	990,474
3	The Treasures of Tutankhamun, 1976–77	835,924
4	Archaeological Finds of the People's Republic of China, 1974–75	684,238
5	Ansel Adams: Classic Images, 1985–86	651,652
6	The Splendor of Dresden, 1978	620,089
7	The Art of Paul Gauguin, 1988	596,058
8	Circa 1492: Art in the Age of Exploration, 1991–92	568,192
9	Andrew Wyeth: The Helga Pictures, 1987	558,433
10	Post Impressionism: Cross Currents in European & American Painting, 1980	557,533

Source: *National Gallery*

TOP 10 | BEST-ATTENDED ART EXHIBITIONS, 2001

	EXHIBITION/VENUE/CITY	DATES	DAILY	TOTAL
1	The Medici and Science, Galleria degli Uffizi, Florence	May 18–Sep 9	4,924	861,865
2	Jacqueline Kennedy: The White House Years, Metropolitan Museum, New York	May 1–July 29	7,178	559,902
3	Vermeer and the Delft School, Metropolitan Museum, New York	Mar 8–May 27	8,033	554,287
4	Giorgio Armani, Guggenheim Bilbao, Bilbao	Mar 24–Sep 2	3,503	528,900
5	Modern Starts: Open Ends, Museum of Modern Art, New York	Sep 28, 2000–Mar 4	3,950	442,500
6	Renaissance Italy, National Museum of Western Art, Tokyo	May 20–July 8	4,403	422,721
7	The Worlds of Nam June Paik, Guggenheim Bilbao, Bilbao	May 22–Dec 2	3,395	417,545
8	Frank Gehry, Guggenheim Museum, New York	May 18–Sep 3	4,151	397,032
9	El Greco, Kunsthistorisches Museum, Vienna	May 4–Sep 16	2,757	375,000
10	Etruscans, Palazzo Grassi, Venice	Nov 26 2000–July 1	1,733	370,926

Source: *The Art Newspaper*

Behind the Mask

Held in the 1970s, the Treasures of Tutankhamun exhibition retains its record as the biggest crowd-pulling art show of all time in both London and New York.

Objects of Desire

 **MOST EXPENSIVE PHOTOGRAPHS**

PHOTOGRAPH*/PHOTOGRAPHER/SALE	PRICE ($)
1 **Noir et Blanche** (1926), Man Ray (American; 1890–1976), Christie's, New York, October 4, 1998	607,500
2 **Paris, Montparnasse** (1993), Andreas Gursky (American; 1955–), Christie's Rockefeller, New York, November 15, 2001	540,000
3 **Light Trap for Henry Moore No. 1** (1967), Bruce Nauman (American; 1941–), Sotheby's, New York, May 17, 2000	480,000
4 **Georgia O'Keeffe: A Portrait – Hands with Thimble** (1930) Alfred Stieglitz (American; 1864–1946), Christie's, New York, October 8, 1993	398,500
5 **Arrival of the Body of Admiral Bruat and Flagship Montebello at Toulon** (1855), Gustave le Gray (French; 1820–82), Bearnes, Exeter, May 6, 2000	380,000 (£250,000)
6 **Noire et Blanche** (1926), Man Ray, Christie's, New York, April 21, 1994	354,500
7 **Vue Perspective de la Seine en Direction de l'Est** (c.1857), Gustave le Gray, Delvaux, Paris, December 15, 2000	341,226 (F.Fr 2,500,000)
8 **Mondrian's Pipe and Glasses** (1926), André Kertész (Hungarian-American; 1894–1985), Christie's, New York, April 17, 1997	340,000
9 **Untitled film still, No. 48** (undated), Cindy Sherman (American; 1954–), Christie's Rockefeller, New York, May 17, 2001	300,000
10 **=Atelier Mondrian, Paris** (undated), André Kertész, Christie's Rockefeller, New York, October 12, 2000	280,000
=Cello Study (undated), André Kertész, Christie's Rockefeller, New York, May 17, 2001	280,000
=Ide Collar, advertisement made for Geo. P. Ide and Co. (1922), Paul Outerbridge Jr. (American; 1896–1958), Christie's Rockefeller, New York, October 12, 2001	280,000

* Single prints only

 **MOST EXPENSIVE PRINTS**

PRINT*/SALE	PRICE ($)
1 **Orange Marilyn#,** Andy Warhol (American; 1928–87), Sotheby's, New York, May 14, 1998	15,750,000
2 **Shot Red Marilyn,** Andy Warhol, Christie's, New York, May 3, 1989	3,700,000
3 **Shot Red Marilyn,** Andy Warhol, Sotheby's, New York, November 2, 1994	3,300,000
4 **Holly,** Andy Warhol, Christie's Rockefeller, New York, November 13, 2001	1,900,000
5 **Homme a la Pipe Assis,** Pablo Picasso, (Spanish; 1881–1973) Christie's Rockefeller, New York, November 6, 2001	1,800,000
6 **Diehard,** Robert Rauschenberg (American; 1925–), Sotheby's, New York, May 2, 1989	1,600,000
7 **Mao,** Andy Warhol (American; 1928–87), Sothebys, London, June 26, 1996	939,400 (£610,000)
8 **Famille Tahitienne,** Paul Gauguin (French; 1848–1903), Francis Briest, Paris, December 4, 1998	806,922 (F.Fr 4,545,010)
9 **=Glider,** Robert Rauschenberg, Christie's, New York, November 14, 1995	750,000
=Mao, Andy Warhol, Christie's Rockefeller, New York, November 13, 2001	750,000

* Included within the classification of prints are silkscreens, lithographs, monotypes, aquatints, woodcuts, engravings, and etchings. Excludes collections.

 # Silkscreen individualized by further ink work

All of these works are single prints by late 19th- and 20th-century artists. *Elles*, a collection of lithographs by French painter and printmaker Henri de Toulouse-Lautrec (1864–1901) holds the record for the highest price for a set of prints, having made $800,000 at Sotheby's, New York, on May 10, 1999.

 **MOST EXPENSIVE DRAWINGS***

DRAWING/ARTIST/SALE	PRICE ($)
1 **Danseuse au Repos,** Edgar Degas (French; 1834–1917), Sotheby's, London, June 28, 1999	25,280,000 (£16,000,000)
2 **Woman,** Willem de Kooning (Dutch; 1904–97), Christie's, New York, November 20, 1996	14,200,000
3 **Famille de l'Arlequin,** Pablo Picasso (Spanish; 1881–1973), Christie's, New York, November 14, 1989	14,000,000
4 **La Moisson en Provence,** Vincent van Gogh (Dutch; 1853–90), Sotheby's, London, June 24, 1997	13,280,001 (£8,000,000)
5 **Danseuse Assise aux Bas Roses,** Henri de Toulouse-Lautrec (French; 1864–1901), Christie's, New York, May 12, 1997	13,200,000
6 **Portrait de Mme. K,** Joan Miró (Spanish; 1893–1983), Christie's Rockefeller, New York, November 6, 2001	11,500,000
7 **The Risen Christ,** Michelangelo (Italian; 1475–1564), Christie's, London, July 4, 2000	11,174,001 (£7,400,000)
8 **Danseuses,** Edgar Degas, Sotheby's, New York, May 13, 1997	10,000,000
9 **Danseuse Espagnole,** Joan Miró, Christie's Rockefeller, New York, November 6, 2001	8,100,000
10 **Study for Head and Hand of an Apostle,** Raphael (Italian; 1483–1520), Christie's, London, December 13, 1996	7,920,000 (£4,800,000)

* Media include pencil, pen, ink, drawing, crayon, and chalk; oil or gouache paintings that have been worked on in these media are also included.

TOP 10 MOST EXPENSIVE WATERCOLORS

WATERCOLOUR/ARTIST/SALE	PRICE ($)
1 **La Moisson en Provence,** Vincent van Gogh (Dutch; 1853–1890), Sotheby's, London, June 24, 1997	13,280,001 (£8,000,000)
2 **Les Toits - 1882,** Vincent van Gogh, Ader Picard & Tajan, Paris, March 20, 1990	4,669,173 (F.Fr 27,000,000)
3 **Red Canoe,** Winslow Homer (American; 1836–1910), Sotheby's, New York, December 1, 1999	4,400,000
4 **Nature Morte au Melon Vert,** Paul Cézanne (French; 1839–1906), Sotheby's, London, April 4, 1989	3,933,000 (£2,300,000)
5 **Die Sangerin L. Ais Fiordiligi,** Paul Klee (Swiss; 1879–1940), Sotheby's, London, November 28, 1989	3,744,000 (£2,400,000)

WATERCOLOUR/ARTIST/SALE	PRICE ($)
6 **=John Biglin in Single Scull,** Thomas Eakins (American; 1844–1916), Christie's, New York, May 23, 1990	3,200,000
=Stony Beach, Maurice Prendergast (American; 1859–1924), Christie's Rockefeller, New York, May 23, 2001	3,200,000
8 **Heidelberg with a Rainbow,** Joseph Mallord William Turner (British; 1775–1851), Sotheby's, London, November 29, 1994	2,590,000 (£1,850,000)
9 **Au Moulin Rouge, La Fille du Roi d'Egypte,** Pablo Picasso (Spanish; 1881–1973), Sotheby's, London, November 29, 1994	2,557,500 (£1,650,000)
10 **Coral Divers,** Winslow Homer, Christie's, New York, December 2, 1998	2,400,000

Prima Ballerina
At a 1999 auction Degas' pastel and gouache study of dancers at rest, owned by the same family over 100 years, broke the world record for a drawing.

Popular Passions

TOP 10 MOST EXPENSIVE TEDDY BEARS SOLD AT AUCTION

BEAR/SALE	PRICE ($)*
1 **"Teddy Girl,"** Steiff cinnamon teddy bear, 1904, Christie's, London, December 5, 1994	169,928 (£110,000)
2 **Black mohair Steiff teddy bear,** c. 1912, Christie's, London, December 4, 2000	132,157 (£91,750)
3 **"Happy,"** dual-plush Steiff teddy bear, 1926, Sotheby's, London, September 19, 1989	85,470 (£55,000)
4 **"Elliot,"** blue Steiff teddy bear, 1908, Christie's, London, December 6, 1993	74,275 (£49,500)
5 **"Teddy Edward,"** golden mohair teddy bear, Christie's, London, December 9, 1996	60,176 (£38,500)
6 **Black mohair Steiff teddy bear,** c.1912, Sotheby's, London, May 18, 1990	45,327 (£24,200)
7 **Blank button,** brown Steiff teddy bear, c.1905, Christie's, London, December 8, 1997	35,948 (£23,000)
8 **Black mohair Steiff teddy bear,** Christie's, London, December 5, 1994	34,331 (£22,000)
9 **"Albert,"** Steiff teddy bear, c.1910, Christie's, London, December 9, 1996	28,759 (£18,400)
10 **Steiff teddy bear,** Christie's, London, December 9, 1996	26,962 (£17,250)

* Including 10 percent buyer's premium, where appropriate

TOP 10 MOST EXPENSIVE ITEMS OF POP MEMORABILIA EVER SOLD AT AUCTION*

ITEM/SALE	PRICE ($)*
1 **John Lennon's 1965 Rolls-Royce Phantom V touring limousine,** Sotheby's, New York, June 29, 1985. Finished in psychedelic paintwork.	2,299,000
2 **John Lennon's Steinway Model Z upright piano,** (on which he composed *Imagine*), Fleetwood-Owen online auction, Hard Rock Café, London and New York, October 17, 2000. Teak veneered, complete with cigarette burns.	2,150,000
3 **"Brownie," one of Eric Clapton's favorite guitars,** Christie's, New York, June 24, 1999. Clapton used the 1956 sunburst Fender to record his definitive guitar track, *Layla*. It was sold to an anonymous telephone bidder for double the expected price, making it the most expensive guitar ever bought at auction.	497,500
4 **Bernie Taupin's handwritten lyrics for the rewritten *Candle In The Wind*,** Christie's, Los Angeles, February 11, 1998. Played by Sir Elton John at the funeral of Diana, Princess of Wales, and sold to Diana's brother Earl Spencer. The sale, part of a charity auction, was a world record for pop lyrics.	400,000
5 **Jimi Hendrix's Fender Stratocaster electric guitar,** Sotheby's, London, April 25, 1990. Hendrix played this guitar at Woodstock in 1969.	370,260 (£198,000)
6 **Paul McCartney's handwritten lyrics for *Getting Better*, 1967,** Sotheby's, London, September 14, 1995	251,643 (£161,000)
7 **Buddy Holly's Gibson acoustic guitar, c.1945,** (in a tooled leather case made by Holly), Sotheby's, New York, June 23, 1990	242,000
8 **John Lennon's 1970 Mercedes-Benz 600 Pullman four-door limousine,** Christie's, London, April 27, 1989	213,125 (£137,500)
9 **John Lennon's 1965 Ferrari 330 GT 2+2 two door coupe, right-hand drive,** Fleetwood-Owen online auction, Hard Rock Cafe, London and New York, October 17, 2000	190,750
10 **Mal Evans' notebook,** compiled 1967–68, Sotheby's, London, September 15, 1998. Includes a draft by Paul McCartney of the lyrics for *Hey Jude*.	185,202 (£111,500)

* Including 10 percent buyer's premium, where appropriate

Pioneered particularly by Sotheby's in London, pop memorabilia has become big business – especially if it involves personal association with megastars such as the Beatles.

Bear the Expense
Happy, a 1926 Steiff, set the first record as the world's most expensive teddy bear when she was bought in 1989 by US collector and author Paul Volpp, for his wife Rosemary.

MOST EXPENSIVE ITEMS OF FILM MEMORABILIA EVER SOLD AT AUCTION

	ITEM/SALE	PRICE ($)
1	**Judy Garland's ruby slippers** from *The Wizard of Oz* (1939), Christie's, New York, May 26, 2000	666,000
2	**Clark Gable's Oscar** for *It Happened One Night*, Christie's, Los Angeles, December 15, 1996	607,500
3	**Vivien Leigh's Oscar** for *Gone with the Wind*, Sotheby's, New York, December 15, 1993	562,500
4	**Poster** for *The Mummy*, 1932, Sotheby's, New York, March 1, 1997	453,500
5	**Statue of the Maltese Falcon** from *The Maltese Falcon* (1941), Christie's Rockefeller, New York, December 5, 1994	398,500
6	**James Bond's Aston Martin DB5** from *Goldfinger*, Sotheby's, New York, June 28, 1986	275,000
7	**Clark Gable's personal script** for *Gone With The Wind*, Christie's, Los Angeles, December 15, 1996	244,500
8	**"Rosebud" sled** from *Citizen Kane*, Christie's, Los Angeles, December 15, 1996	233,500
9	**Herman J. Mankiewicz's scripts** for *Citizen Kane* and *The American*, Christie's, New York, June 21, 1989	231,000
10	**James Bond's Aston Martin DB5** from the 1995 movie of *Goldfinger*, Christie's, London, February 14, 2001	229,315 (£157,750)

This list excludes animated film celluloids or "cels" – the individually painted scenes that are shot in sequence to make up cartoon films – which are now attaining colossal prices: just one of the 150,000 color cels from *Snow White* (1937) was sold in 1991 for $209,000, and in 1989 $286,000 was reached for a black-and-white cel depicting Donald Duck in *Orphan's Benefit* (1934). If memorabilia relating to film stars rather than films is included, Marilyn Monroe's dress that she wore singing "Happy Birthday" to President John F. Kennedy in 1962 would head the list with a world record auction price of $1,267,500 in 1999. Among near-misses are Mel Gibson's broadsword from *Braveheart* (1999) ($170,000), the piano from the Paris scene in *Casablanca* (1942) ($154,000), the posters for two films, *The Mummy* (1932) ($115,000 in 2001), and *Flying Down to Rio* (1933) ($81,000 in 1996).

007's Sporty Number
Equipped with its range of high-tech gadgets, James Bond's Aston Martin DB5 achieved a record price at auction. In 1997 it was stolen from an aircraft hanger in Boca Raton, Florida, and has not been seen since.

FIRST TEDDY BEARS

US PRESIDENT THEODORE ("TEDDY") Roosevelt's refusal to shoot a young bear became the subject of a cartoon by Clifford K. Berryman, published in the *Washington Post* on November 16, 1902. Immediately afterward, Morris Michtom, a New York store owner (and later founder of the Ideal Toy and Novelty Company), began advertising them as "Teddy's Bears." These, and bears made by German toymaker Margarete Steiff, started a craze for bears that has continued over the past 100 years.

FIRST OR LAST

MUSIC & MUSICIANS

Popular Songs

LATEST GRAMMY SONGS OF THE YEAR

YEAR	SONG	SONGWRITER(S)
2001	Fallin'	Alicia Keys
2000	Beautiful Day	U2
1999	Smooth	Itaal Shur and Rob Thomas
1998	My Heart Will Go On	James Horner and Will Jennings
1997	Sunny Came Home	Shawn Colvin
1996	Change the World	Gordon Kennedy, Wayne Kirkpatrick, and Tommy Sims
1995	Kiss From a Rose	Seal
1994	Streets of Philadelphia	Bruce Springsteen
1993	A Whole New World	Alan Menken and Tim Rice
1992	Tears in Heaven	Eric Clapton

TOP 10 US HITS COMPOSED BY GERRY GOFFIN AND CAROLE KING

	SONG	CHARTING ARTIST(S)
1	The Loco-motion	Little Eva, Grand Funk Railroad, Kylie Minogue
2	Go Away Little Girl	Steve Lawrence Happenings, Donny Osmond
3	Will You Love Me Tomorrow	Shirelles, The Four Seasons, Roberta Flack, Melanie, Dana Valery
4	One Fine Day	The Chiffons, Julie, Rita Coolidge, Carole King
5	Up on the Roof	The Drifters, Cryan' Shames, Laura Nyro, James Taylor
6	Take Good Care of My Baby	Bobby Vee, Bobby Vinton
7	Run to Him	Bobby Vee
8	Hey Girl	Freddie Scott, Donny Osmond
9	(You Make Me Feel Like) A Natural Woman	Aretha Franklin, Mary J. Blige
10	I'm into Something Good	Herman's Hermits, Earl-Jean

Gerry Goffin and Carole King began their professional partnership in 1960, composing a huge catalog of hits prior to their 1967 divorce.

TIN PAN ALLEY

FROM THE LATE 19TH CENTURY ONWARD, the US music community centered around New York's West 28th Street. There, in 1903, songwriter and publisher Harry Von Tilzer (1872–1946) was visited by songwriter and journalist Monroe H. Rosenfeld (1861–1918), who told him his piano sounded "like a tin pan." Von Tilzer is reputed to have replied, "Yes, I guess this is tin pan alley." Rosenfeld repeated the comment in an article in the *New York Herald*, and the nickname was born.

FIRST OR LAST

Keystroke
Alicia Keys scooped a total of five Grammys at the 2002 ceremony, honoring recordings in 2001.

TOP 10 DJ REQUESTS IN THE US

	SONG	ARTIST/GROUP
1	Electric Slide	Marcia Griffiths
2	Y.M.C.A.	Village People
3	Cha Cha Slide	DJ Casper
4	Love Shack	B52s
5	Get the Party Started	Pink
6	Amazed	Lonestar
7	Brown Eyed Girl	Van Morrison
8	Old Time Rock and Roll	Bob Seger
9	(You Shook Me) All Night Long	AC/DC
10	Celebration	Kool & the Gang

Source: Mobile Beat Top 200 DJ Song List 2002

Mobile Beat's listing of the 200 most requested songs represents both old favorites – *Brown Eyed Girl* first charted in 1967 and *Y.M.C.A.* in 1979 – as well as newer releases that may prove to have less sustained presence in the all-time list.

TOP 10 SONGWRITERS IN THE US

		CHART HITS
1	John Lennon & Paul McCartney	117
2	=Burt Bacharach & Hal David	103
	=Brian Holland, Lamont Dozier & Eddie Holland	103
4	Curtis Mayfield	85
5	Gerry Goffin & Carole King	83
6	Kenny Gamble & Leon Huff	80
7	Barry Mann & Cynthia Weil	75
8	Diane Warren	73
9	Mick Jagger & Keith Richard	59
10	Jerry Leiber & Mike Stoller	57

Source: *The Music Information Database*

While songwriter partnerships dominate this list, solo composers Curtis Mayfield (1942–99), former singer with The Impressions, and Diane Warren (b.1956), 6-times ASCAP Songwriter of the Year, also feature prominently.

THE 10 LATEST RECIPIENTS OF THE SONGWRITERS HALL OF FAME SAMMY CAHN LIFETIME ACHIEVEMENT AWARD

YEAR	RECIPIENT(S)
2001	Gloria and Emilio Estefan
2000	Neil Diamond
1999	Kenny Rogers
1998	Berry Gordy
1997	Vic Damone
1996	Frankie Laine
1995	Steve Lawrence & Eydie Gorme
1994	Lena Horne
1993	Ray Charles
1992	Nat "King" Cole

Source: *National Academy of Popular Music*

The National Academy of Popular Music was founded in 1969. Its most prestigous award is named for Sammy Cahn, who served for 20 years as the Academy's President.

Mr. Tambourine Man
Bob Dylan has achieved remarkable chart success, not only with his own records but also with a host of hits covered by a diverse range of international artists.

TOP 10 US HITS COMPOSED BY BOB DYLAN

	SONG	CHARTING ARTIST(S)
1	Blowin' in the Wind	Peter, Paul & Mary, Stevie Wonder
2	Mr. Tambourine Man	The Byrds
3	Lay Lady Lay	Bob Dylan, Ferrante & Teicher, The Isley Brothers
4	Like a Rolling Stone	Bob Dylan
5	Rainy Day Women #12 and #35	Bob Dylan
6	Don't Think Twice	Peter, Paul & Mary, Wonder Who?
7	It Ain't Me Babe	Johnny Cash, The Turtles
8	Mighty Quinn (Quinn the Eskimo)	Manfred Mann
9	Knockin' on Heaven's Door	Bob Dylan
10	All I Really Want to Do	The Byrds, Cher

A much-covered songwriter, with hundreds of his titles recorded by other artists, often as album tracks, Bob Dylan has also written material that has proved successful for the likes of Jimi Hendrix (*All Along the Watchtower*), Rod Stewart (*Forever Young*), and even Olivia Newton-John (*If Not For You*). In all, Dylan has penned 52 Hot 100 hits.

Hit Singles

TOP 10 | SINGLES OF 2001 IN THE US

	TITLE	ARTIST/GROUP
1	Loverboy	Mariah Carey
2	Stutter	Joe
3	Get Over Yourself	Eden's Crush
4	All For You	Janet Jackson
5	My Baby	Lil' Romeo
6	What Would You Do?	City High
7	Bizounce	Olivia
8	The Star Spangled Banner	Whitney Houston
9	Superwoman	Lil' Mo
10	Missing You	Case

Source: *Soundscan*

Whitney Houston's *The Star Spangled Banner* was originally released in 1991, and re-released in 2001 to aid victims of the September 11 attacks.

TOP 10 | SINGLES OF 2000 IN THE US

	TITLE	ARTIST/GROUP
1	Maria Maria	Santana featuring the Product G&B
2	Music	Madonna
3	Incomplete	Sisqo
4	Breathe	Faith Hill
5	Get It On ... Tonite	Montell Jordan
6	From the Bottom of My Broken Heart	Britney Spears
7	Thank God I Found You	Mariah Carey with Joe & 98°
8	Hot Boyz	Missy Elliott featuring Nas, Eve & Q-Tip
9	I Like It	Sammie
10	He Wasn't Man Enough	Toni Braxton

Source: *Soundscan*

All of the above sold in excess of 600,000 copies, with *Maria Maria* way out in front with sales of 1.3 million. *Music* and *Incomplete* both topped the million mark.

TOP 10 | SINGLES OF 1999 IN THE US

	TITLE	ARTIST/GROUP
1	Believe	Cher
2	Genie in a Bottle	Christina Aguilera
3	Heartbreak Hotel	Whitney Houston featuring Faith Evans & Kelly Price
4	Summer Girls	LFO
5	Smooth	Santana featuring Rob Thomas
6	If You Had My Love	Jennifer Lopez
7	Livin' La Vida Loca	Ricky Martin
8	Angel of Mine	Monica
9	Bills, Bills, Bills	Destiny's Child
10	All I Have to Give	Backstreet Boys

Source: *Soundscan*

All the singles listed achieved platinum status for sales of over 1 million units during 1999.

TOP 10 | SINGLES OF 1998 IN THE US

	TITLE	ARTIST/GROUP
1	The Boy Is Mine	Brandy & Monica
2	Too Close	Next
3	You're Still the One	Shania Twain
4	Nice & Slow	Usher
5	The First Night	Monica
6	My Way	Usher
7	My All	Mariah Carey
8	Body Bumpin' Yippie-Yi-Yo	Public Announcement
9	No, No, No Part 2	Destiny's Child featuring Wyclef Jean
10	Let's Ride	Montell Jordan featuring Master P & Silkk the Shocker

Source: *Soundscan*

Love Songs
Celine Dion's *Power of Love* and *Because You Loved Me* were both Top 10 hits in the US, but her single of *My Heart Will Go On* from *Titanic* was eclipsed by the 11-million-selling soundtrack album on which it was included.

TOP 10 | SINGLES OF 1997 IN THE US

	TITLE	ARTIST/GROUP
1	Candle in the Wind (1997)/ Something About the Way You Look Tonight	Elton John
2	I'll Be Missing You	Puff Daddy & Faith Evans featuring 112
3	Can't Nobody Hold Me Down	Puff Daddy featuring Mase
4	How Do I Live	LeAnn Rimes
5	You Make Me Wanna	Usher
6	Wannabe	Spice Girls
7	MMMBop	Hanson
8	Return of the Mack	Mark Morrison
9	It's Your Love	Tim McGraw with Faith Hill
10	Mo Money Mo Problems	Notorious B.I.G. featuring Puff Daddy & Mase

Source: *Soundscan*

TOP 10 | SINGLES OF 1996 IN THE US

	TITLE	ARTIST/GROUP
1	Macarena (Bayside Boys Mix)	Los Del Rio
2	How Do U Want It/California Love	2Pac
3	Twisted	Keith Sweat
4	No Diggity	Blackstreet
5	You Mean the World to Me/ I Belong to You	Toni Braxton
6	C'mon N' Ride It (The Train)	Quad City DJ's
7	Because You Loved Me	Celine Dion
8	Loungin	LL Cool J
9	Nobody Knows	Tony Rich Project
10	Un-break My Heart	Toni Braxton

Source: *Soundscan*

While all 10 of these singles went platinum in 1996, *Macarena* sold over 4 million within the year.

TOP 10 | SINGLES OF 1995 IN THE US

	TITLE	ARTIST/GROUP
1	Gangsta's Paradise	Coolio featuring LV
2	Fantasy	Mariah Carey
3	One Sweet Day	Mariah Carey & Boyz II Men
4	Waterfalls	TLC
5	Boombastic/Summer Time	Shaggy
6	Don't Take It Personal (Just One of Dem Days)	Monica
7	One More Chance/ Stay With Me	Notorious B.I.G.
8	Freak Like Me	Adina Howard
9	Exhale (Shoop Shoop)	Whitney Houston
10	This Is How We Do It	Montell Jordan

Source: *Soundscan*

TOP 10 | SINGLES OF 1994 IN THE US

	TITLE	ARTIST/GROUP
1	I'll Make Love to You	Boyz II Men
2	I Swear	All-4-One
3	Bump 'N' Grind	R Kelly
4	The Sign	Ace of Base
5	Tootsee Roll	69 Boyz
6	Fantastic Voyage	Coolio
7	Regulate	Warren G & Nate Dogg
8	The Power of Love	Celine Dion
9	Stay (I Missed You)	Lisa Loeb & Nine Stories
10	Here Comes the Hotstepper	Ini Kamoze

Source: *Soundscan*

The trend of rap/hip-hop/R&B continued, with 7 of the Top 10 in that genre. *I'll Make Love to You* sold 1.6 million copies – 1 of 7 million-sellers during the year.

Hit Albums

TOP 10 ALBUMS OF 2001 IN THE US

	TITLE	ARTIST/GROUP
1	Hybrid Theory	Linkin Park
2	Hotshot	Shaggy
3	Celebrity	*NSYNC
4	A Day Without Rain	Enya
5	Break the Cycle	Staind
6	Songs in A Minor	Alicia Keys
7	Survivor	Destiny's Child
8	Weathered	Creed
9	O Brother Where Art Thou?	Various Artists
10	Now That's What I Call Music! 6	Various Artists

Source: *Soundscan*

All 10 of the best-selling albums of the year achieved multi-platinum (sales of 1,000,000) rank, with Linkin Park's *Hybrid Theory* certified for its first award in January, its fifth by the end of the year, and its seventh by January 2002.

TOP 10 ALBUMS OF 2000 IN THE US

	TITLE	ARTIST/GROUP
1	No Strings Attached	*NSYNC
2	The Marshall Mathers LP	Eminem
3	Oops! ... I Did It Again	Britney Spears
4	Human Clay	Creed
5	Supernatural	Santana
6	1	The Beatles
7	Country Grammar	Nelly
8	Black & Blue	Backstreet Boys
9	2001	Dr. Dre
10	The Writing's on the Wall	Destiny's Child

Source: *Soundscan*

Hot Shot
Grammy Award-winning reggae star Shaggy achieved transatlantic success in 2000 and 2001 with his album *Hotshot*.

TOP 10 ALBUMS OF 1999 IN THE US

#	TITLE	ARTIST/GROUP
1	Millennium	Backstreet Boys
2	... Baby One More Time	Britney Spears
3	Ricky Martin	Ricky Martin
4	Come on Over	Shania Twain
5	Significant Other	Limp Bizkit
6	Supernatural	Santana
7	Devil Without a Cause	Kid Rock
8	Fanmail	TLC
9	Christina Aguilera	Christina Aguilera
10	Wide Open Spaces	Dixie Chicks

Source: *Soundscan*

TOP 10 ALBUMS OF 1998 IN THE US

#	TITLE	ARTIST/GROUP
1	Titanic	Soundtrack
2	Let's Talk About Love	Celine Dion
3	Backstreet Boys	Backstreet Boys
4	Come on Over	Shania Twain
5	*NSYNC	*NSYNC
6	City of Angels	Soundtrack
7	Double Live	Garth Brooks
8	Big Willie Style	Will Smith
9	Savage Garden	Savage Garden
10	Armageddon	Soundtrack

Source: *Soundscan*

TOP 10 ALBUMS OF 1997 IN THE US

#	TITLE	ARTIST/GROUP
1	Spice	Spice Girls
2	Pieces of You	Jewel
3	No Way Out	Puff Daddy & the Family
4	Sevens	Garth Brooks
5	Middle of Nowhere	Hanson
6	Life After Death	Notorious B.I.G.
7	Bringing Down the Horse	Wallflowers
8	Falling into You	Celine Dion
9	Space Jam	Soundtrack
10	You Light Up My Life – Inspirational Songs	LeAnn Rimes

Source: *Soundscan*

TOP 10 ALBUMS OF 1996 IN THE US

#	TITLE	ARTIST/GROUP
1	Jagged Little Pill	Alanis Morissette
2	Falling into You	Celine Dion
3	The Score	The Fugees
4	Tragic Kingdom	No Doubt
5	Daydream	Mariah Carey
6	All Eyez on Me	2Pac
7	Load	Metallica
8	Secrets	Toni Braxton
9	The Woman in Me	Shania Twain
10	(What's the Story) Morning Glory?	Oasis

Source: *Soundscan*

Twain Makes her Mark
Shania Twain's *Come on Over* is the best-selling album in the US by a female artist ever, with sales of more than 18 million in the US and 30 million worldwide.

Chart Hits

TOP 10 ALBUMS OF ALL TIME IN THE US

	TITLE/ARTIST/YEAR	ESTIMATED US SALES
1	**Their Greatest Hits,Eagles 1971–1975,** The Eagles, 1976	27,000,000
2	**Thriller,** Michael Jackson, 1982	26,000,000
3	**Led Zeppelin IV,** Led Zeppelin, 1971	22,000,000
4	**=Back in Black,** AC/DC, 1980	19,000,000
	=Come on Over, Shania Twain, 1997	19,000,000
6	**Rumours,** Fleetwood Mac, 1977	18,000,000
7	**The Bodyguard,** Soundtrack, 1992	17,000,000
8	**=Boston,** Boston, 1976	16,000,000
	=Cracked Rear View, Hootie & The Blowfish, 1994	16,000,000
	=Hotel California, The Eagles, 1976	16,000,000
	=Jagged Little Pill, Alanis Morissette, 1995	16,000,000
	=No Fences, Garth Brooks, 1990	16,000,000

Source: *RIAA*

TOP 10 ALBUMS WITH THE MOST WEEKS ON THE US ALBUM CHART

	TITLE/ARTIST/GROUP	WEEKS
1	**The Dark Side of the Moon,** Pink Floyd	741
2	**Johnny's Greatest Hits,** Johnny Mathis	490
3	**My Fair Lady,** Original Cast	480
4	**Highlights from The Phantom of the Opera,** Original Cast	331
5	**Oklahoma!,** Soundtrack	305
6	**Tapestry,** Carole King	302
7	**Heavenly,** Johnny Mathis	295
8	**MCMXC AD,** Enigma	283
9	**Metallica,** Metallica	281
10	**=Hymns,** Tennessee Ernie Ford	277
	=The King and I, Soundtrack	277

Source: *The Music Information Database*

Monster Hit

Michael Jackson's *Thriller* has sold some 50 million worldwide since its 1982 release, making it the best-selling album of all time.

TOP 10 ARTISTS WITH THE MOST CHART ALBUMS IN THE US

	ARTIST/GROUP	CHART ALBUMS
1	**Elvis Presley**	97
2	**Frank Sinatra**	70
3	**Johnny Mathis**	65
4	**=Ray Conniff**	49
	=James Brown	49
	=Barbra Streisand	49
7	**Willie Nelson**	47
8	**=Mantovani**	45
	=The Beach Boys	45
	=The Temptations	45

Source: *The Music Information Database*

TOP 10 SINGLES OF ALL TIME

TITLE/ARTIST/GROUP/YEAR	SALES EXCEED
1 **Candle in the Wind (1997)/Something About the Way You Look Tonight,** Elton John, 1997	37,000,000
2 **White Christmas,** Bing Crosby, 1945	30,000,000
3 **Rock Around the Clock,** Bill Haley and His Comets, 1954	17,000,000
4 **I Want to Hold Your Hand,** The Beatles, 1963	12,000,000
5 **=Hey Jude,** The Beatles, 1968	10,000,000
=I Will Always Love You, Whitney Houston, 1992	10,000,000
=It's Now or Never, Elvis Presley, 1960	10,000,000
8 **=Diana,** Paul Anka, 1957	9,000,000
=Hound Dog/Don't Be Cruel, Elvis Presley, 1956	9,000,000
10 **=(Everything I Do) I Do It For You,** Bryan Adams, 1991	8,000,000
=I'm a Believer, The Monkees, 1966	8,000,000

TOP 10 SINGLES THAT STAYED LONGEST ON THE US SINGLES CHART

TITLE/ARTIST/GROUP/YEAR	WEEKS
1 **How Do I Live,** LeAnn Rimes, 1997	69
2 **Foolish Games/You Were Meant For Me,** Jewel, 1996	65
3 **Macarena (Bayside Boys Mix),** Los Del Rio, 1996	60
4 **Smooth,** Santana featuring Rob Thomas, 1999	58
5 **Higher,** Creed, 1999	57
6 **I Don't Want to Wait,** Paula Cole, 1997	56
7 **=Amazed,** Lonestar, 1999	55
=Barely Breathing, Duncan Sheik, 1996	55
=Missing, Everything But The Girl, 1996	55
10 **December 1963 (Oh, What a Night),** Four Seasons, 1976*	54

* Re-charted in 1994

Source: *The Music Information Database*

TOP 10 SINGLES OF ALL TIME IN THE US

TITLE/ARTIST/GROUP	ESTIMATED US SALES
1 **Candle in the Wind (1997)/Something About the Way You Look Tonight,** Elton John	11,000,000
2 **=Hey Jude,** The Beatles	4,000,000
=Hound Dog/Don't Be Cruel, Elvis Presley	4,000,000
=I Will Always Love You, Whitney Houston	4,000,000
=We Are the World, USA For Africa	4,000,000
=Whoomp! (There It Is), Tag Team	4,000,000
7 **=(Everything I Do) I Do It For You,** Bryan Adams	3,000,000
=How Do I Live, LeAnn Rimes	3,000,000
=I'll Be Missing You, Puff Daddy and Faith Evans featuring 112	3,000,000
=Love Me Tender/Any Way You Want Me, Elvis Presley	3,000,000
=Macarena, Los Del Rio	3,000,000

Source: *RIAA*

Two of the singles in the Top 10 had special circumstances surrounding them. USA for Africa's 1985 charity single *We are the World* raised some $65 million for famine relief. It took the global response to the death of Princess Diana before the associated single, *Candle in the Wind*, overtook that and every other US release.

To Be Frank
Frank Sinatra is second only to Elvis Presley for the greatest numbers of charting albums.

US Chart Toppers

TOP 10 ONE-HIT WONDERS

	TITLE/ARTIST/GROUP	YEAR
1	**We Are the World**, USA For Africa	1985
2	**Dazzey Duks**, Duice	1993
3	**Gangsta Lean**, D. R. S.	1993
4	**My Body**, LSG	1997
5	**Body Bumpin' Yippie-Yi-Yo**, Public Announcement	1998
6	**I Don't Ever Want to See You Again**, Uncle Sam	1997
7	**Da' Dip**, Freak Nasty	1997
8	**Déjà vu (Uptown Baby)**, Lord Tariq & Peter Gunz	1997
9	**Just a Friend**, Biz Markie	1990
10	**Ditty**, Paperboy	1992

TOP 10 ARTISTS WITH THE MOST CONSECUTIVE NO. 1 SINGLES

	ARTIST	PERIOD	CONSECUTIVE NO. 1 SINGLES
1	**Elvis Presley**	1956–58	9
2	**Whitney Houston**	1985–88	7
3	=**Paula Abdul**	1988–91	6
	=**The Beatles**	1964–66	6
	=**The Bee Gees**	1977–79	6
6	=**Mariah Carey**	1990–91	5
	=**Mariah Carey**	1995–98	5
	=**Michael Jackson**	1987–88	5
	=**The Supremes**	1964–65	5
10	=**Jackson 5**	1970	4
	=**George Michael**	1987–88	4

Source: *The Music Information Database*

Wonderful Achievement

Louis Armstrong's *Hello Dolly!*, a hit song from the Broadway show of the same name, knocked the Beatles off the top slot in May 1964, going on to sell over 2 million copies.

TOP 10 ARTISTS WITH THE MOST NO. 1 SINGLES

	ARTIST	NO. 1 SINGLES
1	**The Beatles**	20
2	**Elvis Presley**	17
3	**Mariah Carey**	15*
4	**Michael Jackson**	13
5	=**Madonna**	12
	=**The Supremes**	12
7	**Whitney Houston**	11
8	=**Janet Jackson**	10
	=**Stevie Wonder**	10
10	=**The Bee Gees**	9
	=**Elton John**	9
	=**Paul McCartney/Wings**	9

* Including duets with Boyz II Men, Joe & 98° and Jay-Z

Source: *The Music Information Database*

TOP 10 OLDEST MALE SINGERS TO HAVE A NO. 1 SINGLE

	ARTIST/YEAR	TITLE	AGE* (YRS)	(MTHS)	(DAYS)
1	**Louis Armstrong**, 1964	Hello Dolly!	63	9	5
2	**Lawrence Welk**, 1961	Calcutta	57	11	14
3	**Morris Stoloff**, 1956	Moonglow and Theme from Picnic	57	10	8
4	**Frank Sinatra#**, 1967	Somethin' Stupid	51	4	24
5	**Lorne Greene**, 1964	Ringo	50	9	23
6	**Elton John**, 1997	Candle in the Wind (1997)/ Something About the Way You Look Tonight	50	9	21
7	**Rod Stewart**, 1994	All For Love	49	0	12
8	**Bill Medley†**, 1987	(I've Had) the Time of My Life	47	2	9
9	**Dean Martin**, 1964	Everybody Loves Somebody	47	2	8
10	**Sammy Davis Jr.**, 1972	The Candy Man	46	6	16

* During last week of No. 1 US single # Duet with Nancy Sinatra

† Duet with Jennifer Warnes

Source: *The Music Information Database*

TOP 10 YOUNGEST FEMALE SINGERS TO HAVE A NO. 1 SINGLE

	SINGER/YEAR	SINGLE	AGE (YRS)	(MTHS)	(DAYS)
1	**Little Peggy March,** 1963	I Will Follow Him	15	1	20
2	**Brenda Lee,** 1960	I'm Sorry	15	7	7
3	**Tiffany,** 1987	I Think We're Alone	16	1	5
4	**Lesley Gore,** 1963	It's My Party	17	0	30
5	**Little Eva,** 1962	The Loco-Motion	17	1	27
6	**Britney Spears,** 1999	...Baby One More Time	17	1	29
7	**Monica,** 1998	The First Night	17	11	9
8	**Shelley Fabares,** 1962	Johnny Angel	18	2	19
9	**Debbie Gibson,** 1988	Foolish Beat	18	6	4
10	**Christina Aguilera,** 1999	Genie in a Bottle	18	7	13

Source: *The Music Information Database*

TOP 10 YOUNGEST MALE SINGERS TO HAVE A NO. 1 SINGLE

	ARTIST/YEAR	TITLE	AGE* (YRS)	(MTHS)	(DAYS)
1	**Stevie Wonder,** 1963	Fingertips	13	2	28
2	**Donny Osmond,** 1971	Go Away Little Girl	13	9	2
3	**Michael Jackson,** 1972	Ben	14	1	15
4	**Laurie London,** 1958	He's Got the Whole World in His Hands	14	3	0
5	**Paul Anka,** 1957	Diana	16	1	16
6	**Brian Hyland,** 1960	Itsy Bitsy Teenie Weenie Yellow Polkadot Bikini	16	9	1
7	**Shaun Cassidy,** 1977	Da Doo Ron Ron	17	9	19
8	**Bobby Vee,** 1961	Take Good Care of My Baby	18	4	24
9	**Usher,** 1998	Nice & Slow	19	4	0
10	**Andy Gibb,** 1977	I Just Want to Be Your Everything	19	4	25

* *During first week of debut No. 1 US single*

Source: *The Music Information Database*

TOP 10 OLDEST FEMALE SINGERS TO HAVE A NO. 1 SINGLE

	ARTIST/YEAR	TITLE	AGE (YRS)	(MTHS)	(DAYS)
1	**Cher,** 1999	Believe	52	9	15
2	**Tina Turner,** 1984	What's Love Got to Do With It	45	9	5
3	**Bette Midler,** 1989	The Wind Beneath My Wings	44	8	24
4	**Madonna,** 2000	Music	42	1	0
5	**Kim Carnes,** 1981	Bette Davis Eyes	35	9	26
6	**Dolly Parton,** 1981	9 to 5	35	1	2
7	**Janet Jackson,** 2001	All For You	34	10	28
8	**Georgia Gibbs,** 1955	Dance With Me Henry	34	8	18
9	**Deniece Williams,** 1985	Let's Hear It For the Boy	33	11	23
10	**Kay Starr,** 1956	Rock and Roll Waltz	33	6	28

Source: *The Music Information Database*

Music Hath Charms
Madonna's *Music*, a 2000 No. 1 in both the US and the UK, also gained her a place among the oldest chart-toppers at the – in pop music terms – venerable age of 42.

Gold & Platinum

TOP 10 **GROUPS WITH THE MOST PLATINUM ALBUMS IN THE US**

	GROUP	PLATINUM ALBUMS*
1	The Beatles	102
2	The Eagles	83
3	Led Zeppelin	78
4	AC/DC	62
5	Aerosmith	58
6	Pink Floyd	51
7	Van Halen	50
8	U2	48
9	Fleetwood Mac	44
10	Alabama	43

By number of album awards, rather than number of albums qualifying for awards; double/triple albums counted once

Gathering No Moss

The Rolling Stones have been releasing best-selling albums for almost 40 years. Among groups, their tally of gold awards in the US runs a close second to the Beatles.

TOP 10 **GROUPS WITH THE MOST GOLD ALBUMS IN THE US**

	GROUP	GOLD ALBUMS
1	The Beatles	41
2	The Rolling Stones	38
3	Kiss	23
4	=Aerosmith	22
	=Alabama	22
	=Rush	22
7	Chicago	21
8	=The Beach Boys	20
	=Jefferson Airplane/Starship	20
10	AC/DC	19

The RIAA's Gold Awards have been presented since 1958 to artists who have sold 500,000 units of a single, album, or multi-disc set. The first single to be so honored was Perry Como's *Catch a Falling Star*, and the first album the soundtrack to *Oklahoma*.

TOP 10 **MALE SOLO ARTISTS WITH THE MOST GOLD ALBUMS IN THE US**

	ARTIST	GOLD ALBUMS
1	Elvis Presley*	65
2	Neil Diamond	36
3	Elton John	34
4	Bob Dylan#	30
5	George Strait	27
6	Frank Sinatra	26
7	Kenny Rogers	25
8	Hank Williams Jr.	22
9	=Eric Clapton	20
	=Rod Stewart	20

*Excluding 16 gold albums for EPs

Excluding 3 gold albums with the Grateful Dead

TOP 10 **FEMALE SOLO ARTISTS WITH THE MOST GOLD ALBUMS IN THE US**

	ARTIST	GOLD ALBUMS
1	Barbra Streisand	42
2	Reba McEntire	20
3	Linda Ronstadt	17
4	Madonna	14
5	=Aretha Franklin	13
	=Anne Murray	13
7	=Amy Grant	12
	=Olivia Newton-John	12
	=Tanya Tucker	12
10	=Natalie Cole	11
	=Donna Summer	11

Barbra Streisand's gold tally spans the 38-year period from 1964 to 2002.

TOP 10 MALE ARTISTS WITH THE MOST PLATINUM ALBUMS IN THE US

	ARTIST	PLATINUM ALBUMS*
1	Garth Brooks	94
2	Billy Joel	66
3	Elton John	64
4	Elvis Presley	62
5	George Strait	59
6	Michael Jackson	55
7	Kenny G	45
8	=Kenny Rogers	42
	=Bruce Springsteen	42
10	Neil Diamond	39

* By number of album awards, rather than number of albums qualifying for awards

Source: *RIAA*

Platinum singles and albums in the US are those that have achieved sales of 1 million units. The award has been made by the Recording Industry Association of America (RIAA) since 1976.

TOP 10 FEMALE ARTISTS WITH THE MOST PLATINUM ALBUMS IN THE US

	ARTIST	PLATINUM ALBUMS*
1	Madonna	58
2	Barbra Streisand	55
3	Mariah Carey	52
4	Whitney Houston	51
5	Celine Dion	40
6	Reba McEntire	32
7	Shania Twain	31
8	Linda Ronstadt	28
9	=Janet Jackson	22
	=Sade	22

* By number of album awards, rather than number of albums qualifying for awards

No Problem for Houston
With total album sales in the US alone topping 52 million, Whitney Houston is ranked 17th in the list of all-time best-selling artists.

All-Time Greats

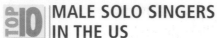

TOP 10 FEMALE SOLO SINGERS IN THE US

	SINGER	CHART SINGLES
1	Aretha Franklin	76
2	=Connie Francis	56
	=Dionne Warwick	56
4	Brenda Lee	55
5	Madonna	48
6	Barbra Streisand	44
7	Patti Page	43
8	=Olivia Newton-John	41
	=Diana Ross	41
10	Janet Jackson	40

Source: *The Music Information Database*

TOP 10 MALE SOLO SINGERS IN THE US

	SINGER	CHART SINGLES
1	Elvis Presley	151
2	James Brown	99
3	Ray Charles	76
4	Elton John	70
5	Frank Sinatra	68
6	Fats Domino	66
7	Stevie Wonder	65
8	=Pat Boone	60
	=Nat King Cole	60
10	Marvin Gaye	57

Source: *The Music Information Database*

TOP 10 "GREATEST HITS" ALBUMS IN THE US

	TITLE	ARTIST OR GROUP	YEAR OF ENTRY
1	Their Greatest Hits 1971–1975	The Eagles	1976
2	Greatest Hits	Elton John	1974
3	Simon & Garfunkel's Greatest Hits	Simon & Garfunkel	1972
4	Greatest Hits	Kenny Rogers	1980
5	James Taylor's Greatest Hits	James Taylor	1976
6	Greatest Hits Volumes I & II	Billy Joel	1985
7	The Immaculate Collection	Madonna	1990
8	The Hits	Garth Brooks	1994
9	Best of The Doobies	Doobie Brothers	1976
10	Greatest Hits	Journey	1988

Source: *The Music Information Database*

All of the above have sold in excess of 10 million copies each, with the Eagles' album the biggest-selling of all time with sales of 27 million. In 1976 it became the first album ever to be awarded the newly-introduced platinum award for sales of 1 million units. By 1990 it had achieved sales of 12 million, adding a further 8 million in the period from December 1993 to June 1995.

Dear John
Elton John (he was knighted by Queen Elizabeth II in 1997) has achieved more chart hits in the US than any other non-American artist.

TOP 10 GARTH BROOKS ALBUMS IN THE US

	ALBUM	YEAR
1	No Fences	1990
2	Ropin' the Wind	1991
3	The Hits	1994
4	Garth Brooks	1990
5	The Chase	1992
6	In Pieces	1993
7	Sevens	1997
8	Double Live	1998
9	Fresh Horses	1995
10	The Garth Brooks Collection	1997

Source: *The Music Information Database*

Success story of the 1990s, Garth Brooks is the best-selling solo singer ever, with total album sales in excess of 104 million, ahead of Elvis Presley's 86.5-million total, and a close runner-up to Led Zeppelin's 105 million and the Beatles' unassailable 164.5 million tally.

TOP 10 RICHEST ROCK STARS

	NAME	EARNINGS IN 2000 ($)
1	The Beatles	70,000,000
2	*NSYNC	42,000,000
3	Britney Spears	38,500,000
4	Backstreet Boys	35,500,000
5	Dr. Dre	31,500,000
6	=Dave Matthews Band	31,000,000
	=Tina Turner	31,000,000
8	Metallica	28,000,000
9	Dixie Chicks	25,000,000
10	Kiss	24,500,000

Source: Forbes

TOP 10 GROUPS IN THE US

	GROUP	CHART SINGLES
1	The Beatles	72
2	The Beach Boys	59
3	The Rolling Stones	57
4	The Temptations	55
5	Chicago	50
6	The Four Seasons	48
7	The Supremes	47
8	Smokey Robinson & the Miracles	46
9	The Four Tops	45
10	The Bee Gees	43

Source: *The Music Information Database*

TOP 10 SINGERS WITH THE MOST POSTHUMOUS HITS IN THE US

	SINGER	CHART SINGLES
1	Otis Redding	8
2	Jim Reeves	7
3	=Sam Cooke	6
	=Jim Croce	6
5	John Lennon	5
6	Elvis Presley	3
7	=Patsy Cline	2
	=Jimi Hendrix	2
	=Roy Orbison	2
	=Ritchie Valens	2

Source: *The Music Information Database*

The Beatles

TOP 10 LONGEST BEATLES TRACKS

	TITLE	DURATION (MINS)	(SECS)
1	Revolution 9	8	15
2	I Want You (She's So Heavy)	7	44
3	Hey Jude	7	15
4	It's All Too Much	6	16
5	A Day in the Life	5	05
6	Within You, Without You	5	00
7	While My Guitar Gently Weeps	4	41
8	I am the Walrus	4	32
9	Helter Skelter	4	28
10	You Know My Name (Look Up the Number)	4	17

Source: *The Music Information Database*

TOP 10 MOST-COVERED BEATLES SONGS

	SONG	YEAR WRITTEN
1	Yesterday	1965
2	Eleanor Rigby	1966
3	Something	1969
4	Hey Jude	1968
5	Let it Be	1969
6	Michelle	1965
7	With a Little Help from My Friends	1967
8	Day Tripper	1965
9	Come Together	1969
10	The Long and Winding Road	1969

Yesterday is one of the most-covered songs of all time, with an estimated 2,500 versions. Although most of these songs are Lennon/McCartney compositions, the No. 3 song, *Something*, was written by George Harrison.

TOP 10 BEST-SELLING BEATLES ALBUMS IN THE US

	TITLE	YEAR
1	Abbey Road	1969
2	The Beatles	1968
3	Sgt. Pepper's Lonely Hearts Club Band	1967
4	The Beatles 1967–1970	1973
5	1	2000
6	The Beatles 1962–1966	1973
7	Revolver	1966
8	Meet The Beatles!	1964
9	A Hard Day's Night	1964
10	Let It Be	1970

Source: *The Music Information Database*

BEATLES ALBUMS THAT STAYED LONGEST ON THE US CHARTS

	TITLE	WEEKS
1	Sgt. Pepper's Lonely Hearts Club Band	176
2	The Beatles 1967–1970	171
3	The Beatles	170
4	The Beatles 1962–1966	161
5	Abbey Road	129
6	Magical Mystery Tour	89
7	Revolver	77
8	Beatles '65	71
9	=Let It Be	59
	=Rubber Soul	59

Source: *The Music Information Database*

YESTERDAY. . .

THE FIRST PUBLIC performance by all four Beatles – John, Paul, George, and Ringo – was at the end of the local Horticultural Society's annual dance on August 18, 1962. Their first TV performance took place on October 17, 1962, from Liverpool's Cavern Club. Their first UK No. 1 single, *From Me to You*, topped the chart on May 4, 1963, beginning a run of 11 consecutive No. 1s. A week later they achieved their first No. 1 album with *Please Please Me*. The worldwide Beatles phenomenon lasted until the end of the decade: the last time they played together was on August 20, 1969.

FIRST OR LAST

BEST-SELLING BEATLES SINGLES IN THE US

	TITLE	YEAR
1	Hey Jude	1968
2	Get Back	1969
3	Let It Be	1970
4	Something	1969
5	Lady Madonna	1968
6	The Long and Winding Road	1970
7	I Want to Hold Your Hand	1964
8	Help!	1965
9	Can't Buy Me Love	1964
10	Yesterday	1965

Source: *The Music Information Database*

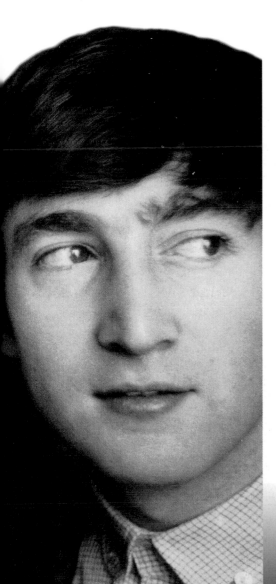

FIRST BEATLES SINGLES RELEASED IN THE US

	TITLE	RELEASE DATE
1	Please Please Me/Ask Me Why	Feb 1963
2	From Me to You/Thank You Girl	May 1963
3	She Loves You/I'll Get You	Sept 1963
4	I Want to Hold Your Hand/I Saw Her Standing There	Jan 1964
5	Please Please Me/From Me to You	Jan 1964
6	Twist and Shout/There's a Place	Mar 1964
7	Can't Buy Me Love/You Can't Do That	Mar 1964
8	Do You Want to Know a Secret/Thank You Girl	Mar 1964
9	Love Me Do/P.S. I Love You	Apr 1964
10	Sie Liebt Dich (She Loves You)/I'll Get You	May 1964

Source: *The Music Information Database*

BEATLES SINGLES THAT STAYED LONGEST IN THE US CHARTS

	TITLE	WEEKS
1	Hey Jude	19
2	Got to Get You into My Life	16
3	=I Want to Hold Your Hand	15
	=She Loves You	15
	=Twist and Shout	15
6	=Love Me Do	14
	=Let It Be	14
8	=Please Please Me	13
	=A Hard Day's Night	13
	=Help!	13

Source: *The Music Information Database*

Fab Four
At their Sixties peak, the Beatles dominated the charts worldwide, establishing numerous best-selling records.

Music Genres

Eminem
Top European single *Stan* by Eminem (Marshall Mathers) sampled *Thank You*, a track from Dido's *No Angel*, which was the top European album for 2001.

TOP 10 SINGLES IN EUROPE, 2001

SINGLE/ARTIST/GROUP

1	**Stan**, Eminem
2	**Can't Get You out of My Head**, Kylie Minogue
3	**It Wasn't Me**, Shaggy featuring Ricardo "Rikrok" Ducent
4	**It's Raining Men**, Geri Halliwell
5	**Can't Fight the Moonlight**, LeAnn Rimes
6	**Daddy DJ**, Daddy DJ
7	**Whole Again**, Atomic Kitten
8	**Lady Marmalade**, Christina Aguilera, Lil' Kim, Mya, & Pink
9	**Angel**, Shaggy featuring Rayvon
10	**Played-A-Live (The Bongo Song)**, Safri Duo

Source: Music & Media

TOP 10 RAP SINGLES IN THE US

	SINGLE/ARTIST/GROUP	YEAR
1	**Whoomp! (There It Is)**, Tag Team	1994
2	**I'll Be Missing You**, Puff Daddy & Faith Evans featuring 112	1997
3	**Gangsta's Paradise**, Coolio featuring L.V.	1995
4	**Can't Nobody Hold Me Down**, Puff Daddy	1997
5	**Dazzey Duks**, Duice	1993
6	**Rump Shaker**, Wreckx-N-Effect	1992
7	**Wild Thing**, Tone Loc	1988
8	**Baby Got Back**, Sir Mix-A-Lot	1992
9	**How Do U Want It**, 2Pac	1996
10	**Tha Crossroads**, Bone Thugs-N-Harmony	1996

Source: *The Music Information Database*

TOP 10 CONTEMPORARY CHRISTIAN ALBUMS IN THE US, 2001

ALBUM/ARTIST/GROUP

1	**WoW-2001 – The Year's 30 Top Christian Artists and Hits**, Various
2	**Songs 4 Worship – Shout to the Lord**, Various
3	**Satellite**, P.O.D.
4	**Live in London and More...**, Donnie McClurkin
5	**Mountain High ... Valley Low**, Yolanda Adams
6	**The Promise**, Plus One
7	**Thankful**, Mary Mary
8	**Offerings – A Worship Album**, Third Day
9	**Intermission – The Greatest Hits**, dc Talk
10	**Free To Fly**, Point of Grace

Source: Billboard

The WoW franchise has sold 8 million copies since its 1995 debut. The growth in popularity of Christian music has prompted the creation of a separate category in the American Society of Composers, Authors, and Publishers (ASCAP) annual awards.

TOP 10 HEAVY METAL SINGLES IN THE US

	SINGLE/ARTIST/GROUP	YEAR
1	**Eye of the Tiger**, Survivor	1982
2	**Keep on Loving You**, REO Speedwagon	1980
3	**I Love Rock 'n' Roll**, Joan Jett & the Blackhearts	1982
4	**Always**, Bon Jovi	1994
5	**I'd Do Anything for Love (But I Won't Do That)**, Meat Loaf	1993
6	**Blaze of Glory**, Jon Bon Jovi	1990
7	**Total Eclipse of the Heart**, Bonnie Tyler	1983
8	**Sweet Child O' Mine**, Guns 'N Roses	1988
9	**Jump**, Van Halen	1984
10	**You Ain't Seen Nothing Yet/Free Wheelin'**, Bachman Turner Overdrive	1974

Source: *The Music Information Database*

The 1980s were clearly the "golden age" of heavy metal, with just 1 single in the all-time Top 10 issued during the past 10 years. Survivor's classic *Eye of the Tiger* benefited from being featured as the theme in the box office blockbuster *Rocky III*, selling over 2 million copies, while all those in the Top 10 have attained gold status (for sales of more than 500,000).

TOP 10 ROCK ALBUMS IN THE US

ALBUM/ARTIST/GROUP	YEAR
1 **Their Greatest Hits 1971–1975,** The Eagles	1976
2 **Led Zeppelin IV,** Led Zeppelin	1973
3 **Rumours,** Fleetwood Mac	1977
4 **Cracked Rear View,** Hootie & the Blowfish	1994
5 **Hotel California,** The Eagles	1976
6 **Physical Graffiti,** Led Zeppelin	1975
7 **Born in the USA,** Bruce Springsteen	1984
8 **Appetite For Destruction,** Guns 'N Roses	1987
9 **The Dark Side of the Moon,** Pink Floyd	1973
10 **Supernatural,** Santana	1999

Source: *The Music Information Database*

TOP 10 ALBUMS IN EUROPE, 2001

ALBUM/ARTIST/GROUP
1 **No Angel,** Dido
2 **1,** The Beatles
3 **Not That Kind,** Anastacia
4 **Hybrid Theory,** Linkin Park
5 **The Marshall Mathers LP,** Eminem
6 **A Day Without Rain,** Enya
7 **All That You Can't Leave Behind,** U2
8 **Survivor,** Destiny's Child
9 **Hotshot,** Shaggy
10 **Music,** Madonna

Source: *Music & Media*

TOP 10 COUNTRY ALBUMS IN THE US

ALBUM/ARTIST	YEAR OF ENTRY
1 **Come on Over,** Shania Twain	1997
2 **No Fences,** Garth Brooks	1990
3 **Ropin' the Wind,** Garth Brooks	1991
4 **The Woman in Me,** Shania Twain	1998
5 **Greatest Hits,** Kenny Rogers	1997
6 **Wide Open Spaces,** Dixie Chicks	1999
7 **The Hits,** Garth Brooks	1994
8 **Fly,** Dixie Chicks	1999
9 **Garth Brooks,** Garth Brooks	1994
10 **Greatest Hits,** Patsy Cline	1998

Source: *The Music Information Database*

No Angel

British singer Dido (Armstrong) recorded her debut album *No Angel* in 1999. It has gained eight platinum awards in the UK, and achieved sales of over 4 million in the US.

The Grammys

 LATEST RECIPIENTS OF THE GRAMMY LIFETIME ACHIEVEMENT AWARD

	ARTIST/GROUP*	YEAR
1	Count Basie	2002
2	Rosemary Clooney	2002
3	Perry Como	2002
4	Al Green	2002
5	Joni Mitchell	2002
6	The Beach Boys	2001
7	Tony Bennett	2001
8	Sammy Davis Jr.	2001
9	Bob Marley	2001
10	The Who	2001

Source: *NARAS*

* Listed alphabetically by year

 ARTISTS WITH MOST GRAMMY AWARDS

	ARTIST	YEARS	AWARDS*
1	Sir Georg Solti	1962–97	38
2	Pierre Boulez	1969–01	29
3	=Vladimir Horowitz	1962–92	26
	=Quincy Jones	1963–93	26
5	Stevie Wonder	1973–98	21
6	=Leonard Bernstein	1961–2001	20
	=Henry Mancini	1958–70	20
8	John T. Williams	1975–2000	18
9	=Eric Clapton	1972–2001	16
	=Itzhak Perlman	1977–95	16

* Excludes Lifetime Achievements

The Grammy awards' ceremony has been held annually in the US since its inauguration on May 4, 1959, and the awards are considered to be the most prestigious in the music industry. The proliferation of classical artists in this Top 10 (not least, conductor Sir George Solti) is largely attributable to the large number of classical award categories at the Grammys, which have only latterly been overshadowed by the rise of pop and rock.

LATEST GRAMMY AWARDS FOR BEST HARD ROCK PERFORMANCE

YEAR	ARTIST/GROUP	TITLE
2001	Linkin Park	Crawling
2000	Rage Against the Machine	Guerrilla Radio
1999	Metallica	Whiskey in the Jar
1998	Robert Plant and Jimmy Page	Most High
1997	Smashing Pumpkins	The End is the Beginning is the End
1996	Smashing Pumpkins	Bullet with Butterfly Wings
1995	Pearl Jam	Spin the Black Circle
1994	Soundgarden	Black Hole Sun
1993	Stone Temple	Plush
1992	Red Hot Chili Peppers	Give It Away

 LATEST GRAMMY MALE POP VOCAL PERFORMANCES OF THE YEAR

YEAR	MALE VOCALIST/SONG
2001	James Taylor, Don't Let Me Be Lonely Tonight
2002	Sting, She Walks this Earth (Soberana Rosa)
1999	Sting, Brand New Day
1998	Eric Clapton, My Father's Eyes
1997	Elton John, Candle in the Wind (1997)
1996	Eric Clapton, Change the World
1995	Seal, Kiss From a Rose
1994	Elton John, Can You Feel the Love Tonight
1993	Sting, If I Ever Lose My Faith in You
1992	Eric Clapton, Tears in Heaven

The first male winner of this award was Perry Como in 1958, for his million-selling *Catch a Falling Star*. James Taylor's most recent award comes 30 years after his first, for *You've Got a Friend* (1971), and 24 years after his second, for *Handy Man* (1977).

LATEST GRAMMY BEST COUNTRY ALBUMS

YEAR*	ALBUM/	ARTIST/GROUP
2001	Timeless – Hank Williams Tribute	Various
2000	Breathe	Faith Hill
1999	Fly	Dixie Chicks
1998	Wide Open Spaces	Dixie Chicks
1997	Unchained	Johnny Cash
1996	The Road to Ensenada	Lyle Lovett
1995	The Woman in Me	Shania Twain
1994	Stones in the Road	Mary Chapin Carpenter
1965	The Return of Roger Miller	Roger Miller
1964	Dang Me/Chug-a-Lug	Roger Miller

*No award was made during 1966–93

LATEST GRAMMY FEMALE POP VOCAL PERFORMANCES OF THE YEAR

YEAR	FEMALE VOCALIST/SONG
2001	Nelly Furtado, I'm Like a Bird
2002	Macy Gray, I Try
1999	Sarah McLachlan, I Will Remember You
1998	Celine Dion, My Heart Will Go On
1997	Sarah McLachlan, Building a Mystery
1996	Toni Braxton, Un-Break My Heart
1995	Annie Lennox, No More "I Love You"s
1994	Sheryl Crow, All I Wanna Do
1993	Whitney Houston, I Will Always Love You
1992	k.d. lang, Constant Craving

The Grammy "Best Pop Vocal Performance – Female" award was introduced in 1971, when it was won by Carole King for *Tapestry*. Whitney Houston's 1993 win was her third in this category and followed awards for *Saving All My Love for You* (1985) and *I Wanna Dance with Somebody* (1987).

 **LATEST GRAMMY RECORDS OF THE YEAR**

YEAR	RECORD	ARTIST/GROUP
2001	Walk On	U2
2000	Beautiful Day	U2
1999	Smooth	Santana featuring Rob Thomas
1998	My Heart Will Go On	Celine Dion
1997	Sunny Came Home	Shawn Colvin
1996	Change the World	Eric Clapton
1995	Kiss From a Rose	Seal
1994	All I Wanna Do	Sheryl Crow
1993	I Will Always Love You	Whitney Houston
1992	Tears in Heaven	Eric Clapton

The Grammys are awarded retrospectively. Thus the 44th awards were presented in 2002 in recognition of musical accomplishment during 2001.

THE 10 | LATEST GRAMMY NEW ARTISTS OF THE YEAR

YEAR	NEW ARTIST(S)
2001	Alicia Keys
2000	Shelby Lynne
1999	Christina Aguilera
1998	Lauryn Hill
1997	Paula Cole
1996	LeeAnn Rimes
1995	Hootie & The Blowfish
1994	Sheryl Crow
1993	Toni Braxton
1992	Arrested Development

Pro Bono
Irish band U2 have won two consecutive Grammy "Records of the Year". In the US they have achieved sales of 45 million albums, *The Joshua Tree* alone having sold over 10 million.

Classical & Opera

TOP 10 MOST PERFORMED OPERAS

	OPERA	PRODUCTIONS	PERFORMANCES*
1	La Bohème	11	52
2	Tosca	12	48
3	Madama Butterfly	9	42
4	Die Zauberflöte	11	37
5	Un Ballo in Maschera	8	35
6	Don Giovanni	9	31
7	Otello	9	30
8	Les Contes d'Hoffmann	7	29
9	Il Barbiere di Siviglia	9	27
10	=La Traviata	8	24
	=Salome	6	24

* Based on a sample of 180 international productions over a 2-month period in 1994

Source: OperaGlass/Alain P. Dornic

TOP 10 CLASSICAL ALBUMS IN THE US

	PERFORMER(S)/ORCHESTRA	TITLE	YEAR
1	Carreras, Domingo, Pavarotti	The Three Tenors in Concert	1990
2	Andrea Bocelli	Romanza	1997
3	Andrea Bocelli	Sogno	1999
4	Charlotte Church	Voice of an Angel	1999
5	Benedictine Monks of Santo Domingo De Silos	Chant	1994
6	Carreras, Domingo, Pavarotti	The Three Tenors in Concert 1994	1994
7	Andrea Bocelli	Sacred Arias	1999
8	Van Cliburn	Tchaikovsky: Piano Concerto No. 1	1958
9	Soundtrack (Philadelphia Orchestra)	Fantasia (50th Anniversary Edition)	1990
10	Placido Domingo	Perhaps Love	1981

Source: The Music Information Database

The 1990s saw a huge increase in sales of classical and opera music, a change that owes much to the influence of tenors such as Placido Domingo and Luciano Pavarotti, whose amazing rise to international stardom has led to opera music becoming a far more accessible genre.

TOP 10 MOST PROLIFIC CLASSICAL COMPOSERS

	COMPOSER	HOURS OF MUSIC
1	Joseph Haydn (Austrian, 1732–1809)	340
2	George Handel (German-English, 1685–1759)	303
3	Wolfgang Amadeus Mozart (Austrian, 1756–91)	202
4	Johann Sebastian Bach (German, 1685–1750)	175
5	Franz Schubert (German, 1797–1828)	134
6	Ludwig van Beethoven (German, 1770–1827)	120
7	Henry Purcell (English, 1659–95)	116
8	Giuseppe Verdi (Italian, 1813–1901)	87
9	Anton Dvorák (Czech, 1841–1904)	79
10	=Franz Liszt (Hungarian, 1811–86)	76
	=Peter Tchaikovsky (Russian, 1840–93)	76

This list is based on a survey conducted by *Classical Music* magazine, which ranked classical composers by the total number of hours of music each composed.

THE FIRST OPERA RECORDINGS ON DISC

LATE IN 1902 IN MILAN, Italy, the great opera singer Enrico Caruso made his first recording of an operatic aria, *Vesti la Giubba* from *I Pagliacci*. The following year other companies followed suit. Then in 1903, HMV in Italy released Verdi's *Ernani*, the first complete opera ever recorded. But such was the technology of the day that the gramophone disks were single-sided and this particular opera required 40 disks to be fully recorded!

FIRST OR LAST

TOP 10 MOST PERFORMED OPERA COMPOSERS

	COMPOSER	PRODUCTIONS*
1	Giuseppe Verdi (Italian, 1813–1901)	58
2	Giacomo Puccini (Italian, 1858–1924)	44
3	Wolfgang Amadeus Mozart (Austrian, 1756–91)	40
4	=Gioacchino Rossini (Italian, 1792–1868)	23
	=Richard Strauss (German, 1864–1949)	23
6	Richard Wagner (German, 1813–83)	22
7	Gaetano Donizetti (Italian, 1797–1848)	21
8	=Leoš Janáček (Czech, 1854–1928)	10
	=Jacques Offenbach (German, 1819–80)	10
10	Georges Bizet (French, 1838–75)	9

* International sample during a 12-month period

TOP 10 CITIES STAGING THE MOST OPERAS

	CITY	PERFORMANCES*
1	Vienna, Austria	32
2	Berlin, Germany	21
3	Prague, Czech Republic	20
4	Paris, France	16
5	Hamburg, Germany	13
6	=London, UK	12
	=Zurich, Switzerland	12
8	=New York, New York	11
	=Munich, Germany	11
10	Hanover, Germany	10

* International sample during a 12-month period

La Bohème

First performed in 1896, Puccini's *La Bohème* is a tale of love and death in bohemian Paris, France. It is one of the world's most popular and most performed operas.

THE 10 | LATEST WINNERS OF THE "BEST OPERA RECORDING" GRAMMY AWARD

YEAR	TITLE/COMPOSER	PRINCIPAL SOLOISTS/ORCHESTRA
2001	**Les Troyens,** Hector Berlioz	Sir Colin Davis, Michelle De Young, Ben Heppner, Petra Lang, Peter Mattei, Stephen Milling, Sara Mingardo, Kenneth Tarver, London Symphony Orchestra
2000	**Doktor Faust,** Busoni	Kent Nagano, Kim Begley, Dietrich Fischer-Dieskau, Dietrich Henschel, Markus Hollop, Eva Jenis
1999	**The Rake's Progress,** Stravinsky	Ian Bostridge, Bryn Terfel, Anne Sofie von Otter, Deborah York, Monteverdi Choir, London Symphony Orchestra
1998	**Bluebeard's Castle,** Bartók	Jessye Norman, Laszlo Polgar, Karl-August Naegler, Chicago Symphony Orchestra
1997	**Die Meistersinger, Von Nürnberg** Richard Wagner	Ben Heppner, Herbert Lippert, Karita Mattila, Alan Opie, Rene Pape, Jose van Dam, Iris Vermillion, Chicago Symphony Chorus, Chicago Symphony Orchestra
1996	**Peter Grimes,** Benjamin Britten	Philip Langridge, Alan Opie, Janice Watson, Opera London, London Symphony Chorus, City of London Sinfonia
1995	**Les Troyens,** Hector Berlioz	Charles Dutoit, Orchestra Symphonie de Montréal
1994	**Susannah,** Carlisle Floyd	Jerry Hadley, Samuel Ramey, Cheryl Studer, Kenn Chester
1993	**Semele,** George Handel	Kathleen Battle, Marilyn Horne, Samuel Ramey, Sylvia McNair, Michael Chance
1992	**Die Frau Ohne Schatten,** Richard Strauss	Placido Domingo, Jose Van Dam, Hildegard Behrens

Source: *NARAS (National Academy of Recording Arts and Sciences)*

Broadcast Music

THE 10 FIRST ARTISTS TO FEATURE IN A COCA-COLA TELEVISION COMMERCIAL

	ARTIST(S)	JINGLE	YEAR
1	McGuire Sisters	Pause for a Coke	1958
2	=Brothers Four*	Refreshing New Feeling	1960
	=Anita Bryant	Refreshing New Feeling	1960
	=Connie Francis	Refreshing New Feeling	1960
5	=Fortunes	Things Go Better With Coke	1963
	=Limeliters*	Things Go Better With Coke	1963
7	Ray Charles	Things Go Better With Coke	1969
8	=Bobby Goldboro	It's The Real Thing	1971
	=New Seekers*	It's The Real Thing	1971
10	Dottie West*	It's The Real Thing (Country Sunshine)	1972

* Artist provided only the audio soundtrack for the commercial

Today's pop audience assumes that the inclusion of George Michael, Elton John, or Paula Abdul in Coke commercials is a new phenomenon. Coca-Cola has, in fact, featured music artists in its promotion since the turn of the last century, when it enlisted the support of popular opera stars. The company went on to sponsor music TV shows in the 1950s for big names like Eddie Fisher and Mario Lanza. Coca-Cola has kept close musical ties, with some of its more popular 1980s ads featuring the Thompson Twins, Robert Plant, Chuck Berry, and even Julio Iglesias.

TOP 10 SINGLES OF TELEVISION THEME TUNES IN THE US

	TITLE/ARTIST	PROGRAM
1	Welcome Back, John Sebastian	Welcome Back Kotter
2	T.S.O.P., MFSB.	Soul Train
3	Theme from S.W.A.T., Rhythm Heritage	S.W.A.T.
4	Theme from "The Greatest American Hero" (Believe It Not), Joey Scarbury	The Greatest American Hero
5	Theme from "The Dukes of Hazzard", Waylon Jennings	The Dukes of Hazzard
6	Makin' It, David Naughton	Makin' It
7	Nadia's Theme (The Young and the Restless), Barry DeVorzon and Perry Botkin, Jr.,	The Young and the Restless
8	How Do You Talk to an Angel, Heights	The Heights
9	Miami Vice Theme, Jan Hammer	Miami Vice
10	Hawaii Five-0, Ventures	Hawaii Five-0

The top 8 hits in this list were all US million-sellers, with theme singles from popular 1970s TV shows predominating. For those too young to remember them, the apparently coded title and artist at No.2 are, respectively, "The Sound of Philadelphia" and "Mother, Father, Sister, Brother".

THE 10 LATEST RECIPIENTS OF THE MTV VMA "BEST GROUP VIDEO" AWARD

YEAR	ARTIST/TITLE
2001	*NSYNC, POP
2000	Blink 182, All the Small Things
1999	TLC, No Scrubs
1998	Backstreet Boys, Everybody (Backstreet's Back)
1997	No Doubt, Don't Speak
1996	Foo Fighters, Big Me
1995	TLC, Waterfalls
1994	Aerosmith, Cryin'
1993	Pearl Jam, Jeremy
1992	U2, Even Better than the Real Thing

Boy Band
Formed in 1995 in Orlando, Florida, boy band *NSYNC scored their first hits in Europe and in the US in 1998, before going on to release hugely successful singles and albums.

TOP 10 MUSIC SHOWS ON US TELEVISION, 2000–1

	PROGRAM	VIEWERS
1	The 34th Annual CMA Awards	11,109,000
2	The American Music Awards	10,620,000
3	The 36th Annual CMA Awards	9,541,000
4	The 11th Annual Billboard Music Awards	7,509,000
5	The 55th Annual Tony Awards	6,467,000
6	The World Music Awards	5,605,000
7	AFI Tribute: Barbara Streisand	4,104,000
8	The 2000 Radio Music Awards	3,496,000
9	The Source Hip-Hop Awards 2001	3,297,000
10	The Alma Awards	2,993,000

* Period covered Oct 2, 2000 to Sep 23, 2001

© 2000, Nielsen Media Research

THE 10 LATEST RECIPIENTS OF THE MTV VMA "BEST MALE VIDEO" AWARD

YEAR	ARTIST/TITLE
2001	Moby/Gwen Stefani, South Side
2000	Eminem, The Real Slim Shady
1999	Will Smith, Miami
1998	Will Smith, Just the Two of Us
1997	Beck, The Devil's Haircut
1996	Beck, Where It's At
1995	Tom Petty and the Heartbreakers, You Don't Know How It Feels
1994	Tom Petty and the Heartbreakers, Mary Jane's Last Dance
1993	Lenny Kravitz, Are You Gonna Go My Way
1992	Eric Clapton, Tears in Heaven (performance)

THE 10 LATEST RECIPIENTS OF THE MTV VMA "BEST FEMALE VIDEO" AWARD

YEAR	ARTIST/TITLE
2001	Eve/Gwen Stefani, Let Me Blow Ya Mind
2000	Aaliyah, Try Again
1999	Lauryn Hill, Doo Wop (That Thing)
1998	Madonna, Ray of Light
1997	Jewel, You Were Meant for Me
1996	Alanis Morissette, Ironic
1995	Madonna, Take a Bow
1994	Janet Jackson, If
1993	k.d. lang, Constant Crying
1992	Annie Lennox, Why

Whale of a Time
Award-winning and highly versatile artist Moby (Richard Melville Hall) is named after his great-great-granduncle Herman Melville, the author of the whaling novel, *Moby Dick*.

Movie Music

 ## LATEST DISNEY "BEST SONG" OSCAR WINNERS

YEAR	SONG	FILM
2001	If I Didn't Have You	Monster's Inc.
1999	You'll Be in My Heart	Tarzan
1996	You Must Love Me	Evita
1995	Colors of the Wind	Pocahontas
1994	Can You Feel the Love Tonight	The Lion King
1992	Whole New World	Aladdin
1991	Beauty and The Beast	Beauty and The Beast
1990	Sooner or Later (I Always Get My Man)	Dick Tracy
1989	Under the Sea	The Little Mermaid
1964	Chim Chim Cher-ee	Mary Poppins

The first Disney "Best Song" Oscar was won by *When You Wish Upon a Star* from the film *Pinocchio*, in 1940.

FILM MUSICALS ADAPTED FROM STAGE VERSIONS

	MUSICAL	THEATER OPENING	FILM RELEASE
1	Grease	1972	1978
2	The Sound of Music	1959	1965
3	Evita	1978	1996
4	The Rocky Horror Picture Show	1973	1975
5	Fiddler on the Roof	1964	1971
6	My Fair Lady	1956	1964
7	The Best Little Whorehouse in Texas	1978	1982
8	Annie	1977	1982
9	West Side Story	1957	1961
10	Cabaret	1967	1972

Turning stage musicals into films is a long tradition. Recent years have seen the reverse, with popular stage shows based on films and cartoons, such as *42nd Street* (stage 1980/film 1933), *The Lion King* (1997/1994), and *Beauty and the Beast* (1994/1991).

POP MUSIC FILMS

	FILM	YEAR
1	Spice World	1997
2	Purple Rain	1984
3	The Blues Brothers	1980
4	La Bamba	1987
5	What's Love Got to Do With It	1993
6	The Doors	1991
7	Blues Brothers 2000	1998
8	The Wall	1982
9	The Commitments	1991
10	Sgt. Pepper's Lonely Hearts Club Band	1978

These films are pop star biographies or vehicles. *La Bamba* told the Ritchie Valens story; *What's Love Got to Do With It*, Tina Turner's. Other films showcased a real pop star, such as Prince, or imaginary group (*The Commitments*), or duo (*The Blues Brothers*). Film Nos. 8 and 10 were both based on an album.

MUSICAL FILMS

	FILM	YEAR
1	Grease	1978
2	Saturday Night Fever	1977
3	The Sound of Music	1965
4	Evita	1996
5	The Rocky Horror Picture Show	1975
6	Staying Alive	1983
7	American Graffiti	1973
8	Mary Poppins	1964
9	Flashdance	1983
10	Fantasia 2000	2000

Traditional musicals (films in which the cast actually sing) and films in which a musical soundtrack is a major component of the film are included here. The era of the blockbuster musical film may be over, but in recent years, animated films with an important musical content appear to have taken over from them – *Beauty and the Beast, Aladdin, The Lion King, Pocahontas, The Prince of Egypt*, and *Tarzan* all won "Best Original Song" Oscars – while the film soundtrack album of *Titanic* is the best-selling of all time.

ELVIS PRESLEY FILMS

	FILM	YEAR
1	Viva Las Vegas	1964
2	Blue Hawaii	1961
3	Love Me Tender	1956
4	G. I. Blues	1960
5	Jailhouse Rock	1957
6	Loving You	1957
7	Girls! Girls! Girls!	1962
8	Tickle Me	1965
9	Roustabout	1964
10	Girl Happy	1965

Big Brothers
Dan Aykroyd as Elwood Blues and John Belushi as "Joliot" Jake Blues re-form their band to raise money for an orphanage in the cult film *The Blues Brothers*.

TOP 10 ORIGINAL CAST RECORDING ALBUMS IN THE US

	SHOW TITLE*	YEAR OF RELEASE
1	Les Misèrables	1987
2	My Fair Lady	1956
3	Highlights from The Phantom of the Opera, London	1990
4	The Phantom of the Opera, London	1988
5	Fiddler on the Roof	1964
6	A Chorus Line	1975
7	The Music Man	1958
8	Rent	1996
9	Annie	1977
10	Cats	1983

* All shows performed on Broadway, unless otherwise indicated

The 1950s and early 1960s were clearly the golden era of musicals when cast albums regularly outperformed the burgeoning number of rock 'n' roll artists.

TOP 10 SOUNDTRACK ALBUMS IN THE US

	SOUNDTRACK	YEAR OF RELEASE	SALES
1	The Bodyguard	1992	17,000,000
2	Purple Rain	1984	13,000,000
3	Forrest Gump	1994	12,000,000
4	=Dirty Dancing	1987	11,000,000
	=Titanic	1997	11,000,000
6	The Lion King	1994	10,000,000
7	Top Gun	1986	9,000,000
8	=Footloose	1984	8,000,000
	=Grease	1978	8,000,000
10	Saturday Night Fever	1977	7,500,000

Source: RIAA

TOP 10 JAMES BOND FILM THEMES IN THE US

	TITLE (FILM*)/ARTIST	YEAR
1	A View to a Kill, Duran Duran	1985
2	Nobody Does It Better (from The Spy Who Loved Me), Carly Simon	1977
3	Live and Let Die, Paul McCartney and Wings	1973
4	For Your Eyes Only, Sheena Easton	1981
5	Goldfinger, Shirley Bassey	1965
6	Thunderball, Tom Jones	1966
7	All Time High (from Octopussy), Rita Coolidge	1983
8	You Only Live Twice, Nancy Sinatra	1967
9	Diamonds are Forever, Shirley Bassey	1972
10	Goldfinger, John Barry	1965

* If different from song title

By no means all the James Bond themes have been major US hits, especially those from the later movies which failed to register at all. Every song listed here reached the Top 100, but only the first 7 made the Top 40, and only Duran Duran had a Bond-associated US No. 1 hit. Note two appearances for *Goldfinger* – a vocal version by Shirley Bassey and an instrumental by John Barry; the film also produced the biggest-selling Bond film soundtrack LP during the same year.

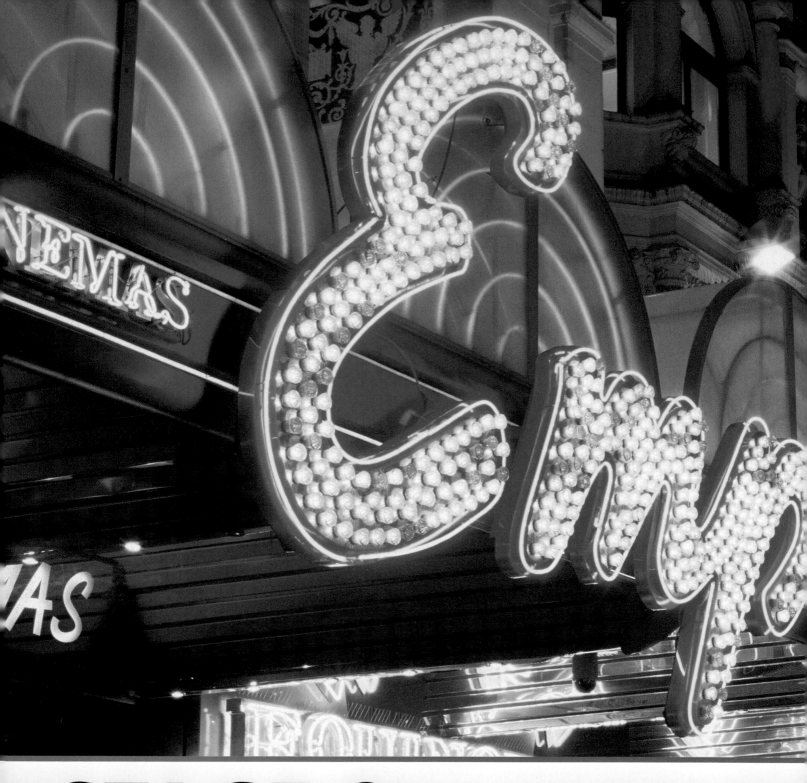

STAGE & SCREEN

Encore! Encore!

TOP 10 LONGEST-RUNNING MUSICALS ON BROADWAY

MUSICAL/YEARS	PERFORMANCES
1 Cats (1982–2000)	7,485
2 A Chorus Line (1975–90)	6,137
3 Les Misérables* (1987–)	6,101
4 The Phantom of the Opera* (1988–)	5,804
5 Miss Saigon (1991–2001)	4,095
6 42nd Street (1980–89)	3,486
7 Grease (1972–80)	3,388
8 Fiddler on the Roof (1964–72)	3,242
9 Beauty and the Beast* (1994–)	3,130
10 Hello Dolly! (1964–71)	2,844

Still running; total as of January 1, 2002

Source: *The League of American Theatres and Producers*

Off Broadway, the musical show *The Fantasticks* finally closed at the Sullivan Street Playhouse, New York, on January 13, 2002, after 17,162 performances during its 42-year run.

TOP 10 LONGEST-RUNNING COMEDIES ON BROADWAY

COMEDY/YEARS	PERFORMANCES
1 Life with Father (1939–47)	3,224
2 Abie's Irish Rose (1922–27)	2,327
3 Gemini (1977–81)	1,819
4 Harvey (1944–49)	1,775
5 Born Yesterday (1946–49)	1,642
6 Mary, Mary (1961–64)	1,572
7 The Voice of the Turtle (1943–48)	1,557
8 Barefoot in the Park (1963–67)	1,530
9 Same Time Next Year (1975–78)	1,454
10 Brighton Beach Memoirs (1983–86)	1,299

Source: *The League of American Theatres and Producers*

TOP 10 LONGEST-RUNNING THRILLERS ON BROADWAY

THRILLER/YEARS	PERFORMANCES
1 Deathtrap (1978–82)	1,793
2 Arsenic and Old Lace (1941–44)	1,444
3 Angel Street (1941–1944)	1,295
4 Sleuth (1970–73)	1,222
5 Dracula (1977–80)	925
6 Witness for the Prosecution (1954–56)	644
7 Dial M for Murder (1952–54)	552
8 Sherlock Holmes (1975–76)	479
9 An Inspector Calls (1994–95)	454
10 Ten Little Indians (1944–45)	424

Source: *The League of American Theatres and Producers*

TOP 10 LONGEST-RUNNING NONMUSICALS ON BROADWAY

NONMUSICAL/YEARS	PERFORMANCES
1 Oh! Calcutta! (1976–89)	5,959
2 Life with Father (1939–47)	3,224
3 Tobacco Road (1933–41)	3,182
4 Abie's Irish Rose (1922–27)	2,327
5 Gemini (1977–81)	1,819
6 Deathtrap (1978–82)	1,793
7 Harvey (1944–49)	1,775
8 Born Yesterday (1946–49)	1,642
9 Mary, Mary (1961–64)	1,572
10 The Voice of the Turtle (1943–48)	1,557

Source: *The League of American Theatres and Producers*

Off Broadway, these records have all been broken by *The Drunkard*, which was performed at the Mart Theater, Los Angeles, from July 1933 to September 1953, and then re-opened with a musical adapation from September 1953 until October 1959.

LONGEST-RUNNING ROGERS AND HAMMERSTEIN PRODUCTIONS ON BROADWAY

PRODUCTION/YEARS	PERFORMANCES
1 Oklahoma! (1943–1948)	2,212
2 South Pacific (1949–1954)	1,925
3 The Sound of Music (1959–1963)	1,443
4 The King and I (1951–1954)	1,246
5 Carousel (1945–1947)	890
6 The King and I (1996–1998)	780
7 The King and I (1977–1978)	695
8 The Flower Drum Song (1958–1960)	600
9 The Sound of Music (1998–1999)	533
10 Carousel (1994–1995)	337

LONGEST-RUNNING MUSICALS IN THE UK

MUSICAL/YEARS	PERFORMANCES
1 Cats (1981–2002)	8,949
2 Starlight Express (1984–2002)	7,406
3 Les Misérables* (1985–)	6,670
4 The Phantom of the Opera* (1986–)	6,327
5 Miss Saigon (1989–99)	4,263
6 Oliver! (1960–69)	4,125
7 Jesus Christ Superstar (1972–80)	3,357
8 Evita (1978–86)	2,900
9 The Sound of Music (1961–67)	2,386
10 Salad Days (1954–60)	2,283

* Still running; total as of January 1, 2002

Cats closed on May 12, 2002, its 21st birthday. Since May 12, 1989, it held the record as the UK's longest-running musical.

LONGEST-RUNNING NONMUSICALS IN THE UK

MUSICAL/YEARS	PERFORMANCES
1 The Mousetrap* (1952–)	20,432
2 No Sex, Please – We're British (1971–81; 1982–86; 1986–87)	6,761
3 The Woman in Black* (1989–)	5,175
4 Oh! Calcutta! (1970–1974; 1974–1980)	3,918
5 The Complete Works of William Shakespeare (abridged)* (1996–)	2,916
6 Run For Your Wife (1983–91)	2,638
7 There's a Girl in My Soup (1966–69; 1969–72)	2,547
8 Pyjama Tops (1969–1975)	2,498
9 Sleuth (1970; 1972; 1973–75)	2,359
10 Worm's Eye View (1945–51)	2,245

* Still running; total as of January 1, 2002

LONGEST-RUNNING COMEDIES IN THE UK

COMEDY/YEARS	PERFORMANCES
1 No Sex, Please – We're British (1971–81; 1982–86; 1986–87)	6,761
2 The Complete Works of William Shakespeare (abridged)* (1996–)	2,916
3 Run For Your Wife (1983–91)	2,638
4 There's A Girl in My Soup (1966–69; 1969–72)	2,547
5 Pyjama Tops (1969–75)	2,498
6 Worm's Eye View (1945–51)	2,245
7 Boeing Boeing (1962–65; 1965–67)	2,035
8 Blithe Spirit (1941–42; 1942; 1942–46)	1,997
9 Dirty Linen (1976–80)	1,667
10 Reluctant Heroes (1950–54)	1,610

* Still running; total as of January 1, 2002

No Sex, Please – We're British is the world's longest-running comedy. It opened at the Strand Theatre, London, UK, on June 3, 1971, and after transfers to the Garrick and Duchess Theatres, finally closed on September 5, 1987.

Stage Fright

With the closure in 2002 of Andrew Lloyd Webber's Cats and Starlight Express, The Phantom of the Opera musical is set to become his longest-running show in the UK.

LATEST RECIPIENTS OF THE NEW YORK DRAMA LEAGUE DISTINGUISHED PERFORMANCE AWARD

YEAR	ACTOR/ACTRESS
2002	Liam Neeson
2001	=Mary-Louis Parker
	=Gary Sinise
2000	Eileen Heckart
1999	Kathleen Chalfant
1998	Brian Stokes Mitchell
1997	=Charles Durning
	=Bebe Neuwirth
1996	Uta Hagan
1995	Cherry Jones

The Distinguished Performance Award is the oldest award given in American theater, first presented in 1935, and predating the Tony Awards by 12 years. A recipient may be given the award only once.

LATEST NEW YORK DRAMA CRITICS CIRCLE AWARDS FOR BEST FOREIGN PLAY

YEAR	PLAY	PLAYWRIGHT
2000	Copenhagen	Michael Frayn
1999	Closer	Patrick Marber
1997	Skylight	Joan Marcus
1996	Molly Sweeney	Brian Friel
1995	Someone Who'll Watch Over Me	Frank McGuinness
1994	Our Country's Good	Timberlake Wertenbaker
1990	Privates on Parade	Peter Nichols
1989	Aristocrats	Brian Friel
1988	The Road to Mecca	Athol Fugard
1987	Les Misérables	Claude-Michel Schönberg and Alain Boublil

No awards in 2001, 1998, 1991–93

LATEST DRAMA DESK AWARDS FOR AN ACTOR

YEAR	ACTOR	PLAY
2001	Richard Easton	The Invention of Love
2000	Stephen Dillane	The Real Thing
1999	Brian Dennehy	Death of a Salesman
1998	Anthony LaPaglia	A View From the Bridge
1997	=David Morse	How I Learned to Drive
	=Christopher Plummer	Barrymore
1996	Frank Langella	The Father
1995	Ralph Fiennes	Hamlet
1994	Stephen Spinella	Angels in America Part II: Perestroika
1993	Ron Leibman	Angels in America Part I: Millennium Approaches

Closer
British playwright Patrick Marber won two Evening Standard "Best Comedy" awards in the 1990s, with *Closer* also winning acclaim and awards on Broadway.

LATEST DRAMA DESK AWARDS FOR AN ACTRESS

YEAR	ACTRESS	PLAY
2001	Mary-Louise Parker	Proof
2000	Eileen Heckart	The Waverly Gallery
1999	Kathleen Chalfant	Wit
1998	Cherry Jones	Pride's Crossing
1997	Janet McTeer	A Doll's House
1996	Zoë Caldwell	Master Class
1995	Glenn Close	Sunset Boulevard
1994	Myra Carter	Three Tall Women
1993	Jane Alexander	The Sisters Rosensweig
1992	Laura Esterman	Marvin's Room

Source: *New York Drama Desk*

August Presence
Set in a cab office in 1970s Pittsburgh, August Wilson's *Jitney* won accolades and awards in both the US and the UK.

THE 10 LATEST NEW YORK DRAMA CRITICS CIRCLE AWARDS FOR BEST NEW PLAY*

YEAR	PLAY	AUTHOR
2001	The Invention of Love	Tom Stoppard
2000	Jitney	August Wilson
1999	Wit	Margaret Edson
1998	Art	Yasmina Reza
1997	How I Learned to Drive	Paula Vogel
1996	Seven Guitars	August Wilson
1995	Arcardia	Tom Stoppard
1994	Three Tall Women	Edward Albee
1993	Angels in America: Millennium Approaches	Tony Kushner
1992	Dancing At Lughnasa	Brian Friel

* Award was for "Best Play" prior to 1996

THE 10 LATEST TONY AWARDS FOR AN ACTOR

YEAR	ACTOR	PLAY
2001	Richard Easton	The Invention of Love
2000	Stephen Dillane	The Real Thing
1999	Brian Dennehy	Death of a Salesman
1998	Anthony LaPaglia	A View From the Bridge
1997	Christopher Plummer	Barrymore
1996	George Grizzard	A Delicate Balance
1995	Ralph Fiennes	Hamlet
1994	Stephen Spinella	Angels in America Part II: Perestroika
1993	Ron Leibman	Angels in America Part I: Millennium Approaches
1992	Judd Hirsch	Conversations with My Father

Film of the Year

TOP 10 FILMS OF THE 1990s

YEAR	FILM
1999	Star Wars: Episode I – The Phantom Menace
1998	Armageddon
1997	Titanic
1996	Independence Day
1995	Die Hard: With a Vengeance
1994	The Lion King
1993	Jurassic Park
1992	Aladdin
1991	Terminator 2: Judgement Day
1990	Home Alone

TOP 10 FILMS OF THE 1970s

YEAR	FILM
1979	Moonraker
1978	Grease
1977	Star Wars
1976	Rocky
1975	Jaws
1974	Blazing Saddles
1973	The Exorcist
1972	The Godfather
1971	Diamonds Are Forever
1970	Love Story

TOP 10 FILMS OF THE 1960s

YEAR	FILM
1969	Butch Cassidy and the Sundance Kid
1968	The Graduate
1967	The Jungle Book
1966	Hawaii
1965	The Sound of Music
1964	Goldfinger
1963	Cleopatra
1962	Dr. No
1961	One Hundred and One Dalmatians
1960	Let's Make Love

TOP 10 FILMS OF THE 1980s

YEAR	FILM
1989	Indiana Jones and the Last Crusade
1988	Rain Man
1987	Fatal Attraction
1986	Top Gun
1985	Back to the Future
1984	Indiana Jones and the Temple of Doom
1983	Star Wars: Episode VI – Return of the Jedi
1982	ET: the Extra-Terrestrial
1981	Raiders of the Lost Ark
1980	Star Wars: Episode V – The Empire Strikes Back

Keeping up with the Joneses
All three Indiana Jones films figure in the Top 10 of the 1980s. Harrison Ford starred in them, as well as appearing in the two *Star Wars* films released in the same decade.

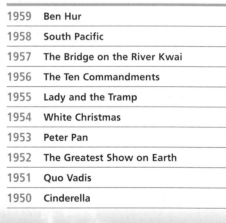

TOP 10 FILMS OF THE 1950s

YEAR	FILM
1959	Ben Hur
1958	South Pacific
1957	The Bridge on the River Kwai
1956	The Ten Commandments
1955	Lady and the Tramp
1954	White Christmas
1953	Peter Pan
1952	The Greatest Show on Earth
1951	Quo Vadis
1950	Cinderella

TOP 10 FILMS OF THE 1940s

YEAR	FILM
1949	Samson & Delilah
1948	The Red Shoes
1947	Welcome Stranger
1946	Song of the South
1945	The Bells of St. Mary's
1944	Mom and Dad
1943	This is the Army
1942	Bambi
1941	Sergeant York
1940	Pinocchio

Monster Smash

Frankenstein was the film hit of 1931. In the film, British actor Boris Karloff (born William Henry Pratt) created one of the most enduring screen images ever, in his definitive portrayal of the monster.

TOP 10 FILMS OF THE 1930s

YEAR	FILM
1939	Gone with the Wind
1938	Boys Town
1937	Snow White and the Seven Dwarfs
1936	San Francisco
1935	The Woman in Red
1934	Viva Villa!
1933	42nd Street
1932	The Kid from Spain
1931	Frankenstein
1930	All Quiet on the Western Front

Film Hits

TOP 10 HIGHEST-GROSSING FILMS

FILM	YEAR	GROSS INCOME ($) US	WORLD TOTAL
1 Titanic	1997	600,800,000	1,835,400,000
2 Harry Potter and the Sorcerer's Stone	2001	317,000,000	954,700,000
3 Star Wars: Episode I – The Phantom Menace	1999	431,100,000	925,500,000
4 Jurassic Park	1993	357,100,000	920,100,000
5 The Lord of the Rings: The Fellowship of the Ring	2001	305,800,000	816,800,000
6 Independence Day	1996	306,200,000	809,400,000
7 Star Wars	1977/97	461,000,000	798,000,000
8 The Lion King	1994	312,900,000	771,900,000
9 E.T.: The Extra-Terrestrial	1982	431,200,000	735,500,000
10 Forrest Gump	1994	329,700,000	679,700,000

TOP 10 FILM SEQUELS THAT EARNED THE GREATEST AMOUNT MORE THAN THE ORIGINAL*

ORIGINAL	HIGHEST-EARNING SEQUEL
1 The Terminator	Terminator 2: Judgment Day
2 First Blood	Rambo: First Blood Part II
3 Lethal Weapon	Lethal Weapon 3
4 Austin Powers: International Man of Mystery	Austin Powers: The Spy Who Shagged Me
5 Die Hard	Die Hard: With a Vengeance
6 Rocky	Rocky IV
7 Toy Story	Toy Story 2
8 Star Wars	Star Wars: Episode I – The Phantom Menace
9 Raiders of the Lost Ark	Indiana Jones and the Last Crusade
10 Ace Ventura: Pet Detective	Ace Ventura: When Nature Calls

Ranked by differential between original and highest-earning sequel by global box office income

TOP 10 OPENING WEEKENDS IN THE US

FILM	RELEASE DATE	OPENING WEEKEND GROSS ($)
1 Spider-Man	May 3, 2002	114,844,116
2 Harry Potter and the Sorcerer's Stone	Nov 16, 2001	90,294,621
3 The Lost World: Jurassic Park	May 23, 1997	90,161,880
4 Men in Black	Jul 4, 1997	84,133,900
5 Pearl Harbor	May 25, 2001	75,177,654
6 Mission: Impossible II	May 26, 2000	70,816,215
7 Planet of the Apes	Jul 27, 2001	68,532,960
8 The Mummy Returns	May 4, 2001	68,139,035
9 Rush Hour 2	Aug 3, 2001	67,408,222
10 The Lord of the Rings: The Fellowship of the Ring	Dec 21, 2001	66,114,741

A high-earning opening weekend (generally 3 days, Friday to Sunday, but sometimes a 4-day holiday weekend) in the US is usually a pointer to the ongoing success of a film, but does not guarantee it. Conversely, a film may start its run relatively quietly and then gather momentum: *Titanic* earned only $28,638,131 on its opening weekend (December 19, 1997), but has gone on to become the highest-earning film of all time. In 2002, *Spider-Man* broke all records, becoming the first film ever to earn more than $100 million in its opening weekend.

TOP 10 FILM SERIES

FILM SERIES	RELEASE YEARS
1 Star Wars/The Empire Strikes Back/Return of the Jedi/Star Wars: Episode I – The Phantom Menace	1977–99
2 Jurassic Park/The Lost World: Jurassic Park/ Jurassic Park III	1993–2001
3 Batman/Batman Returns/Batman Forever/ Batman & Robin	1989–97
4 Raiders of the Lost Ark/Indiana Jones and the Temple of Doom/Indiana Jones and the Last Crusade	1981–89
5 Mission: Impossible/Mission: Impossible 2	1996–2000
6 Star Trek I–VI/Generations/First Contact/Insurrection	1979–98
7 Back to the Future I–III	1985–90
8 Lethal Weapon 1–4	1987–98
9 Toy Story/Toy Story 2	1995–99
10 The Mummy/The Mummy Returns	1995–2001

Based on total earnings of the original film and all its sequels up to 1999, Steven Spielberg's *Star Wars* sequence beats his *Jurassic Park* and its sequels *The Lost World: Jurassic Park* and *Jurassic Park III*. Each of the other series films in the Top 10 have achieved cumulative global earnings of more than $800 million, and have made a total of $12,500 million between them. The James Bond films are not presented as sequels, but if they were taken into account, their overall world earnings would easily place them at the head of this list.

TOP 10 FILMS OF 2001* IN THE US

	FILM	US BOX OFFICE GROSS ($)
1	Harry Potter and the Sorcerer's Stone	317,000,000
2	The Lord of the Rings: The Fellowship of the Ring	305,800,000
3	Shrek	267,700,000
4	Monsters, Inc.	253,000,000
5	Rush Hour 2	226,100,000
6	The Mummy Returns	202,200,000
7	Pearl Harbor	198,500,000
8	Jurassic Park III	181,200,000
9	Planet of the Apes	180,000,000
10	Hannibal	165,100,000

* Release year; earnings of some continued into 2002

Fairy-tale Film
Shrek, the ogre voiced by Mike Myers, is the eponymous hero of the award-winning computer-animated blockbuster.

Film Genres

TOP 10 FILMS ADAPTED FROM COMICS

	FILM*	COMIC FIRST PUBLISHED	FILM RELEASED
1	Men in Black	1990	1997
2	Batman	1939	1989
3	The Mask	1991	1994
4	Superman	1938	1978
5	X-Men	1963	2000
6	Casper	1949	1995#
7	Teenage Mutant Ninja Turtles	1984	1990
8	The Addams Family	1937	1991
9	Dick Tracy	1931	1990
10	Blade	1994	1998

* If series, highest earning only

 # Original film made 1946

The transition from cartoons and comic strips to film has been commonplace since the 1920s, and there are many popular predecessors to those appearing in the Top 10 (each of which earned over $125 million at the global box office), from *Flash Gordon* (comic strip 1934, first film 1936) to *Barbarella* (1962/1967).

TOP 10 SPORTS FILMS

	FILM/SPORT	YEAR OF RELEASE
1	Rocky IV, boxing	1985
2	Jerry Maguire, football	1996
3	Space Jam, basketball	1996
4	The Waterboy, football	1998
5	Days of Thunder, stock car racing	1990
6	Cool Runnings, bobsled	1993
7	A League of Their Own, baseball	1992
8	Remember the Titans, football	2000
9	Rocky III, boxing	1982
10	Rocky V, boxing	1990

Protecting the Earth
Agents K and J (Tommy Lee Jones and Will Smith) save the world from destruction in *Men in Black*, the most successful of all comic-to-screen adaptations.

TOP 10 HORROR FILMS

	FILM	YEAR
1	Jurassic Park	1993
2	The Sixth Sense	1999
3	The Lost World: Jurassic Park	1997
4	Jaws	1975
5	The Mummy Returns	2001
6	The Mummy	1999
7	Godzilla	1998
8	Hannibal	2001
9	The Exorcist	1973
10	Scary Movie	2000

Each of the films listed has earned $275 million or more at the world box office.

FIRST WESTERNS

TWO MILESTONE FILMS, BOTH dating from 100 years ago, mark the beginning of the Western as a film genre. The first, *Kit Carson*, presented a series of scenes, but did not follow a narrative, whereas *The Great Train Robbery* was notable as the first film to tell a story.

FIRST OR LAST

TOP 10 COWBOY AND WESTERN FILMS

	FILM	YEAR
1	Dances with Wolves	1990
2	The Mask of Zorro	1998
3	Wild Wild West	1999
4	Maverick	1994
5	City Slickers	1991
6	Legends of the Fall	1994
7	Unforgiven	1992
8	Blazing Saddles	1974
9	Butch Cassidy and the Sundance Kid	1969
10	Shanghai Noon	2000

TOP 10 | MAGIC, WITCHES, AND WIZARDS FILMS

	FILM	YEAR
1	Harry Potter and the Sorcerer's Stone	2001
2	The Lord of the Rings: The Fellowship of the Ring	2001
3	Shrek*	2001
4	Beauty and the Beast*	1991
5	The Blair Witch Project	1999
6	Sleepy Hollow	1999
7	Snow White and the Seven Dwarfs*	1937
8	Practical Magic	1998
9	Fantasia*	1940
10	The Witches of Eastwick	1987

* Animated

Ringing Success
Ian MacKellen, seen here as the wizard Gandalf the Grey, starred in the first film in *The Lord of the Rings* trilogy, which earned international success.

TOP 10 | WAR FILMS

	FILM	YEAR
1	Saving Private Ryan	1998
2	Pearl Harbor	2001
3	Schindler's List	1993
4	The Patriot	2000
5	Braveheart	1995
6	Hot Shots!	1991
7	Born on the Fourth of July	1999
8	Platoon	1986
9	Good Morning, Vietnam	1987
10	U-571	2000

Until the hugely successful *Saving Private Ryan*, surprisingly few war films appeared in the high-earning bracket in recent years, leading some to feel that the days of big-budget films in this genre were over. Recent blockbusters, including "historical" war films such as Mel Gibson's 2 notable successes, *Braveheart* and *The Patriot*, and *Pearl Harbor*, appear to have disproved this prediction. This list excludes successful films that are not technically "war" films but which have military themes, such as *Top Gun* (1986), which would otherwise appear in the Top 10.

Comedy Strip

Gross Income
There's Something About Mary is the leader among gross-out classics. Its international appeal has earned it box office income in excess of $350 million worldwide.

TOP 10 GROSS-OUT COMEDY FILMS

FILM	YEAR
1 There's Something About Mary	1998
2 Austin Powers: The Spy Who Shagged Me	1999
3 Scary Movie	2000
4 Dumb & Dumber	1994
5 Big Daddy	1999
6 American Pie	1999
7 The Waterboy	1998
8 Nutty Professor II: The Klumps	2000
9 Me, Myself & Irene	2000
10 American Pie 2	2001

"Gross-out" films represent a new wave of films featuring outrageous juvenile comedy for teens and adults, generally revolving around disgusting behavior and often involving bodily functions.

TOP 10 COMEDY FILMS

FILM	YEAR
1 Forrest Gump	1994
2 Men in Black	1997
3 Home Alone	1990
4 Ghost	1990
5 Pretty Woman	1990
6 Mrs. Doubtfire	1993
7 What Women Want	2001
8 Notting Hill	1999
9 There's Something About Mary	1998
10 Flintstones	1995

Since the earliest days of Hollywood, comedy has consistently performed well at the box office. Of the Top 10, each of the first 4 has earned in excess of half a billion dollars globally, while the rest lag not far behind.

TOP 10 JIM CARREY FILMS

FILM	YEAR
1 Batman Forever	1995
2 The Mask	1994
3 Dr. Seuss' How the Grinch Stole Christmas	2000
4 Liar Liar	1997
5 The Truman Show	1998
6 Dumb & Dumber	1994
7 Ace Ventura: When Nature Calls	1995
8 Me, Myself & Irene	2000
9 The Cable Guy	1996
10 Ace Ventura: Pet Detective	1994

Canadian-born Carrey has appeared in more than 20 Hollywood films – 9 of them earning over $100 million each.

CHARLIE CHAPLIN

At the age of 14, British-born Charlie Chaplin (1889–1977) made his debut in London 100 years ago. He appeared as Sammy in the play *Jim, A Romance of Cockayne*, which opened on July 6, 1903 at the Royal County Theatre, Kingston, England. He then got the part of Billy, a newspaper boy, in *Sherlock Holmes*, which started its run at the Pavilion Theatre in London's East End before going on tour. Chaplin's stage experience coincided with the early years of film, and a decade later he arrived in Hollywood, destined to become the most famous comedy star of the silent screen.

TOP 10 WHOOPI GOLDBERG FILMS

	FILM	YEAR
1	Ghost	1990
2	Sister Act	1992
3	The Color Purple*	1985
4	Star Trek: Generations	1994
5	Made in America	1993
6	In & Out	1997
7	Sister Act 2: Back in the Habit	1993
8	Rat Race	2001
9	The Little Rascals	1994
10	How Stella Got Her Groove Back	1998

* Academy Award nomination for "Best Actress"

Whoopi Goldberg provided the voice of Shenzi in *The Lion King* (1994). If that were taken into account, it would appear in the No. 1 position in her Top 10. Her voice was also that of Ranger Margaret in *The Rugrats Movie* (1998), which would appear in fourth position.

TOP 10 ROBIN WILLIAMS FILMS

	FILM	YEAR
1	Mrs. Doubtfire	1993
2	Hook	1991
3	Jumanji	1995
4	Dead Poets' Society	1989
5	Good Will Hunting*	1997
6	Patch Adams	1998
7	The Birdcage	1995
8	Flubber	1997
9	Nine Months	1995
10	Good Morning, Vietnam	1987

* Academy Award for "Best Supporting Actor"

Robin Williams (born July 21, 1952, Chicago, Illinois) first came to public attention on TV through his appearances in *Rowan and Martin's Laugh-In* and as the alien Mork in *Mork and Mindy*. Since then he has made numerous films, typically playing crazed individuals – such as the DJ in *Good Morning, Vietnam*, and the down-and-out in *The Fisher King*.

TOP 10 PETER SELLERS FILMS

	FILM	YEAR
1	The Revenge of the Pink Panther	1978
2	The Return of the Pink Panther	1974
3	The Pink Panther Strikes Again	1976
4	Murder by Death	1976
5	Being There	1979
6	Casino Royale	1967
7	What's New, Pussycat?	1965
8	A Shot in the Dark	1964
9	The Pink Panther	1963
10	=Dr. Strangelove	1963
	=The Fiendish Plot of Dr. Fu Manchu	1980

In the Pink
Peter Sellers' role as the bungling Inspector Clouseau earned the *Pink Panther* films five of the places in his Top 10 most popular films list.

Animated Films

THE 10 | LATEST OSCAR-WINNING ANIMATED FILMS*

YEAR	FILM	DIRECTOR/COUNTRY
2001	For the Birds	Ralph Eggleston, US
2000	Father and Daughter	Michael Dudok de Wit, Netherlands
1999	The Old Man and the Sea	Aleksandr Petrov, US
1998	Bunny	Chris Wedge, US
1997	Geri's Game	Jan Pinkava, US
1996	Quest	Tyron Montgomery, UK
1995	Wallace & Gromit: A Close Shave	Nick Park, UK
1994	Bob's Birthday	David Fine and Alison Snowden, UK
1993	Wallace & Gromit: The Wrong Trousers	Nick Park, UK
1992	Mona Lisa Descending a Staircase	Joan C. Gratz, US

In the category "Short Films (Animated)"

TOP 10 | ANIMATED FILM BUDGETS

	FILM	YEAR	BUDGET ($)
1	Tarzan	1999	150,000,000
2	Final Fantasy: The Spirits Within	2001	137,000,000
3	Dinosaur	2000	128,000,000
4	Monsters, Inc.	2001	115,000,000
5	The Emperor's New Groove	2000	100,000,000
6	=The Road to El Dorado	2000	95,000,000
	=Space Jam*	1996	95,000,000
8	=Atlantis: The Lost Empire	2001	90,000,000
	=Toy Story 2	1999	90,000,000
10	Fantasia/2000	1999	80,000,000

Part animated, part live action

Animated film budgets have come a long way since *Snow White and the Seven Dwarfs* (1937) established a record of $1,490,000. The $2,600,000 budget for *Pinocchio* (1940), and $2,280,000 for the original *Fantasia* (1940) were the 2 biggest of the 1940s, while *Sleeping Beauty* (1959) cost $6 million – the highest of the 1950s. *The Lord of the Rings* (the animated version from 1978) was probably the first animated film with a budget of over $10 million.

Short but Sweet
Although only eight minutes long, Dudok de Wit's film *Father and Daughter* has been hailed for its moving story, and is a rare example of a non-US or -UK animated Oscar winner.

TOP 10 WALT DISNEY ANIMATED FILMS

	FILM	YEAR
1	The Lion King	1994
2	Monsters, Inc.	2001
3	Aladdin	1992
4	Toy Story 2	1999
5	Tarzan	1999
6	Toy Story	1995
7	A Bug's Life	1998
8	Beauty and the Beast*	1991
9	Who Framed Roger Rabbit	1988
10	Dinosaur	2000

Part animated, part live action

Within just 2 months of its November 2, 2001 opening, *Monsters, Inc.* had earned almost $250 million at the US box office. It more than doubled that figure after its international release.

THE 10 FIRST BUGS BUNNY CARTOONS

	FILM	FIRST THEATRICAL RELEASE
1	Porky's Hare Hunt	Apr 30, 1938
2	Hare-um Scare-um	Aug 12 ,1939
3	Elmer's Candid Camera	Mar 2, 1940
4	A Wild Hare	Jul 27, 1940
5	Elmer's Pet Rabbit	Jan 4, 1941
6	Tortoise Beats Hare	Mar 15, 1941
7	Hiawatha's Rabbit Hunt	Jun 7, 1941
8	The Heckling Hare	Jul 5, 1941
9	All This and Rabbit Stew	Sep 13, 1941
10	Wabbit Twouble	Dec 20, 1941

Bugs Bunny's debut was as a costar alongside Porky Pig in *Porky's Hare Hunt*, but he was not named until the release of *Elmer's Pet Rabbit*. *A Wild Hare* was the first in which he said the line that became his trademark – "Eh, what's up, Doc?". This film was also nominated for an Oscar, as was *Hiawatha's Rabbit Hunt*. The first Bugs Bunny film to win an Oscar was *Knighty-Knight Bugs* (1958).

TOP 10 NON-DISNEY ANIMATED FEATURE FILMS

	FILM	PRODUCTION COMPANY	YEAR
1	Shrek	DreamWorks	2001
2	Space Jam*	Warner Bros.	1996
3	The Prince of Egypt	DreamWorks	1998
4	Chicken Run	DreamWorks	2000
5	Antz	DreamWorks	1998
6	Pokémon the First Movie: Mewtwo Strikes Back	4 Kids Entertainment/ Warner Bros.	1999
7	Anastasia	20th Century Fox	1997
8	Cats & Dogs	Warner Bros.	2001
9	Pokémon: Power of One (aka Pocket Monsters Revelation Lugia)	4 Kids Entertainment/ Warner Bros.	1999
10	Rugrats in Paris: The Movie	Klasky-Csupo/ Paramount Pictures	2000

Part animated, part live action

Fowl Play
Doyen of claymation, Aardman Animations was responsible for creating *Chicken Run*, which earned back over four times its $42 million budget at the world box office.

Leading Men

TOP 10 NICOLAS CAGE FILMS

	FILM TITLE	YEAR
1	The Rock	1996
2	Face/Off	1997
3	Gone in 60 Seconds	2000
4	Con Air	1997
5	City of Angels	1998
6	The Family Man	2000
7	Snake Eyes	1998
8	8MM	1999
9	Moonstruck	1987
10	Leaving Las Vegas*	1995

* Won Academy Award for "Best Actor"

TOP 10 RUSSELL CROWE FILMS

	FILM TITLE	YEAR
1	Gladiator*	2000
2	A Beautiful Mind#	2001
3	L.A. Confidential	1997
4	The Insider#	1999
5	The Quick and the Dead	1995
6	Proof of Life	2000
7	Virtuosity	1995
8	Mystery, Alaska	1999
9	The Sum of Us	1994
10	Proof	1991

* Won Academy Award for "Best Actor"

 # Nominated for Academy Award for "Best Actor"

TOP 10 MEL GIBSON FILMS

	FILM TITLE	YEAR
1	What Women Want	2000
2	Ransom	1996
3	Lethal Weapon 4	1998
4	The Patriot	2000
5	Braveheart*	1995
6	Payback	1999
7	Lethal Weapon 2	1989
8	Lethal Weapon 3	1992
9	Conspiracy Theory	1997
10	Forever Young	1992

* Won Academy Award for "Best Director" and "Best Picture" (shared with Alan Ladd Jr. and Bruce Davey)

Mel Gibson also provided the voices of John Smith in *Pocahontas* (1995) and Rocky Rhodes, the Rhode Island Red Rooster, in *Chicken Run* (2000), and appeared, uncredited, as himself in *Casper* (1995). If included, these would all merit prominent inclusion in his Top 10 films, each of which has earned more than $100 million at the world box office.

TOP 10 TOM CRUISE FILMS

	FILM TITLE	YEAR
1	Mission: Impossible II	2000
2	Mission: Impossible	1996
3	Rain Man	1988
4	Top Gun	1986
5	Jerry Maguire*	1996
6	The Firm	1993
7	A Few Good Men	1992
8	Interview with the Vampire: The Vampire Chronicles	1994
9	Vanilla Sky	2001
10	Days of Thunder	1990

* Nominated for Academy Award for "Best Actor"

Mind Games
Russell Crowe stars as game theory mathematician John Forbes Nash in "Best Picture" Oscar winner, *A Beautiful Mind*.

TOP 10 HUGH GRANT FILMS

	FILM TITLE	YEAR
1	Notting Hill	1999
2	Bridget Jones's Diary	2001
3	Four Weddings and a Funeral	1994
4	Sense and Sensibility	1995
5	Nine Months	1995
6	Mickey Blue Eyes	1999
7	The Remains of the Day	1993
8	Extreme Measures	1996
9	Small Time Crooks	2000
10	The Englishman Who Went Up a Hill But Came Down a Mountain	1995

TOP 10 TOM HANKS FILMS

	FILM TITLE	YEAR
1	Forrest Gump*	1994
2	Saving Private Ryan#	1998
3	Cast Away#	2000
4	Apollo 13	1995
5	The Green Mile	1999
6	You've Got M@il	1998
7	Sleepless in Seattle	1993
8	Philadelphia*	1993
9	Big#	1988
10	A League of Their Own	1992

* Won Academy Award for "Best Actor"

Nominated for Academy Award for "Best Actor"

Tom Hanks also appeared in a voice-only part as Woody in *Toy Story 2* (1999) and *Toy Story* (1995). If included, these would be ranked in third and fifth places respectively in his personal Top 10, every one of which has earned more than $100 million worldwide.

Leading Ladies

TOP 10 DREW BARRYMORE FILMS

FILM	YEAR
1 E.T.: The Extra-Terrestrial	1982
2 Batman Forever	1995
3 Charlie's Angels	2000
4 Scream	1996
5 The Wedding Singer	1998
6 Ever After	1998
7 Never Been Kissed	1999
8 Wayne's World 2	1993
9 Everyone Says I Love You	1996
10 Riding in Cars with Boys	2001

Angel Face
Even popular films such as *Charlie's Angels* cannot match the success of *E.T.*, which Drew Barrymore made at the age of seven.

TOP 10 JULIANNE MOORE FILMS

FILM	YEAR
1 The Lost World: Jurassic Park	1997
2 The Fugitive	1993
3 Hannibal	2001
4 Nine Months	1995
5 The Hand That Rocks the Cradle	1992
6 Assassins	1995
7 Evolution	2001
8 Magnolia	1999
9 Boogie Nights*	1997
10 The Big Lebowski	1998

* Nominated for Academy Award for "Best Supporting Actress"

Julianne Moore was also nominated for a "Best Actress" Oscar for her role in *The End of the Affair* (1999), a movie that fails to make her Top 10.

TOP 10 JULIA ROBERTS FILMS

FILM	YEAR
1 Pretty Woman*	1990
2 Ocean's Eleven	2001
3 Notting Hill	1999
4 Hook	1991
5 My Best Friend's Wedding	1997
6 Runaway Bride	1999
7 Erin Brockovich#	2000
8 The Pelican Brief	1993
9 Sleeping with the Enemy	1991
10 Stepmom	1998

* Nominated for Academy Award for "Best Actress"
\# Won Academy Award for "Best Actress"

Although one of the earliest films in Julia Roberts' meteoric movie career, *Pretty Woman* remains her most successful. It is the 30th highest-earning film of all time.

TOP 10 KATE WINSLET FILMS

FILM TITLE	YEAR
1 Titanic*	1997
2 Sense and Sensibility#	1995
3 Quills	2000
4 A Kid in King Arthur's Court	1995
5 Enigma	2001
6 Iris†	2001
7 Hamlet	1996
8 Holy Smoke	1999
9 Heavenly Creatures	1994
10 Hideous Kinky	1998

* Nominated for Academy Award for "Best Actress"
\# Nominated for Academy Award for "Best Supporting Actress"
† Nominated for Academy Award for "Best Supporting Actress"

TOP 10 CAMERON DIAZ FILMS

FILM	YEAR
1 There's Something About Mary	1998
2 The Mask	1994
3 My Best Friend's Wedding	1997
4 Charlie's Angels	2000
5 Vanilla Sky	2001
6 Any Given Sunday	1999
7 Being John Malkovich	1999
8 A Life Less Ordinary	1997
9 She's the One	1996
10 Fear and Loathing in Las Vegas	1998

Cameron Diaz's career took off immediately when her debut *The Mask* became a box office smash and saw her nominated for three MTV movie awards. Cameron Diaz provided the voice of Princess Fiona in the animated blockbuster *Shrek* (2001), which, if included, would appear at No. 1.

FILM	YEAR
1 Se7en	1995
2 Hook	1991
3 Shakespeare in Love*	1998
4 A Perfect Murder	1998
5 The Talented Mr. Ripley	1999
6 Shallow Hal	2001
7 Sliding Doors	1998
8 Great Expectations	1998
9 The Royal Tenenbaums	2001
10 Malice	1993

* Won Academy Award for "Best Actress"

Although Gwyneth Paltrow's debut *Shout* (1991) failed to achieve commercial success, her subsequent career has seen her become one of the few actresses today capable of commanding a salary of over $10 million per movie.

NICOLE KIDMAN
FILMS

FILM	YEAR
1 Batman Forever	1995
2 Moulin Rouge!*	2001
3 The Others	2001
4 Days of Thunder	1990
5 Eyes Wide Shut	1999
6 The Peacemaker	1997
7 Practical Magic	1998
8 Far and Away	1992
9 Malice	1993
10 To Die For	1995

* Nominated for Academy Award for "Best Actress"

Here's Looking at you, Kidman
Nicole Kidman appeared as Satine in Baz Luhrmann's award-winning Bohemian spectacular, *Moulin Rouge!*

173

Yesterday's Stars

TOP 10 FILMS DIRECTED BY BILLY WILDER

	FILM	YEAR
1	Some Like It Hot	1959
2	Irma la Douce	1963
3	The Front Page	1974
4	The Apartment	1960
5	The Seven Year Itch	1955
6	The Lost Weekend	1945
7	The Emperor Waltz	1948
8	Sabrina	1954
9	Witness for the Prosecution	1957
10	Stalag 17	1953

TOP 10 AUDREY HEPBURN FILMS

	FILM	YEAR
1	My Fair Lady	1964
2	Always	1989
3	Wait until Dark	1967
4	Charade	1963
5	War and Peace	1956
6	The Nun's Story	1959
7	Bloodline	1979
8	How to Steal a Million	1966
9	Breakfast at Tiffany's	1961
10	Robin and Marian	1976

TOP 10 JOHN WAYNE FILMS

	FILM	YEAR
1	How the West Was Won	1962
2	The Longest Day	1962
3	True Grit	1969
4	The Green Berets	1968
5	The Alamo	1960
6	The Cowboys	1972
7	Big Jake	1971
8	Rooster Cogburn	1975
9	Hatari!	1962
10	The Greatest Story Ever Told	1965

John Wayne was one of Hollywood's most prolific actors, making more than 150 films during a career that spanned 48 years. He is chiefly remembered for his tough-guy roles as a soldier or cowboy. Curiously, in many of his roles he had a Scottish name: for example, his title roles in *Big Jim McLain* (1952), *McLintock* (1963), and *McQ* (1974). Occasionally he found himself badly miscast – one prime example of miscasting was when he played Genghis Khan in *The Conqueror* (1955).

TOP 10 MARILYN MONROE FILMS

	FILM	YEAR
1	Some Like It Hot	1959
2	How to Marry a Millionaire	1953
3	The Seven Year Itch	1955
4	Gentlemen Prefer Blondes	1953
5	There's No Business Like Show Business	1954
6	Bus Stop	1956
7	The Misfits	1961
8	River of No Return	1954
9	All About Eve	1950
10	Let's Make Love	1960

Ladies First
Tony Curtis disguised as "Josephine" and Jack Lemmon as "Daphne," shown here in Billy Wilder's *Some Like It Hot*. This film was voted "The Funniest Film Ever Made" by the American Film Institute.

TOP 10 FILMS DIRECTED BY ALFRED HITCHCOCK

	FILM	YEAR
1	Psycho	1960
2	Rear Window	1954
3	North by Northwest	1959
4	Family Plot	1976
5	Torn Curtain	1966
6	Frenzy	1972
7	Vertigo	1958
8	The Man Who Knew Too Much	1956
9	The Birds	1963
10	Spellbound	1945

TOP 10 CARY GRANT FILMS

	FILM	YEAR
1	That's Entertainment!	1974
2	Operation Petticoat	1959
3	That Touch of Mink	1962
4	North by Northwest	1959
5	Charade	1963
6	The Bachelor and the Bobby-Soxer	1947
7	Father Goose	1964
8	Notorious	1946
9	To Catch a Thief	1955
10	I Was a Male War Bride	1949

Psycho-killer
Anthony Perkins played the chilling and now legendary role of Norman Bates, hotelier and murderer, in *Psycho* – Alfred Hitchcock's most successful film.

FIRST MOVIE STAR

THE FIRST MOVIE star and first cowboy hero emerged exactly 100 years ago in 1903, when Gilbert Max "Broncho Billy" Anderson appeared in the Thomas Edison Company's film *The Great Train Robbery*. The first Western and the first film to tell a story, it was made in New Jersey with a budget of just $150. Anderson (1880–1971) took three parts in the film and went on to star as Broncho Billy in hundreds of Westerns up to 1916.

FIRST OR LAST

Today's Directors

THE 10 | LATEST WINNERS OF THE DIRECTORS GUILD OF AMERICA LIFETIME ACHIEVEMENT AWARD*

YEAR	RECIPIENT
2000	Steven Spielberg
1998	Francis Ford Coppola
1997	Stanley Kubrick
1996	Woody Allen
1995	James Ivory
1994	Robert Altman
1993	Sidney Lumet
1992	Akira Kurosawa
1990	Ingmar Bergman

* The D. W. Griffith Award for Distinguished Achievement in Motion Picture Directing until 1999

The DGA's Lifetime Achievement Award is a highly prestigious award that is presented at irregular intervals. Its name was changed in 1999 because of concerns over D. W. Griffith's promotion of racial stereotypes, although his importance as a pioneering filmmaker remains undisputed.

TOP 10 | FILMS DIRECTED BY ACTORS

FILM/YEAR	DIRECTOR
1 **Armageddon,** 1998	Michael Bay
2 **Pretty Woman,** 1990	Garry Marshall
3 **Dances With Wolves,** 1990	Kevin Costner
4 **The Bodyguard,** 1992	Kevin Costner
5 **Pearl Harbor,** 2001	Michael Bay
6 **Dr. Seuss's How the Grinch Stole Christmas,** 2000	Ron Howard
7 **Apollo 13,** 1995	Ron Howard
8 **The Rock,** 1996	Michael Bay
9 **Ransom,** 1996	Ron Howard
10 **Rocky IV,** 1985	Sylvester Stallone

The role of actor-director has a long tradition, including such names as Charlie Chaplin, Buster Keaton, Orson Welles, and John Huston. All those in the Top 10 have combined the two professions in films that have each earned more than $300 million at the world box office.

TOP 10 | FILMS DIRECTED BY WOMEN

FILM/YEAR	DIRECTOR
1 **Shrek,** 2001	Vicky Jenson
2 **Deep Impact,** 1998	Mimi Leder
3 **Look Who's Talking,** 1989	Amy Heckerling
4 **Doctor Dolittle,** 1998	Betty Thomas
5 **Sleepless in Seattle,** 1993	Nora Ephron
6 **The Prince of Egypt,** 1998	Brenda Chapman*
7 **What Women Want,** 2000	Nancy Meyers
8 **The Birdcage,** 1996	Elaine May
9 **Bridget Jones's Diary,** 2001	Sharon Maguire
10 **You've Got M@il,** 1998	Nora Ephron

* Codirector

Woman directors worked in the film industry from its early years. Dorothy Arzner (1897–1979) was the first woman to direct a talkie (*The Wild Party,* 1929), as well as introducing the overhead ("boom") microphone. Her successors have been responsible for many major blockbusters – all those movies listed here have earned more than $100 million each worldwide.

TOP 10 | FILMS DIRECTED BY RON HOWARD

FILM	YEAR
1 **Dr. Seuss's How the Grinch Stole Christmas**	2000
2 **Apollo 13**	1995
3 **Ransom**	1996
4 **A Beautiful Mind***	2001
5 **Backdraft**	1991
6 **Parenthood**	1989
7 **Cocoon**	1985
8 **Splash**	1984
9 **Far and Away**	1992
10 **Willow**	1988

* Won Academy Award for "Best Director" and "Best Picture"

You Better Watch Out

Ron Howard's most successful film, *Dr. Seuss's How the Grinch Stole Christmas,* has taken over $340 million worldwide.

Breaking the Silence
Anthony Hopkins receives direction from Ridley Scott on the set of *Hannibal*, the sequel to *The Silence of the Lambs*.

TOP 10 | FILMS DIRECTED BY RIDLEY SCOTT

	FILM	YEAR
1	Gladiator	2000
2	Hannibal	2001
3	Alien	1979
4	Black Hawk Down	2001
5	Black Rain	1989
6	G.I. Jane	1997
7	Thelma & Louise	1991
8	Blade Runner	1982
9	Legend	1985
10	White Squall	1996

British director Ridley Scott began his career in television, but has been directing films since the late 1970s, when *Alien* started a run of box office successes.

TOP 10 | FILMS DIRECTED BY ROBERT ZEMECKIS

	FILM	YEAR
1	Forrest Gump	1994
2	Back to the Future	1985
3	Who Framed Roger Rabbit	1988
4	Back to the Future Part II	1989
5	Cast Away	2000
6	What Lies Beneath	2000
7	Back to the Future Part III	1990
8	Contact	1997
9	Death Becomes Her	1992
10	Romancing the Stone	1984

Prolific writer-director Zemeckis is notable for his use of special effects in his impressive catalog of comedy and science-fiction blockbusters.

TOP 10 | FILMS DIRECTED BY CHRISTOPHER COLUMBUS

	FILM	YEAR
1	Harry Potter and the Sorcerer's Stone	2001
2	Home Alone	1990
3	Mrs. Doubtfire	1993
4	Home Alone 2: Lost in New York	1992
5	Stepmom	1998
6	Nine Months	1995
7	Bicentennial Man	1999
8	Adventures in Babysitting	1987
9	Only the Lonely	1991
10	Heartbreak Hotel	1988

The Studios

TOP 10 DREAMWORKS FILMS

	FILM	YEAR
1	Saving Private Ryan*	1998
2	Shrek	2001
3	Gladiator*	2000
4	Deep Impact*	1998
5	American Beauty	1999
6	What Lies Beneath*	2000
7	Artificial Intelligence: AI	2001
8	The Prince of Egypt	1998
9	The Haunting	1990
10	Chicken Run	2000

Coproduction with another studio

TOP 10 UNIVERSAL FILMS

	FILM	YEAR
1	Jurassic Park	1993
2	E.T. the Extra-Terrestrial	1982
3	The Lost World: Jurassic Park	1997
4	Jaws	1975
5	The Mummy Returns	2001
6	The Mummy	1999
7	The Flintstones	1994
8	Notting Hill	1999
9	Back to the Future	1985
10	Dr. Seuss's How the Grinch Stole Christmas	2000

Universal Pictures was founded in 1912 by Carl Laemmle, who soon developed it into the world's largest film studio. After changing hands a number of times, it was sold to MCA and developed its strengths as a TV production company, inaugurating the studio tours that are now one of the leading tourist attractions in the US. Films from artists like Alfred Hitchcock and Clint Eastwood were followed by some of the highest-earning films of all time.

War Winner
Tom Hanks played Captain John Miller in *Saving Private Ryan*. Dreamworks' most successful film was a coproduction with Paramount Pictures and Amblin.

TOP 10 DIMENSION FILMS

	FILM	YEAR
1	Scary Movie	2000
2	Scream	1996
3	Scream 2	1997
4	Scream 3	2000
5	Scary Movie 2	2001
6	Spy Kids	2001
7	Halloween H2O	1998
8	The Faculty	1998
9	From Dusk Till Dawn	1996
10	Wes Craven Presents Dracula 2000	2000

TOP 10 STUDIOS/ DISTRIBUTORS, 2001

STUDIO	US BOX OFFICE GROSS IN 2001 ($)	MARKET SHARE %
1 Warner Bros.	1,266,300,000	15.00
2 Universal	1,004,300,000	11.90
3 Paramount	966,600,000	11.45
4 20th Century Fox	937,200,000	11.10
5 Buena Vista	925,500,000	10.97
6 Sony	744,500,000	8.82
7 New Line	558,100,000	6.61
8 MGM/United Artists	445,200,000	5.28
9 DreamWorks	400,400,000	4.74
10 Dimension	350,200,000	4.15

Total US gross for all studios/distributors in 2001 was estimated as $8,439,081,112 (an increase of more than $1 billion over the previous years), of which the Top 10 earned $7,598,300,000, or 90 percent of the total. The former clear-cut distinction between production companies, studios, and distributors is becoming increasingly blurred, with, for example, certain studios acting as distributors for films made by other studios.

Sweet Success
Juliet Binoche was nominated for a "Best Actress" Oscar for her role in the Miramax film *Chocolat*.

TOP 10 WARNER BROS. FILMS

FILM	YEAR
1 Harry Potter and the Sorcerer's Stone	2001
2 Twister	1996
3 The Matrix	1999
4 Batman	1989
5 The Bodyguard	1992
6 Robin Hood: Prince of Thieves	1991
7 The Fugitive	1993
8 Batman Forever	1995
9 The Perfect Storm	2000
10 Lethal Weapon 3	1992

Founded in 1923 by the Warner brothers, the studio was responsible for such classic films as *Casablanca* and *The Jazz Singer*.

TOP 10 MIRAMAX FILMS

FILM	YEAR
1 Shakespeare in Love	1998
2 The English Patient	1996
3 Good Will Hunting	1997
4 Pulp Fiction	1994
5 The Others	2001
6 Chocolat	2000
7 The Talented Mr. Ripley	1999
8 She's All That	1999
9 The Cider House Rules	1999
10 Jackie Brown	1997

The Weinstein brothers founded Miramax in 1979, naming it after their parents Mira and Max. Its first major success was in 1994 with *Pulp Fiction*.

TOP 10 NEW LINE FILMS

FILM	YEAR
1 The Lord of the Rings: The Fellowship of the Ring	2001
2 Se7en	1995
3 Rush Hour 2	2001
4 The Mask	1994
5 Austin Powers: The Spy who Shagged Me	1999
6 Dumb and Dumber	1994
7 Rush Hour	1998
8 Teenage Mutant Ninja Turtles	1990
9 Lost in Space	1998
10 Blade	1998

Oscar-Winning Films

The Winner
Ben-Hur won in every one of the 12 Oscar categories for which it was nominated, with the exception of "Best Adapted Screenplay."

TOP 10 FILMS TO WIN THE MOST OSCARS*

	FILM	YEAR	NOMINATIONS	AWARDS
1	=Ben-Hur	1959	12	11
	=Titanic	1997	14	11
3	West Side Story	1961	11	10
4	=Gigi	1958	9	9
	=The Last Emperor	1987	9	9
	=The English Patient	1996	12	9
7	=Gone With the Wind	1939	13	8#
	=From Here to Eternity	1953	13	8
	=On the Waterfront	1954	12	8
	=My Fair Lady	1964	12	8
	=Cabaret	1972	10	8
	=Gandhi	1982	11	8
	=Amadeus	1984	11	8

* *Oscar® is a Registered Trademark*

\# *Plus 2 special awards*

Nine other films have won 7 Oscars each: *Going My Way* (1944), *The Best Years of Our Lives* (1946), *The Bridge on the River Kwai* (1957), *Lawrence of Arabia* (1962), *Patton* (1970), *The Sting* (1973), *Out of Africa* (1985), *Dances With Wolves* (1991), and *Schindler's List* (1993) – each of the last 2 films being nominated for 12 awards. *Titanic* (1997) matched the 14 nominations of *All About Eve* (1950), but outshone it by winning 11, compared with the latter's 6.

THE 10 LATEST OSCARS FOR "BEST SCREENPLAY WRITTEN DIRECTLY FOR THE SCREEN"

YEAR	FILM	WRITER(S)
2001	Gosford Park	Julian Fellowes
2000	Almost Famous	Cameron Crowe
1999	American Beauty	Alan Ball
1998	Shakespeare in Love	Marc Norman, Tom Stoppard
1997	Good Will Hunting	Ben Affleck, Matt Damon
1996	Fargo	Ethan Coen, Joel Coen
1995	The Usual Suspects	Christopher McQuarrie
1994	Pulp Fiction	Roger Avary, Quentin Tarantino
1993	The Piano	Jane Campion
1992	The Crying Game	Neil Jordan

Class Act
Actor-turned-screenwriter Julian Fellowes gained a "Best Screenplay" Oscar for his debut film (directed by Robert Altman) *Gosford Park*.

THE 10 | LATEST "BEST DIRECTOR" OSCAR WINNERS

YEAR	DIRECTOR	FILM
2001	Ron Howard	A Beautiful Mind*
2000	Steven Soderbergh	Traffic
1999	Sam Mendes	American Beauty*
1998	Steven Spielberg	Saving Private Ryan
1997	James Cameron	Titanic*
1996	Antony Minghella	The English Patient*
1995	Mel Gibson	Braveheart*
1994	Robert Zemeckis	Forrest Gump*
1993	Steven Spielberg	Schindler's List*
1992	Clint Eastwood	Unforgiven*

* Winner of "Best Picture" Oscar

THE 10 | LATEST "BEST PICTURE" OSCAR WINNERS

YEAR	FILM
2001	A Beautiful Mind
2000	Gladiator
1999	American Beauty
1998	Shakespeare in Love
1997	Titanic
1996	The English Patient
1995	Braveheart
1994	Forrest Gump
1993	Schindler's List
1992	Unforgiven

TOP 10 | HIGHEST-EARNING "BEST PICTURE" OSCAR WINNERS

	FILM	YEAR
1	Titanic	1997
2	Forrest Gump	1994
3	Gladiator	2000
4	Dances With Wolves	1990
5	Rain Man	1988
6	Schindler's List	1993
7	Shakespeare in Love	1998
8	The English Patient	1996
9	American Beauty	1999
10	A Beautiful Mind	2001

Oscar-Winning Stars

TOP 10 | ACTORS AND ACTRESSES WITH THE MOST OSCAR NOMINATIONS

	ACTOR/ACTRESS/NOMINATION YEARS	NOMINATIONS
1	**Katharine Hepburn,** 1932–33*; 1935; 1940; 1942; 1951; 1955; 1956; 1959; 1962; 1967*; 1968*(shared); 1981*	12
2	**=Jack Nicholson,** 1969#; 1970; 1973; 1974; 1975*; 1981#; 1983*; 1985; 1987; 1992#; 1997*	11
	=Meryl Streep, 1978#; 1979*; 1981; 1982*; 1983; 1985; 1987; 1988; 1990; 1995; 1998	11
4	**=Bette Davis,** 1935*; 1938*; 1939; 1940; 1941; 1942; 1944; 1950; 1952; 1962	10
	=Laurence Olivier, 1939; 1940; 1946; 1948*; 1956; 1960; 1965; 1972; 1976#; 1978	10
6	**Spencer Tracy,** 1936; 1937*; 1938*; 1950; 1955; 1958; 1960; 1961; 1967	9
7	**=Marlon Brando,** 1951; 1952; 1953; 1954*; 1957; 1972*; 1973; 1989#	8
	=Jack Lemmon, 1955#; 1959; 1960; 1962; 1973*; 1979; 1980; 1982	8
	=Paul Newman†, 1958; 1961; 1963; 1967; 1981; 1982; 1986*; 1994	8
	=Al Pacino, 1972#; 1973; 1974; 1975; 1979; 1990#; 1992*; 1992#	8
	=Geraldine Page, 1953#; 1961; 1962; 1966; 1972; 1978; 1984; 1985*	8

* Won Academy Award in "Best" or "Best Supporting" category

\# Nomination but no win in "Best Supporting Actor" or "Best Supporting Actress"

† Also won an honorary Oscar in 1985

TOP 10 | OLDEST OSCAR-WINNING ACTORS AND ACTRESSES

	ACTOR/ACTRESS	AWARD/FILM	YEAR	AGE*
1	Jessica Tandy	"Best Actress" (Driving Miss Daisy)	1989	80
2	George Burns	"Best Supporting Actor" (The Sunshine Boys)	1975	80
3	Melvyn Douglas	"Best Supporting Actor" (Being There)	1979	79
4	John Gielgud	"Best Supporting Actor" (Arthur)	1981	77
5	Don Ameche	"Best Supporting Actor" (Cocoon)	1985	77
6	Peggy Ashcroft	"Best Supporting Actress" (A Passage to India)	1984	77
7	Henry Fonda	"Best Actor" (On Golden Pond)	1981	76
8	Katharine Hepburn	"Best Actress" (On Golden Pond)	1981	74
9	Edmund Gwenn	"Best Supporting Actor" (Miracle on 34th Street)	1947	72
10	Ruth Gordon	"Best Supporting Actress" (Rosemary's Baby)	1968	72

* At time of Award ceremony; those of apparently identical age have been ranked according to their precise age in days at the time of the ceremony

TOP 10 | YOUNGEST OSCAR WINNERS

	ACTOR/ACTRESS	AWARD/FILM (WHERE SPECIFIED)	YEAR	AGE*
1	Shirley Temple	Special Award – outstanding contribution during 1934	1934	6
2	Margaret O'Brien	Special Award (Meet Me in St. Louis, etc.)	1944	8
3	Vincent Winter	Special Award (The Little Kidnappers)	1954	8
4	Ivan Jandl	Special Award (The Search)	1948	9
5	Jon Whiteley	Special Award (The Little Kidnappers)	1954	10
6	Tatum O'Neal	"Best Supporting Actress" (Paper Moon)	1973	10
7	Anna Paquin	"Best Supporting Actress" (The Piano)	1993	11
8	Claude Jarman Jr.	Special Award (The Yearling)	1946	12
9	Bobby Driscoll	Special Award (The Window)	1949	13
10	Hayley Mills	Special Award (Pollyanna)	1960	13

* At the time of the Award ceremony; those of apparently identical age have been ranked according to their precise age in days at the time of the ceremony

THE 10 LATEST "BEST ACTOR" OSCAR WINNERS

YEAR	ACTOR	FILM
2001	**Denzel Washington**	Training Day
2000	**Russell Crowe**	Gladiator
1999	**Kevin Spacey**	American Beauty*
1998	**Roberto Benigni**	Life Is Beautiful
1997	**Jack Nicholson**	As Good as It Gets#
1996	**Geoffrey Rush**	Shine
1995	**Nicolas Cage**	Leaving Las Vegas
1994	**Tom Hanks**	Forrest Gump*
1993	**Tom Hanks**	Philadelphia
1992	**Al Pacino**	Scent of a Woman

* Winner of "Best Picture" Oscar

 # Winner of "Best Actress" Oscar

Training to Win

Denzel Washington's first award was for "Best Supporting Actor" in *Glory* (1989), and his latest for "Best Actor" in *Training Day*.

THE 10 LATEST "BEST ACTRESS" OSCAR WINNERS

YEAR	ACTRESS	FILM
2001	**Halle Berry**	Monster's Ball
2000	**Julia Roberts**	Erin Brockovich
1999	**Hilary Swank**	Boys Don't Cry
1998	**Gwyneth Paltrow**	Shakespeare in Love*
1997	**Helen Hunt**	As Good as It Gets
1996	**Frances McDormand**	Fargo
1995	**Susan Sarandon**	Dead Man Walking
1994	**Jessica Lange**	Blue Sky
1993	**Holly Hunter**	The Piano
1992	**Emma Thompson**	Howards End

* Winner of "Best Picture" Oscar

Monster Advance

Halle Berry's "Best Actress" Oscar for *Monster's Ball* is the first awarded to a Black actress in the 74-year history of the Academy Awards.

And the Winner is...

 LATEST GOLDEN GLOBE AWARDS FOR "BEST MOTION PICTURE – DRAMA"

YEAR	FILM
2002	**A Beautiful Mind**
2001	**Billy Elliott**
2000	**American Beauty**
1999	**Saving Private Ryan**
1998	**Titanic**
1997	**The English Patient**
1996	**Sense and Sensibility**
1995	**Forrest Gump**
1994	**Schindler's List**
1993	**Scent of a Woman**

The Hollywood Foreign Press Association inaugurated what was to become the Golden Globe Awards in 1944. They are announced earlier in the year than the Academy Awards, to which they often act as a pointer.

 LATEST GOLDEN GLOBE AWARDS FOR "BEST DIRECTOR"

YEAR	DIRECTOR	FILM
2002	**Robert Altman**	Gosford Park
2001	**Ang Lee**	Crouching Tiger, Hidden Dragon
2000	**Sam Mendes**	American Beauty
1999	**Steven Spielberg**	Saving Private Ryan
1998	**James Cameron**	Titanic
1997	**Milos Foreman**	The People vs. Larry Flynt
1996	**Mel Gibson**	Braveheart
1995	**Robert Zemeckis**	Forrest Gump
1994	**Steven Spielberg**	Schindler's List
1993	**Clint Eastwood**	Unforgiven

The "Best Director" Golden Globe dates from 1945, the second year of the Awards, when Leo McCarey won for the 1944 release *Going My Way* – which also won "Best Picture".

LATEST GOLDEN GLOBE AWARDS FOR "BEST MOTION PICTURE – MUSICAL OR COMEDY"

YEAR	FILM
2002	**Moulin Rouge**
2001	**Almost Famous**
2000	**Toy Story 2**
1999	**Shakespeare in Love**
1998	**As Good as It Gets**
1997	**Evita**
1996	**Babe**
1995	**The Lion King**
1994	**Mrs. Doubtfire**
1993	**The Player**

THE 10 LATEST WINNERS OF THE SUNDANCE GRAND JURY PRIZE – DRAMATIC

YEAR	FILM/FILMMAKER
2002	**Personal Velocity**, Rebecca Miller
2001	**The Believer**, Henry Bean
2000	**=Girlfight**, Karyn Kusama
	=You Can Count on Me, Kenneth Lunergan
1999	**Three Seasons**, Tony Bui
1998	**Slam**, Marc Levin
1997	**Sunday**, Jonathan Nossiter
1996	**Welcome to the Dollhouse**, Todd Solondz
1995	**The Brothers McMullen**, Edward Burns
1994	**What Happened Was...**, Tom Noonan

THE 10 LATEST RECIPIENTS OF THE AMERICAN FILM INSTITUTE LIFETIME ACHIEVEMENT AWARD

YEAR	ACTOR/ACTRESS/DIRECTOR
2002	**Tom Hanks**
2001	**Barbra Streisand**
2000	**Harrison Ford**
1999	**Dustin Hoffman**
1998	**Robert Wise**
1997	**Martin Scorsese**
1996	**Clint Eastwood**
1995	**Steven Spielberg**
1994	**Jack Nicholson**
1993	**Elizabeth Taylor**

THE 10 LATEST WINNERS OF THE GOLDEN RASPBERRY AWARD FOR WORST PICTURE

YEAR	FILM
2001	**Freddy Got Fingered**
2000	**Battlefield Earth**
1999	**Wild Wild West**
1998	**An Alan Smithee Film: Burn, Hollywood, Burn!**
1997	**The Postman**
1996	**Striptease**
1995	**Showgirls**
1994	**Color of Night**
1993	**Indecent Proposal**
1992	**Shining Through**

Founded in 1981 as a parody of such prestigious awards as the Golden Globes and the Academy Awards (which they pre-empt by being announced the day before), the Golden Raspberry or "Razzie" Awards are anti-accolades or "Dis-Honors for Worst Achievements in Film". Its categories include Worst Picture, Actor, and Actress, and such less familiar ones as Worst Remake and Worst Screen Couple.

THE 10 LATEST WINNERS OF THE CANNES PALME D'OR FOR BEST FILM

YEAR	FILM/COUNTRY
2001	**The Son's Room,** Italy
2000	**Dancer in the Dark,** Denmark
1999	**Rosetta,** France
1998	**Eternity and a Day,** Greece
1997	**=The Eel,** Japan
	=The Taste of Cherries, Iran
1996	**Secrets and Lies,** UK
1995	**Underground,** Yugoslavia
1994	**Pulp Fiction,** US
1993	**=Farewell My Concubine,** China
	=The Piano, Australia

A "Grand Prize," first awarded at the Cannes Film Festival in 1949, has been known since 1955 as the "Palme d'Or."

Golden Prize
Nanni Moretti celebrates winning the prestigious Palme d'Or for *The Son's Room* – which he starred in, wrote, produced, and directed.

Out Takes

TOP 10 MOST EXPENSIVE FILMS EVER MADE

	FILM	YEAR	WORLD GROSS ($)	BUDGET ($)
1	Titanic	1997	1,835,400,000	200,000,000
2	=Waterworld	1995	255,200,000	175,000,000
	=Wild Wild West	1999	213,800,000	175,000,000
4	Pearl Harbor	2001	389,000,000	153,000,000
5	Speed 2: Cruise Control	1997	155,100,000	150,000,000
6	Tarzan*	1999	435,300,000	145,000,000
7	=Armageddon	1998	554,400,000	140,000,000
	=Lethal Weapon 4	1998	285,400,000	140,000,000
9	Spider-Man	2002	n/a	139,000,000
10	Final Fantasy: The Spirits Within*	2001	74,400,000	137,000,000

* Animated

It is coincidental that several of the most expensive films ever made are water-based. Large casts and large-scale special effects, such as those featured in *Titanic*, are major factors in escalating budgets. The two blockbuster films of 2001, *Harry Potter and the Sorcerer's Stone* and *The Lord of the Rings: The Fellowship of the Ring*, had budgets of $125 million and $109 million respectively, and hence do not make the Top 10.

TOP 10 FILM-PRODUCING COUNTRIES (PER CAPITA)

	COUNTRY	FILMS PRODUCED PER MILLION PEOPLE IN 2000
1	Hong Kong	27.78
2	Iceland	21.21
3	Luxembourg	6.81
4	Ireland	5.80
5	Denmark	4.47
6	Switzerland	4.33
7	Norway	3.13
8	Austria	2.92
9	France	2.88
10	US	2.76

Source: Screen Digest

While these countries produced the most feature films in relation to their populations, the actual number of films varies enormously: in 2000 Iceland made just six, while Hong Kong made 185 (but it has a population over 24 times the size of that of Iceland). Although India made the greatest number in total, it equates with only 1.17 per million, and hence does not appear in the Top 10.

TOP 10 FILM-PRODUCING COUNTRIES

	COUNTRY	FILMS PRODUCED IN 2000
1	India	855
2	US	762
3	Japan	282
4	Hong Kong	185
5	France	171
6	=Italy	103
	=Philippines	103
8	Bangladesh	100
9	Spain	98
10	=Germany	90
	=UK	90
	World total	*3, 569*

Source: Screen Digest

Of the 3,569 feature films produced worldwide in 2000, a total of 1,085 were made in India and other countries in Asia, 815 in North America, 754 in Europe, 638 in the Far East, 93 in Central and South America, 92 in Central and Eastern Europe, and 40 in Australasia. The remainder were made in Egypt, Israel, and South Africa.

TOP 10 FILMS WITH THE MOST EXTRAS

	FILM/COUNTRY/YEAR	EXTRAS
1	Gandhi, UK, 1982	300,000
2	Kolberg, Germany, 1945	187,000
3	Monster Wang-magwi, South Korea, 1967	157,000
4	War and Peace, USSR, 1967	120,000
5	Ilya Muromets, USSR, 1956	106,000
6	Tonko, Japan, 1988	100,000
7	The War of Independence, Romania, 1912	80,000
8	Around the World in 80 Days, US, 1956	68,894
9	=Intolerance, US, 1916	60,000
	=Dny Zrady, Czechoslovakia, 1972	60,000

Unhappy Returns

One of the blockbuster films of 2001, comedy horror movie *The Mummy Returns* benefited from extensive advertising on the Internet.

TOP 10 FILMS ADVERTISED ON THE INTERNET

	FILM	HITS*
1	Pearl Harbor	434,800,000
2	The Mummy Returns	157,000,000
3	Atlantis: The Lost Empire	79,400,000
4	The Fast and the Furious	75,000,000
5	Hannibal	70,500,000
6	AntiTrust	50,700,000
7	Operation: Swordfish	39,900,000
8	Head Over Heels	35,800,000
9	Heartbreakers	32,200,000
10	One Night at McCool's	28,500,000

* Number of times advertisement viewed, Jan–July 2001

Source: AdRelevance/Screen Digest

TOP 10 | COUNTRIES WITH THE MOST BOX OFFICE REVENUE

	COUNTRY	BOX OFFICE REVENUE IN 2000 ($)
1	US	7,661,000,000
2	Japan	1,585,000,000
3	UK	1,025,300,000
4	France	893,200,000
5	Germany	824,700,000
6	Italy	566,500,000
7	Spain	536,300,000
8	India	468,400,000
9	Canada	439,500,000
10	Australia	401,200,000

Source: Screen Digest

TOP 10 | CINEMA-GOING COUNTRIES

	COUNTRY	TOTAL ATTENDANCE IN 2000
1	India	3,100,000,000
2	US	1,420,800,000
3	France	165,960,000
4	Germany	152,500,000
5	UK	143,610,000
6	=Japan	135,390,000
	=Spain	135,390,000
8	Mexico	123,550,000
9	China	115,000,000
10	Italy	108,600,000

Source: Screen Digest

TOP 10 | COUNTRIES SPENDING THE MOST ON CINEMA VISITS

	COUNTRY	SPENDING PER INHABITANT IN 2000 ($)
1	Iceland	45.57
2	US	27.96
3	Australia	21.21
4	Singapore	20.86
5	Ireland	18.65
6	Hong Kong	18.56
7	Switzerland	16.93
8	Luxembourg	16.43
9	UK	15.96
10	Canada	14.38

Source: Screen Digest

Top Video

TOP 10 BEST-SELLING DVDS IN THE US, 2001

	TITLE
1	Gladiator
2	Crouching Tiger, Hidden Dragon
3	Cast Away
4	X-Men
5	Gone in 60 Seconds
6	Traffic
7	Star Wars: Episode 1 – The Phantom Menace
8	The Matrix
9	The Patriot
10	Meet the Parents

Source: Billboard

DVD was launched in the US in March 1997. By the end of 2001, DVD-player penetration had reached close to a quarter of the US market. It is predicted that by 2005 DVD will account for 43 percent of the US video market and that, worldwide, shipments of DVDs will rise to over 2 billion by 2005.

Parent Power

Ben Stiller is subjected to a lie detector test at the hands of prospective father-in-law Robert De Niro in the smash hit movie and video *Meet the Parents*.

TOP 10 MOST-RENTED VIDEOS OF ALL TIME IN THE US

	TITLE	REVENUE ($ MILLIONS)
1	Cast Away	102,340,000
2	Unbreakable	96,880,000
3	Enemy of the State	95,940,000
4	The Green Mile	92,740,000
5	Crouching Tiger, Hidden Dragon	89,580,000
6	Meet The Parents	89,120,000
7	Hannibal	88,080,000
8	The Family Man	87,220,000
9	Gladiator	83,880,000
10	The Perfect Storm	78,860,000

Source: Video Store Magazine

TOP 10 BEST-SELLING VIDEOS IN THE US, 2001

	TITLE
1	The Emperor's New Groove
2	Chicken Run
3	The Silence of the Lambs
4	Coyote Ugly
5	Miss Congeniality
6	Bring It On
7	Gladiator
8	102 Dalmatians
9	Toy Story 2
10	Meet the Parents

Source: Billboard

TOP 10 MOST-RENTED DVDS IN THE US, 2001

	VIDEO
1	Shrek
2	Pearl Harbor
3	Dr. Seuss's How The Grinch Stole Christmas*
4	Star Wars I – The Phantom Menace
5	The Mummy Returns*
6	Rush Hour 2
7	Crouching Tiger Hidden Dragon
8	Planet Of The Apes
9	Jurassic Park 3*
10	Gladiator

* Chart position has been determined by combining two versions of the same title

Source: *VideoScan (a service of VNU and ACNielsen)*

TOP 10 BEST-SELLING CHILDREN'S VIDEOS IN THE US, 2001

TITLE

1 Mary-Kate & Ashley – Our Lips Are Sealed

2 Lady and the Tramp II – Scamp's Adventure

3 The Book of Pooh – Stories from the Heart

4 Blue's Clues – Playtime with Periwinkle

5 Dora the Explorer – Wish on a Star

6 Mary-Kate & Ashley – Winning London

7 The Little Mermaid II – Return to the Sea

8 Fantasia 2000

9 Bob the Builder – Can We Fix It?

10 Power Rangers – In 3-D

Source: Billboard

Pirated Pie

The comedy *American Pie* secured the dubious honor of being the most pirated film on the internet.

TOP 10 PIRATED VIDEOS ON THE INTERNET

FILM	PIRATE COPIES AVAILABLE ONLINE*
1 American Pie	1,663
2 The Fast and the Furious	1,056
3 Shrek	957
4 Jurassic Park III	908
5 The Matrix	812
6 Planet of the Apes	756
7 Crouching Tiger, Hidden Dragon	738
8 Swordfish	697
9 Traffic	695
10 Fight Club	643

* During August 2001, ranked by frequency of pirated copies available online

Source: *MediaForce*

TOP 10 VIDEO-BUYING COUNTRIES

COUNTRY	PRERECORDED VIDEOS PURCHASED PER 1,000 INHABITANTS* IN 2000
1 Canada	2,646.0
2 US	2,302.4
3 Australia	1,958.6
4 New Zealand	1,767.8
5 UK	1,554.6
6 Japan	1,008.2
7 Ireland	983.9
8 Sweden	802.3
9 Italy	752.8
10 France	677.3

* In those countries for which data available

Source: *Euromonitor*

Sound & Vision

TOP 10 TV-OWNING COUNTRIES

	COUNTRY	TVS PER 1,000 POPULATION IN 1999
1	US	844
2	Latvia	741
3	Japan	719
4	Canada	715
5	Australia	706
6	UK	652
7	Norway	648
8	Finland	643
9	France	623
10	Denmark	621
	World average	268

Source: *International Telecommunication Union*, World Telecommunication Development Report 2000/01

TV Age
The proliferation of terrestrial and satellite television in recent years has transformed both the industry and the skylines of today's cities.

TOP 10 RADIO-OWNING COUNTRIES

	COUNTRY	RADIOS PER 1,000 POPULATION IN 1999
1	US	2,146
2	Finland	1,563
3	UK	1,435
4	Australia	1,378
5	Denmark	1,318
6	Canada	1,047
7	South Korea	1,033
8	Switzerland	1,000
9	New Zealand	989
10	Netherlands	981

Source: *International Telecommunication Union,* World Telecommunication Development Report 2000/01

TRANSATLANTIC RADIO

THE YEAR 1903 SAW THE FIRST use of the word "radio" in print. It was also the year in which the first transatlantic radio message was transmitted. On January 18, 1903, President Roosevelt sent a greeting on behalf of the American people to the inhabitants of the British Empire. It was sent by Morse code from a station in South Wellfleet, Massachusetts, and was received by King Edward VII via the Marconi radio station at Polhdu, Cornwall. The King replied from Sandringham, Norfolk, the following day.

FIRST OR LAST

TOP 10 RADIO FORMATS IN THE US

	FORMAT	NO. OF STATIONS
1	Country	2,190
2	News/Talk	1,139
3	Oldies	786
4	Adult Contemporary	709
5	Spanish	574
6	Adult Standards	569
7	CHR (Top 40)	468
8	Soft Adult Contemporary	375
9	Hot Adult Contemporary	369
10	Religion (teaching and variety)	356

Source: *M Street*

TOP 10 RADIO STATIONS IN THE US

	STATION/LOCATION	FORMAT	AQH*
1	WLTW-FM, New York	Soft Adult Contemporary	153,900
2	WQHT-FM, New York	Black/Urban	146,000
3	WHTZ-FM, New York	CHR	106,900
4	WCBS-FM, New York	Oldies	101,300
5	WKTU-FM, New York	Dance/CHR	96,800
6	WABC-AM, New York	Talk	94,000
7	WSKQ-FM, New York	Hispanic CHR	94,700
8	KROQ-FM, Los Angeles	Modern Rock	86,500
9	WBLS-FM, New York	Black/Urban	86,500
10	WINS-AM, New York	News	84,700

* Average Quarter Hour statistic based on number of listeners aged 12+ listening between Monday and Sunday 6:00 am to midnight, from Arbitron data

Source: *Duncan's American Radio/Arbitron, Inc.*

TOP 10 | PRIMETIME PROGRAMS ON NETWORK TELEVISION, 2000–01

	PROGRAM	NETWORK	AUDIENCE
1	Survivor II	CBS	17,759,000
2	Who Wants to be a Millionaire (Wednesdays)	ABC	13,999,000
3	NFL Monday Night Football	ABC	12,986,000
4	E.R.	NBC	12,454,000
5	CBS NFL National Post Gun	CBS	12,244,000
6	Who Wants to be a Millionaire (Tuesdays)	ABC	11,757,000
7	Everybody Loves Raymond	CBS	11,551,000
8	Law and Order	NBC	11,322,000
9	Friends	NBC	11,282,000
10	Who Wants to be a Millionaire (Sundays)	ABC	11,263,000

© 2002 Nielsen Media Research

TOP 10 | SYNDICATED PROGRAMS ON US TELEVISION, 2000–01

	PROGRAM	AUDIENCE %	AUDIENCE TOTAL
1	Wheel of Fortune	9.7	9,892,000
2	Jeopardy	8.1	8,257,000
3	World Wrestling Federation	7.2	7,367,000
4	MMN Home Team Baseball	6.7	6,871,000
5	Judge Judy	6.0	6,125,000
6	ESPN NFL Regular Season	6.0	6,117,000
7	Entertainment Tonight	5.9	6,046,000
8	The Oprah Winfrey Show	5.9	6,037,000
9	Century 16: Home Alone (movie)	5.9	5,986,000
10	Friends	5.5	5,590,000

© Copyright 2002 – Nielsen Media Research

TOP 10 | MOVIES ON US TELEVISION, 2000–01

	MOVIE/PROGRAM	DATE	AUDIENCE
1	Life with Judy Garland: Me and My Shadows (Pt. 1), ABC Premiere Event	Feb 25, 2001	14,105,000
2	Oprah Winfrey presents Amy & Isabel, ABC Original	Mar 4, 2001	13,658,000
3	Dr. Dolittle, ABC Sun Picture Show	Feb 11, 2001	9,245,000
4	Anne Frank (Pt. 1), ABC Premiere Event	May 20, 2001	8,934,000
5	Jackie, Ethel, Joan: The Women of Camelot, NBC Movie of the Week	Mar 5, 2001	8,676,000
6	Glimmer Man, ABC Monday Night Movie	Sep 3, 2001	8,381,000
7	Rush Hour, Fox Movie Special	Sep 23, 2001	8,248,000
8	The Ten Commandments, ABC Big Picture Show	Apr 8, 2001	8,229,000
9	Sister Act 2: Back, in the Habit, ABC Sun Picture Show	Oct 15, 2000	8,172,000
10	True Lies, Fox Movie Special	Mar 25, 2001	8,120,000

© Copyright 2002 – Nielsen Media Research

TOP 10 | TV AUDIENCES IN THE US

	PROGRAM	DATE	AUDIENCE TOTAL	AUDIENCE %
1	M*A*S*H Special	Feb 28, 1983	50,150,000	60.2
2	Dallas	Nov 21, 1980	41,470,000	53.3
3	Roots Part 8	Jan 30, 1977	36,380,000	51.1
4	Super Bowl XVI	Jan 24, 1982	40,020,000	49.1
5	Super Bowl XVII	Jan 30, 1983	40,480,000	48.6
6	XVII Winter Olympics	Feb 23, 1994	45,690,000	48.5
7	Super Bowl XX	Jan 26, 1986	41,490,000	48.3
8	Gone With the Wind Pt.1	Nov 7, 1976	33,960,000	47.7
9	Gone With the Wind Pt.2	Nov 8, 1976	33,750,000	47.4
10	Super Bowl XII	Jan 15, 1978	34,410,000	47.2

© Copyright 2002 – Nielsen Media Research

Historically, as more households acquired television sets (there are currently 105,500,000 "TV households" in the US), audiences generally increased. However, the rise in channel choice and the use of VCRs has somewhat checked this trend. Listing the Top 10 according to percentage of households viewing provides a clearer picture of who watches what.

TV & Radio Awards

 LATEST WINNERS OF THE PRIMETIME EMMY "OUTSTANDING LEAD ACTOR IN A COMEDY SERIES" AWARD

SEASON ENDING	ACTOR	PROGRAM
2001	Eric McCormack	Will & Grace
2000	Michael J. Fox	Spin City
1999	John Lithgow	3rd Rock from the Sun
1998	Kelsey Grammer	Frasier
1997	John Lithgow	3rd Rock from the Sun
1996	John Lithgow	3rd Rock from the Sun
1995	Kelsey Grammer	Frasier
1994	Kelsey Grammer	Frasier
1993	Ted Danson	Cheers
1992	Craig T. Nelson	Coach

 LATEST WINNERS OF THE PRIMETIME EMMY "OUTSTANDING LEAD ACTRESS IN A COMEDY SERIES" AWARD

SEASON ENDING	ACTRESS	PROGRAM
2001	Patricia Heaton	Everybody Loves Raymond
2000	Patricia Heaton	Everybody Loves Raymond
1999	Helen Hunt	Mad About You
1998	Helen Hunt	Mad About You
1997	Helen Hunt	Mad About You
1996	Helen Hunt	Mad About You
1995	Candice Bergen	Murphy Brown
1994	Candice Bergen	Murphy Brown
1993	Roseanne	Roseanne
1992	Candice Bergen	Murphy Brown

LATEST WINNERS OF THE PRIMETIME EMMY "OUTSTANDING DRAMA" AWARD

SEASON ENDING	PROGRAM
2001	The West Wing
2000	The West Wing
1999	The Practice
1998	The Practice
1997	Law & Order
1996	ER
1995	NYPD Blue
1994	Picket Fences
1993	Picket Fences
1992	Northern Exposure

The first Emmy awards were presented on January 25, 1949. Emmy awards are awarded by the National Academy of Television Arts and Sciences and are considered the ultimate accolade for those in American television.

 LATEST WINNERS OF THE PRIMETIME EMMY "OUTSTANDING COMEDY SERIES" AWARD

SEASON ENDING	PROGRAM
2001	Sex and the City
2000	Will and Grace
1999	Ally McBeal
1998	Frasier
1997	Frasier
1996	Frasier
1995	Frasier
1994	Frasier
1993	Seinfeld
1992	Murphy Brown

 LATEST GEORGE FOSTER PEABODY AWARDS FOR BROADCASTING WON BY NATIONAL PUBLIC RADIO*

SEASON ENDING	PROGRAM
2001	=Coverage of September 11, 2001
	=Jazz Profiles
2000	The NPR 100
1999	=Lost & Found Sound
	=Morning Edition with Bob Edwards
1998	=Coverage of Africa
	=I Must Keep Fightin': The Art of Paul Robeson
	=Performance Today
1997	Jazz from Lincoln Center
1996	Remorse: The 14 Stories of Eric Morse

* Includes only programs made or coproduced by NPR

Source: *Peabody Awards*

LATEST WINNERS OF THE NAB MARCONI "LEGENDARY STATION OF THE YEAR" AWARD

YEAR	STATION/LOCATION
2001	KNIX, Pheonix, Arizona
2000	WEBN, Cincinnati, Ohio
1999	KOA, Denver, Colorado
1998	WCBS-FM, New York, New York
1997	KVIL-FM, Dallas, Texas
1996	WJR-AM, Detroit, Michigan
1995	KGO-AM, San Francisco, California
1994	KDKA-AM, Pittsburgh, Pennsylvania
1993	WHO-AM, Des Moines, Iowa
1992	WCCO-AM, Minneapolis, Minnesota

Unlike the National Association of Broadcasters' other awards (which are concerned with a station or personality's achievements during the preceeding year), the "Legendary Station" award can be presented only once to a station. It recognizes overall excellence in radio, and considers the station's history and heritage.

Hitting the High Note
James Gandolfini wins an Emmy for his starring role in *The Sopranos*. The statuette of a winged woman holding an atom, designed in 1948, represents the fusion of arts and sciences.

THE 10 LATEST WINNERS OF THE PRIMETIME EMMY "OUTSTANDING LEAD ACTOR IN A DRAMA SERIES" AWARD

SEASON ENDING	ACTOR	PROGRAM
2001	James Gandolfini	The Sopranos
2000	James Gandolfini	The Sopranos
1999	Dennis Franz	NYPD Blue
1998	Andre Braugher	Homicide: Life on the Street
1997	Dennis Franz	NYPD Blue
1996	Dennis Franz	NYPD Blue
1995	Mandy Patinkin	Chicago Hope
1994	Dennis Franz	NYPD Blue
1993	Tom Skerritt	Picket Fences
1992	Christopher Lloyd	Avonlea

THE 10 LATEST WINNERS OF THE PRIMETIME EMMY "OUTSTANDING LEAD ACTRESS IN A DRAMA SERIES" AWARD

SEASON ENDING*	ACTRESS	PROGRAM
2001	Edie Falco	The Sopranos
2000	Sela Ward	Once and Again
1999	Edie Falco	The Sopranos
1998	Christine Lahti	Chicago Hope
1997	Gillian Anderson	The X Files
1995	Kathy Baker	Picket Fences
1994	Sela Ward	Sisters
1993	Kathy Baker	Picket Fences
1992	Dana Delaney	China Beach
1991	Patricia Wettig	thirtysomething

* No award 1996

COMMERCIAL
WORLD

World Finance

TOP 10 RICHEST COUNTRIES

	COUNTRY	GDP* PER CAPITA IN 1999 ($)
1	Luxembourg	42,769
2	US	31,872
3	Norway	28,433
4	Iceland	27,835
5	Switzerland	27,171
6	Canada	26,251
7	Ireland	25,918
8	Denmark	25,869
9	Belgium	25,443
10	Austria	25,089
	World total	6,980

* Gross Domestic Product

Source: *United Nations,* Human Development Indicators, 2001

THE 10 POOREST COUNTRIES

	COUNTRY	GDP* PER CAPITA IN 1999 ($)
1	Sierra Leone	448
2	Tanzania	501
3	Burundi	578
4	Malawi	586
5	Ethiopia	628
6	Sudan	664
7	Guinea-Bissau	678
8	Congo	727
9	=Mali	753
	=Niger	753

* Gross Domestic Product

Source: *United Nations,* Human Development Indicators, 2001

TOP 10 FASTEST-GROWING ECONOMIES

	COUNTRY	GDP PER CAPITA IN 1999 ($)	GDP PER CAPITA ANNUAL GROWTH RATE FROM 1990–99 (%)
1	Equatorial Guinea	4,676	16.3
2	China	3,617	9.5
3	Vietnam	1,860	6.2
4	Ireland	25,918	6.1
5	Lebanon	4,705	5.7
6	Chile	8,652	5.6
7	Guyana	3,640	5.2
8	=Malaysia	8,209	4.7
	=Singapore	20,767	4.7
	=South Korea	15,712	4.7

Source: *United Nations,* Human Development Indicators, 2001

Certain countries in Africa, Asia, Europe, and South America have bucked the trend by achieving above-average growth.

THE 10 FASTEST-SHRINKING ECONOMIES

	COUNTRY	GDP PER CAPITA IN 1999* ($)	GDP PER CAPITA ANNUAL GROWTH RATE FROM 1990–99* (%)
1	Moldova	2,037	-10.8
2	Azerbaijan	2,850	-10.7
3	Ukraine	3,458	-10.3
4	Turkmenistan	3,347	-9.6
5	Dem. Rep. of Congo	801	-8.1
6	Kyrgyzstan	2,573	-6.4
7	Russia	7,473	-5.9
8	Kazakhstan	4,951	-4.9
9	=Armenia	2,215	-3.9
	=Lithuania	6,656	-3.9

* In those countries for which data are available

Source: *United Nations,* Human Development Indicators, 2001

Most former Soviet bloc countries are notable for economic slowdown since the transition from centralized to market economies.

TOP 10 CORPORATIONS IN THE US

	CORPORATION	SALES IN 2001 ($)
1	Wal-Mart Stores, Inc.	217,799,000,000
2	Exxon Mobil	187,510,000,000
3	General Motors Corp.	177,260,000,000
4	Ford Motor Company	162,412,000,000
5	Enron Corp.*	138,718,000,000
6	General Electric	125,679,000,000
7	Citigroup Inc.	112,022,000,000
8	ChevronTexaco Corp.	106,245,000,000
9	Philip Morris Companies Inc.	89,924,000,000
10	International Business Machines Corp.	85,866,000,000

* Revenue for 9 months Jan–Sept 2001; filed for bankruptcy December 2, 2001

Source: Fortune

TOP 10 GLOBAL INDUSTRIAL COMPANIES

	COMPANY/LOCATION	REVENUE IN 2001 ($)
1	Wal-Mart Stores, Inc., US	217,799,000,000
2	Exxon Mobil, US	187,510,000,000
3	Royal Dutch/Shell Group, Netherlands/UK	177,281,000,000
4	General Motors Corp., US	177,260,000,000
5	Ford Motor Co., US.	162,412,000,000
6	DaimlerChrysler AG, Germany	152,446,000,000
7	BP plc, UK	148,062,000,000
8	Enron Corp.*, US	138,718,000,000
9	General Electric, US	125,679,000,000
10	Mitsubishi Corp., Japan	110,787,000,000

* Revenue for 9 months Jan–Sept 2001; filed for bankruptcy December 2 , 2001

Source: Fortune

Sam Walton opened his first Wal-Mart store in Rogers, Arkansas, in 1962. It has expanded in the past 40 years, to become the world's no. 1 company.

TOP 10 LARGEST BANKS (BY ASSETS)

	BANK/COUNTRY	ASSETS* ($)
1	Deutsche Bank, Germany	841,796,920,000
2	Bank of Tokyo-Mitsubishi, Japan	729,249,600,000
3	BNP Paribas, France	700,232,030,000
4	Bank of America Corp., US	632,574,000,000
5	UBS, Switzerland	613,198,370,000
6	Fuji Bank, Japan	567,899,800,000
7	HSBC Holdings, UK	567,793,290,000
8	Sumitomo Bank, Japan	524,227,780,000
9	Dai-Ichi Kangyo Bank, Japan	506,980,440,000
10	HypoVereinsbank, Germany	504,412,630,000

* In latest year for which data are available

Source: Fortune Global 500, April 14, 2001

You Can Bank on It
The headquarters of the world's largest bank, the Deutsche Bank, occupies twin 509-ft (155-m) towers in Frankfurt, Germany.

TOP 10 OLDEST ESTABLISHED BUSINESSES IN THE US

	COMPANY*/LOCATION/BUSINESS	FOUNDED
1	White Horse Tavern, Newport, RI, Dining	1673
2	J. E. Rhoads & Sons, Branchburg, NJ, Conveyor belts	1702
3	Wayside Inn, Sudbury, MA, Inn	1716
4	Elkridge Furnace Inn, Elkridge, MD, Inn	1744
5	Moravian Book Shop, Bethlehem, PA, Retail, Books	1745
6	Pennsylvania Hospital, Philadelphia, PA, Hospital	1751
7	Philadelphia Contributorship, Philadelphia, PA, Insurance	1752
8	New Hampshire Gazette, Portsmouth, NH, Newspaper	1756
9	Hartford Courant, Hartford, CT, Newspaper	1764
10	Bachman Funeral Home, Strasburg, PA, Funeral home	1769

* Excluding mergers and transplanted companies

Workers of the World

A Woman's Work
Rwanda is notable for its exceptionally high level of female employment in its urban areas.

TOP 10 COUNTRIES WITH THE HIGHEST FEMALE EMPLOYMENT

	COUNTRY	PERCENTAGE OF WOMEN AGED OVER 14 EMPLOYED*
1	Rwanda	85#
2	=Burundi	83
	=Tanzania	83
4	Solomon Islands	82
5	=Ghana	81
	=Uganda	81
7	Malawi	79
8	Guinea	78
9	Burkina Faso	77
10	=Cambodia	76
	=East Timor	76
	US	60†

* In latest year and in those countries for which data available

Urban areas only   † Aged over 16

Source: International Labor Organization

TOP 10 COUNTRIES WITH THE HIGHEST MALE EMPLOYMENT

	COUNTRY	PERCENTAGE OF MEN AGED OVER 14 EMPLOYED*
1	=Burundi	93
	=Niger	93
3	Qatar	92
4	=Guinea-Bissau	91
	=Mozambique	91
	=Uganda	91
7	=Angola	90
	=Bhutan	90
	=Burkina Faso	90
	=The Gambia	90
	=Mali	90
	US	75#

* In latest year and in those countries for which data available

Aged over 16

Source: International Labor Organization

COUNTRIES WITH THE MOST FARMERS

	COUNTRY	AGRICULTURAL LABOR FORCE IN 2000
1	China	510,796,000
2	India	263,691,000
3	Indonesia	49,596,000
4	Bangladesh	38,732,000
5	Vietnam	27,527,000
6	Pakistan	24,521,000
7	Ethiopia	22,891,000
8	Thailand	21,103,000
9	Myanmar	18,033,000
10	Nigeria	15,030,000
	World total	*1,318,628,000*
	US	*3,027,000*

Source: *Food and Agriculture Organization of the United Nations*

All the Tea in China
Five Chinese women tea pickers engage in one of the world's most labor-intensive activities.

COUNTRIES WITH THE MOST WORKERS

	COUNTRY	WORKERS* IN 2000
1	China	766,889,000
2	India	442,156,000
3	US	145,105,000
4	Indonesia	102,561,000
5	Brazil	79,247,000
6	Russia	78,041,000
7	Bangladesh	69,611,000
8	Japan	68,369,000
9	Pakistan	52,077,000
10	Nigeria	45,129,000

* Based on people aged 15–64 who are currently employed; unpaid groups are not included

Source: *Food and Agriculture Organization of the United Nations*

In practice, it is difficult to count the employed and unemployed accurately, especially in countries where thousands of people may be involved in subsistence agriculture, unrecorded or informal activities, or underemployed (working a few hours a week).

COUNTRIES WITH THE HIGHEST PROPORTION OF CHILD WORKERS

	COUNTRY	PERCENTAGE OF CHILDREN WHO WORKED IN 1999*
1	Mali	52
2	Burundi	49
3	Burkina Faso	45
4	=Niger	44
	=Uganda	44
6	Nepal	43
7	=Ethiopia	41
	=Rwanda	41
9	Kenya	40
10	Eritrea	39

* Based on percentage of children working aged 10–14 years

Source: *World Bank*, World Development Indicators 2001

While child labor is officially claimed not to exist, rural economies, especially in Africa, employ large numbers of boys and girls.

SERVICE INDUSTRY COUNTRIES

	COUNTRY	PERCENTAGE OF LABOR FORCE IN SERVICES* FEMALE	MALE#
1	Colombia	78	68
2	Peru	86	66
3	Singapore	77	66
4	Argentina	88	65
5	Australia	86	64
6	=Canada	87	63
	=Ecuador	84	63
	=US	86	63
9	Paraguay	87	62
10	=Israel	85	60
	=UK	86	60

* Service industries include wholesale and retail trade, restaurants and hotels; transportation, storage, and communications; financing, insurance, real estate, and business services; and community, social, and personal services

Ranked by percentage of male labor force

Source: *World Bank*, World Development Indicators 2001

Advertising & Brands

TOP 10 CORPORATE ADVERTISERS IN THE US

	CORPORATION	AD SPENDING IN 2000 ($)
1	General Motors Corporation	3,934,800,000
2	Philip Morris Companies	2,602,900,000
3	Procter & Gamble Company	2,363,500,000
4	Ford Motor Company	2,345,200,000
5	Pfizer	2,265,300,000
6	PepsiCo	2,100,700,000
7	DaimlerChrysler	1,984,000,000
8	AOL Time Warner Inc.	1,770,100,000
9	Walt Disney Company	1,757,500,000
10	Verizon Communications	1,612,900,000

Source: *Crain Communications Inc.*/Advertising Age

TOP 10 TYPES OF ADVERTISING MEDIA IN THE US

	MEDIUM	AD SPENDING IN 2000 ($)
1	Network television	18,417,000,000
2	Newspapers (excluding nationals)	18,817,000,000
3	Magazines (excluding Sundays)	16,697,000,000
4	Spot television	17,107,000,000
5	Yellow Pages	13,228,000,000
6	Cable television networks	9,506,000,000
7	Internet	4,333,000,000
8	National newspapers	3,785,000,000
9	Syndicated television	2,804,000,000
10	National spot radio	2,672,000,000

Source: *Taylor Nelson Sofres' Competitive Media Reporting*/Advertising Age

FIRST GILLETTE RAZOR

KING CAMP GILLETTE (1855–1932), an amateur inventor, invented the disposable blade. He had experimented for several years before meeting William E. Nickerson, who refined the design. In 1901, Gillette formed a company, set up a factory in Boston, and patented his invention. In 1903, the first year the Gillette safety razor went on sale, just 51 razors and 168 blades were sold. The following year, Gillette sold 90,844 razors and 123,648 blades, launching the company and its products into a world-dominating position.

TOP 10 GLOBAL MARKETERS

	COMPANY/BASE	MEDIA SPENDING IN 2000 ($)
1	Procter & Gamble Company, US	4,152,000,000
2	General Motors Corporation, US	3,979,000,000
3	Unilever, Netherlands/UK	3,664,000,000
4	Ford Motor Company, US	2,323,000,000
5	Philip Morris Companies, US	2,311,000,000
6	Toyota Motor Corporation, Japan	2,135,000,000
7	DaimlerChrysler, Germany/US	2,111,000,000
8	Nestlé, Switzerland	1,886,000,000
9	AOL Time Warner, US	1,842,000,000
10	Volkswagen, Germany	1,714,000,000

Source: Ad Age Global

Automobile Production

As one of the costliest of all items of consumer expenditure, advertising budgets for automobiles figure prominently among the highest for any products.

TOP 10 BRAND ADVERTISERS IN THE US

	BRAND/PARENT COMPANY	AD SPENDING IN 2000 ($)
1	**Chevrolet vehicles,** General Motors Corporation	819,200,000
2	**AT&T telephone services,** AT&T Corporation	787,900,000
3	**Verizon telephone services,** Verizon Communications	709,700,000
4	**McDonald's restaurants,** McDonald's Corporation	663,400,000
5	**Sprint telephone services,** Sprint Corporation	660,500,000
6	**Dodge vehicles,** DaimlerChrysler	660,400,000
7	**Toyota vehicles,** Toyota Motor Corporation	595,800,000
8	**Ford vehicles,** Ford Motor Company	545,500,000
9	**Sears department stores,** Sears, Roebuck & Company	491,300,000
10	**Nissan vehicles,** Nissan Motor Company	489,000,000

Source: *Taylor Nelson Sofres' Competitive Media Reporting/Advertising Age*

TOP 10 MOST VALUABLE GLOBAL BRANDS

	BRAND NAME*	INDUSTRY	BRAND VALUE IN 2001 ($)
1	**Coca-Cola**	Beverages	68,945,000,000
2	**Microsoft**	Technology	65,068,000,000
3	**IBM**	Technology	52,752,000,000
4	**General Electric**	Diversified	42,396,000,000
5	**Nokia,** Finland	Technology	35,035,000,000
6	**Intel**	Technology	34,665,000,000
7	**Disney**	Leisure	32,591,000,000
8	**Ford**	Automobiles	30,092,000,000
9	**McDonald's**	Food retail	25,289,000,000
10	**AT&T**	Telecommunications	22,828,000,000

* All US-owned unless otherwise stated

Source: *Interbrand*

Brand consultants Interbrand use a method of estimating value that takes into account the profitability of individual brands within a business (rather than the companies that own them), as well as such factors as their potential for growth. Well over half of the 75 most valuable global brands surveyed by Interbrand are US-owned, with Europe accounting for another 30 percent.

Things Go Better...
The Coca-Cola brand stands apart as a symbol of American culture, the most valued international beverage and one of the best-selling products in the world.

Shopping Lists

TOP 10 RETAILERS

	COMPANY/COUNTRY	RETAIL SALES IN 2000 ($)
1	**Wal-Mart**, US	191,329,000,000
2	**Carrefour**, France	59,703,000,000
3	**Kroger Company**, US	49,000,000,000
4	**Home Depot**, US	45,738,000,000
5	**METRO AG**, Germany	42,439,000,000
6	**Ahold**, Netherlands	41,539,000,000
7	**Kmart**, US	37,028,000,000
8	**Albertson's**, US	36,762,000,000
9	**Sears, Roebuck**, US	36,548,000,000
10	**Target**, US	36,362,000,000

Source: Stores' Top 200 Global Retailers

In 1887 watch retailer Richard Sears entered a partnership with watchmaker Alvah C. Roebuck to form Sears, Roebuck. It flourished to become the world's largest mail-order company before opening its first stores in the 1920s.

TOP 10 COUNTRIES WITH THE MOST STORES

	COUNTRY	STORES IN 2000
1	**China**	19,306,800
2	**India**	10,537,080
3	**Brazil**	1,595,062
4	**Japan**	1,240,237
5	**Mexico**	1,087,995
6	**Spain**	780,247
7	**Vietnam**	727,268
8	**South Korea**	704,032
9	**Italy**	697,853
10	**US**	685,367
	World total	*44,443,840*

Source: *Euromonitor*

Less developed countries tend to have a high ratio of small stores to population: China has 1 store per 67 people, and India 1 to 92, whereas the ratio in the US, where stores are generally larger, is 1 to 400.

Nation of Shopkeepers
India's tradition of entrepreneurship and trade has given rise to a culture in which small shops play a prominent part.

TOP 10 WORLD RETAIL SECTORS

	SECTOR	COMPANIES*
1	**Supermarket**	95
2	**Specialty**	90
3	**Department**	58
4	**Hypermarket**	56
5	**=Convenience**	38
	=Discount	38
7	**Mail order**	25
8	**Restaurant**	21
9	**Drug**	18
10	**Home Improvement**	17

* *Of those listed in* Stores' Top 200 Global Retailers *(stores can operate in more than one sector)*

Source: Stores

TOP 10 ITEMS BOUGHT ON THE INTERNET

	ITEM	% OF INTERNET USERS WHO HAVE PURCHASED
1	**Computer software**	43
2	**Computer hardware**	37
3	**Books**	23
4	**Music CDs**	17
5	**=Consumer electronics**	14
	=Travel	14
7	**Games**	11
8	**Clothing**	8
9	**Flowers**	7
10	**Information**	6

Source: *NOP survey*

In terms of value of sales, travel has emerged as the No.1 online commodity, followed by computer hardware and books.

TOP 10 INTERNET RETAILERS

	COMPANY	WEBSITE	EST. US SALES ($)*
1	eBay	eBay.com	3,500–3,700,000,000
2	Amazon.com	amazon.com	1,700–1,900,000,000
3	Dell	dell.com	1,100–1,300,000,000
4	buy.com	buy.com	700–800,000,000
5	=Egghead.com	Egghead.com (formerly) OnSale.com	500–600,000,000
	=Gateway	Gateway.com	500–600,000,000
7	Quixtar	Quixtar.com	400–450,000,000
8	=Barnes & Noble	bn.com	275–325,000,000
	=uBid.com	uBid.com	275–325,000,000
10	=Cyberian Outpost	Outpost.com	200–250,000,000
	=MicroWarehouse	MicroWarehouse.com	200–250,000,000
	=Value America#	va.com	200–250,000,000

* In latest financial year   *# Ceased retail operations*

Source: *Stores/Verifone and Russell Reynold Associates' Top 100 Internet Retailers, Sept 2001 © NRF Enterprises, Inc.*

TOP 10 SPECIALTY RETAILERS

	COMPANY*	SPECIALTY	RETAIL SALES IN 2000 ($)
1	Home Depot, Inc.	Home improvement supplies	47,738,000,000
2	AutoNation, Inc.	Automobile dealers	20,610,000,000
3	Lowe's Companies, Inc.	Home improvement supplies	18,779,000,000
4	Best Buy	Consumer electronics	15,327,000,000
5	The Gap, Inc.	Clothing	13,673,000,000
6	Circuit City Stores, Inc.	Consumer electronics	12,959,000,000
7	Toys'R'Us, Inc.	Toys	11,332,000,000
8	The Limited, Inc.	Clothing	10,105,000,000
9	Staples, Inc.	Office supplies	9,992,000,000
10	TJX Companies, Inc.	Clothing and accessories	9,579,000,000

* All have their headquarters in the US

Source: *Fortune*

TOP 10 SHOPPING COUNTRIES

	COUNTRY	RETAIL SPENDING PER CAPITA IN 2000 ($)
1	Japan	8,622
2	US	8,098
3	Switzerland	6,827
4	Norway	6,563
5	Germany	5,841
6	Denmark	5,778
7	Finland	5,569
8	UK	5,356
9	Sweden	5,261
10	France	5,191
	World	*1,540*

Source: *Euromonitor*

The biggest retail spenders are the countries with the highest per capita incomes, but even those at the bottom end of the Top 10 spend more than 3 times as much each as the global average. There are also many countries far beneath that figure, especially rural and barter-based economies where people spend relatively little on retail purchases: Indonesia's annual average is just $123 per capita, and that of the Ukraine estimated at only $102.

Wealth & Riches

 **RICHEST WOMEN***

	NAME/COUNTRY	NET WORTH ($)
1	**Alice L. Walton,** US	20,500,000,000
2	**Helen R. Walton,** US	20,400,000,000
3	**Liliane Bettencourt,** France	15,600,000,000
4	**=Barbara Cox Anthony,** US	10,100,000,000
	=Anne Cox Chambers, US	10,100,000,000
6	**Jacqueline Badger Mars,** US	9,000,000,000
7	**Abigail Johnson,** US	8,600,000,000
8	**Charlene de Carvalho,** Netherlands	4,300,000,000
9	**=Ann Walton Kroenke,** US	2,800,000,000
	=Nancy Walton Laurie, US	2,800,000,000

Excluding rulers and fortunes shared with family

Source: Forbes

This list is led by 2 members of the same family: Alice L. Walton is the daughter of Sam Walton, founder of the Wal-Mart chain of stores, while Helen Robson Walton is his widow.

 **RICHEST MEN***

	NAME/COUNTRY	NET WORTH ($)
1	**William H. Gates III,** US	52,800,000,000
2	**Warren Edward Buffett,** US	35,000,000,000
3	**Paul Gardner Allen,** US	25,200,000,000
4	**Lawrence Joseph Ellison,** US	23,500,000,000
5	**Jim C. Walton,** US	20,800,000,000
6	**John T. Walton,** US	20,700,000,000
7	**S. Robson Walton,** US	20,500,000,000
8	**Prince Alwaleed Bin Talal Alsaud,** Saudi Arabia	20,000,000,000
9	**Steven Anthony Ballmer,** US	14,800,000,000
10	**Ingvar Kamprad,** Sweden	13,400,000,000

Excluding rulers and fortunes shared with family

Source: Forbes

The German billionaires Theo and Karl Albrecht have a joint net worth of $26,800 million, but are excluded from the list because their fortune is joint, and therefore neither of them can lay claim to the full amount as an individual. The Canadian publisher Kenneth Thomson is also excluded, because his $14,900 million fortune is shared with his family.

BEST PAID CEOs IN THE US

	CEO/COMPANY	EARNINGS ($)*
1	**Michael Dell,** Dell Computer	235,912,000
2	**Sanford Weill,** Citigroup	216,183,000
3	**Gerald Levin,** AOL Time Warner	164,388,000
4	**John Chambers,** Cisco Systems	157,305,000
5	**Henry Silverman,** Cendant	137,447,000
6	**Louis Gerstner Jr.,** IBM	103,410,000
7	**Joseph Nacchio,** Qwest Communications	97,387,000
8	**Walter Sanders III,** Advanced Micro	92,246,000
9	**Steven Jobs,** Apple Computer	90,000,000
10	**Jeffrey Skilling,** Enron#	84,449,000

Data as of April 6, 2001, based on earnings for latest financial year available; includes earnings from company stocks

Enron filed for bankruptcy on December 2, 2001

Source: Forbes

US STATES WITH THE MOST BILLIONAIRES

	STATE	NET WORTH OF BILLIONAIRES	BILLIONAIRES*
1	**California**	163,315,000,000	92
2	**New York**	104,025,000,000	49
3	**Texas**	78,553,000,000	36
4	**Florida**	24,350,000,000	20
5	**Illinois**	31,785,000,000	15
6	**=Pennsylvania**	19,850,000,000	14
	=Washington	109,495,000,000	14
8	**Michigan**	12,575,000,000	11
9	**=Colorado**	9,600,000,000	10
	=Massachusetts	33,200,000,000	10

Individuals and families with a net worth of $1,000 million or more

Source: Forbes

The dollar billionaire is a relatively recent phenomenon. In 1992, *Forbes* estimated there to be 73 billionaires in the US – 19 fewer than there are now in the state of California alone. The nation's principal centers of commerce – California's Silicon Valley, New York's Wall Street, and the oilfields of Texas – have inevitably produced the greatest number of billionaires, as the boom of the past decade increased the net worth of many, created newcomers to the list, and elevated numerous former humble millionaires to billionaire status.

TOP 10 RICHEST PEOPLE UNDER 40

	NAME/COUNTRY	AGE	SOURCE	ASSETS ($)
1	**Michael Dell,** US	37	Dell Computer Corp.	11,100,000,000
2	**Ernesto Bertarelli and family,** Switzerland	36	Biotechnology	8,400,000,000
3	**Pierre Omidyar,** US	34	eBay	4,500,000,000
4	**Lorenzo Mendoza and family,** Venezuela	36	Beer	4,400,000,000
5	**Mikhail Khodorkovsky,** Russia	38	Oil	3,700,000,000
6	**William Wrigley, Jr.,** US	39	Chewing gum	3,400,000,000
7	**Roman Abramovich,** Russia	35	Oil	3,000,000,000
8	**Ferit Sahenk and family,** Turkey	38	Banking	2,500,000,000
9	**=Mikhail Fridmann,** Russia	37	Oil	2,200,000,000
	=Jeffrey S. Skoll, Canada	37	eBay	2,200,000,000

Source: Forbes

This list includes billionaires who inherited successful family businesses, as well as entrepreneurs who started young, such as Michael S. Dell, who in 1984 with capital of just $1,000 founded the company that bears his name, Dell Computer Corp.

TOP 10 COUNTRIES WITH THE MOST DOLLAR BILLIONAIRES

	COUNTRY	$ BILLIONAIRES*
1	**US**	242
2	**Germany**	29
3	**Japan**	25
4	**Switzerland**	21
5	**UK**	17
6	**=Canada**	14
	=China (Hong Kong 13)	14
8	**=Italy**	12
	=France	12
	=Mexico	12

Individuals and families with a net worth of $1,000 million or more

Source: Forbes

TOP 10 HIGHEST-EARNING CELEBRITIES

	CELEBRITY	PROFESSION	EARNINGS IN 2000 ($)
1	**George Lucas**	Film producer/director	250,000,000
2	**Oprah Winfrey**	TV host/producer	150,000,000
3	**=The Beatles**	Rock band	70,000,000
	=Bruce Willis	Actor	70,000,000
5	**David Copperfield**	Illusionist	60,000,000
6	**Michael Schumacher**	Racing driver	59,000,000
7	**Tiger Woods**	Golfer	53,000,000
8	**Steven Spielberg**	Film producer/director	51,000,000
9	**Siegfried & Roy**	Illusionists	50,000,000
10	**Mike Tyson**	Boxer	48,000,000

Source: Forbes

Young Tycoon
The personal fortune of Swiss billionaire Ernesto Bertarelli, of the pharmaceutical company Serono, ranks him as the 31st richest in the world and the second richest under 40.

TOP 10 LARGEST UNCUT DIAMONDS

DIAMOND	CARATS
1 Cullinan	3,106.00

Measuring approximately 4 x 2½ x 2 in (100 x 65 x 50 mm), and weighing 1 lb 6 oz (621 g), the Cullinan was unearthed in 1905. Bought by the Transvaal government for £150,000 ($730,500), it was presented to King Edward VII. The King had it cut and the most important of the separate gems are now among the British Crown Jewels.

2 Excelsior	995.20

Found at the Jagersfontein Mine, South Africa, on June 30, 1893, it was cut by the celebrated Amsterdam firm of I.J. Asscher in 1903. The Excelsior produced 21 superb stones, which were sold mainly through Tiffany's of New York.

3 Star of Sierra Leone	968.90

Found in Sierra Leone on St. Valentine's Day, 1972, the uncut diamond weighed 8 oz (225 g) and measured 2½ x 1½ in (63.5 x 38.1 mm).

4 Incomparable	890.00

Discovered in 1980 at the village of Mbuji-Mayi, or "Goat Water," in the Dem. Rep. of Congo (then Zaïre). The four-year cutting process yielded a stone of 407.48 carats and 14 "satellite" gems.

5 Great Mogul	787.50

When found in 1650 in the Kollur Diggings, India, this diamond was presented to Shah Jahan, the builder of the Taj Mahal.

6 De Beers Millennium Star	777.00

Recently discovered near Mbuji-Mayi, Dem. Rep. of Congo (then Zaïre), the dimensions of the rough diamond from which the Millennium Star was cut are shrouded in secrecy. The polished stone, which was featured in the celebrations at the Millennium Dome, London (where it was the object of a failed heist), is 203.04 carats and measures 2 x 1½ x ¾ in (50.06 x 36.56 x 18.5 mm).

7 Woyie River	770.00

Found in 1945 beside the river in Sierra Leone whose name it now bears, it was cut into 30 stones. The largest of these, known as Victory and weighing 31.35 carats, was auctioned at Christie's, New York, in 1984 for $880,000.

8 Golden Jubilee	755.50

Found in 1986 in the Premier Mine (the home of the Cullinan), the polished diamond cut from it is, at 545.67 carats, the largest in the world.

9 Presidente Vargas	726.60

Discovered in the San Antonio River, Brazil, in 1938, it was named after the then President, Getúlio Dornelles Vargas.

10 Jonker	726.00

In 1934 this massive diamond was found on a claim owned by Johannes Jacobus Jonker, after it had been exposed by a heavy storm. Acquired by diamond dealer Harry Winston, it was exhibited in the American Museum of Natural History and attracted enormous crowds.

Source: *De Beers*

The weight of diamonds is measured in carats (the word derives from the carob bean, which was once used as a measure). There are approximately 142 carats to the ounce. Fewer than 1,000 rough diamonds weighing more than 100 carats have ever been recorded.

Jewel in the Crown
Cut from the Cullinan, the square-shaped Second Star of Africa is set in the British Imperial State Crown, beneath the Black Prince's Ruby.

TOP 10 MOST EXPENSIVE SINGLE DIAMONDS SOLD AT AUCTION

DIAMOND/SALE	PRICE ($)
1 Star of the Season, pear-shaped 100.10 carat D* IF# diamond, Sotheby's, Geneva, May 17, 1995	16,548,750 (SF19,858,500)
2 The Mouawad Splendor, pear-shaped 101.84 carat D IF diamond, Sotheby's, Geneva, Nov 14, 1990	12,760,000 (SF15,950,000)
3 Star of Happiness, cut cornered rectangular-cut 36 carat D IF diamond, Sotheby's, Geneva, Nov 17, 1993	11,882,333 (SF17,823,500)
4 Fancy blue emerald-cut 20.17 carat diamond VS2#, Sotheby's, New York, Oct 18, 1994	9,902,500
5 Eternal Light, pear-shaped 85.91 carat D, IF# diamond, Sotheby's, New York, Apr 19, 1988	9,130,000
6 Rectangular-cut fancy deep-blue 13.49 carat IF diamond, Christie's, New York, Apr 13, 1995	7,482,500
7 Rectangular-cut 52.59 carat D, IF diamond, Christie's, New York, Apr 20, 1988	7,480,000
8 Fancy pink rectangular-cut 19.66 carat diamond VVS2#, Christie's, Geneva, Nov 17, 1994	7,421,318 (SF9,573,500)
9 The Jeddah Bride, rectangular-cut 80.02 carat D, IF diamond, Sotheby's, New York, Oct 24, 1991	7,150,000
10 The Agra Diamond, fancy light pink cushion-shaped 32.24 carat diamond VS1#, Christie's, London, Jun 20, 1990	6,959,700 (£4,070,000)

* A color grade given to a diamond for its whiteness, D being the highest grade

\# A clarity grade, which gives the relative position of a diamond on a flawless-to-imperfect scale. IF = internally flawless, VS = very slightly flawed, VVS = very, very slightly flawed. The numbers indicate the degree of the flaw.

TOP 10 COUNTRIES MAKING GOLD JEWELRY

	COUNTRY	GOLD USED IN 2001 (TONNES)
1	India	654.0
2	Italy	478.7
3	China	161.0
4	US	158.0
5	Saudi Arabia and Yemen	137.3
6	Turkey	132.8
7	Indonesia	97.0
8	Egypt	96.5
9	Malaysia	81.0
10	South Korea	76.0
	World total	3,005.8

Source: *Gold Fields Mineral Services Ltd*, Gold Survey 2002

In 2001 the gold jewelry manufacturing nations of the world consumed 3,006 tonnes of gold (including recycled scrap). The Top 10 accounted for over 5 times as much gold as the entire production of South Africa, the world's foremost producer, and only 532 tonnes less than the entire world mined production for the whole year.

TOP 10 LARGEST POLISHED GEM DIAMONDS

	DIAMOND/LAST KNOWN WHEREABOUTS OR OWNER	CARATS
1	**Golden Jubilee,** King of Thailand	545.67
2	**Great Star of Africa/Cullinan I,** British Crown Jewels	530.20
3	**Incomparable/Zale,** auctioned in New York, 1988	407.48
4	**Second Star of Africa/Cullinan II,** British Crown Jewels	317.40
5	**Centenary,** privately owned	273.85
6	**Jubilee,** Paul-Louis Weiller	245.35
7	**De Beers,** sold in Geneva, 1982	234.50
8	**Red Cross,** sold in Geneva, 1973	205.07
9	**De Beers Millennium Star,** De Beers	203.04
10	**Black Star of Africa,** unknown	202.00

Source: *De Beers*

The *De Beers Millennium Star* achieved celebrity on November 7, 2000, when it was on display as part of a $500-million (£350-million) collection in the Millennium Dome, London. Armed raiders smashed their way in, intent on stealing the jewels. They were caught by police and jailed, but had they succeeded they would have been disappointed: following a tip-off, all the diamonds had been replaced by replicas.

CUTTING EDGE

AN UNNAMED WORKER found the Excelsior diamond on June 30, 1893, as he loaded a truck at the Jagersfontein Mine in South Africa. He took it directly to the mine manager, who rewarded him with a horse, a saddle and bridle, and £500 ($2,440). In 1903, the Excelsior was delivered to the celebrated Amsterdam firm of I. J. Asscher for cutting – the first time a diamond of this size had ever been cut. It took until well into the next year for the work of cutting and polishing to be completed. The Excelsior yielded 10 large gems ranging in size from 69.68 carats down to less than one carat. They were sold through Tiffany's of New York and other dealers, and entered private ownership. The largest, Excelsior I, last changed hands in 1996, when it was bought by jeweler and collector Robert Mouawad, who owns the diamond to this day.

TOP 10 COUNTRIES MAKING SILVER JEWELRY*

	COUNTRY	SILVER USED IN 2000 (OZ)
1	India	84,600,000
2	Italy	54,200,000
3	Thailand	30,000,000
4	US	13,700,000
5	Mexico	13,200,000
6	Germany	9,300,000
7	China	6,700,000
8	Bangladesh and Nepal	6,000,000
9	Turkey	5,900,000
10	South Korea	4,900,000
	World total	281,700,000

* Jewelry and silverware

Source: *The Silver Institute*, World Survey 2001

Silver Service
Silver on sale at a market in Taxco, silver capital of Mexico, one of the world's foremost manufacturers of silver jewelry.

Energy & Environment

TOP 10 PAPER-RECYCLING COUNTRIES

	COUNTRY	PRODUCTION PER 1,000 PEOPLE IN 2000 (TONNES)
1	Austria	163.49
2	Sweden	159.69
3	Switzerland	158.58
4	Netherlands	155.95
5	US	148.35
6	Germany	134.02
7	Finland	132.44
8	Japan	116.77
9	France	97.54
10	South Korea	82.78

Source: *Food and Agriculture Organization of the United Nations*

TOP 10 HYDROELECTRICITY-CONSUMING COUNTRIES

	COUNTRY	PERCENTAGE CHANGE FROM 1999–2000	CONSUMPTION* IN 2000
1	Canada	+4.3	30,800,000
2	Brazil	+4.1	26,200,000
3	US	-14.1	23,400,000
4	China	+13.4	19,000,000
5	Russia	+2.7	14,200,000
6	Norway	+16.7	12,200,000
7	Japan	-1.3	7,900,000
8	Sweden	+9.7	6,800,000
9	India	-6.4	6,600,000
10	France	-6.1	6,200,000
	World total	+1.7	230,400,000

* Tonnes of oil equivalent

Source: BP Statistical Review of World Energy 2001

TOP 10 CARBON DIOXIDE-EMITTING COUNTRIES

	COUNTRY	CO_2 EMISSIONS PER CAPITA IN 1999 (TONNES OF CARBON)
1	Qatar	14.2
2	United Arab Emirates	11.2
3	Bahrain	8.2
4	Singapore	6.4
5=	Guam	5.8
	=Kuwait	5.8
7	USA	5.6
8	Trinidad and Tobago	5.5
9	Luxembourg	5.4
10	Australia	5.0

Source: *Energy Information Administration*

CO_2 emissions derive from 3 principal sources – fossil fuel burning, cement manufacturing, and gas flaring.

TOP 10 ENERGY-CONSUMING COUNTRIES

	COUNTRY	ENERGY CONSUMPTION IN 2000*					
		OIL	GAS	COAL	NUCLEAR	HEP#	TOTAL
1	US	897.4	588.9	564.1	204.7	23.4	2,278.6
2	China	226.9	22.3	480.1	4.3	19.0	752.7
3	Russia	123.5	339.5	110.4	33.7	14.2	621.3
4	Japan	253.5	68.6	98.9	82.5	7.9	511.3
5	Germany	129.5	71.3	82.7	43.8	2.1	329.4
6	India	97.6	22.5	163.4	4.1	6.6	294.2
7	France	95.1	35.6	14.0	107.3	6.2	258.2
8	Canada	82.9	70.1	29.3	18.7	30.8	231.8
9	UK	77.6	86.1	37.7	24.0	0.7	226.1
10	South Korea	101.8	18.9	42.9	28.1	0.5	192.3
	World	3,503.6	2,164.0	2,186.0	668.6	230.4	8,752.4

* Millions of tonnes of oil equivalent
# Hydroelectric power

Source: BP Statistical Review of World Energy 2001

Paper Chase

Every ton of recycled paper uses 64 percent less energy, 50 percent less water, causes 74 percent less air pollution, and saves 17 trees compared with the same quantity derived from new wood pulp.

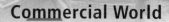

TOP 10 COUNTRIES MOST RELIANT ON NUCLEAR POWER

	COUNTRY	NUCLEAR ELECTRICITY AS PERCENTAGE OF TOTAL IN 2000
1	France	76.4
2	Lithuania	73.7
3	Belgium	56.8
4	Slovak Republic	53.4
5	Ukraine	47.3
6	Bulgaria	45.0
7	Hungary	42.2
8	South Korea	40.7
9	Sweden	39.0
10	Switzerland	38.2

Source: *International Atomic Energy Agency*

TOP 10 WIND POWER COUNTRIES

	COUNTRY	PRODUCTION IN 1997 (MEGAWATTS)
1	Germany	1,939
2	Denmark	1,061
3	Spain	406
4	Netherlands	336
5	UK	330
6	Sweden	108
7	Italy	100
8	Ireland	46
9	Greece	29
10	=Austria	20
	=Portugal	20

Source: *Energy Information Administration*

Wind Power
Turbines on a Spanish hillside contribute to the country's electricity production. Although environmentally friendly, wind power provides only a small percentage of the world's energy demands.

209

TOP 10 COMPUTER COMPANIES

COMPANY/COUNTRY	ANNUAL SALES ($)*
1 IBM, US	88,396,000,000
2 Fujitsu, Japan	49,603,490,000
3 Hewlett-Packard, US	48,782,000,000
4 Compaq Computer, US	42,383,000,000
5 Dell Computer, US	31,888,000,000
6 Canon, Japan	25,805,960,000
7 Xerox, US	18,632,000,000
8 Sun Microsystems, US	15,721,000,000
9 Ricoh, Japan	13,912,700,000
10 Gateway, US	9,600,600,000

In latest year for which figures are available

Source: Fortune 500/Fortune Global 500

Chips with Everything
Microchips have revolutionized all aspects of daily life, also becoming the focus of some of the world's foremost businesses.

TOP 10 COUNTRIES WITH THE MOST COMPUTERS

COUNTRY	PERCENTAGE OF WORLD COMPUTERS	TOTAL IN 2000
1 US	30.64	168,840,000
2 Japan	8.71	48,000,000
3 Germany	5.73	31,590,000
4 UK	4.70	25,910,000
5 France	3.96	21,810,000
6 China	3.87	21,310,000
7 Canada	3.12	17,200,000
8 Italy	3.11	17,170,000
9 South Korea	2.70	14,860,000
10 Brazil	2.04	11,230,000

Source: *Computer Industry Almanac, Inc.*

Computer industry estimates put the number of computers in the world at 98 million in 1990, 222 million in 1995, and over 625 million by the end of 2001, with the Top 10 countries owning over 70 percent of the total.

TOP 10 COUNTRIES THAT REGISTER THE MOST PATENTS

COUNTRY	PATENTS REGISTERED IN 1999
1 US	153,487
2 Japan	150,059
3 South Korea	62,635
4 Germany	49,548
5 France	44,287
6 UK	40,683
7 Italy	32,476
8 Netherlands	21,403
9 Spain	20,066
10 Russia	19,508

Source: *World Intellectual Property Organization*

A patent is an exclusive license to manufacture and exploit a unique product or process for a fixed period. The number of patents granted during 1999 represents a mere fraction of patents applied for.

TOP 10 COUNTRIES THAT REGISTER THE MOST TRADEMARKS

COUNTRY	TRADEMARKS REGISTERED IN 1999
1 Japan	123,656
2 China	115,654
3 US	87,431
4 Spain	67,214
5 Germany	62,923
6 Argentina	53,555
7 UK	53,472
8 Italy	41,591
9 Mexico	40,314
10 South Korea	32,968

Source: *World Intellectual Property Organization*

This list includes all trademarks (product names that are thereby legally protected) and service marks (which apply to company and other names applied to services rather than products) that were actually registered in 1999. The business of creating unique names for new goods and services has developed into a major international industry.

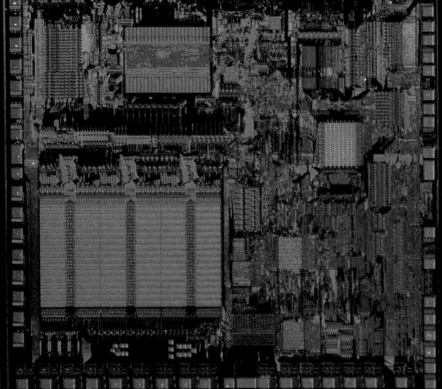

TOP 10 WORLD INDUSTRIES FOR RESEARCH AND DEVELOPMENT

	INDUSTRY	R&D SPENDING IN 2000 ($)
1	IT hardware	76,093,005,000
2	Automobiles and parts	50,109,924,000
3	Pharmaceuticals	43,145,151,000
4	Electronic and electrical	26,625,617,000
5	Chemicals	12,110,789,000
6	Aerospace and defense	10,903,064,000
7	Software and IT services	10,500,117,000
8	Engineering and machinery	5,968,971,000
9	Telecommunications	5,707,976,000
10	Health	5,122,678,000

Source: *The Financial Times Ltd., 2001*

Early Learning

Sales of computers simple enough for small children to operate have exceeded the dreams of the industry's pioneers, making the development of both hardware and software into huge global concerns.

TOP 10 PATENT COMPANIES IN THE US

	COMPANY	PATENTS IN 2000
1	IBM Corp.	2,886
2	NEC Corporation	2,020
3	Canon Kabushiki Kaisha	1,890
4	Samsung Electronics Co., Ltd.	1,441
5	Lucent Technologies Inc.	1,411
6	Sony Corporation	1,385
7	Micron Technology Inc.	1,304
8	Toshiba Corporation	1,232
9	Motorola Inc.	1,196
10	Fujitsu Limited	1,147

Source: *US Patent and Trademark Office*

TOP 10 INTERNATIONAL COMPANIES FOR RESEARCH AND DEVELOPMENT

	COMPANY/COUNTRY	INDUSTRY	R&D SPENDING IN 2000 ($)
1	BAE Systems, UK	Aerospace and defense	10,903,064,000
2	Ford Motor, US	Automobiles and parts	6,800,000,000
3	General Motors, US	Automobiles and parts	6,600,000,000
4	DaimlerChrysler, Germany	Automobiles and parts	5,949,476,000
5	Siemens, Germany	Electronic and electrical	5,250,973,000
6	IBM, US	IT hardware	4,901,000,000
7	Matsushita Electric, Japan	Electronic and electrical	4,602,074,000
8	Ericsson, Sweden	IT hardware	4,442,886,000
9	Motorola, US	IT hardware	4,437,000,000
10	Pfizer, US	Pharmaceuticals	4,435,000,000

Source: *The Financial Times Ltd., 2001*

Keep in Touch

TOP 10 COUNTRIES WITH THE HIGHEST RATIO OF CELLULAR MOBILE PHONE USERS

	COUNTRY	SUBSCRIBERS IN 2000	CELLULAR PHONES PER 100 INHABITANTS
1	Finland	3,893,000	75.2
2	=Austria	6,150,000	75.0
	=Taiwan	16,650,000	75.0
4	Italy	42,383,000	73.9
5	Sweden	6,477,000	73.0
6	Norway	3,139,000	70.2
7	UK	40,065,000	67.3
8	Switzerland	4,798,000	67.0
9	Portugal	6,522,000	65.4
10	Denmark	3,478,000	65.3
	US	110,547,000	40.1

Source: *Siemens AG*, International Telecom Statistics, 2001

There were approximately 727,911,100 cellular phone users in the world at the beginning of 2000, an increase of over 50 percent in just 1 year.

THE FIRST FAX

FIRST OR LAST

ALTHOUGH THE FAX MACHINE is a modern invention, its technology dates back 100 years or more. In 1903, Arthur Korn (1870–1945), a physics professor at Munich University, Germany, demonstrated the first practical photoelectric facsimile system, or photoelectric telephotography. A scanned image was converted into a varying electric current, enabling images to be transmitted by telephone.

TOP 10 COUNTRIES WITH THE BIGGEST INCREASE IN CELLULAR MOBILE PHONE USERS

	COUNTRY	SUBSCRIBERS IN 2000 INCREASE	% INCREASE
1	Morocco	2,510,000	652
2	=Bulgaria	408,000	124
	=Czech Republic	2,403,000	124
4	Germany	24,850,000	107
5	Philippines	2,920,000	103
6	Turkey	8,128,000	101
7	=China	41,790,000	96
	=India	1,523,000	96
9	Hungary	1,473,000	91
10	Mexico	6,831,000	88
	US	24,500,000	3.9

Source: *Siemens AG*, International Telecom Statistics, 2001

TOP 10 COUNTRIES WITH THE MOST TELEPHONES

COUNTRY	TELEPHONE LINES*
1 US	202,176,000
2 China	136,800,000
3 Japan	74,100,000
4 Germany	51,157,000
5 UK	34,748,000
6 France	34,656,000
7 India	31,300,000
8 Brazil	31,100,000
9 Russia	27,450,000
10 Italy	27,040,000

*As of January 1, 2001

Source: *Siemens AG,* International Telecom Statistics, 2001

It is estimated that there are some 990,728,000 telephone lines in use in the world, of which 316,850,000 are in Europe, 229,800,000 in North and South America, 338,592,000 in Asia, 21,149,000 in Africa, and 14,337,000 in Oceania.

TOP 10 COUNTRIES WITH THE BIGGEST INCREASE IN TELEPHONE LINES

COUNTRY	% INCREASE IN 2000
1 El Salvador	34.5
2 China	25.8
3 Brazil	24.5
4 Sudan	23.3
5 Saudi Arabia	18.6
6 Vietnam	18.3
7 India	18.1
8 Guatemala	14.6
9 Tunisia	11.7
10 Bangladesh	11.6
US	3.9

Source: *Siemens AG,* International Telecom Statistics, 2001

TOP 10 COUNTRIES RECEIVING THE MOST LETTERS FROM ABROAD

COUNTRY	ITEMS OF MAIL RECEIVED IN 2000*
1 India	849,270,000
2 Germany	702,000,000
3 UK	521,791,463
4 US	474,347,500
5 France	468,300,000
6 Netherlands	299,000,000
7 Japan	290,375,000
8 Saudi Arabia	252,645,000
9 Algeria	231,415,000
10 Italy	222,744,602

*Or latest year for which data available

Source: *Universal Postal Union*

TOP 10 COUNTRIES SENDING THE MOST LETTERS ABROAD

COUNTRY	ITEMS OF MAIL SENT ABROAD IN 2000*
1 UK	928,511,545
2 US	904,600,000
3 France	597,900,000
4 Germany	402,600,000
5 Saudi Arabia	244,540,000
6 Russia	221,800,000
7 India	196,860,000
8 Belgium	193,793,831
9 Australia	192,700,000
10 Italy	162,328,532

*Or latest year for which data available

Source: *Universal Postal Union*

Phone Home
Morocco has experienced an unprecedented increase in cellular phone usage. Cellular phones are especially popular in Africa, where landlines are sparse and unreliable.

TOP 10 LETTER-MAILING COUNTRIES

COUNTRY	AVERAGE NO. OF MAILED ITEMS PER INHABITANT IN 2000*
1 Vatican City	6,125.00
2 US	734.36
3 Sweden	502.89
4 Norway	467.43
5 France	447.57
6 Netherlands	442.75
7 Austria	371.63
8 Luxembourg	346.59
9 Finland	344.58
10 Belgium	344.05

*Or latest year for which data available

Source: *Universal Postal Union*

Official church missives account for much of the mail posted in the Vatican City (population about 750), but Romans have also discovered that mail sent from there with Vatican stamps gets priority status.

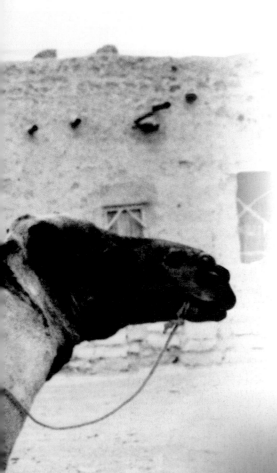

World Wide Web

TOP 10 COUNTRIES WITH THE HIGHEST PROPORTION OF INTERNET USERS

	COUNTRY	INTERNET USERS PER 1,000 IN 1999
1	Canada	428.20
2	Sweden	414.15
3	Finland	408.04
4	US	406.49
5	Iceland	403.46
6	Denmark	395.97
7	Norway	379.59
8	Australia	343.27
9	Singapore	310.77
10	New Zealand	264.90
	World average	46.75

Source: *Internet Industry Almanac, Inc.*

TOP 10 USES OF THE INTERNET

	ACTIVITY	% OF INTERNET USERS*
1	Email	90
2	General information	77
3	Surfing	69
4	Reading	67
5	Hobbies	63
6	Product information	62
7	Travel information	54
8	Work/business	46
9	=Entertainment/games	36
	=Buying	36

* Based on US sample survey, 2000

Source: *Stanford Institute for the Quantitative Study of Society*

Other uses include stock quotes (27 percent), job search (26 percent), chat rooms (24 percent), homework (21 percent), and auctions (13 percent).

TOP 10 SEARCH ENGINES

	SEARCH ENGINE	US AUDIENCE REACH (%)*
1	Yahoo!	64.9
2	MSN	58.2
3	Lycos	44.9
4	Go.com	29.4
5	Google	24.4
6	Netscape	18.6
7	Excite	14.0
8	Ask Jeeves	12.1
9	iWon	11.2
10	NBCi	8.1

* Percentage of surfers who visit the search engine site each month; based on sample of US web surfers, December 2001

Source: *Jupiter Media Metrix*

TOP 10 MOST COMMON TYPES OF INTERNET FRAUD

	CATEGORY	AVERAGE LOSS ($)	% OF ALL COMPLAINTS IN 2001
1	Auctions	478	63
2	Online shopping	845	11
3	Nigerian money offers	6,542	9
4	=Information/adult services	234	3
	=Internet access	568	3
6	=Computer equipment/software	1,102	2
	=Work-at-home plans	120	2
8	Advance-fee loans	1,209	1
9	Credit card offers	412	0.6
10	Business opportunities	16,031	0.4

Source: *National Fraud Information Center, National Consumers League*

TOP 10 MOST VISITED WEBSITES IN THE US

WEBSITE	UNIQUE VISITORS IN US*
1 AOL Time Warner	39,458,234
2 Yahoo!	32,514,019
3 MSN	28,971,380
4 Microsoft	11,749,833
5 Amazon	8,975,025
6 eBay	8,816,073
7 About-Primedia	7,985,457
8 Google	7,589,240
9 Lycos Network	4,894,339
10 Walt Disney Internet Group	6,605,811

* Total number of unique visitors during week ending December 16, 2001

Source: Nielsen/NetRatings Audience Measurement Service

TOP 10 MOST WIRED CITIES

CITY/COUNTRY
1 **New York,** New York, US
2 **London,** UK
3 **Amsterdam,** Netherlands
4 **Paris,** France
5 **San Francisco,** California, US
6 **Tokyo,** Japan
7 **Washington DC,** US
8 **Miami,** Florida
9 **Los Angeles,** California
10 **Copenhagen,** Denmark

Source: TeleGeography

These are the top cities in the world for connection to the internet. New York has direct connections with 71 countries and the highest bandwidth capacity of any city in the world.

TOP 10 SEARCHES ON LYCOS IN 2001

SEARCH TERM
1 **Dragonball**
2 **Britney Spears**
3 **Napster**
4 **Tattoos**
5 **Osama bin Laden**
6 **IRS**
7 **Pokémon**
8 **World Trade Center**
9 **Nostradamus**
10 **WWF**

Source: Lycos 50

Popular search engine Lycos mirrored the fluctuating concerns of its users in internet searches during 2001. While Japanese cult cartoon Dragonball remained top overall, after the events of September 11 it was eclipsed by Osama bin Laden, who remained the No.1 search term for 5 weeks.

TOP 10 COUNTRIES WITH THE MOST INTERNET USERS

COUNTRY	USERS*
1 US	134,600,000
2 Japan	33,900,000
3 China	22,500,000
4 Germany	19,900,000
5 South Korea	19,000,000
6 UK	16,800,000
7 Canada	15,400,000
8 Italy	12,500,000
9 France	9,000,000
10 Australia	7,600,000
World total	413,700,000

* As of the end of 2000

Source: Computer Industry Almanac, Inc.

Chinese Internet Café

These young internet club members are using computers at Beijing Airport.

Hazards at Home & Work

THE 10 MOST ACCIDENT-PRONE COUNTRIES

	COUNTRIES	ACCIDENT DEATH RATE PER 100,000*
1	Latvia	104.2
2	Estonia	103.0
3	Belarus	99.6
4	Russia	98.8
5	Lithuania	88.0
6	Ukraine	76.4
7	Moldova	63.2
8	Kazakhstan	59.6
9	Romania	56.0
10	South Korea	53.9
	US	35.7

* In those countries/the latest year for which data available

Source: UN Demographic Yearbook

THE 10 MOST COMMON CAUSES OF DOMESTIC FIRE IN THE US*

	CAUSE	FIRES
1	Cooking equipment	95,300
2	Heating equipment	65,900
3	Incendiary or suspicious causes	50,700
4	Other equipment	43,900
5	Electrical distribution system	39,200
6	Appliance, tool, or air conditioning	30,100
7	Smoking materials	22,000
8	Open flame, torch	20,500
9	Child playing	19,800
10	Exposure (to other hostile fire)	15,700

* Based on a survey conducted by the National Fire Incidence Reporting System (NFIRS) and National Fire Protection Association (NFPA) covering the period 1993–97

THE 10 MOST DANGEROUS OCCUPATIONS IN THE US

	OCCUPATION	ACCIDENTAL DEATHS IN 2000
1	Truck drivers	852
2	Handlers, equipment cleaners, helpers, and laborers	617
3	Construction trades (except supervisors)	504
4	Management/administrative executives	397
5	Sales occupations	386
6	Mechanics and repairers	322
7	=Farmers and farm managers	320
	=Other farm workers (including supervisors)	320
9	Construction laborers	288
10	Protective services (police, firefighters, guards)	257

Source: US Department of Labor, Bureau of Labor Statistics

THE 10 MOST ACCIDENT-PRONE PRIVATE INDUSTRIES IN THE US

	INDUSTRY	INJURIES PER 100 FULL-TIME EMPLOYEES IN 2000
1	Meat-packing plants	24.7
2	Motor vehicles and car bodies	22.7
3	Ship building and repairing	22.0
4	Gray and ductile iron foundries	21.7
5	Mobile homes	19.7
6	Truck and bus bodies	19.4
7	Aluminum foundries	18.3
8	=Industrial furnaces and ovens	18.1
	=Travel trailers and campers	18.1
10	Metal sanitary ware	17.5

Source: US Bureau of Labor Statistics

With an all-industry average injury rate of 6.1 per 100, it is evident that, other than the meat-packing industry, the US's most dangerous trades involve metal working – some of which report injury rates almost double those of workers who are handling other materials.

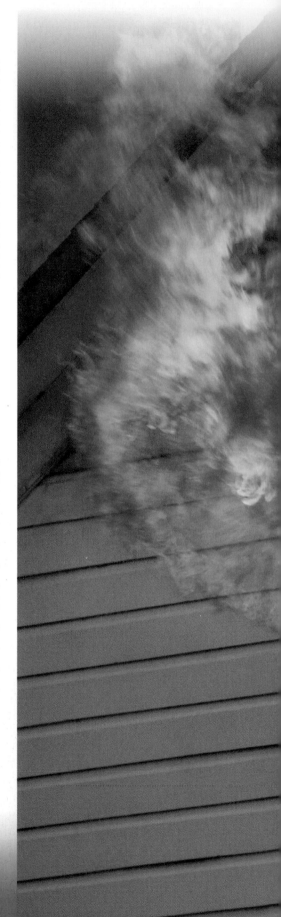

TOP 10 PRODUCTS MOST OFTEN INVOLVED IN ACCIDENTS IN THE US

	PRODUCT GROUP*	ESTIMATED NUMBER OF INJURIES IN 2000
1	Stairs, ramps, landings, and floors	2,086,689
2	Beds, mattresses, and pillows	487,352
3	Chairs, sofas, and sofabeds	433,793
4	Doors and panels (non-glass)	363,149
5	Tables	311,208
6	Bathroom structures and fixtures	277,510
7	Cans and other containers	253,451
8	Desks, cabinets, shelves, and racks	248,458
9	Ladders and stools	197,198
10	Toys	184,483

* Excluding sport and recreational equipment

Source: *US Consumer Product Safety Commission/NEISS (National Electronic Injury Surveillance System)*

These figures are based on the results of a survey of injuries caused by some 15,000 types of product, based on a sample of 100 US hospitals during 2000. The highest rate of injury recorded is for people aged 65 and over, who hurt themselves on stairs, ramps, landings, and floors at a rate of 1,653.6 per 100,000.

THE 10 MOST COMMON CAUSES OF UNNATURAL DEATH IN THE US

	CAUSE	TOTAL	DEATH RATE PER 100,000 IN 1999
1	Traffic accident	40,965	15.02
2	Poisoning	19,741	7.23
3	Suicide – firearm	16,599	6.09
4	Suicide – non-firearm	12,600	4.61
5	Falling	13,931	5.11
6	Suffocation	11,748	4.31
7	Homicide – firearm	10,828	3.94
8	Fire – burns and flames	7,689	2.82
9	Homicide – non-firearm	6,061	2.20
10	Drowning	4,153	1.50
	Total deaths from injury and adverse effects	*151,109*	*55.36*

Source: *National Center for Injury Prevention and Control*

Home Fires Burning
Fires associated with cooking are among the most common domestic accidents, and result in the most serious personal injuries and property damage.

Food for Thought

TOP 10 BREAD CONSUMERS

	COUNTRY	CONSUMPTION PER CAPITA IN 2000		
		(LB)	(OZ)	(KG)
1	Turkey	440	1	199.6
2	Serbia and Montenegro	297	10	135.0
3	Bulgaria	293	7	133.1
4	Slovakia	292	9	132.7
5	Latvia	258	13	117.4
6	Egypt	245	13	111.5
7	Saudi Arabia	233	4	105.8
8	Estonia	226	7	102.7
9	Romania	220	14	100.2
10	Lithuania	206	2	93.5
	US	*46*	*15*	*21.3*

Source: *Euromonitor*

Our Daily Bread
Turkey has been identified as the world's foremost consumer of bread – Turkish people eat more than three times their own body weight in bread annually.

TOP 10 BAKED BEAN CONSUMERS

	COUNTRY	CONSUMPTION PER CAPITA IN 1999		
		(LB)	(OZ)	(KG)
1	UK	11	11	5.3
2	Ireland	11	4	5.1
3	Mexico	9	4	4.2
4	New Zealand	4	14	2.2
5	=Australia	4	0	1.8
	=France	4	0	1.8
7	Switzerland	3	5	1.5
8	Saudi Arabia	3	1	1.4
9	=Canada	2	14	1.3
	=US	2	14	1.3

Source: *Euromonitor*

TOP 10 BREAKFAST CEREAL CONSUMERS

	COUNTRY	CONSUMPTION PER CAPITA IN 2000		
		(LB)	(OZ)	(KG)
1	Sweden	22	15	10.4
2	Canada	17	3	7.8
3	Australia	16	1	7.3
4	UK	15	3	6.9
5	=Nauru	14	2	6.4
	=New Zealand	14	2	6.4
7	Ireland	11	14	5.4
8	US	11	7	5.2
9	Finland	9	11	4.4
10	Denmark	7	1	3.2

Source: *Euromonitor*

TOP 10 FROZEN-FOOD CONSUMERS

	COUNTRY	CONSUMPTION PER CAPITA IN 1999		
		(LB)	(OZ)	(KG)
1	Norway	78	8	35.6
2	Denmark	71	10	32.5
3	UK	68	2	30.9
4	Israel	63	8	28.8
5	Czech Republic	46	15	21.3
6	Sweden	44	12	20.3
7	Ireland	41	11	18.9
8	Belgium	39	4	17.8
9	Finland	36	10	16.6
10	US	35	15	16.3

Source: *Euromonitor*

TOP 10 | LARGEST CHEESES EVER MADE

WEIGHT

1 **57,508 lb (26,085 kg)**
In his book, *Natural History*, the Roman historian Pliny the Elder (AD 23–79) describes a 1,000-lb (454-kg) cheese that was made in Italy. The current world record holder is this monster cheddar made in 1995 in Quebec, Canada, by Loblaws Supermarkets and Agropur Dairies.

2 **40,060 lb (18,171 kg)**
This former world record holder was manufactured on March 13–14, 1988, by Simon's Specialty Cheese of Little Chute, Wisconsin. It was then taken on tour in a refrigerated "cheesemobile."

3 **34,591 lb (15,690 kg)**
Made on January 20–22, 1964, for the World's Fair, New York, by the Wisconsin Cheese Foundation, this cheese was 14 ft 6 in (4.4 m) long, 6 ft 6 in (2.0 m) wide, and 6 ft (1.8 m) high and took 183 tons (202 tonnes) of milk.

4 **22,000 lb (9,970 kg)**
Made for the Colombian Exposition in Chicago in 1893, this 11-ton (12-tonne) monster had a circumference of 28 ft (8.5 m) and used the equivalent of a day's milk from 10,000 cows. It was made at several factories in Canada. On arrival at the fair, it fell through the floor.

5 **13,440 lb (6,096 kg)**
This cheese was made in 1937 with the milk from 6,000 cows and was exhibited at the New York State Fair in Syracuse.

6 **11,815 lb (5,359 kg)**
This cheddar was made in January 1957 in Flint, Michigan, from the milk pooled by a group of 367 farmers from their 6,600 cows.

7 **8,000 lb (3,629 kg)**
This large Canadian cheddar was made for the 1883 Toronto Fair, and is the subject of the *Ode On the Mammoth Cheese* by poet James McIntyre.

8 **7,300 lb (3,311 kg)**
This "Big Cheese" was made at the James Harris Cheese Factory, Ingersoll, Canada, in 1866. It measured 3 ft (0.9 m) high and 7 ft (2.1 m) in diameter, and was exhibited at the New York State Fair, Saratoga, before being shipped to Liverpool, UK, and exhibited all over England.

9 **1,474 lb (669 kg)**
A cheese 13 ft (4.0 m) in circumference made by James Elgar of Northamptonshire, UK, in 1849.

10 **1,400 lb (653 kg)**
A cheddar given to President Andrew Jackson on his inauguration in Washington, DC, in 1825.

TOP 10 | MOST SUCCESSFUL FAST-FOOD COMPANIES

COMPANY/COUNTRY	FAST FOOD MARKET SHARE % IN 1999
1 **McDonald's Corporation,** US	21.9
2 **Tricon Global Restaurants, Inc.,** US	10.7
3 **Diageo plc,** UK	7.1
4 **Wendy's International, Inc.,** US	3.8
5 **=Allied Domecq plc,** UK	2.3
=Doctor's Associates, Inc., US	2.3
7 **CKE Restaurants, Inc.,** US	2.0
8 **Domino's Pizza, Inc.,** US	1.8
9 **Berkshire Hathaway, Inc.,** US	1.5
10 **Triarc Corporation,** US	1.3

Source: *Euromonitor*

TOP 10 | COUNTRIES WITH THE MOST FAST-FOOD RESTAURANTS

COUNTRY	RESTAURANTS IN 1999
1 **China**	554,170
2 **US**	177,125
3 **India**	38,598
4 **Japan**	38,429
5 **UK**	26,189
6 **Germany**	23,616
7 **Brazil**	17,955
8 **Canada**	17,036
9 **Italy**	16,598
10 **Russia**	10,228

Source: *Euromonitor*

Fast-Food for Thought
The appeal of the hamburger has enabled McDonald's to establish its unique role in the shaping of the world's eating habits: its 29,000 restaurants in 121 countries serve 45 million people every day.

Sweet Treats

TOP 10 SUGAR CONFECTIONERY CONSUMERS

	COUNTRY	CONSUMPTION PER CAPITA IN 2000 (LB)	(OZ)	(KG)
1	Denmark	18	5	8.3
2	Netherlands	13	7	6.1
3	Sweden	13	4	6.0
4	Finland	12	5	5.6
5	Russia	10	6	4.7
6	Norway	10	2	4.6
7	US	9	15	4.5
8	Iceland	9	11	4.4
9	Luxembourg	9	4	4.2
10	Andorra	9	1	4.1
	World	2	0	0.9

Source: *Euromonitor*

TOP 10 CHOCOLATE CONFECTIONERY CONSUMERS

	COUNTRY	CONSUMPTION PER CAPITA IN 2000 (LB)	(OZ)	(KG)
1	Switzerland	25	6	11.5
2	Liechtenstein	22	15	10.4
3	Luxembourg	22	11	10.3
4	UK	21	10	9.8
5	Belgium	18	15	8.6
6	Norway	17	3	7.8
7	=Germany	17	0	7.7
	=Ireland	17	0	7.7
9	Iceland	16	12	7.6
10	Austria	13	14	6.3
	World	2	3	1.0
	US	12	9	5.7

Source: *Euromonitor*

TOP 10 CHOCOLATE CANDY BARS IN THE US

	BRAND/MANUFACTURER	SALES* ($)
1	M&Ms, Mars	97,404,576
2	Hershey's Milk Chocolate, Hershey Chocolate	81,296,784
3	Reese's Peanut Butter Cups, Hershey Chocolate	54,391,268
4	Snickers, Mars	53,695,428
5	KitKat, Hershey Chocolate (under licence from Nestlé)	38,168,580
6	Twix, Mars	33,174,400
7	York Peppermint Patty, York Cone Company	25,494,038
8	Peter Paul Almond Joy, Hershey Chocolate	23,721,998
9	Butterfinger, Nestlé	22,804,380
10	Three Musketeers, Mars	19,834,244

* 3.5 oz candy bars only; 52 weeks to Jan 27, 2002

Source: *Information Resources, Inc.*

TOP 10 SUGAR PRODUCERS

	COUNTRY	PRODUCTION IN TONS* 2001
1	India	21,274,625
2	Brazil	18,777,888
3	China	9,149,682
4	US	8,509,850
5	Thailand	5,682,419
6	Mexico	5,566,677
7	Germany	5,015,520
8	France	4,624,200
9	Australia	4,608,767
10	Cuba	3,951,789
	World total	141,111,859

* Raw centrifugal sugar

Source: *Food and Agriculture Organization of the United Nations*

Short and Sweet

The world's leading crop by weight, sugar cane, along with sugar beet, fuels the planet's insatiable appetite for sweet foods.

Cream Topping
Ice cream consumption varies greatly around the world. Factors affecting the amount purchased and eaten include wealth, national taste, and dietary traditions.

FIRST HERSHEY FACTORY

PENNSYLVANIA-BORN Milton Snavely Hershey (1857–1945) began his apprenticeship as a candy maker at the age of 15, and in 1883 he established the Lancaster Caramel Company. At the Colombian Exposition in 1893, he bought German chocolate-making equipment and sold his caramel business for $1 million, so that he could turn his attention to making chocolate. In 1903, he began to build what was to become the world's largest chocolate manufacturing plant. Like Cadbury, in England, Hershey was a good employer who built a town for his employees. He named the town after himself, and even gave its avenues names like Cocoa and Chocolate.

FIRST OR LAST

TOP 10 SUGAR CONSUMERS

COUNTRY	CONSUMPTION PER CAPITA* IN 1999 (LB)	(OZ)	(KG)
1 Delize	138	0	62.6
2 Cuba	129	3	58.6
3 Barbados	117	5	53.2
4 Brazil	112	3	50.9
5 Iceland	111	5	50.5
6 =Costa Rica	110	8	50.4
=Trinidad and Tobago	110	8	50.4
8 Macedonia	110	0	49.9
9 New Zealand	109	2	49.5
10 Swaziland	106	7	48.3
World	41	7	18.8
US	67	4	30.5

* Refined equivalent

Source: *Food and Agriculture Organization of the United Nations*

Each citizen of Belize, the current world leader in the sweet-tooth stakes, would appear to consume a quantity equal to more than the 2.2 lb (1 kg) bag of sugar every week.

TOP 10 ICE CREAM CONSUMERS

COUNTRY	CONSUMPTION PER CAPITA IN 2000 (PINTS)	(LITERS)
1 Australia	29.2	16.6
2 Italy	25.0	14.2
3 US	24.5	13.9
4 New Zealand	23.2	13.2
5 Sweden	21.5	12.2
6 Ireland	18.1	10.3
7 Norway	16.2	9.2
8 Canada	16.0	9.1
9 Israel	15.8	9.0
10 Finland	15.5	8.8

Source: *Euromonitor*

TOP 10 CHEWING GUM CONSUMERS

COUNTRY	CONSUMPTION PER CAPITA IN 2000 (LB)	(OZ)	(KG)
1 =Andorra	2	0	900
=Iceland	2	0	900
=Norway	2	0	900
4 =Israel	1	9	700
=Liechtenstein	1	9	700
=Switzerland	1	9	700
=US	1	9	700
8 =St. Kitts and Nevis	1	5	600
=Spain	1	5	600
=Turkey	1	5	600

Source: *Euromonitor*

Drink Up

TOP 10 FRESH COFFEE DRINKERS

COUNTRY	CONSUMPTION PER CAPITA IN 1999			
	(LB)	(OZ)	(KG)	(CUPS*)
1 Sweden	13	14	6.3	945
2 =Finland	12	12	5.8	870
=Norway	12	12	5.8	870
4 Iceland	12	2	5.5	825
5 Switzerland	11	3	5.1	765
6 =Denmark	10	2	4.6	690
=Liechtenstein	10	2	4.6	690
=Netherlands	10	2	4.6	690
9 Austria	9	14	4.5	675
10 Germany	8	13	4.0	600
US	3	15	1.8	270

* Based on 150 cups per 2 lb 3 oz (1 kg)

Source: *Euromonitor*

Café Society

The world's most enthusiastic coffee drinkers are all Europeans – led by Scandinavians, who consume two or more cups each a day.

TOP 10 ALCOHOL CONSUMERS

COUNTRY	CONSUMPTION PER CAPITA* IN 2000	
	(PINTS)	(LITERS)
1 Ireland	21.6	12.3
2 Luxembourg	21.2	12.1
3 Romania	20.5	11.7
4 Portugal	19.0	10.8
5 Czech Republic	18.6	10.6
6 =France	18.4	10.5
=Germany	18.4	10.5
8 Spain	17.5	10.0
9 Denmark	16.7	9.5
10 Austria	16.5	9.4

* Pure alcohol

Source: *Productschap voor Gedistilleerde Dranken*

A country's alcohol intake is measured by the amount of pure alcohol consumed within beer, wine, or spirits. Western European countries lead the world, with an average consumption of 15.1 pints (8.6 liters) per person per annum, compared with a world average of 5.9 pints (3.4 liters).

TOP 10 BEER DRINKERS

COUNTRY	CONSUMPTION PER CAPITA IN 2000	
	(PINTS)	(LITERS)
1 Czech Republic	281.5	160.0
2 Ireland	269.0	152.9
3 Germany	220.8	125.5
4 Austria	190.2	108.1
5 Luxembourg	189.8	107.9
6 Denmark	175.4	99.7
7 Belgium	172.8	98.2
8 UK	167.8	95.4
9 Australia	167.1	95.0
10 Slovak Republic	153.9	87.5

Source: *Productschap voor Gedistilleerde Dranken*

While no African countries appear in this list – or even in the Top 50 countries – this does not mean that people in Africa do not drink beer. Bottled beer is often prohibitively expensive, so people tend to consume homemade beers sold in local markets, which are excluded from national statistics.

DECAFFEINATED COFFEE

IN 1903 IN BREMEN, Germany, coffee importer Ludwig Roselius (1874–1943) received a batch of coffee beans that appeared to have been ruined by contamination with seawater. Research indicated that they had lost their caffeine content, which inspired Roselius to perfect a way of removing the caffeine from coffee without spoiling its flavor. He marketed this new product as Sanka (from "sans café," French for without coffee). Roselius founded Kaffee Hag in 1906, made a fortune from his business, and became a leading art collector, acquiring many treasures that are today exhibited in a museum in his native Bremen.

TOP 10 BOTTLED WATER DRINKERS*

	COUNTRY	CONSUMPTION PER CAPITA IN 1999 (PINTS)	(LITERS)
1	Andorra	287.3	163.3
2	Italy	242.8	138.0
3	Monaco	.235.8	134.0
4	Luxembourg	230.1	130.8
5	France	228.9	130.1
6	Spain	197.9	112.5
7	Belgium	191.8	109.0
8	Germany	182.6	103.8
9	Switzerland	167.8	95.4
10	Liechtenstein	151.1	85.9
	US	64.2	36.5

* Includes carbonated, still, and flavored water

Source: Euromonitor

TOP 10 CARBONATED SOFT DRINK CONSUMERS

	COUNTRY	CONSUMPTION PER CAPITA IN 1999 (PINTS)	(LITERS)
1	US	377.9	214.8
2	United Arab Emirates	279.4	158.8
3	Mexico	279.2	158.7
4	Andorra	237.2	134.8
5	Bahrain	225.6	128.2
6	St. Lucia	220.4	125.3
7	Dominica	218.5	124.2
8	Luxembourg	210.4	119.6
9	Belize	210.1	119.4
10	Norway	208.0	118.2

Source: Euromonitor

TOP 10 WINE DRINKERS

	COUNTRY	CONSUMPTION PER CAPITA IN 2000 (PINTS)	(LITERS)
1	Luxembourg	106.9	60.8
2	France	98.5	56.0
3	Italy	89.7	51.0
4	Portugal	87.9	50.0
5	Switzerland	76.5	43.5
6	Romania	64.5	36.7
7	Argentina	61.4	34.9
8	Greece	59.8	34.0
9	Ireland	58.4	33.2
10	Spain	58.0	33.0
	US	7.6	13.3

Source: Productschap voor Gedistilleerde Dranken

TOP 10 TEA DRINKERS

	COUNTRY	ANNUAL CONSUMPTION PER CAPITA* (LB)	(OZ)	(KG)	(CUPS#)
1	Ireland	5	15	2.69	1,184
2	Libya	5	6	2.44	1,074
3	Kuwait	5	6	2.43	1,069
4	Turkey	5	5	2.40	1,056
5	UK	5	2	2.33	1,025
6	Qatar	4	14	2.21	972
7	Iraq	4	8	2.03	893
8	Morocco	3	1	1.40	616
9	Sri Lanka	2	13	1.28	563
10	Tunisia	2	12	1.25	550
	US	0	12	0.34	149

* 1998–2000

Based on 440 cups per 2 lb 3 oz (1 kg)

Source: International Tea Committe Ltd., London, England

Recorded figures for tea consumption vary enormously around the world, from the current world-leading Irish figure down to 3 oz/0.08 kg (35 cups) in Italy and Tanzania.

Wine Appreciation
Each of the Top 5 wine-drinking countries consumes the equivalent of a bottle of wine per capita every week.

TRANSPORTATION
& TOURISM

Speed Freaks

THE 10 LATEST HOLDERS OF THE LAND SPEED RECORD

	DRIVER/COUNTRY/CAR	DATE	SPEED (MPH)	(KM/H)
1	**Andy Green** (UK) Thrust SSC*	Oct 15, 1997	763.04	1,227.99
2	**Richard Noble** (UK) Thrust 2*	Oct 4, 1983	633.47	1,013.47
3	**Gary Gabelich** (US) The Blue Flame	Oct 23, 1970	622.41	995.85
4	**Craig Breedlove** (US) Spirit of America – Sonic 1	Nov 15, 1965	600.60	960.96
5	**Art Arfons** (US) Green Monster	Nov 7, 1965	576.55	922.48
6	**Craig Breedlove** (US) Spirit of America – Sonic 1	Nov 2, 1965	555.48	888.76
7	**Art Arfons** (US) Green Monster	Oct 27, 1964	536.71	858.73
8	**Craig Breedlove** (US) Spirit of America	Oct 15, 1964	526.28	842.04
9	**Craig Breedlove** (US) Spirit of America	Oct 13, 1964	468.72	749.95
10	**Art Arfons** (US) Green Monster	Oct 5, 1964	434.02	694.43

* Location, Black Rock Desert, Nevada; all other speeds were achieved at Bonneville Salt Flats, Utah

THE 10 FIRST AMERICAN HOLDERS OF THE LAND SPEED RECORD

	DRIVER*/CAR/LOCATION	DATE	(MPH)	(KM/H)
1	**William Vanderbilt,** Mors, Albis, France	Aug 5, 1902	76.08	122.44
2	**Henry Ford#,** Ford Arrow, Lake St. Clair, Michigan	Jan 12, 1904	91.37	147.05
3	**Fred Marriott#,** Stanley Rocket, Daytona Beach, Florida	Jan 23, 1906	121.57	195.65
4	**Barney Oldfield#,** Benz, Daytona Beach, Florida	Mar 16, 1910	131.27	211.26
5	**Bob Burman#,** Benz, Daytona Beach, Florida	Apr 23, 1911	141.37	227.51
6	**Ralph de Palma#,** Packard, Daytona Beach, Florida	Feb 17, 1919	149.87	241.19
7	**Tommy Milton#,** Duesenberg, Daytona Beach, Florida	Apr 27, 1920	156.03	251.11
8	**Ray Keech,** White Triplex, Daytona Beach, Florida	Apr 22, 1928	207.55	334.02
9	**Craig Breedlove#,** Spirit of America, Bonneville Salt Flats, Utah	Aug 5, 1963	407.45	655.73
10	**Tom Green,** Wingfoot Express, Bonneville Salt Flats, Utah	Oct 2, 1964	413.20	664.98

* Excluding those who subsequently broke their own records

Record not recognized in Europe

THE 10 LATEST HOLDERS OF THE MOTORCYCLE SPEED RECORD

	RIDER	MOTORCYCLE	YEAR	(MPH)	(KM/H)
1	**Dave Campos**	Twin 91 cu in/1,491 cc Ruxton Harley-Davidson *Easyriders*	1990	322.15	518.45
2	**Donald A. Vesco**	Twin 1,016 cc Kawasaki *Lightning Bolt*	1978	318.60	512.73
3	**Donald A. Vesco**	1,496 cc Yamaha *Silver Bird*	1975	302.93	487.50
4	**Calvin Rayborn**	1,480 cc Harley-Davidson	1970	264.96	426.40
5	**Calvin Rayborn**	1480 cc Harley-Davidson	1970	254.99	410.37
6	**Donald A. Vesco**	700 cc Yamaha	1970	251.82	405.25
7	**Robert Leppan**	1,298 cc Triumph	1966	245.62	395.27
8	**William A. Johnson**	667 cc Triumph	1962	224.57	361.40
9	**Wilhelm Herz**	499 cc NSU	1956	210.08	338.08
10	**Russell Wright**	998 cc Vincent HRD	1955	184.95	297.64

* All records were achieved at the Bonneville Salt Flats, US, except No.10, attained at Christchurch, New Zealand

TOP 10 PRODUCTION CARS WITH THE FASTEST 0–100 KM/H TIMES

	MODEL*	COUNTRY OF MANUFACTURE	SECONDS TAKEN#
1	**Westfield Megabusa**	UK	3.3
2	**Caterham 7 Superlight R500**	UK	3.5
3	**Lamborghini Diablo GT Coupé**	Italy	3.7
4	**TVR Cerbera 4.5**	UK	4.0
5	**Porsche 911 GT2**	Germany	4.1
6	**Ferrari 550 Maranello**	Italy	4.3
7	**=BMW Z8**	Germany	4.7
	=Lotus Exige	UK	4.7
9	**=Audi RS4**	Germany	4.9
	=Nissan Skyline GT-R	Japan	4.9

* Currently in production

May vary according to specification modifications to meet national legal requirements

THE 10 LATEST AIR SPEED RECORDS HELD BY JETS*

	PILOT/COUNTRY	LOCATION	AIRCRAFT	SPEED (MPH)	(KM/H)	DATE
1	**Eldon W. Joersz/George T. Morgan Jr.,** US	Beale AFB#, California	Lockheed SR-71A	2,193.167	3,529.560	Jul 28, 1976
2	**Robert L. Stephens/Daniel Andre,** US	Edwards AFB, California	Lockheed YF-12A	2,070.102	3,331.507	May 1, 1965
3	**Georgi Mossolov,** USSR	Podmoskownoe, USSR	Mikoyan E-166	1,665.896	2,681.000	Jul 7, 1962
4	**Robert B. Robinson,** US	Edwards AFB, California	McDonnell F4H-1F Phantom II	1,606.509	2,585.425	Nov 22, 1961
5	**Joseph W. Rogers,** US	Edwards AFB, California	Convair F-106A Delta Dart	1,525.924	2,455.736	Dec 15, 1959
6	**Georgi Mossolov,** USSR	Jukowski-Petrowskol, USSR	Mikoyan E-66	1,483.834	2,388.000	Oct 31, 1959
7	**Walter W. Irwin,** US	Edwards AFB, California	Lockheed YF-104A Starfighter	1,404.012	2,259.538	May 16, 1958
8	**Adrian E. Drew,** US	Edwards AFB, California	McDonnell F-101A Voodoo	1,207.635	1,943.500	Dec 12, 1957
9	**Peter Twiss,** UK	Chichester, UK	Fairey Delta Two	1,132.138	1,822.000	Mar 10, 1956
10	**Horace A. Hanes,** US	Palmdale, California	North American F-100C Super Saber	822.268	1,323.312	Aug 20, 1955

* Ground-launched only, hence excludes X-15 records   *# Air Force Base*

The flight of Horace A. Hanes was the first official supersonic record-holder. The next holder, that of Peter Twiss, was the greatest ever incremental increase – 309.870 mph (498.688 km/h). It should be noted that although air records are traditionally expressed to 3 decimal places, few flights have ever been recorded to such a level of accuracy.

Bye-Bye Blackbird
Although set over a quarter of a century ago, the speed record established by the Lockheed Blackbird SR-71A still stands. The aircraft attained Mach 3.31 (over three times the speed of sound) and a record height of 16 miles (26 km).

Long Distance

TOP 10 COUNTRIES WITH THE LONGEST ROAD NETWORKS

LOCATION	LENGTH (MILES)	(KM)
1 US	3,958,191	6,370,031
2 India	2,062,731	3,319,644
3 Brazil	1,230,315	1,980,000
4 China	869,919	1,400,000
5 Japan	715,948	1,152,207
6 Russia	591,545	952,000
7 Australia	567,312	913,000
8 Canada	560,416	901,902
9 France	554,822	892,900
10 Germany	407,706	656,140

Source: *Central Intelligence Agency*

Totals include both paved and unpaved roads. Around the world, the proportion of paved to unpaved varies considerably: India's overall total, for example, comprises 942,668 miles (1,517,077 km) paved and 1,120,063 miles (1,802,567 km) unpaved. Only 114,419 miles (184,140 km), or 9 percent, of Brazil's and 168,578 miles (271,300 km), or 19 percent, of China's total are paved. Some 90 percent of the US total is paved, while the entire road network of certain countries, such as Bermuda, Jordan, Morocco, Switzerland, and the United Arab Emirates is paved.

Get Your Kicks on Route 66
America's highways form the world's longest road network and include 3,562,380 miles (5,733,028 km) of paved roads, of which 46,038 miles (74,091 km) are expressways.

TOP 10 COUNTRIES WITH THE LONGEST RAILROAD NETWORKS

LOCATION	TOTAL RAIL LENGTH (MILES)	(KM)
1 US	140,274	225,750
2 Russia	92,584	149,000
3 China	41,957	67,524
4 India	39,093	62,915
5 Germany	25,368	40,826
6 Canada	22,440	36,114
7 Australia	21,014	33,819
8 Argentina	20,967	33,744
9 France	19,846	31,939
10 Mexico	19,292	31,048

Source: *Central Intelligence Agency*

The total of the world's railroad networks is today thought to be 746,476 miles (1,201,337 km). Of this, 148,775 miles (239,430 km) is narrow gauge and some 118,061 to 121,167 miles (190,000 to 195,000 km) electrified. Europe has the most electrified lines – 91,814 miles (147,760 km) – compared with 15,229 miles (24,509 km) in the Far East, 6,866 miles (11,050 km) in Africa, 2,624 miles (4,223 km) in South America, and 2,585 miles (4,160 km) in North America.

TOP 10 COUNTRIES WITH THE LONGEST INLAND WATERWAY NETWORKS*

LOCATION	LENGTH (MILES)	(KM)
1 China	68,351	110,000
2 Russia	59,589	95,900
3 Brazil	31,069	50,000
4 US#	25,482	41,009
5 Indonesia	13,409	21,579
6 Colombia	11,272	18,140
7 Vietnam	11,000	17,702
8 India	10,054	16,180
9 Dem. Rep. of Congo	9,321	15,000
10 France	9,278	14,932

* Canals and navigable rivers

 # Excluding Great Lakes

Source: *Central Intelligence Agency*

The navigability of the world's waterways varies greatly: only 2,256 miles (3,631 km) of those in India, for example, are navigable by large ocean-going vessels.

THE FIRST SUSPENSION BRIDGE WITH STEEL TOWERS

THE CONSTRUCTION OF THE WILLIAMSBURG BRIDGE linking Manhattan with Williamsburg, Brooklyn, started in 1896 and finished in 1903. It was once the longest (1,600 ft/488 m) and heaviest suspension bridge in the world, and the first with towers made entirely of steel. The towers stand 310 ft (95 m) above water and support four 4,344-ton (3,941-tonne) main cables, 18¾ in (48 cm) in diameter, each containing 37 strands of 208 wires – a total of almost 17,500 miles (28,164 km). The bridge, which cost $30 million to build, remained the world's longest until 1924, when it was overtaken by Bear Mountain Bridge, which crosses the Hudson River near Albany, New York, and has since been relegated to 39th place in the world list.

FIRST OR LAST

TOP 10 | LONGEST BRIDGES IN THE US

BRIDGE/LOCATION	YEAR COMPLETED	LENGTH OF MAIN SPAN (FT)	(M)
1 Verrazano Narrows, New York	1964	4,260	1,298
2 Golden Gate, San Francisco, California	1937	4,200	1,280
3 Mackinac Straits, Michigan	1957	3,800	1,158
4 George Washington, New York	1931/62*	3,500	1,067
5 Tacoma Narrows II, Washington	1950	2,800	853
6 Transbay, San Francisco, California†	1936	2,310	704
7 Bronx-Whitestone, New York	1939	2,300	701
8 Delaware Memorial, Wilmington, Delaware†	1951/68	2,150	655
9 Walt Whitman, Philadelphia, Pennsylvania	1957	2,000	610
10 Ambassador, Detroit, Michigan	1929	1,850	564

* Lower deck added   *† Twin spans*

All are suspension bridges. The US also has the 2 longest steel arch bridges in the world: the New River Gorge Bridge, Fayetteville, West Virginia (1977: 1,700 ft/ 518 m) and the Bayonne at Bayonne, New Jersey (1931: 1,675 ft/511 m).

TOP 10 | LONGEST STEEL ARCH BRIDGES

BRIDGE/LOCATION	YEAR COMPLETED	LONGEST SPAN (FT)	(M)
1 New River Gorge, Fayetteville, West Virginia	1977	1,700	518
2 Kill van Kull, Bayonne, New Jersey/ Staten Island, New York	1931	1,652	504
3 Sydney Harbour, Australia	1932	1,650	503
4 Wanxian, Yangtse River, China	1997	1,378	420
5 Fremont, Portland, Oregon	1973	1,257	383
6 Port Mann, Vancouver, Canada	1964	1,200	366
7 Thatcher Ferry, Panama Canal	1962	1,128	344
8 Laviolette, Quebec, Canada	1967	1,100	335
9 Zdákov, Lake Orlik, Czech Republic	1967	1,083	330
10 Runcorn-Widnes, UK	1961	1,082	330

TOP 10 | LONGEST CABLE-STAYED BRIDGES

BRIDGE/LOCATION	YEAR COMPLETED	LENGTH OF MAIN SPAN (FT)	(M)
1 Tatara, Onomichi-Imabari, Japan	1999	2,920	890
2 Pont de Normandie, Le Havre, France	1994	2,808	856
3 Qinghzhou Minjiang, Fozhou, China	1996	1,985	605
4 Yang Pu, Shanghai, China	1993	1,975	602
5 =Meiko-chuo, Nagoya, Japan	1997	1,936	590
=Xu Pu, Shanghai, China	1997	1,936	590
7 Skarnsundet, Trondheim Fjord, Norway	1991	1,739	530
8 Tsurumi Tsubasa, Yokohama, Japan	1994	1,673	510
9 =Ikuchi, Onomichi-Imabari, Japan	1994	1,608	490
=Öresund, Copenhagen-Malmö, Denmark/Sweden	2000	1,608	490

TOP 10 | LONGEST SUSPENSION BRIDGES

BRIDGE/LOCATION	YEAR COMPLETED	LENGTH OF MAIN SPAN (FT)	(M)
1 Akashi-Kaikyo, Kobe-Naruto, Japan	1998	6,532	1,991
2 Great Belt, Denmark	1997	5,328	1,624
3 Humber Estuary, UK	1980	4,626	1,410
4 Jiangyin, China	1998	4,544	1,385
5 Tsing Ma, Hong Kong, China	1997	4,518	1,377
6 Verrazano Narrows, New York	1964	4,260	1,298
7 Golden Gate, San Francisco, California	1937	4,200	1,280
8 Höga Kusten (High Coast), Veda, Sweden	1997	3,970	1,210
9 Mackinac Straits, Michigan	1957	3,800	1,158
10 Minami Bisan-seto, Kojima-Sakaide, Japan	1988	3,609	1,100

The Messina Strait Bridge between Sicily and Calabria, Italy, remains a speculative project, but if constructed according to plan it will have by far the longest center span of any bridge at 10,827 ft (3,300 m). At 12,828 ft (3,910 m), Japan's Akashi-Kaikyo bridge, completed in 1998, and with a main span of 6,529 ft (1,990 m), is the world's longest overall. Turkey's equally speculative Izmit Bay Bridge has a proposed length of 5,338 ft (1,627 m).

Going Underground

 **LONGEST RAIL TUNNELS**

	TUNNEL/LOCATION	YEAR COMPLETED	LENGTH (FT)	(M)
1	**Seikan,** Japan	1988	176,673	53,850
2	**Channel Tunnel,** France/England	1994	165,518	50,450
3	**Moscow Metro** (Medvedkovo/Belyaevo section), Russia	1979	100,722	30,700
4	**London Underground** (East Finchley/Morden, Northern Line), UK	1939	91,339	27,840
5	**Dai-Shimizu,** Japan	1982	72,904	22,221
6	**Simplon II,** Italy/Switzerland	1922	65,039	19,824
7	**Simplon I,** Italy/Switzerland	1906	64,970	19,803
8	**Vereina,** Switzerland	1999	62,526	19,058
9	**Shinkanmon,** Japan	1975	61,394	18,713
10	**Appennino,** Italy	1934	60,718	18,507

The first passenger rail tunnel was the 2,514-ft (766-m) Tyler Hill Tunnel in Kent, UK, opened on May 4, 1830. The first underwater rail tunnel was the Thames Tunnel, Wapping, London, UK, opened on December 7, 1869. The longest rail tunnel built in the 19th century is the 9.32-mile (15-km) St. Gotthard Tunnel, Switzerland, opened on May 20, 1882.

LONGEST ROAD TUNNELS

	TUNNEL/LOCATION	YEAR COMPLETED	LENGTH (FT)	(M)
1	**Laerdal,** Norway	2000	80,413	24,510
2	**St. Gotthard,** Switzerland	1980	55,505	16,918
3	**Arlberg,** Austria	1978	45,850	13,972
4	**Pinglin Highway,** Taiwan	U/C 2003*	42,323	12,900
5	**Fréjus,** France/Italy	1980	42,306	12,895
6	**Mont Blanc,** France/Italy	1965	38,255	11,660
7	**Gudvanga,** Norway	1991	37,493	11,428
8	**Folgefonn,** Norway	2001	36,516	11,130
9	**Kan-Etsu II,** Japan	1991	36,270	11,055
10	**Kan-Etsu I,** Japan	1985	35,846	10,926

Under construction; scheduled completion date

The first 3 tunnels on this list, as well as No. 6, have all held the record for "The world's longest road tunnel." Previous record-holders include the 19,206-ft (5,854-m) Gran San Bernardo (Italy/Switzerland; 1964); the 16,841-ft (5,133-m) Alfonso XIII or "Viella" (Spain; 1948); the 11,253-ft (3,430-m) Mersey Tunnel (connecting Liverpool and Birkenhead, UK; 1934), and the 10,584-ft (3,226-m) Col de Tende (France/Italy; 1882), originally built as a rail tunnel.

TOP 10 OLDEST UNDERGROUND RAILROAD SYSTEMS

	CITY	OPENED
1	**London**, UK	1863
2	**Budapest**, Hungary	1896
3	**Glasgow**, UK	1896
4	**Boston**, Massachusetts	1897
5	**Paris**, France	1900
6	**Berlin**, Germany	1902
7	**New York**, New York	1904
8	**Philadelphia**, Pennsylvania	1907
9	**Hamburg**, Germany	1912
10	**Buenos Aires**, Argentina	1913

Channel Tunnel
The Channel Tunnel was first proposed over 200 years ago, but only became technologically feasible in the late 20th century. The Tunnel was officially opened by Queen Elizabeth and President Mitterrand on May 6, 1994.

THE 10 FIRST CITIES IN NORTH AMERICA TO HAVE SUBWAY SYSTEMS

	CITY	YEAR OPENED
1	**Chicago**, Illinois	1892
2	**Boston**, Massachusetts	1901
3	**New York**, New York	1904
4	**Philadelphia**, Pennsylvania	1907
5	**Toronto**, Ontario, Canada	1954
6	**Cleveland**, Ohio	1955
7	**Montreal**, Quebec, Canada	1966
8	**San Francisco**, California	1972
9	**Washington**, DC	1976
10	**Atlanta**, Georgia	1979

Named after its inventor Alfred Ely Beach, the Beach Pneumatic Underground Railway was demonstrated in New York in 1867 and opened to the public on February 26, 1870. Limited to a single 312-ft (95-m) tunnel and one 22-seat car, it was a commercial failure and closed within 3 years.

TOP 10 LONGEST CANAL TUNNELS

	TUNNEL	CANAL/LOCATION	LENGTH (FT)	(M)
1	**Le Rôve**	Canal de Marseille au Rhône, France	23,360	7,120
2	**Bony** ("Le Grand Souterrain")	Canal de St. Quentin, France	18,625	5,677
3	**Standedge**	Huddersfield Narrow, UK	17,093	5,210
4	**Mauvages**	Canal de la Marne au Rhin Ouest, France	16,306	4,970
5	**Balesmes**	Canal de la Marne à la Saône, France	15,748	4,800
6	**Ruyaulcourt**	Canal du Nord, France	14,764	4,500
7	**Strood***	Thames and Medway, UK	11,837	3,608
8	**Lapal**	Birmingham, UK	11,713	3,570
9	**Sapperton**	Thames and Severn, UK	11,444	3,488
10	**Pouilly-en-Auxois**	Canal de Bourgogne, France	10,935	3,333

* Later converted to a rail tunnel

Construction of the Rôve tunnel on the Canal de Marseilles au Rhône was delayed by World War I, but it was completed in 1927.

TOP 10 LONGEST UNDERGROUND RAILROAD NETWORKS

	CITY	OPENED	STATIONS	TOTAL TRACK LENGTH (MILES)	(KM)
1	**London**, UK	1863	267	244	392
2	**New York**, New York	1904	468	231	371
3	**=Moscow**, Russia	1935	150	163	262
	=Tokyo, Japan*	1927	237	163	262
5	**Paris**, France#	1900	297	125	201
6	**Mexico City**, Mexico	1969	154	112	178
7	**Chicago**, Illinois	1943	140	108	173
8	**Copenhagen**, Denmark†	1934	80	106	170
9	**Seoul**, South Korea	1974	114	90	144
10	**Berlin**, Germany	1902	172	89	143

* Through-running extensions raise total to 391 miles (683 km), with 502 stations

Metro and RER

† Only partly underground

Source: Tony Pattison, Centre for Environmental Initiatives Researcher

On the Road

Keep on Trucking
The total annual production of heavy trucks approaches two million, with China and South Korea poised to enter the Top 10.

THE 10 WORST MOTOR VEHICLE AND TRAFFIC DISASTERS

LOCATION/DATE	NO. OF PEOPLE KILLED
1 Afghanistan, November 3, 1982 Following a collision with a Soviet army truck, a gasoline tanker exploded in the 1.7-mile (2.7-km) Salang Tunnel. Some authorities have put the death toll from the explosion, fire, and fumes as high as 3,000.	over 2,000
2 Colombia, August 7, 1956 Seven army ammunition trucks exploded at night in the center of Cali, destroying 8 city blocks, including a barracks where 500 soldiers were sleeping.	1,200
3 Thailand, February 15, 1990 A dynamite truck exploded.	over 150
4 Nigeria, November 4, 2000 A gasoline tanker collided with a line of parked cars on the Ile-Ife-Ibadan Expressway, exploding and burning many to death. Some 96 bodies were recovered, but some estimates put the final toll as high as 200.	150
5 Nepal, November 23, 1974 Hindu pilgrims were killed when a suspension bridge over the River Mahahali collapsed.	148
6 Egypt, August 9, 1973 A bus drove into an irrigation canal.	127
7 Togo, December 6, 1965 Two trucks collided with dancers during a festival at Sotouboua.	over 125
8 Spain, July 11, 1978 A liquid gas tanker exploded in a camping site at San Carlos de la Rapita.	over 120
9 South Korea, April 28, 1995 An undergound explosion destroyed vehicles and caused about 100 cars and buses to plunge into the pit it created.	110
10 Kenya, early December 1992 A bus carrying 112 skidded, hit a bridge, and plunged into a river.	106

TOP 10 | TRUCK PRODUCERS

	COUNTRY	LORRY PRODUCTION IN 2001
1	Japan	595,403
2	US	252,767
3	China	157,073
4	Germany	132,200
5	India	115,000
6	Brazil	77,342
7	Mexico	64,000
8	France	47,955
9	Russia	40,772
10	Italy	40,605

Source: *OICA Correspondents' Survey*

TOP 10 | CAR PRODUCERS

	COUNTRY	CAR PRODUCTION IN 2001
1	Japan	8,117,563
2	Germany	5,299,700
3	US	4,879,119
4	France	3,181,549
5	South Korea	2,471,444
6	Spain	2,211,172
7	UK	1,492,138
8	Brazil	1,481,975
9	Canada	1,274,853
10	Italy	1,271,763
	World total	39,538,157

Source: *OICA Correspondents' Survey*

TOP 10 | CARS OF 2001 IN THE US

	CAR	SALES
1	Honda Accord	414,718
2	Toyota Camry	390,449
3	Ford Taurus	353,560
4	Honda Civic	331,780
5	Ford Focus	264,414
6	Toyota Corolla	245,023
7	Chevrolet Cavalier	233,298
8	Chevrolet Impala	208,395
9	Pontiac Grand Am	182,046
10	Chevrolet Malibu	176,583

Source: *Ward's AutoInfoBank*

Crash Test Dummy
The introduction of seat belts over 30 years ago, and more recent developments such as the advent of airbags, have improved driver and passenger safety.

THE 10 | FIRST COUNTRIES TO MAKE SEAT BELTS COMPULSORY

	COUNTRY	INTRODUCED
1	Czechoslovakia	Jan 1969
2	Ivory Coast	Jan 1970
3	Japan	Dec 1971
4	Australia	Jan 1972
5	=Brazil	Jun 1972
	=New Zealand	Jun 1972
7	Puerto Rico	Jan 1974
8	Spain	Oct 1974
9	Sweden	Jan 1975
10	=Belgium	Jun 1975
	=Luxembourg	Jun 1975
	=Netherlands	Jun 1975

Seat belts, long in use in airplanes, were not designed for use in private cars until the 1950s. They were optional extras in most cars until the 1970s.

All at Sea

BUSIEST PORTS

PORT/COUNTRY	CONTAINER TRAFFIC IN TEUS* IN 1999
1 **Hong Kong,** China	16,211,000
2 **Singapore,** Singapore	15,945,000
3 **Kaohsiung,** Taiwan	6,985,361
4 **Rotterdam,** Netherlands	6,400,000
5 **Busan,** South Korea	6,310,664
6 **Long Beach,** California	4,408,480
7 **Shanghai,** China	4,210,000
8 **Los Angeles,** California	3,828,851
9 **Hamburg,** Germany	3,738,307
10 **Antwerp,** Belgium	3,614,246

* 20-foot Equivalent Units

Source: *American Association of Port Authorities*

Free Trade

On an average day, more than 100 ocean-going ships load and discharge their cargoes in Hong Kong, the world's busiest deepwater port.

LARGEST CRUISE SHIPS

SHIP	YEAR BUILT	COUNTRY BUILT	PASSENGER CAPACITY	GROSS TONNAGE
1 **Navigator of the Seas**	2002*	Finland	3,840	142,000
2 **Explorer of the Seas**	2000	Finland	3,840	137,308
3 **Adventure of the Seas**	2001	Finland	3,840	137,300
4 **Voyager of the Seas**	1999	Finland	3,840	137,276
5 **Carnival Conquest**	2002*	Italy	2,974	111,000
6 **Star Princess**	2002*	Italy	3,300	108,977
7 **Golden Princess**	2001	Italy	3,300	108,865
8 **Grand Princess**	1998	Italy	3,300	108,806
9 **Carnival Victory**	2000	Italy	3,470	101,509
10 **Carnival Destiny**	1996	Italy	3,336	101,353

* Still under construction as of January 24, 2002

Source: *Lloyd's Register-Fairplay Ltd.*

While the day of the passenger liner may be over, that of the cruise liner has dawned, with ever-larger vessels joining the world's cruise line fleets in the 21st century.

LARGEST OIL TANKERS*

	TANKER	YEAR BUILT	COUNTRY	GROSS TONNAGE#	DEADWEIGHT TONNAGE†
1	Jahre Viking	1979	Japan	260,851	564,650
2	Sea Giant	1979	France	261,862	555,051
3	Kapetan Giannis	1977	Japan	247,160	516,895
4	Kapetan Michalis	1977	Japan	247,160	516,423
5	Sea World	1978	Sweden	237,768	491,120
6	Arctic Blue (formerly *Nissei Maru*)	1975	Japan	234,287	484,276
7	Stena King	1978	Taiwan	218,593	457,927
8	Stena Queen	1977	Taiwan	218,593	457,841
9	Kapetan Panagiotis	1977	Japan	218,447	457,328
10	Kapetan Giorgis	1976	Japan	218,447	457,154

* *As of January 1, 2002*

The weight of the ship when empty

† *The total weight of the vessel, including its cargo, crew, passengers, and supplies*

Source: *Lloyd's Register-Fairplay Ltd.*

The 1,504-ft (485.45-m) long *Jahre Viking* (formerly called *Happy Giant* and *Seawise Giant*) is the longest vessel ever built – as long as more than 20 tennis courts end-to-end and 226 ft (68.86 m) wide.

WORST OIL TANKER SPILLS

	TANKER/LOCATION	DATE	APPROX. SPILLAGE IN TONNES
1	Atlantic Empress and Aegean Captain, Trinidad	Jul 19, 1979	273,875
2	Castillio de Bellver, Cape Town, South Africa	Aug 6, 1983	255,125
3	Olympic Bravery, Ushant, France	Jan 24, 1976	250,000
4	Amoco Cadiz, Finistère, France	Mar 16, 1978	223,275
5	Odyssey, Atlantic, off Canada	Nov 10, 1988	140,075
6	Haven, off Genoa, Italy	Apr 11, 1991	136,500
7	Torrey Canyon, Scilly Isles, UK	Mar 18, 1967	124,150
8	Sea Star, Gulf of Oman	Dec 19, 1972	123,175
9	Irenes Serenade, Pilos, Greece	Feb 23, 1980	118,950
10	Texaco Denmark, North Sea, off Belgium	Dec 7, 1971	102,375

Source: *Environmental Technology Center,* Oil Spill Intelligence Report

In addition to these major slicks, it is estimated that an average of 2,000,000 tonnes of oil is spilled into the world's seas every year. The grounding of the *Exxon Valdez* in Prince William Sound, Alaska, on March 24, 1989, ranks outside the 10 worst at about 35,000 tonnes, but resulted in major ecological damage. All these accidents were caused by collision, grounding, fire, or explosion; worse tanker oil spills have been caused by military action: between January and June 1942, for example, German U-Boats torpedoed a number of tankers off the east coast of the US with a loss of some 600,000 tonnes of oil, and in 1991, during the Gulf War, various tankers were sunk in the Persian Gulf, spilling a total of more than 1,000,000 tonnes of oil.

WORST MARINE DISASTERS

	LOCATION/DATE/INCIDENT	APPROX. NO. KILLED
1	**Off Gdansk,** Poland, January 30, 1945 The German liner *Wilhelm Gustloff*, laden with refugees, was torpedoed by a Soviet submarine, S-13. The precise death toll remains uncertain, but is in the range of 5,348 to 7,800.	up to 7,800
2	**Off Cape Rixhöft** (Rozeewie), Poland, April 16, 1945 The German ship *Goya*, carrying evacuees from Gdansk, was torpedoed in the Baltic.	6,800
3	**Off Yingkow,** China, December 3, 1948 The boilers of an unidentified Chinese troopship carrying Nationalist soldiers from Manchuria exploded, detonating ammunition.	over 6,000
4	**Lübeck,** Germany, May 3, 1945 The German ship *Cap Arcona*, carrying concentration camp survivors, was bombed and sunk by British aircraft.	5,000
5	**Off St. Nazaire,** France, June 17, 1940 The British troop ship *Lancastria* sank.	3,050
6	**Off Stolpmünde** (Ustka), Poland, February 9, 1945 German war-wounded and refugees were lost when the *Steuben* was torpedoed by the same Russian submarine that had sunk the *Wilhelm Gustloff*.	3,000
7	**Tablas Strait,** Philippines, December 20, 1987 The ferry *Dona Paz* was struck by oil tanker *MV Victor*.	up to 3,000
8	**Woosung,** China, December 3, 1948 The overloaded steamship *Kiangya*, carrying refugees, struck a Japanese mine.	over 2,750
9	**Lübeck,** Germany, May 3, 1945 The refugee ship *Thielbeck* sank during the British bombardment of Lübeck harbor in the closing weeks of World War II.	2,750
10	**South Atlantic,** September 12, 1942 The British passenger vessel *Laconia*, carrying Italian prisoners-of-war, was sunk by German U-boat *U-156*.	2,279

Recent reassessments of the death tolls in marine disasters mean that the most famous of all, the *Titanic*, the British liner that struck an iceberg in the North Atlantic and sank on April 15, 1912, with the loss of 1,517 lives, no longer ranks in the Top 10. It remains one of the worst-ever peacetime disasters.

Up & Away

BUSIEST INTERNATIONAL AIRPORTS

	AIRPORT	LOCATION	INTERNATIONAL PASSENGERS IN 2000
1	London Heathrow	London, UK	56,860,000
2	Charles de Gaulle	Paris, France	43,616,000
3	Frankfurt	Frankfurt, Germany	40,243,000
4	Schiphol	Amsterdam, Netherlands	39,100,000
5	Hong Kong	Hong Kong, China	32,131,000
6	London Gatwick	Gatwick, UK	29,024,000
7	Singapore International	Singapore	26,964,000
8	Narita International	Tokyo, Japan	24,022,000
9	Brussels National	Zaventem, Belgium	21,515,000
10	Kloten	Zurich, Switzerland	21,192,000

Source: *Air Transport Intelligence at www.rati.com*

Flying Start

The waits at airport check-ins have become increasingly familiar, as the world's leading airports process as many as 200,000 passengers a day.

BUSIEST AIRPORTS IN THE US

	AIRPORT	LOCATION	TOTAL PASSENGERS* IN 2000
1	Atlanta Hartsfield International	Atlanta, Georgia	80,162,000
2	Chicago O'Hare International	Chicago, Illinois	72,144,000
3	Los Angeles International	Los Angeles, California	66,425,000
4	Dallas/Fort Worth International	Irving, Texas	60,687,000
5	San Francisco International	San Francisco, California	41,041,000
6	Denver International	Denver, Colorado	38,752,000
7	McCarran International	Las Vegas, Nevada	36,866,000
8	Minneapolis/St. Paul International	St. Paul, Minnesota	36,752,000
9	Phoenix Sky Harbor International	Phoenix, Arizona	36,040,000
10	Detroit Metropolitan	Wayne County, Michigan	35,535,000

* Includes international, domestic, and in transit

Source: *Air Transport Intelligence at www.rati.com*

FIRST AIRCRAFT FLIGHT

ONE OF THE MOST momentous milestones of the 20th century, powered flight, dates back to December 17, 1903, when, at Kitty Hawk, North Carolina, at 10:35 a.m., Orville Wright (1871–1948) took off in the *Wright Flyer I*. This epic event – the culmination of years of dedicated research – lasted just 12 seconds, covered 120 ft (37 m), and was witnessed by only five people, but it was from this beginning that modern aviation developed.

FIRST OR LAST

TOP 10 | AIRLINERS IN SERVICE

	AIRCRAFT MODEL	NO. IN SERVICE
1	Boeing B-737-300	985
2	Airbus A-320-200	960
3	Boeing B-757-200	813
4	Boeing B-737-200 Advanced	479
5	Boeing B-737-400	464
6	Boeing B-767-300ER	422
7	Boeing B-747-400	405
8	McDonnell Douglas DC-9-30	308
9	Raytheon Beech 1900D	278
10	Boeing B-727-200 Advanced	270

Source: *Air Transport Intelligence at www.rati.com*

The first Boeing B-737, a B-737-100, flew in 1967. Such was the appeal of its successor, the versatile twin-engined 737-300, to the world's airlines that by 1987 it had become the best-selling airliner in aviation history.

TOP 10 | COUNTRIES WITH THE MOST AIRPORTS

	COUNTRY	AIRPORTS
1	US	14,720
2	Brazil	3,264
3	Russia	2,743
4	Mexico	1,848
5	Canada	1,417
6	Argentina	1,359
7	Bolivia	1,093
8	Colombia	1,091
9	Paraguay	915
10	South Africa	741

Source: *CIA*

Airports, as defined by the Central Intelligence Agency (which monitors them for strategic reasons), range in size and quality from those with paved runways over 3,048 m (10,000 ft) in length to those with only short landing strips. European countries with the most airports are Germany (613), the UK (489), and France (475).

TOP 10 | AIRLINES WITH THE HIGHEST REVENUES

	GROUP/AIRLINE/COUNTRY	REVENUE IN 2000 ($)
1	UAL/United Airlines, US	19,352,000,000
2	AMR Corp/American Airlines, US	17,115,000,000
3	Delta Air Lines, US	16,741,000,000
4	FedEx, US	15,534,000,000
5	Japan Airlines, Japan	15,372,100,000
6	Lufthansa Group, Germany	14,013,500,000
7	British Airways, UK	13,700,000,000
8	Northwest Airlines, US	11,240,000,000
9	Air France Group, France	11,148,000,000
10	ANA Group/ All Nippon, Japan	10,913,885,000

Source: Airline Business/*Air Transport Intelligence at www.rati.com*

World Tourism

TOP 10 TOURIST DESTINATIONS

	COUNTRY	TOTAL VISITORS IN 2000
1	France	74,500,000
2	US	52,690,000
3	Spain	48,500,000
4	Italy	41,182,000
5	China	31,236,000
6	UK	24,900,000
7	Russia	22,783,000
8	Canada	20,423,000
9	Mexico	20,000,000
10	Germany	18,916,000

Source: *World Tourism Organization*

The World Tourism Organization's estimate for 2000 puts the total number of international tourists at a record high of 698 million, nearly 50 million more than in 1999.

TOP 10 TOURISM CITIES IN THE US

	CITY/STATE	PERCENTAGE OF MARKET	ESTIMATED OVERSEAS VISITORS IN 2000
1	New York, New York	22.0	5,714,000
2	Los Angeles, California	13.6	3,533,000
3	Orlando, Florida	11.6	3,013,000
4	Miami, Florida	11.3	2,935,000
5	San Francisco, California	10.9	2,831,000
6	Las Vegas, Nevada	8.7	2,260,000
7	Oahu/Honolulu, Hawaii	8.6	2,234,000
8	Washington, DC (Metro)	5.7	1,481,000
9	Chicago, Illinois	5.2	1,351,000
10	Boston, Massachusetts	5.1	1,325,000

Source: *Tourism Industries, International Trade Administration*

TOP 10 COUNTRIES WITH THE BIGGEST INCREASE IN TOURISM

	COUNTRY	PERCENTAGE GROWTH INTERNATIONAL ARRIVALS* IN 2001
1	Malaysia	23.3
2	Bulgaria	14.4
3	Slovakia	13.0
4	=Croatia	12.4
	=Turkey	12.4
6	Slovenia	11.0
7	Vietnam	10.2[#]
8	Estonia	9.0
9	Tunisia	7.6[#]
10	China	6.2

* Based on preliminary data collected in January 2002

[#] January–November 2001

Source: *World Tourism Organization*

TOP 10 WORLDWIDE AMUSEMENT AND THEME PARKS, 2001

	PARK/LOCATION	ATTENDANCE
1	Tokyo Disneyland, Tokyo, Japan	17,708,000
2	The Magic Kingdom, at Walt Disney World, Lake Buena Vista, Florida, USA	14,784,000*
3	Disneyland, California, USA	12,350,000*
4	Disneyland Paris, Marne-La-Vallée, France	12,200,000
5	Everland, Kyonggi-Do, South Korea	9,028,000
6	Epcot at Walt Disney World, Lake Buena Vista, Florida, USA	9,010,000*
7	Universal Studios Japan, Osaka, Japan	9,000,000*
8	Disney-MGM Studios at Walt Disney World, Lake Buena Vista, Florida, USA	8,366,000*
9	Disney's Animal Kingdom at Walt Disney World, Lake Buena Vista, Florida, USA	7,771,000*
10	Lotte World, Seoul, South Korea	7,450,000*

* Estimated

Source: Amusement Business

TOP 10 MOST VISITED NATIONAL PARKS IN THE US

	PARK/LOCATION	RECREATION VISITS IN 2001
1	Great Smoky Mountains National Park, North Carolina/Tennessee	9,197,697
2	Grand Canyon National Park, Arizona	4,104,809
3	Yosemite National Park, California	3,368,731
4	Olympic National Park, Washington	3,416,069
5	Rocky Mountain National Park, Colorado	3,139,685
6	Cuyuhoga Valley National Park, near Cleveland and Akron, Ohio	3,123,353
7	Yellowstone National Park, Wyoming	2,758,526
8	Grand Teton National Park, Wyoming	2,535,108
9	Acadia National Park, Maine	2,516,551
10	Zion National Park, Utah	2,217,779

The total number of recreation visits to the US National Park System in 2001 was 279,873,926 – more than the population of the US.

THE 10 COUNTRIES WITH THE BIGGEST DECREASE IN TOURISM

	COUNTRY	PERCENTAGE DECREASE INTERNATIONAL ARRIVALS* IN 2001
1	Israel	50.0
2	Nepal	22.0
3	Sri Lanka	16.1
4	Egypt	15.6
5	Macau (China)	12.7
6	US	12.6
7	Poland	12.0[#]
8	Philippines	10.4[#]
9	Guam	10.0
10	Argentina	8.9
	UK	6.6[#]

* Based on preliminary data collected in January 2002

[#] January–November 2001

Source: *World Tourism Organization*

Especially after 11 September, strife-torn regions and those dependant on air travelers suffered from a decline in visitors, as many tourists switched from long-haul destinations to those accessible by road and rail.

FASTEST ROLLER-COASTERS

	ROLLER-COASTER/LOCATION	YEAR OPENED	SPEED (MPH)	(KM/H)
1	**Dodonpa,** Fujikyu Highland, ShinNishihara, FujiYoshida-shi, Japan	2001	106.9	172
2	**=Superman The Escape,** Six Flags Magic Mountain, Valencia, California	1997	100	161
	=Tower of Terror, Dreamworld, Gold Coast, Australia	1997	100	161
4	**Steel Dragon 2000,** Nagshima Spa Land, Nagshima, Japan	2000	95	153
5	**Millennium Force,** Cedar Point, Sandusky, Ohio	2000	93	149
6	**=Goliath,** Six Flags Magic Mountain, Valencia, California	2000	85	137
	=Titan, Six Flags Over Texas, Arlington, Texas	2001	85	137
8	**Phantom's Revenge,** Kennywood Park, West Mifflin, Pennsylvania	2001	82	132
9	**Fujiyama,** Fujikyu Highland, ShinNishihara, FujiYoshida-shi, Japan	1996	80.8	130
10	**=Desperado,** Buffalo Bill's Resort and Casino, Primm, Nevada	1994	80	129
	=HyperSonic XLC, Paramount's Kings Dominion, Doswell, Virginia	2001	80	129
	=Nitro, Six Flags Great Adventure, Jackson, New Jersey	2001	80	129

Superman The Escape is also the world's tallest roller-coaster at 415 ft (126.5 m), and shares the record for the greatest drop with The Tower of Terror at 328 ft 1 in (100 m). The Steel Dragon 2000 is the longest at 8,133 ft 2 in (2,479 m).

COUNTRIES OF ORIGIN OF VISITORS TO THE US

	COUNTRY	VISITORS IN 2001
1	**Canada**	13,518,159
2	**UK**	4,199,159
3	**Japan**	4,124,450
4	**Mexico**	3,895,794
5	**Germany**	1,346,822
6	**France**	935,322
7	**South Korea**	626,669
8	**Venezuela**	570,521
9	**Brazil**	569,687
10	**Italy**	491,330

White Knuckle Ride
The 170-ft (52-m) high, 3,900-ft (1,189-m) long Dodonpa roller-coaster accelerates from 0 to 106.9 mph (172 km/h) in 1.8 seconds.

SPORT &
LEISURE

Summer Olympics

SUMMER OLYMPICS ATTENDED BY THE MOST COMPETITORS, 1896–2000

	LOCATION	YEAR	COUNTRIES REPRESENTED	COMPETITORS
1	Sydney	2000	199	10,651
2	Atlanta	1996	197	10,310
3	Barcelona	1992	169	9,364
4	Seoul	1988	159	8,465
5	Munich	1972	121	7,123
6	Los Angeles	1984	140	6,797
7	Montréal	1976	92	6,028
8	Mexico City	1968	112	5,530
9	Rome	1960	83	5,346
10	Moscow	1980	80	5,217

The first Games in 1896 were attended by just 211 competitors, representing 14 countries. Women took part for the first time 4 years later at the Paris Games. At the 2000 Games, 4,069 were women. Other totals for numbers of competitors are higher, because they include managers and trainers, and count the same competitor more than once if he/she competes in 2 or more events.

Australian Victory
More than 50 times as many competitors took part in the 2000 Sydney Olympics as attended the inaugural modern games in Athens, Greece, in 1896.

SPORTS WHERE THE US GAINED THE MOST OLYMPIC MEDALS

	SPORT	GOLD	SILVER	BRONZE	TOTAL
1	Track and field	309	220	183	712
2	Swimming*	192	138	104	434
3	Diving	47	40	41	128
4	Wrestling	47	44	25	119
5	Boxing	47	23	37	107
6	Shooting	46	26	23	95
7	Rowing	29	29	21	79
8	Gymnastics	26	23	28	77
9	Yachting	17	21	17	55
10	Speed skating	22	16	10	48

* Not including diving, water polo, or synchronized swimming

TOP 10 GOLD MEDAL-WINNING COUNTRIES

	COUNTRY	GOLD MEDALS
1	US	872
2	USSR*	485
3	France	189
4	Great Britain	188
5	Italy	179
6	Germany#	165
7	East Germany	151
8	Hungary	150
9	Sweden	138
10	Australia	103

* Including Unified Team of 1992; not including Russia since then

 # Not including West/East Germany 1968–88

TOP 10 COUNTRIES AT THE SYDNEY OLYMPICS WITH THE HIGHEST RATIO OF MEDALS TO POPULATION

	COUNTRY	MEDALS PER MILLION POPULATION
1	Bahamas	6.80
2	Barbados	3.76
3	Iceland	3.65
4	Australia	3.09
5	Jamaica	2.72
6	Cuba	2.61
7	Norway	2.26
8	Estonia	2.07
9	Hungary	1.68
10	Belarus	1.66
	US	*0.36*

Source: *eCountries*

TOP 10 SUMMER OLYMPICS FOR DISTRIBUTION OF GOLD MEDALS AMONG THE MOST COUNTRIES

	VENUE	YEAR	COUNTRIES WINNING GOLD MEDALS
1	Atlanta	1996	53
2	Sydney	2000	51
3	Barcelona	1992	37
4	Seoul	1988	31
5	Mexico City	1968	30
6	Amsterdam	1928	28
7	Helsinki	1952	27
8	=Montréal	1976	26
	=Tokyo	1964	26
10	=Melbourne	1956	25
	=Moscow	1980	25
	=Munich	1972	25

All-American Dream
American athlete Michael Johnson adds another gold to the unrivaled tally the US has won in the 27 Summer Olympics in which it has participated.

TOP 10 OLYMPIC MEDAL-WINNING COUNTRIES THAT HAVE NEVER WON A GOLD

	COUNTRY	MEDALS			
		GOLD	SILVER	BRONZE	TOTAL
1	Mongolia	0	5	9	14
2	Taipei	0	4	6	10
3	=Chile	0	6	3	9
	=Philippines	0	2	7	9
5	Georgia	0	0	8	8
6	=Latvia	0	5	2	7
	=Slovenia	0	2	5	7
8	Puerto Rico	0	1	5	6
9	=Ghana	0	1	3	4
	=Israel	0	1	3	4
	=Lebanon	0	2	2	4
	=Moldavia	0	2	2	4
	=Namibia	0	4	0	4
	=Nigeria	0	1	3	4

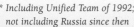

Winter Olympics

Laurel
Olympic medal-winning German, Norwegian, and Swiss ski teams celebrate their respective victories in Salt Lake City, 2002.

TOP 10 WINTER OLYMPIC MEDAL-WINNING COUNTRIES, 1924–2002*

	COUNTRY	GOLD	SILVER	BRONZE	TOTAL
1	Soviet Union#	113	82	78	273
2	Norway	94	93	73	260
3	US	70	70	51	191
4	Austria	41	57	65	163
5	Germany†	54	51	37	142
6	Finland	41	51	49	141
7	East Germany	39	37	35	111
8	Sweden	36	28	38	102
9	Switzerland	32	33	36	101
10	Canada	30	28	37	95

* Includes medals won at figure skating and ice hockey included in the Summer Games prior to the launch of the Winter Olympics in 1924

\# Includes Unified Team of 1992; excludes Russia since then

† Not including East/West Germany 1968–88

TOP 10 GOLD MEDALLISTS AT THE WINTER OLYMPICS (MEN)

	MEDALLIST/COUNTRY	SPORT	GOLD MEDALS
1	**Bjørn Dählie,** Norway	Nordic skiing	8
2	**=Eric Heiden,** US	Speed skating	5
	=Clas Thunberg, Norway	Speed skating	5
4	**=Ivar Ballangrud,** Norway	Speed skating	4
	=Yevgeny Grishin, Soviet Union	Speed skating	4
	=Sixten Jernberg, Sweden	Nordic skiing	4
	=Johann Olav Koss, Norway	Speed skating	4
	=Matti Nykänen, Finland	Ski jumping	4
	=Alexander Tikhonov, Soviet Union	Biathlon	4
	=Thomas Wassberg, Sweden	Nordic skiing	4
	=Nikolai Zimyatov, Soviet Union	Nordic skiing	4
	=Gunde Svan, Sweden	Nordic skiing	4

TOP 10 GOLD MEDALLISTS AT THE WINTER OLYMPICS (WOMEN)

	MEDALLIST/COUNTRY	SPORT	GOLD MEDALS
1	**=Lydia Skoblikova,** Soviet Union	Speed skating	6
	=Lyubov Egorova, EUN*/Russia	Nordic skiing	6
3	**=Bonnie Blair,** US	Speed skating	5
	=Larissa Lazutina, EUN*/Russia	Nordic skiing	5
5	**=Galina Kulakova,** Soviet Union	Nordic skiing	4
	=Lee-Kyung Chun, South Korea	Short track speed skating	4
	=Claudia Pechstein, Germany	Speed skating	4
	=Raisa Smetanina, EUN*/Russia	Nordic skiing	4
9	**=Claudia Boyarskikh,** Soviet Union	Nordic skiing	3
	=Marja-Liisa Kirvesniemi (née Hämäläinen), Finland	Nordic skiing	3
	=Sonja Henie, Norway	Figure skating	3
	=Karin Kania (née Enke), East Germany	Speed skating	3
	=Gunda Niemann-Stirnemann, Germany	Speed skating	3
	=Anfisa Reztsova, Soviet Union/EUN*	Nordic skiing/biathlon	3
	=Irina Rodnina, Soviet Union	Figure skating	3
	=Vreni Schneider, Switzerland	Alpine skiing	3
	=Katja Seizinger, Germany	Alpine skiing	3
	=Elena Valbe, EUN*/Russia	Nordic skiing	3
	=Yvonne van Gennip, Netherlands	Speed skating	3

* Unified Team, Commonwealth of Independent States, 1992

TOP10 MEDAL-WINNING COUNTRIES AT THE 2002 SALT LAKE WINTER OLYMPICS

	COUNTRY	GOLD	MEDALS SILVER	BRONZE	TOTAL
1	Germany	12	16	7	35
2	US	10	13	11	34
3	Norway	11	7	6	24
4	Canada	6	3	8	17
5	=Austria	2	4	10	16
	=Russia	6	6	4	16
7	Italy	4	4	4	12
8	=France	4	5	2	11
	=Switzerland	3	2	6	11
10	=China	2	2	4	8
	=Netherlands	3	5	0	8

Red Hot Team
The German four-man bobsleigh hurtles to Olympic gold at the 2002 Winter Games.

TOP10 INDIVIDUAL MEDAL WINNERS AT THE WINTER OLYMPICS

	MEDALLIST/COUNTRY	SPORT	YEARS	GOLD	MEDALS SILVER	BRONZE	TOTAL
1	Bjørn Dählie, Norway	Nordic skiing	1992–98	8	4	0	12
2	Raisa Smetanina, Soviet Union	Nordic skiing	1976–92	4	5	1	10
3	=Stefania Belmondo, Italy	Nordic skiing	1992–2002	2	3	4	9
	=Sixten Jernberg, Sweden	Nordic skiing	1956–64	4	3	2	9
	=Lyubov Egorova, EUN*/Russia	Nordic skiing	1992–94	6	3	0	9
	=Larisa Lazutina, EUN*/Russia	Nordic skiing	1992–2002	5	3	1	9
7	=Karin Kania (née Enke), East Germany	Speed skating	1980–88	3	4	1	8
	=Galina Kulakova, Soviet Union	Nordic skiing	1968–80	4	2	2	8
	=Gunda Neimann-Stirnemann, East Germany/Germany	Speed skating	1992–98	3	4	1	8
10	=Ivar Ballangrud, Norway	Speed skating	1928–36	4	2	1	7
	=Andrea Ehrig (née Mitscherlich; formerly Schöne), East Germany	Speed skating	1976–88	1	5	1	7
	=Veikko Hakulinen, Finland	Nordic skiing	1952–60	3	3	1	7
	=Marja-Liisa Kirvesniemi (née Hämäläinen), Finland	Nordic skiing	1980–98	3	0	4	7
	=Eero Mäntyranta, Finland	Nordic skiing	1960–68	3	2	2	7
	=Bogdan Musiol, East Germany/Germany	Bobsledding	1986–92	1	5	1	7
	=Claudia Pechstein, Germany	Speed skating	1992–2002	4	1	2	7
	=Clas Thunberg, Norway	Speed skating	1924–28	5	1	1	7
	=Elena Valbe, EUN*/Russia	Nordic skiing	1992–98	3	0	4	7

* EUN = Unified Team (Commonwealth of Independent States 1992)

Winter Sports

TOP 10 ALPINE SNOWBOARDERS (FEMALE)

	SNOWBOARDER/COUNTRY	TOTAL POINTS*
1	**Ursula Bruhin**, Switzerland	1,662.00
2	**Milena Meisser**, Switzerland	1,626.25
3	**Heidi Jaufenthaler**, Austria	1,595.00
4	**Daniela Meuli**, Switzerland	1,542.28
5	**Brigitte Koeck**, Austria	1,511.25
6	**Steffi von Siebenthal**, Switzerland	1,461.00
7	**Jana Sedova**, Slovakia	1,385.44
8	**Nadia Livers**, Switzerland	1,359.18
9	**Babsi Hoffmann**, Austria	1,320.76
10	**Polona Zupan**, Slovenia	1,299.76

Ranked by best four results in 52-week period to February 21, 2002

Source: *International Snowboard Federation*

TOP 10 ALPINE SNOWBOARDERS (MALE)

	SNOWBOARDER/COUNTRY	TOTAL POINTS*
1	**Gilles Jaquet**, Switzerland	3,842.41
2	**Siegfried Grabner**, Austria	3,627.00
3	**Philipp Schoch**, Switzerland	3,604.70
4	**Ueli Kestnholz**, Switzerland	3,536.11
5	**Christophe Segura**, France	3,440.95
6	**Urs Eiselin**, Switzerland	3,404.81
7	**Simon Schoch**, Switzerland	3,288.93
8	**André Gruetter**, Switzerland	3,089.03
9	**Sascha Duff**, Switzerland	2,779.56
10	**Rok Flander**, Slovenia	2,755.71

Ranked by best four results in 52 week period to February 21, 2002

Source: *International Snowboard Federation*

TOP 10 OLYMPIC BOBSLEDDING COUNTRIES

	COUNTRY	MEDALS			
		GOLD	SILVER	BRONZE	TOTAL
1	**Switzerland**	9	10	9	28
2	**US**	6	5	6	17
3	**East Germany**	5	6	3	14
4	**=Germany***	4	3	6	13
5	**Italy**	4	4	3	11
6	**West Germany**	3	2	2	7
7	**Great Britain**	1	1	2	4
8	**=Austria**	1	2	0	3
	=Soviet Union#	1	0	2	3
10	**=Belgium**	0	1	1	2
	=Canada	2	0	0	2

Not including West or East Germany 1968–88

Includes United Team of 1992; excludes Russia since then

Snow Queen
Ursula Bruhin is the highest-ranking female snowboarder. A recent sport, snowboarding was first competed at the Olympics in 1998.

TOP 10 SKIERS IN THE 2001/02 ALPINE WORLD CUP (MALE)

	SKIER/COUNTRY	OVERALL POINTS*
1	**Stephen Eberharter,** Austria	1,702
2	**Kjetil Andre Aamodt,** Norway	1,096
3	**Didier Cuche,** Switzerland	1,064
4	**Bode Miller,** US	952
5	**Frizt Strobl,** Austria	846
6	**Lasse Kjus,** Norway	680
7	**Ivica Kostelic,** Croatia	677
8	**Fredrik Nyberg,** Sweden	584
9	**Benjamin Raich,** Austria	526
10	**Kristian Ghedina,** Italy	505

* Awarded for performances in slalom, giant slalom,
super giant, downhill, and combination disciplines

Source: *International Ski Federation*

Speed Skater
Canadian Jeremy Wotherspoon holds the
world record over 1,000 meters.

TOP 10 FASTEST SPEED SKATERS

	SKATER/COUNTRY	LOCATION	DATE	TIME FOR 500 M (SECS)
1	**Hiroyasu Shimizu,** Japan	Salt Lake City, Utah	Mar 10, 2001	34.32
2	**Casey FitzRandolph,** US	Salt Lake City	Feb 11, 2002	34.42
3	**Jeremy Wotherspoon,** Canada	Salt Lake City	Mar 10, 2001	34.52
4	**Toyoki Takeda,** Japan	Calgary, Canada	Dec 9, 2001	34.62
5	**=Joey Cheek,** US	Salt Lake City	Dec 19, 2001	34.66
	=Michael Ireland, Canada	Calgary, Canada	Mar 18, 2000	34.66
7	**Kip Carpenter,** US	Salt Lake City	Feb 11, 2002	34.68
8	**=Jan Bos,** Netherlands	Salt Lake City	Feb 12, 2002	34.72
	=Gerard van Velde, Netherlands	Salt Lake City	Feb 11, 2002	34.72
10	**Lee Kyu-Hyuk,** South Korea	Salt Lake City	Feb 11, 2002	34.74

Source: *International Skating Union*

The 500-m speed skating record has improved remarkably over the past century.
The first record was set in 1891 by Swedish skater Oscar Grund, with 50.8
seconds over 500 metres – equivalent to 35.43 km/h (22.02 mph). Hiroyasu
Shimuzu's current record is equal to 52.45 km/h (32.59 mph).

TOP 10 FASTEST WINNING TIMES OF THE IDITAROD DOG SLED RACE

	WINNER	YEAR	TIME (DAYS)	(HRS)	(MINS)	(SECS)
1	**Martin Buser**	2002	8	22	46	2
2	**Doug Swingley**	2000	9	0	58	6
3	**Doug Swingley**	1995	9	2	42	19
4	**Jeff King**	1996	9	5	43	19
5	**Jeff King**	1998	9	5	52	26
6	**Martin Buser**	1997	9	8	30	45
7	**Doug Swingley**	1999	9	14	31	7
8	**Doug Swingley**	2001	9	19	55	50
9	**Martin Buser**	1994	10	13	2	39
10	**Jeff King**	1993	10	15	38	15

Source: *Iditarod Trail Committee*

The race, which has been held annually since 1973, follows an old mail route
from Anchorage to Nome, Alaska, and covers 1,158 miles (1,864 km). Iditarod
is a deserted mining village along the route. The race commemorates an
emergency operation in 1925 to get medical supplies to Nome following a
diphtheria epidemic.

Field Athletics

TOP 10 FIELD ATHLETES (FEMALE)

	ATHLETE/COUNTRY	EVENT	SCORE
1	Stacy Dragila, US	Pole vault	1,462
2	Svetlana Feofanova, Russia	Pole vault	1,420
3	Osleidys Menendez, Cuba	Javelin throw	1,399
4	Hestrie Storbeck-Cloete, Russia	High jump	1,393
5	Tatyana Lebedeva, Russia	Triple jump	1,392
6	Yelena Prokhorova, Russia	Heptathlon	1,389
7	Inga Babakova, Ukraine	High jump	1,381
8	Kajsa Bergqvist, Sweden	High jump	1,373
9	Tereza Marinova, Bulgaria	Triple jump	1,360
10	Tatyana Kotova, Russia	Long jump	1,341

* As of April 8, 2002

Source: International Association of Athletics Federations

TOP 10 FIELD ATHLETES (MALE)

	ATHLETE/COUNTRY	EVENT	SCORE
1	Tomás Dvorák, Czech Republic	Decathlon	1,412
2	Jan Zelezny, Czech Republic	Javelin throw	1,403
3	Virgilijus Alekna, Lithuania	Discus throw	1,394
4	Erki Nool, Estonia	Decathlon	1,392
5	Iván Pedroso, Cuba	Long jump	1,377
6	Jonathan Edwards, Great Britain	Triple jump	1,375
7	=John Godina, US	Shot put, discus throw	1,373
	=Koji Murofushi, Japan	Hammer throw	1,373
9	Dmitriy Markov, Australia	Pole vault	1,366
10	Constantinos Gatsioudis, Greece	Javelin throw	1,356

* As of April 8, 2002

Source: International Association of Athletics Federations

TOP 10 HIGHEST HIGH JUMPS*

	ATHLETE/COUNTRY	YEAR	HEIGHT (M)
1	Javier Sotomayor, Cuba	1993	2.45
2	=Patrik Sjöberg, Sweden	1987	2.42
	=Carlo Thränhardt, West Germany#	1988	2.42
4	Igor Paklin, USSR	1985	2.41
5	=Rudolf Povarnitsyn, USSR	1985	2.40
	=Sorin Matei, Romania	1990	2.40
	=Charles Austin, US	1991	2.40
	=Hollis Conway, US#	1991	2.40
	=Vyochaslav Voronin, Russia	2000	2.40
10	=Jianhua Zhu, China	1984	2.39
	=Dietmar Mögenburg, West Germany#	1985	2.39
	=Hollis Conway, US	1989	2.39
	=Ralph Sonn, Germany#	1991	2.39

* Highest by each athlete only

Indoor

TOP 10 HIGHEST POLE VAULTS*

	ATHLETE/COUNTRY	YEAR	HEIGHT (M)
1	Sergei Bubka, Ukraine#	1993	6.15
2	=Maksim Tarasov, Russia	1999	6.05
	=Dmitri Markov, Australia	2001	6.05
4	=Okkert Brits, South Africa	1995	6.03
	=Jeff Hartwig, US	2000	6.03
6	Radion Gataullin, USSR#	1989	6.02
7	Igor Trandenkov, Russia	1996	6.01
8	=Jeane Galfione, France#	1999	6.00
	=Tim Lobinger, Germany	1997	6.00
	=Danny Ecker, Germany#	2001	6.00

* Highest by each athlete only

Indoor

TOP 10 LONGEST HAMMER THROWS*

	ATHLETE/COUNTRY	YEAR	DISTANCE (M)
1	Yuriy Sedykh, Ukraine	1986	86.74
2	Sergey Litvinov, Russia	1986	86.04
3	Igor Astapkovich, Bulgaria	1992	84.62
4	Igor Nikulin, USSR	1990	84.48
5	Juri Tamm, Estonia	1984	84.40
6	Tibor Gécsek, Hungary	1998	83.68
7	Koji Murofushi, Japan	2001	83.47
8	Andrey Abduvaliyev, Tajikistan	1990	83.46
9	Ralf Haber, Germany	1988	83.40
10	Adrián Annus, Hungary	2001	83.39

* Longest by each athlete only

TOP 10 LONGEST JAVELIN THROWS*

	ATHLETE/COUNTRY	YEAR	DISTANCE (M)
1	Jan Zelezny, Czech Republic	1996	98.48
2	Aki Parviainen, Finland	1999	93.09
3	Raymond Hecht, Germany	1995	92.60
4	Konstadinós Gatsioúdis, Greece	2000	91.69
5	Steve Backley, Great Britain	1992	91.46
6	Seppo Räty, Finland	1992	90.60
7	Boris Henry, Germany	1997	90.44
8	Sergey Makarov, Russia	1999	89.93
9	Tom Petranoff, US	1991	89.16
10	Patrik Bodén, Sweden	1990	89.10

* Longest by each athlete only

TOP 10 LONGEST TRIPLE JUMPS*

	ATHLETE/COUNTRY	YEAR	DISTANCE (M)
1	**Jonathan Edwards,** Great Britain	1995	18.29
2	**Kenny Harrison,** US	1996	18.09
3	**Willie Banks,** US	1985	17.97
4	=**Khristo Markov,** Bulgaria	1987	17.92
	=**James Beckford,** Jamaica	1995	17.92
6	**Vladimir Inozemtsev,** Ukraine	1990	17.90
7	**João Carlos de Oliveira,** Brazil	1975	17.89
8	**Mike Conley,** US	1987	17.87
9	**Charles Simpkins,** US	1985	17.86
10	**Yoelbi Quesada,** Cuba	1997	17.85

* Longest by each athlete only included

One Jump Ahead

In Lille, France, on June 25, 1995, Jonathan Edwards broke the triple jump record twice, becoming the first person ever to break the 18-meter barrier.

TOP 10 LONGEST LONG JUMPS*

	ATHLETE/COUNTRY	YEAR	DISTANCE (M)
1	**Mike Powell,** US	1991	8.95
2	**Bob Beamon,** US	1968	8.90
3	**Carl Lewis,** US	1991	8.87
4	**Robert Emmiyan,** USSR	1987	8.86
5	=**Larry Myricks,** US	1988	8.74
	=**Erick Walder,** US	1994	8.74
7	**Iván Pedroso,** Cuba	1995	8.71
8	**Kareem Streete-Thompson,** US	1994	8.63
9	**James Beckford,** Jamaica	1997	8.62
10	**Yago Lamela,** Spain#	1999	8.56

* Longest by each athlete only included
 # Indoor

Going the Distance

TOP 10 TRACK ATHLETES (MALE)

	ATHLETE/COUNTRY	EVENT	SCORE*
1	**Hicham El Guerrouj,** Morocco	1,500 m	1,467
2	**Maurice Greene,** US	100 m	1,449
3	**Tim Montgomery,** US	100 m	1,432
4	**Allen Johnson,** US	110 m hurdles	1,431
5	**Anier Garcia,** Cuba	110 m hurdles	1,425
6	**André Bucher,** Switzerland	800 m	1,421
7	**Reuben Kosgei,** Kenya	300 m steeplechase	1,416
8	**=Bernard Lagat,** Kenya	1,500 m	1,415
	=Brahim Boulami, Morocco	3,000 m steeplechase	1,415
10	**Felix Sánchez,** Dominican Republic	400 m hurdles	1,408

* As at April 8, 2002

Source: *International Association of Athletics Federations*

TOP 10 TRACK ATHLETES (FEMALE)

	ATHLETE/COUNTRY	EVENT	SCORE*
1	**Marion Jones,** US	100 m, 200 m	1,445
2	**Olga Yegorova,** Russia	5,000 m	1,424
3	**Maria Lurdes Mutola,** Mozambique	800 m	1,405
4	**Gabriela Szabo,** Romania	1,500 m, 5,000 m	1,404
5	**Violetta Beclea-Szekely,** Romania	1,500 m	1,398
6	**Nezha Bidouane,** Morocco	400 m hurdles	1,390
7	**Stephanie Graf,** Austria	800 m	1,389
8	**Gail Devers,** US	100 m hurdles	1,385
9	**Zhanna Pintusevich,** Ukraine	100 m	1,381
10	**Gete Wami,** Ethiopia	500 m, 10,000 m	1,379

* As at April 8 2002

Source: *International Association of Athletics Federations*

These athletes have been ranked by the IAAF, according to their Ranking Score. The Ranking Score is the average points achieved by the athlete. After each competition, athletes' Performance Scores, which consist of points awarded for results and placing, are calculated. Athletes are then ranked by taking the average of their top 5 Performance Scores.

Front Runner

Moroccan runner Hicham El Guerrouj, the fastest person ever to run a mile (3 mins, 43.13 secs), also holds the world indoor and outdoor 1,500-meter records.

TOP 10 FASTEST MARATHONS (MALE)

	ATHLETE*/COUNTRY	VENUE	YEAR	TIME (HR:MIN:SEC)
1	Khalid Khannouchi, US	London, UK	2002	2:05:38
2	Khalid Khannouchi	Chicago, US	1999	2:05:42
3	Ronaldo da Costa, Brazil	Berlin, Germany	1998	2:06:05
4	Gert Thys, Russia	Tokyo, Japan	1999	2:06:33
5	António Pinto, Portugal	London, UK	2000	2:06:36
6	Josephat Kiprono, Kenya	Berlin, Germany	1999	2:06:44
7	Fred Kiprop, Kenya	Amsterdam, Netherlands	1999	2:06:47
8	=Belayneh Dinsamo, Ethiopia	Rotterdam, Netherlands	1988	2:06:50
	=Josephat Kiprono	Rotterdam, Netherlands	2001	2:06:50
10	Atsushi Fujita, Japan	Fukuoka, Japan	2000	2:06:51

* Winners only listed

TOP 10 FASTEST MARATHONS (FEMALE)

	ATHLETE*/COUNTRY	VENUE	YEAR	TIME (HRS:MINS:SECS)
1	Catherine Ndereba, Kenya	Chicago, US	2001	2:18:47
2	Paula Radcliffe, UK	London, UK	2002	2:18:56
3	Naoko Takahashi, Japan	Berlin, Germany	2001	2:19:46
4	Tegla Loroupe, Kenya	Berlin, Germany	1999	2:20:43
5	Tegla Loroupe	Rotterdam, Netherlands	1998	2:20:47
6	Ingrid Christensen-Kristiansen, Norway	London, UK	1985	2:21:06
7	Joan Samuelson (née Benoit), US	Chicago, US	1985	2:21:21
8	Catherine Ndereba	Chicago, US	2000	2:21:33
9	Uta Pippig, Germany	Boston, US	1994	2:21:45
10	Naoko Takahashi	Bangkok, Thailand	1998	2:21:47

* Winners only listed

TOP 10 FASTEST MEN EVER*

	ATHLETE/COUNTRY	YEAR	TIME (SECONDS)
1	Maurice Greene, US	1999	9.79
2	=Donovan Bailey, Canada	1996	9.84
	=Bruny Surin, Canada	1999	9.84
	=Tim Montgomery, US	2001	9.84
5	Leroy Burrell, US	1994	9.85
6	=Ato Boldon, Trinidad	1998	9.86
	=Frank Fredericks, Namibia	1996	9.86
	=Carl Lewis, US	1991	9.86
9	=Linford Christie, UK	1993	9.87
	=Obadele Thompson, Barbados	1998	9.87

* Based on fastest time for the 100 meters

Many would argue that Michael Johnson (US) should be in this category with his remarkable 200-meter record of 19.32 seconds in 1996 (equivalent to a 100-meter time of 9.66 seconds), but his best 100-meter time is only 10.09 seconds.

TOP 10 FASTEST WOMEN EVER*

	ATHLETE/COUNTRY	YEAR	TIME (SECONDS)
1	Florence Griffith Joyner, US	1988	10.49
2	Marlon Jones, US	1998	10.65
3	Christine Arron, France	1998	10.73
4	Merlene Ottey, Jamaica	1996	10.74
5	Evelyn Ashford, US	1984	10.76
6	Irina Privalova, Russia	1994	10.77
7	Dawn Sowell, US	1989	10.78
8	=Xuemei Li, China	1997	10.79
	=Inger Miller, US	1999	10.79
10	Marlies Oelsner-Göhr, East Germany	1983	10.81

* Based on fastest time for the 100 meters

World's Fastest

US athlete Marion Jones, the fastest woman on Earth, receives the second of the three gold medals she won at the 2000 Sydney Olympics (100 meters, 200 meters, and 4 x 400 meters relay) – as well as two bronze medals.

251

Football

TOP 10 TEAMS WHO HAVE PLAYED IN THE MOST SUPER BOWLS

	TEAM	WON	LOST	TOTAL
		FINALS PLAYED		
1	Dallas Cowboys	5	3	8
2	Denver Broncos	2	4	6
3	=Miami Dolphins	2	3	5
	=San Francisco 49ers	5	0	5
	=Washington Redskins	3	2	5
6	=Buffalo Bills	0	4	4
	=Green Bay Packers	3	1	4
	=Minnesota Vikings	0	4	4
	=Oakland/Los Angeles Raiders	3	1	4
	=Pittsburgh Steelers	4	0	4

Source: *National Football League*

TOP 10 PLAYERS WITH THE MOST CAREER TOUCHDOWNS

	PLAYER	TOUCHDOWNS
1	Jerry Rice*	196
2	Emmitt Smith*	159
3	Marcus Allen	145
4	Cris Carter*	130
5	Jim Brown	126
6	Walter Payton	125
7	John Riggins	116
8	Lenny Moore	113
9	Marshall Faulk*	110
10	Barry Sanders	109

* Still active at end of 2001 season

Source: *National Football League*

TOP 10 RUSHERS IN AN NFL CAREER

	PLAYER	TOTAL YARDS GAINED RUSHING
1	Walter Payton	16,726
2	Emmitt Smith*	16,187
3	Barry Sanders	15,269
4	Eric Dickerson	13,259
5	Tony Dorsett	12,739
6	Jim Brown	12,312
7	Marcus Allen	12,243
8	Franco Harris	12,120
9	Thurman Thomas	12,074
10	John Riggins	11,352

* Still active at end of 2001 season

Source: *National Football League*

Super Bowl Stars

Between 1966 and 1985, the Dallas Cowboys had 20 consecutive winning seasons, also achieving the best record of any football team in the Super Bowl.

TOP 10 LONGEST CAREERS OF CURRENT NFL PLAYERS

	PLAYER	TEAM	YEARS*
1	=Morten Andersen	Atlanta Falcons	20
	=Gary Anderson	Minnesota Vikings	20
3	=Darrell Green	Washington Redskins	19
	=Trey Junkin	Arizona Cardinals	19
	=Bruce Matthews	Tennessee Titans	19
6	=Lomas Brown	New York Giants	17
	=Lee Johnson	Minnesota Vikings	17
	=Sean Landeta	Philadelphia Eagles	17
	=Jerry Rice	Oakland Raiders	17
	=Bruce Smith	Washington Redskins	17

* As at end of 2001 season

Source: *National Football League*

Danish-born Morten Andersen joined New Orleans Saints in 1982. Gary Anderson was born in South Africa and also started his pro career in 1982 when he was selected by Buffalo. Although both Andersen and Anderson are closing on his total, they fall short of the 26-year record career of quarterback George Blanda. He played from 1949 to 1975, retiring at the age of 49 having played 340 games – another NFL record.

Best Foot Forward

In a 20-year career, Minnesota Vikings kicker Gary Anderson has achieved more career points than any other player in NFL history, as well as scoring the most field goals and most consecutive field goals.

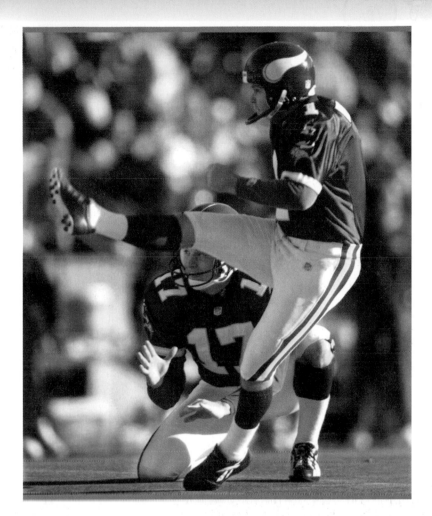

FIRST STADIUM

THE FIRST STADIUM built for football, and the first for US college sports, was the Harvard University stadium. Designed by Charles McKim and George Bruno de Gersdorff, it was built using reinforced concrete – the largest building made from this material up to this time – at a cost of $175,000. It was opened on November 14, 1903, when the home team was beaten by Dartmouth, 11–0. In 1906, when the design prevented the field from being widened, college football rules were changed to allow forward passes.

FIRST OR LAST

TOP 10 PLAYERS WITH THE MOST CAREER POINTS

	PLAYER	POINTS
1	Gary Anderson*	2,133
2	Morten Andersen*	2,036
3	George Blanda	2,002
4	Norm Johnson	1,736
5	Nick Lowery	1,711
6	Jan Stenerud	1,699
7	Eddie Murray	1,594
8	Al Del Greco	1,584
9	Pat Leahy	1,470
10	Jim Turner	1,439

* Still active at end of 2001 season

Source: *National Football League*

TOP 10 MOST SUCCESSFUL COACHES IN AN NFL CAREER

	COACH	GAMES WON
1	Don Shula	347
2	George Halas	324
3	Tom Landry	270
4	Curly Lambeau	229
5	Chuck Noll	209
6	Chuck Knox	193
7	Dan Reeves*	186
8	Paul Brown	170
9	Bud Grant	168
10	Marv Levy	154

* Still active at end of 2001 season

Source: *National Football League*

Basketball Bests

THE 10 WORST WIN/LOSS RECORDS IN A SEASON

	TEAM	YEAR	RECORD	% GAMES WON
1	Philadelphia 76ers	1972–73	9–73	11.0
2	Providence Steamrollers	1947–48	6–42	12.5
3	=Dallas Mavericks	1992–93	11–71	13.4
	=Denver Nuggets	1997–98	11–71	13.4
5	Los Angeles Clippers	1986–87	12–70	14.6
6	Dallas Mavericks	1993–94	13–69	15.9
7	Vancouver Grizzlies	1998–99	8–42	16.0
8	=Houston Rockets	1982–83	14–68	17.1
	=Vancouver Grizzlies	1996–97	14–68	17.1
10	Philadelphia Warriors	1952–53	12–57	17.4

TOP 10 BEST WIN/LOSS RECORDS IN A SEASON

	TEAM	YEAR	RECORD	% GAMES WON
1	Chicago Bulls	1995–96	72–10	87.8
2	=Chicago Bulls	1996–97	69–13	84.1
	=Los Angeles Lakers	1971–72	69–13	84.1
4	Philadelphia 76ers	1966–67	68–13	84.0
5	Boston Celtics	1972–73	68–14	82.9
6	=Boston Celtics	1985–86	67–15	81.7
	=Chicago Bulls	1991–92	67–15	81.7
	=Los Angeles Lakers	1999–2000	67–15	81.7
	=Washington Capitols	1946–47	49–11	81.7
10	Milwaukee Bucks	1970–71	66–16	80.5

TOP 10 EARNERS IN THE NBA IN 2001-02

	PLAYER/TEAM	EARNINGS ($)
1	Kevin Garnett, Minnesota Timberwolves	22,400,000
2	Shaquille O'Neal, Los Angeles Lakers	21,430,000
3	Alonzo Mourning, Miami Heat	18,766,000
4	Juwan Howard, Denver Nuggets	18,750,000
5	Scottie Pippen, Portland Trail Blazers	18,100,000
6	Karl Malone, Utah Jazz	17,500,000
7	Rasheed Wallace, Portland Trail Blazers	14,400,000
8	Dikembe Mutombo, Philadelphia 76ers	14,320,000
9	Gary Payton, Seattle Supersonics	12,930,000
10	=Allan Houston, New York Knicks	12,750,000
	=Chris Webber, Sacramento Kings	12,750,000

Source: *InsideHoops.com*

Kevin Garnett was the fifth pick overall in the 1995 Draft, and joined the Minnesota Timberwolves. In 1998 he became the first Timberwolves player to start the NBA All-Star game. He has twice had 40-pointer games, and in 1996–97 led the Timberwolves to their first playoff. He completed 7 seasons with them in 2002, ending the season with a career total of 9,994 points. The Timberwolves' total team payroll for the 2001–02 season was $54,509,632 (the League leader was New York Knicks on $85,253,575). Both are technically in excess of the official total salary cap, but there are various exceptions that permit payrolls and individual salaries well in excess of these.

TOP 10 POINTS AVERAGES IN AN NBA SEASON

	PLAYER	CLUB	SEASON	AVERAGE
1	Wilt Chamberlain	Philadelphia 76ers	1961–62	50.4
2	Wilt Chamberlain	San Francisco Warriors	1962–63	44.8
3	Wilt Chamberlain	Philadelphia 76ers	1960–61	38.4
4	Elgin Baylor	Los Angeles Lakers	1961–62	38.3
5	Wilt Chamberlain	Philadelphia 76ers	1959–60	37.6
6	Michael Jordan	Chicago Bulls	1986–87	37.1
7	Wilt Chamberlain	San Francisco Warriors	1963–64	36.9
8	Rick Barry	San Francisco Warriors	1966–67	35.6
9	Michael Jordan	Chicago Bulls	1987–88	35.0
10	=Elgin Baylor	Los Angeles Lakers	1960–61	34.8
	=Kareem Abdul-Jabbar	Milwaukee Bucks	1971–72	34.8

Source: *NBA*

Elgin Baylor was the runner-up to Wilt Chamberlain in the scoring list in both 1960–61 and 1961–62. Chamberlain's dominance meant that Baylor never once topped the list, even though his averages would have enabled him to do so in almost any other NBA season. Baylor spent his entire pro career of 15 seasons with the Minneapolis-Los Angeles Lakers, and led them to eight NBA finals, including 1962 against the Celtics when he scored 61 points in a game – a record for an NBA final. Between them, Michael Jordan and Wilt Chamberlain topped the annual scoring average 17 times. Jordan was in top place on 10 occasions with Chicago between 1987 and 1998, while Chamberlain topped it 7 times, with Philadelphia and San Francisco, all consecutive, between 1960 and 1966.

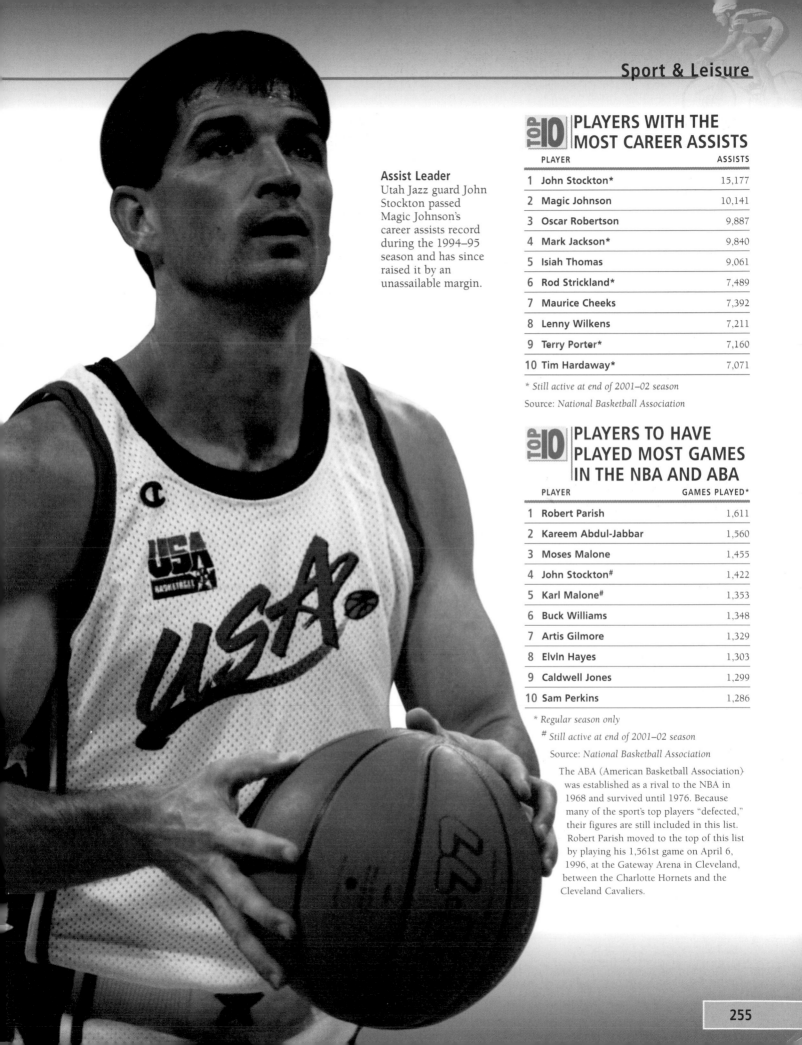

Assist Leader
Utah Jazz guard John Stockton passed Magic Johnson's career assists record during the 1994–95 season and has since raised it by an unassailable margin.

TOP 10 PLAYERS WITH THE MOST CAREER ASSISTS

	PLAYER	ASSISTS
1	John Stockton*	15,177
2	Magic Johnson	10,141
3	Oscar Robertson	9,887
4	Mark Jackson*	9,840
5	Isiah Thomas	9,061
6	Rod Strickland*	7,489
7	Maurice Cheeks	7,392
8	Lenny Wilkens	7,211
9	Terry Porter*	7,160
10	Tim Hardaway*	7,071

* Still active at end of 2001–02 season

Source: *National Basketball Association*

TOP 10 PLAYERS TO HAVE PLAYED MOST GAMES IN THE NBA AND ABA

	PLAYER	GAMES PLAYED*
1	Robert Parish	1,611
2	Kareem Abdul-Jabbar	1,560
3	Moses Malone	1,455
4	John Stockton#	1,422
5	Karl Malone#	1,353
6	Buck Williams	1,348
7	Artis Gilmore	1,329
8	Elvin Hayes	1,303
9	Caldwell Jones	1,299
10	Sam Perkins	1,286

* Regular season only

 # Still active at end of 2001–02 season

Source: *National Basketball Association*

The ABA (American Basketball Association) was established as a rival to the NBA in 1968 and survived until 1976. Because many of the sport's top players "defected," their figures are still included in this list. Robert Parish moved to the top of this list by playing his 1,561st game on April 6, 1996, at the Gateway Arena in Cleveland, between the Charlotte Hornets and the Cleveland Cavaliers.

Baseball Teams

THE 10 TEAMS WITH THE WORST ERA, 2001

	TEAM	ERA
1	Texas Rangers	5.71
2	Colorado Rockies	5.29
3	Pittsburgh Pirates	5.05
4	Detroit Tigers	5.01
5	Tampa Bay Devil Rays	4.94
6	Kansas City Royals	4.87
7	Cincinnati Reds	4.77
8	Montreal Expos	4.68
9	Baltimore Orioles	4.67
10	=Cleveland Indians	4.64
	=Milwaukee Brewers	4.64

Source: *Major League Baseball*

TOP 10 TEAMS WITH THE BEST ERA, 2001

	TEAM	ERA
1	Seattle Mariners	3.54
2	=Atlanta Braves	3.59
	=Oakland Athletics	3.59
4	Arizona Diamondbacks	3.87
5	St. Louis Cardinals	3.93
6	New York Yankees	4.02
7	Chicago Cubs	4.03
8	New York Mets	4.07
9	=Boston Red Sox	4.15
	=Philadelphia Philles	4.15

Source: *Major League Baseball*

TOP 10 BASEBALL TEAM PAYROLLS

	TEAM	TOTAL PAYROLL IN 2002 ($)
1	New York Yankees	125,928,583
2	Boston Red Sox	108,366,060
3	Texas Rangers	105,302,124
4	Arizona Diamondbacks	102,820,000
5	Los Angeles Dodgers	94,850,952
6	New York Mets	94,633,593
7	Atlanta Braves	93,470,367
8	Seattle Mariners	80,282,668
9	Cleveland Indians	78,909,448
10	San Francisco Giants	78,299,835

Source: *Associated Press*

TOP 10 BIGGEST SINGLE GAME WINS IN THE WORLD SERIES

	TEAMS*/GAME	DATE	SCORE
1	New York Yankees vs New York Giants (Game 2)	Oct 2, 1936	18–4
2	=New York Yankees vs Pittsburgh Pirates (Game 2)	Oct 6, 1960	16–3
	=Arizona Diamondbacks vs New York Yankees (Game 6)	Nov 3, 2001	15–2
4	=New York Yankees vs New York Giants (Game 5)	Oct 9, 1951	13–1
	=New York Yankees vs Pittsburgh Pirates (Game 6)	Oct 12, 1960	12–0
	=Detroit Tigers vs St. Louis Cardinals (Game 6)	Oct 9, 1968	13–1
	=New York Yankees vs Milwaukee Brewers (Game 6)	Oct 19, 1982	13–1
8	=New York Yankees vs Philadelphia Athletics (Game 6)	Oct 26, 1911	13–2
	=St. Louis Cardinals vs Detroit Tigers (Game 7)	Oct 9, 1934	11–0
	=Chicago White Sox vs Los Angeles Dodgers (Game 1)	Oct 1, 1959	11–0
	=Kansas City Royals vs St. Louis Cardinals (Game 7)	Oct 27, 1985	11–0
	=Atlanta Braves vs New York Yankees (Game 1)	Oct 20, 1996	12–1

* Winners listed first

Source: *Major League Baseball*

Having lost the first game in the 1936 World Series to the Giants, the Yankees won the second game with their record score, and then went on to build up a 3–1 series lead before capturing their fifth crown 4–2. However, it was a different story when they set the second best mark in game 2 in 1960. They had lost the first game but then went into a 2–1 series lead, eventually losing to the Pirates who won their first World Series since 1925.

THE 10 LATEST WINNERS OF THE WORLD SERIES

YEAR*	WINNER/LEAGUE	LOSER/LEAGUE	SCORE
2001	Arizona Diamondbacks (N)	New York Yankees (A)	4-3
2000	New York Yankees (A)	New York Mets (N)	4-1
1999	New York Yankees (A)	Atlanta Braves (N)	4-0
1998	New York Yankees (A)	San Diego Padres (N)	4-0
1997	Florida Marlins (N)	Cleveland Indians (A)	4-3
1996	New York Yankees (A)	Atlanta Braves (N)	4-2
1995	Atlanta Braves (N)	Cleveland Indians (A)	4-2
1993	Toronto Blue Jays (A)	Philadelphia Phillies (N)	4-2
1992	Toronto Blue Jays (A)	Atlanta Braves (N)	4-2
1991	Minnesota Twins (A)	Atlanta Braves (N)	4-2

* The 1994 event was canceled due to a players' strike

A = American League

N = National League

Source: *Major League Baseball*

TOP 10 OLDEST STADIUMS IN MAJOR LEAGUE BASEBALL

	STADIUM	HOME CLUB	DATE OF FIRST GAME
1	Fenway Park	Boston Red Sox	Apr 20, 1912
2	Wrigley Field	Chicago Cubs	Apr 23, 1914
3	Yankee Stadium	New York Yankees	Apr 18, 1923
4	Dodger Stadium	Los Angeles Dodgers	Apr 10, 1962
5	Shea Stadium	New York Mets	Apr 17, 1964
6	Edison International Field of Anaheim*	Anaheim Angels	Apr 19, 1966
7	Busch Stadium	St. Louis Cardinals	May 12, 1966
8	Qualcomm Stadium#	San Diego Padres	Apr 5, 1968
9	Network Associates Coliseum†	Oakland Athletics	Apr 17, 1968
10	Cinergy Field	Cincinnati Reds	Jun 30, 1970

* Formerly known as Anaheim Stadium

Formerly known as Jack Murphy Stadium

† Formerly known as Oakland-Alameda County Coliseum

Source: Major League Baseball

TOP 10 MOST EXPENSIVE US BASEBALL TEAM SALES

	TEAM	BUYER	YEAR	COST ($)
1	Boston Red Sox	John Henry	2001	700,000,000
2	Cleveland Indians	Larry Dolan	2000	323,000,000
3	Los Angeles Dodgers	News Corp.	1998	311,000,000
4	Texas Rangers	Tom Hicks	1998	250,000,000
5	Baltimore Orioles	Peter Angelos	1993	173,000,000
6	=Florida Marlins	John Henry	1999	150,000,000
	=St. Louis Cardinals	William DeWitt, Jr.	1995	150,000,000
8	=Arizona Diamondbacks	Jerry Colangelo	1995	130,000,000
	=Tampa Bay Devil Rays	Vincent Naimoli	1995	130,000,000
10	Houston Astros	Drayton McLane, Jr.	1992	115,000,000

Source: Bonham Group

When the consortium led by John Henry, the former owner of the Florida Marlins, bought the Red Sox in 2001, it ended the Yawkey family's 70-year association with the team. It is hoped that Henry will be able to change the fortunes of this team – one of the most famous names in the sport – since they have not won the World Series since 1918.

TOP 10 TEAMS WITH THE MOST HOME RUNS, 2001

	TEAM	HOME RUN TOTAL
1	Texas Rangers	246
2	San Francisco Giants	235
3	Chicago White Sox	214
4	Colorado Rockies	213
5	Cleveland Indians	212
6	Milwaukee Brewers	209
7	=Arizona Diamondbacks	208
	=Houston Astros	208
9	Los Angeles Dodgers	206
10	New York Yankees	203

Source: Major League Baseball

Home runs do not always win matches, and that was certainly true for the Texas Rangers in 2001. They may well have slugged more homers than any other team, but they finished bottom of the American League West Division, with a 73–89 record. Coach Johnny Oates quit partway through his seventh season with the club when they were on 11–17.

TOP 10 TEAMS WITH THE MOST WORLD SERIES WINS

	TEAM*	WINS
1	New York Yankees	26
2	=Philadelphia/Kansas City/Oakland Athletics	9
	=St. Louis Cardinals	9
4	Brooklyn/Los Angeles Dodgers	6
5	=Boston Red Sox	5
	=Cincinnati Reds	5
	=New York/San Francisco Giants	5
	=Pittsburgh Pirates	5
9	Detroit Tigers	4
10	=Boston/Milwaukee/Atlanta Braves	3
	=St. Louis/Baltimore Orioles	3
	=Washington Senators/Minnesota Twins	3

* Teams separated by / indicate changes of franchise and are regarded as the same team for Major League record purposes

Source: Major League Baseball

TOP 10 AVERAGE ATTENDANCES, 2001

	TEAM	AVERAGE ATTENDANCE
1	Seattle Mariners	43,300
2	San Francisco Giants	40,888
3	New York Yankees	40,811
4	Cleveland Indians	39,694
5	Colorado Rockies	39,096
6	Baltimore Orioles	38,685
7	St. Louis Cardinals	38,389
8	Los Angeles Dodgers	37,248
9	Houston Astros	35,855
10	Chicago Cubs	35,183

Source: Major League Baseball

Of those team in the list, the Giants filled their ballpark to the biggest percentage with an average of 98.9 percent of the Pacific Bell Park stadium being filled for each of their 81 home games. Despite their fanatical following the Giants never made it to the play-offs. The Dodgers had the worst percentage of those on the list with their stadium being filled to only 66.51 percent of capacity.

Baseball Stars

TOP 10 | PLAYERS WITH THE MOST CAREER STRIKEOUTS

	PLAYER	STRIKEOUTS
1	Nolan Ryan	5,714
2	Steve Carlton	4,136
3	Roger Clemens*	3,717
4	Bert Blyleven	3,701
5	Tom Seaver	3,640
6	Don Sutton	3,574
7	Gaylord Perry	3,534
8	Walter Johnson	3,508
9	Randy Johnson*	3,412
10	Phil Niekro	3,342

Still active at end of 2001 season

Source: *Major League Baseball*

TOP 10 | PLAYERS MOST AT-BAT IN A CAREER

	PLAYER	AT-BAT
1	Pete Rose	14,053
2	Hank Aaron	12,364
3	Carl Yastrzemski	11,988
4	Cal Ripken Jr.	11,551
5	Ty Cobb	11,434
6	Eddie Murray	11,336
7	Robin Yount	11,008
8	Dave Winfield	11,003
9	Stan Musial	10,972
10	Willie Mays	10,881

Source: *Major League Baseball*

As well as appearing second in this list, Hank Aaron collected more bases than any other player in baseball history, overtaking Stan Musial's previous record of 6,134 in 1972, and going on to reach 6,856 in 1976.

TOP 10 | PLAYERS WHO PLAYED THE MOST GAMES IN A CAREER

	PLAYER	GAMES
1	Pete Rose	3,562
2	Carl Yastrzemski	3,308
3	Hank Aaron	3,298
4	Ty Cobb	3,034
5	=Eddie Murray	3,026
	=Stan Musial	3,026
7	Cal Ripken Jr.	3,001
8	Willie Mays	2,992
9	Rickey Henderson	2,979
10	Dave Winfield	2,973

Source: *Major League Baseball*

Pete Rose is the only player to appear in over 500 games in 5 different positions: he was at first base in 939 games, second in 628, third in 634, and right field in 595.

TOP 10 | HIGHEST-PAID BASEBALL PLAYERS*

	PLAYER	TEAM	LENGTH OF CONTRACT	AVERAGE ANNUAL SALARY ($)
1	Alex Rodriguez	Texas Rangers	2001–10	25,200,000
2	Manny Ramirez	Boston Red Sox	2001–08	20,000,000
3	Derek Jeter	New York Yankees	2001–10	18,900,000
4	=Barry Bonds	San Francisco Giants	2002–06	18,000,000
	=Sammy Sosa	Chicago Cubs	2002–05	18,000,000
6	Jason Giambi	New York Yankees	2002–08	17,142,857
7	=Jeff Bagwell	Houston Astros	2002–06	17,000,000
	=Carlos Delgado	Toronto Blue Jays	2001–04	17,000,000
9	Todd Helton	Colorado Rockies	2003–11	15,722,222
10	Roger Clemens	New York Yankees	2001–02	15,450,000

Ranked by average annual value of contract

Source: Sports Illustrated

Alex Rodriguez set a new record in 2001 when he signed a contract worth $252 million over 10 years. He is also eligible for such bonuses as $500,000 for his first MVP award, $1 million for a second, and $1.5 million for subsequent MVPs.

TOP 10 | PLAYERS WITH THE MOST HOME RUNS IN A SEASON

	PLAYER	TEAM	YEAR	RUNS
1	Barry Bonds	San Francisco Giants	2001	73
2	Mark McGwire	St. Louis Cardinals	1998	70
3	Sammy Sosa	Chicago Cubs	1998	66
4	Mark McGuire	St. Louis Cardinals	1999	65
5	Sammy Sosa	Chicago Cubs	2001	64
6	Sammy Sosa	Chicago Cubs	1999	63
7	Roger Maris	New York Yankees	1961	61
8	Babe Ruth	New York Yankees	1927	60
9	Babe Ruth	New York Yankees	1921	59
10	=Jimmie Foxx	Philadelphia Phillies	1932	58
	=Hank Greenberg	Detroit Tigers	1938	58
	=Mark McGuire	St. Louis Cardinals	1997	58

Source: *Major League Baseball*

George Herman "Babe" Ruth set a new home run record in 1919 by hitting 29, and then broke it during the next season, hitting 54. The progression of season bests since then has seen the total rise to 259.

 LATEST
PERFECT GAMES

	PLAYER	MATCH	DATE
1	David Cone	New York Yankees vs Montreal Expos	Jul 18, 1999
2	David Wells	New York Yankees vs Minnesota Twins	May 17, 1998
3	Kenny Rogers	Texas Rangers vs California Angels	Jul 28, 1994
4	Dennis Martinez	Montreal Expos vs Los Angeles Dodgers	Jul 28, 1991
5	Tom Browning	Cincinnati Reds vs Los Angeles Dodgers	Sep 16, 1988
6	Mike Witt	California Angels vs Texas Rangers	Sep 30, 1984
7	Len Barker	Cleveland Indians vs Toronto Blue Jays	May 15, 1981
8	Catfish Hunter	Oakland Athletics vs Minnesota Twins	May 8, 1968
9	Sandy Koufax	Los Angeles Dodgers vs Chicago Cubs	Sep 9, 1965
10	Jim Bunning	Philadelphia Phillies vs New York Mets	Jun 21, 1964

Seventeen pitchers have thrown perfect games; that is, they have pitched in all 9 innings, dismissing 27 opposing batters, and without conceding a run. The first player to pitch a perfect innings was Lee Richmond, for Worcester against Cleveland, on June 12, 1880.

Source: *Major League Baseball*

THE 10 LATEST WINNERS OF THE CY YOUNG AWARD

	AMERICAN LEAGUE PLAYER/TEAM	NATIONAL LEAGUE PLAYER/TEAM
2001	Roger Clemens, New York Yankees	Randy Johnson, Arizona Diamondbacks
2000	Pedro Martinez, Boston Red Sox	Randy Johnson, Arizona Diamondbacks
1999	Pedro Martinez, Boston Red Sox	Randy Johnson, Arizona Diamondbacks
1998	Roger Clemens, Toronto Blue Jays	Tom Glavine, Atlanta Braves
1997	Roger Clemens, Toronto Blue Jays	Pedro Martinez, Montreal Expos
1996	Pat Hentgen, Toronto Blue Jays	John Smoltz, Atlanta Braves
1995	Randy Johnson, Seattle Mariners	Greg Maddux, Atlanta Braves
1994	David ConeKansas, City Royals	Greg Maddux, Atlanta Braves
1993	Jack McDowell, Chicago White Sox	Greg Maddux, Atlanta Braves
1992	Dennis Eckersley, Oakland Athletics	Greg Maddux, Chicago Cubs

Source: *Major League Baseball*

TOP 10 PITCHERS WITH THE MOST CAREER WINS

	PLAYER	WINS
1	Cy Young	511
2	Walter Johnson	417
3	=Grover Alexander	373
	=Christy Mathewson	373
5	Pud Galvin	365
6	Warren Spahn	363
7	Kid Nichols	361
8	Tim Keefe	342
9	Steve Carlton	329
10	John Clarkson	328

Source: *Major League Baseball*

In the 1925 season, Walter Johnson became the only pitcher to win 20 games and achieve a batting average for the season of 0.433 in 97 "at bats" – the highest of any pitcher in baseball history.

THE 10 LATEST BATTING CHAMPIONS

	AMERICAN LEAGUE PLAYER/TEAM	BATTING AVERAGE	NATIONAL LEAGUE PLAYER/TEAM	BATTING AVERAGE
2001	Ichiro Suzuki, Seattle Mariners	.350	Larry Walker, Colorado Rockies	.350
2000	Nomar Garciaparra, Boston Red Sox	.372	Todd Helton, Colorado Rockies	.372
1999	Nomar Garciaparra, Boston Red Sox	.357	Larry Walker, Colorado Rockies	.379
1998	Bernie Williams, New York Yankees	.339	Larry Walker, Colorado Rockies	.363
1997	Frank Thomas, Chicago White Sox	.347	Tony Gwynn, San Diego Padres	.372
1996	Alex Rodriguez, Seattle Mariners	.358	Tony Gwynn, San Diego Padres	.353
1995	Edgar Martinez, Seattle Mariners	.356	Tony Gwynn, San Diego Padres	.368
1994	Paul O'Neill, New York Yankees	.359	Tony Gwynn, San Diego Padres	.394
1993	John Olerud, Toronto Blue Jays	.363	Andres Galarraga, Colorado Rockies	.370
1992	Edgar Martinez, Seattle Mariners	.343	Gary Sheffield, San Diego Padres	.330

Source: *Major League Baseball*

The first Japanese hitter to join the majors, Ichiro Suzuki vindicated his critics with one of the finest rookie seasons of all time, gaining the American League Rookie of the Year Award, the junior circuit's MVP honors, and a Gold Glove.

International Soccer

TOP 10 TRANSFERS IN INTERNATIONAL SOCCER

	PLAYER/COUNTRY	FROM	TO	YEAR	FEE ($)
1	**Zinedine Zidane,** France	Juventus, Italy	Real Madrid, Spain	2001	67,100,000
2	**Luis Figo,** Portugal	Barcelona, Spain	Real Madrid, Spain	2000	56,700,000
3	**Hernan Crespo,** Argentina	Parma, Italy	Lazio, Italy	2000	54,100,000
4	**Gianluigi Buffon,** Italy	Parma, Italy	Juventus, Italy	2001	46,200,000
5	**Gaizka Mendieta,** Spain	Valencia, Spain	Lazio, Italy	2001	40,600,000
6	**Juan Sebastian Veron,** Argentina	Lazio, Italy	Manchester United, England	2001	39,600,000
7	**Rui Costa,** Portugal	Fiorentina, Italy	AC Milan, Italy	2001	39,400,000
8	**Christian Vieri,** Italy	Lazio, Italy	Inter Milan, Italy	1999	38,500,000*
9	**Nicolas Anelka,** France	Arsenal, England	Real Madrid, Spain	1999	37,400,000
10	**Pavel Nedved,** Czech Republic	Lazio, Italy	Juventus, Italy	2001	36,800,000

Vieri's transfer was part of a package deal with Nicola Ventola, who was valued at $11.2 million. Vieri was valued at $38.5 million.

TOP 10 BIGGEST WORLD CUP SCORES

	MATCH (WINNER FIRST)*	DATE	SCORE
1	**Australia vs American Samoa**	Apr 11, 2001	31–0
2	**Australia# vs Tonga**	Apr 9, 2001	22–0
3	**Iran vs Guam**	Nov 24, 2000	19–0
4	**Iran# vs Maldives**	Jun 2, 1997	17–0
5	**Tajikistan vs Guam**	Nov 26, 2000	16–0
6	**=New Zealand vs Fiji**	Aug 16, 1981	13–0
	=Australia vs Solomon Islands	Jun 11, 1997	13–0
	=Fiji vs American Samoa	Apr 7, 2001	13–0
9	**=West Germany vs Cyprus**	May 21, 1969	12–0
	=Syria# vs Maldives	Jun 4, 1997	12–0
	=Oman vs Laos	Apr 30, 2001	12–0
	=Syria vs Philippines	Apr 30, 2001	12–0
	=United Arab Emirates# vs Brunei	Apr 14, 2001	12–0

*All matches are qualifiers

# Denotes away team. Australia vs Tonga was the "away" fixture but was played on Australian soil

TEAMS IN THE WORLD CUP

	TEAM	GAMES WON	POINTS*
1	Brazil	53	120
2	Germany#	45	107
3	Italy	38	92
4	Argentina	29	68
5	England	20	53
6	France	21	48
7	Spain	16	42
8	Yugoslavia	16	40
9	Uruguay	15	38
10	=Netherlands	14	37
	=Sweden	14	37

* 2 points for a win and 1 for a draw in all matches played in the final stages; up to and including the 1998 Cup

\# Including West Germany

TEAMS IN THE AFRICAN NATIONS CUP

	TEAM	GAMES WON	POINTS*
1	Egypt	35	81
2	Ghana	31	77
3	Nigeria	29	73
4	Cameroon	28	72
5	Côte d'Ivoire	21	56
6	Algeria	17	49
7	Zambia	19	48
8	Congo-Kinshasa	15	44
9	Morocco	13	42
10	=Senegal	12	31
	=Tunisia	9	31

* 2 points for a win and 1 for a draw in all matches played in the final stage; up to and including the 2002 Cup

One-sided Match

The Australian team defeated American Samoa 31–0, the greatest margin of victory in an international match.

TEAMS IN THE EUROPEAN CHAMPIONSHIP

	TEAM	GAMES WON	POINTS*
1	Germany	17	44
2	Netherlands	15	36
3	France	12	30
4	Italy	10	29
5	Soviet Union/Russia	9	25
6	Spain	7	22
7	England	7	21
8	Czechoslovakia/ Czech Republic	7	20
9	Portugal	7	17
10	Yugoslavia	5	15

* 2 points for a win and 1 for a draw in all matches played in the final stages; up to and including 2000 championship

TEAMS IN THE COPA AMÉRICA

	TEAM	GAMES WON	POINTS*
1	Argentina	102	234
2	Uruguay	98	222
3	Brazil	88	203
4	Paraguay	57	143
5	Chile	53	139
6	Peru	44	116
7	Colombia	32	83
8	Bolivia	19	58
9	Ecuador	14	47
10	Mexico	11	30

* 2 points for a win and 1 for a draw in all matches played in the final stages; up to and including the 2001 Cup

The first South American Championship was staged in 1916 and is now held every 2 years. The only other countries to have competed are Costa Rica, Honduras, Japan, Venezuela, and the US.

Hockey Highlights

TOP 10 TEAMS WITH THE MOST STANLEY CUP WINS

	TEAM	WINS*
1	Montreal Canadiens	23
2	Toronto Maple Leafs	13
3	Detroit Red Wings	9
4	=Boston Bruins	5
	=Edmonton Oilers	5
6	=New York Islanders	4
	=New York Rangers	4
9	Chicago Black Hawks	3
10	=Colorado Avalanche	2
	=Montreal Maroons	2
	=New Jersey Devils	2
	=Philadelphia Flyers	2
	=Pittsburgh Penguins	2

* 1927 to 2001 inclusive

THE 10 LATEST STANLEY CUP WINNERS

YEAR	WINNER
2001	Colorado Avalanche
2000	New Jersey Devils
1999	Dallas Stars
1998	Detroit Red Wings
1997	Detroit Red Wings
1996	Colorado Avalanche
1995	New Jersey Devils
1994	New York Rangers
1993	Montreal Canadiens
1992	Pittsburgh Penguins

The Colorado Avalanche became only the fifth team in NHL history to trail 3–2 in the Stanley Cup and yet go on to win. The last team to perform the feat before them were the Montreal Canadiens who overturned the deficit to beat Chicago in 1971.

TOP 10 GOALIES IN AN NHL CAREER

	PLAYER	SEASONS	GAMES WON*
1	Patrick Roy#	18	516
2	Terry Sawchuk	21	447
3	Jacques Plante	18	434
4	Tony Esposito	16	423
5	Glenn Hall	18	407
6	Grant Fuhr	19	403
7	Mike Vernon#	19	385
8	John Vanbiesbrouck#	21	374
9	Andy Moog	18	372
10	Tom Barrasso#	18	368

* Regular season only

Still active at end 2001–02 season

Source: National Hockey League

TOP 10 BIGGEST NHL ARENAS

	STADIUM	HOME TEAM	CAPACITY
1	Molson Centre, Montreal	Montreal Canadiens	21,273
2	United Center, Chicago	Chicago Blackhawks	20,500
3	Ice Palace, Tampa Bay	Tampa Bay Lightning	19,758
4	First Union Center, Philadelphia	Philadelphia Fliers	19,523
5	National Car Rental Center, Sunrise, Florida	Florida Panthers	19,250
6	Continental Airlines Arena, East Rutherford, New Jersey	New Jersey Devils	19,040
7	SAVVIS Center, St. Louis	St. Louis Blues	19,022
8	Air Canada Centre, Toronto	Toronto Maple Leafs	18,819
9	Entertainment & Sports Arena, Raleigh	Carolina Hurricanes	18,730
10	MCI Center, Washington, DC	Washington Capitals	18,672

Source: NHL Official Guide & Record Book 2002

TOP 10 GOALIES WITH THE BEST SAVES PERCENTAGES IN THE NHL, 2001–02

	PLAYER*	TEAM	GAMES PLAYED	TOTAL SAVES	SAVES %
1	=David Aebischer	Colorado Avalanche	21	501	0.931
	=Jose Theodore	Montreal Canadiens	67	1,836	0.931
3	Patrick Roy	Columbus Blue Jackets	63	1,507	0.925
4	=Roman Cechmanek	Philadelphia Fliers	46	1,042	0.921
	=Marty Turco	Dallas Stars	31	617	0.921
6	=Sean Burke	Phoenix Coyotes	60	1,574	0.920
	=J. Giguere	Mighty Ducks of Anaheim	53	1,273	0.920
	=Nikolai Khabibulin	Tampa Bay Lightning	70	1,761	0.920
9	Evgeni Nabokov	San Jose Sharks	67	1,669	0.918
10	Kevin Weekes	Carolina Hurricanes	21	468	0.916

* Minimum qualification 20 games; regular season only

Source: National Hockey League

TOP 10 GOALSCORERS IN AN NHL CAREER

	PLAYER	SEASONS	GOALS*
1	Wayne Gretzky	20	894
2	Gordie Howe	26	801
3	Marcel Dionne	18	731
4	Phil Esposito	18	717
5	Mike Gartner	19	708
6	Brett Hull#	17	679
7	=Mark Messier#	23	658
	=Steve Yzerman#	19	658
9	Mario Lemieux#	14	654
10	Luc Robitaille	16	620

* Regular season only

\# Still active at end of 2001–02 season

Source: *National Hockey League*

TOP 10 ASSISTS IN AN NHL CAREER

	PLAYER	SEASONS	ASSISTS*
1	Wayne Gretzky	20	1,963
2	Ron Francis#	20	1,187
3	Ray Bourque	26	1,169
4	Mark Messier#	23	1,146
5	Paul Coffey	29	1,135
6	Gordie Howe	26	1,049
7	Marcel Dionne	18	1,040
8	Adam Oates#	19	1,027
9	Steve Yzerman#	19	1,004
10	Mario Lemiux	14	947

* Regular season only

\# Still active at end of 2001–02 season

Source: *National Hockey League/Hockey Database*

TOP 10 GOALSCORERS IN THE NHL, 2001–02*

	PLAYER/TEAM	GOALS*
1	Jarome Iginla, Calgary Flames	52
2	=Bill Guerin, Boston Bruins	41
	=Glen Murray, Boston Bruins	41
	=Mats Sundin, Toronto Maple Leafs	41
5	Markus Naslund, Vancouver Canucks	40
6	Peter Bondra, Washington Capitals	39
7	=Eric Daze, Chicago Black Hawks	38
	=Keith Tkachuk, St. Louis Blues	38
9	=Daniel Alfredsson, Ottawa Senators	37
	=Eric Lindros, Ottawa Senators	37
	=Miroslav Satan, Buffalo Sabres	37
	=Brendan Shanahan, Detroit Red Wings	37

* Regular season only

Source: *National Hockey League*

TOP 10 GOALSCORERS IN AN NHL SEASON

	PLAYER	TEAM	SEASON	GOALS
1	Wayne Gretzky	Edmonton Oilers	1981–82	92
2	Wayne Gretzky	Edmonton Oilers	1983–84	87
3	Brett Hull	St. Louis Blues	1990–91	86
4	Mario Lemieux	Pittsburgh Penguins	1988–89	85
5	=Phil Esposito	Boston Bruins	1970–71	76
	=Alexander Mogilny	Buffalo Sabers	1992–93	76
	=Teemu Selanne	Winnipeg Jets	1992–93	76
8	Wayne Gretzky	Edmonton Oilers	1984–85	73
9	Brett Hull	St. Louis Blues	1989–90	72
10	=Wayne Gretzky	Edmonton Oilers	1982–83	71
	=Jari Kurri	Edmonton Oilers	1984–85	71

Source: *National Hockey League*

TOP 10 GOAL-SCORING ROOKIES IN THE NHL, 2001–02*

	PLAYER	TEAM	GAMES PLAYED	GOALS
1	Ilya Kovalchuk	Atlanta Thrashers	65	29
2	Dany Heatley	Atlanta Thrashers	82	26
3	Kristian Huselius	Florida Panthers	79	23
4	Radim Vrbata	Colorado Avalanche	52	18
5	Erik Cole	Carolina Hurricanes	81	16
6	Pascal Dupuis	Minnesota Wild	76	15
7	Mark Bell	Chicago Black Hawks	80	12
8	=Pavel Datsyuk	Detroit Red Wings	70	11
	=Krystofer Kolanos	Phoenix Coyotes	57	11
10	=Kris Beech	Pittsburgh Penguins	79	10
	=Pierre Dagenais	Florida Panthers	42	10
	=Niklas Hagman	Florida Panthers	78	10
	=Chris Neil	Ottawa Senators	72	10

* Regular season only

Source: *National Hockey League*

Racket Sports

TOP 10 PLAYERS WITH THE MOST BADMINTON WORLD TITLES

	PLAYER/COUNTRY	MALE/FEMALE	TITLES*
1	Park Joo-bong, South Korea	M	5
2	=Han Aiping, China	F	3
	=Li Lingwei, China	F	3
	=Guan Weizhan, China	F	3
	=Lin Ying, China	F	3
6	=Tian Bingyi, China	M	2
	=Christian Hadinata, Indonesia	M	2
	=Lene Köppen, Denmark	F	2
	=Kim Moon-soo, South Korea	M	2
	=Chung Myung-hee, South Korea	F	2
	=Nora Perry, England	F	2
	=Yang Yang, China	M	2
	=Li Yongbo, China	M	2

* Includes singles, doubles, mixed doubles

Source: *International Badminton Federation*

The World Championship was launched as recently as 1977. Originally it was held every 3 years but since 1985 it has been a biennial event.

GRAND SLAM FIRST

100 YEARS AGO, IN 1903, Hugh Lawrence Doherty (1875–1919) achieved the first ever Grand Slam, by taking both the men's singles and, with his brother Reginald Frank Doherty (1872–1910), the doubles titles in the US Open and Wimbledon in the same year. Although a notable tennis first, the Dohertys' achievement was limited because at this time, these were the only two international open tennis competitions. When the French championship became an open event in 1925, and players also competed in the Australian Open, the notion of a Grand Slam including all four was born, and the term was first used in 1938.

FIRST OR LAST

TOP 10 TABLE TENNIS WORLD CHAMPIONSHIP GOLD MEDAL WINNERS

	COUNTRY	MEN'S	WOMEN'S	TOTAL*
1	China	41.5	48	89.5
2	Hungary	42	26	68
3	Japan	23.5	23.5	47
4	Czechoslovakia	17.5	10.5	28
5	Romania	-	17	17
6	=England	8	6	14
	=Sweden	14	-	14
8	US	5	5	10
9	Austria	3	3	6
10	Germany	1	4	5
	All countries	161	154	315

* Includes team events, singles, doubles, and mixed; 0.5 golds were possible when doubles pairs could be of different nationalities – today, only players of the same nationality can play in pairs

Source: *International Table Tennis Federation (ITTF)*

The ITTF was formed in Berlin in 1926 and the first table tennis world championships were played that year in London, UK. The sport was dominated by the Hungarians until World War II.

TOP 10 FEMALE SQUASH PLAYERS

	PLAYER/COUNTRY	AVERAGE POINTS*
1	Sarah Fitz-Gerald, Australia	2,713.125
2	Leilani Joyce, New Zealand	1,537.750
3	Carol Owens, New Zealand	1,134.063
4	Cassie Campion, England	913.688
5	Linda Charman-Smith, England	843.375
6	Fiona Geaves, England	770.813
7	Stephani Brind, England	677.063
8	Rachael Grinham, Australia	660.625
9	Suzanne Horner, England	642.313
10	Rebecca Macree, England	534.219

* As of January 2002

Source: *WISPA World Rankings*

TOP 10 WINNERS OF WOMEN'S GRAND SLAM SINGLES TITLES

	PLAYER/COUNTRY	A	F	W	US	TOTAL
1	Margaret Court (née Smith), Australia	11	5	3	5	24
2	Steffi Graf, Germany	4	6	7	5	22
3	Helen Wills-Moody, US	0	4	8	7	19
4	=Chris Evert-Lloyd, US	2	7	3	6	18
	=Martina Navratilova, Cze/US	3	2	9	4	18
6	=Billie Jean King (née Moffitt), US	1	1	6	4	12
	=Suzanne Lenglen, France	0	6	6	0	12
8	=Maureen Connolly, US	1	2	3	3	9
	=Monica Seles, Yug/US	4	3	0	2	9
10	Molla Mallory (née Bjurstedt), US	0	0	0	8	8

A – Australian Open; F – French Open; W – Wimbledon; US – US Open

TOP 10 MALE SQUASH PLAYERS

	PLAYER/COUNTRY	AVERAGE POINTS*
1	Peter Nicol, England	1,048.438
2	David Palmer, Australia	1,009.375
3	John White, Scotland	547.656
4	Jonathon Power, Canada	521.125
5	Thierry Lincou, France	481.250
6	Stewart Boswell, Australia	480.469
7	Ong Beng Hee, Malaysia	375.000
8	David Evans, Wales	350.781
9	Paul Price, Australia	341.406
10	Mark Chaloner, England	325.694

* As of January 2002

Source: *Dunlop PSA World Rankings*

The players' rankings have been decided by taking the total points they have scored and dividing it by the number of tournaments in which they have competed.

TOP 10 WINNERS OF MEN'S GRAND SLAM TENNIS SINGLES TITLES

	PLAYER/NATIONALITY	A	F	W	US	TOTAL
1	**Pete Sampras**, US	2	0	7	4	13
2	**Roy Emerson**, Australia	6	2	2	2	12
3	**=Bjorn Borg**, Sweden	0	6	5	0	11
	=Rod Laver, Australia	3	2	4	2	11
5	**Bill Tilden**, US	0	0	3	7	10
6	**=Jimmy Connors**, US	1	0	2	5	8
	=Ivan Lendl, Cze/US	2	3	0	3	8
	=Fred Perry, Great Britain	1	1	3	3	8
	=Ken Rosewall, Australia	4	2	0	2	8
10	**=Andre Agassi**, US	3	1	1	2	7
	=Henri Cochet, France	0	4	2	1	7
	=René Lacoste, France	0	3	2	2	7
	=Bill Larned, US	0	0	0	7	7
	=John McEnroe, US	0	0	3	4	7
	=John Newcombe, Australia	2	0	3	2	7
	=Willie Renshaw, Great Britain	0	0	7	0	7
	=Richard Sears, US	0	0	0	7	7
	=Mats Wilander, Sweden	3	3	0	1	7

A – Australian Open; F – French Open;
W – Wimbledon; US – US Open

For Pete's Sake
Pete Sampras holds more Grand Slam singles titles than any other man in the history of the sport.

Golfing Greats

TOP 10 MONEY-WINNING GOLFERS (MALE)

	GOLFER*	CAREER WINNINGS# ($)
1	Tiger Woods	28,876,727
2	Phil Mickelson	19,553,860
3	Davis Love III	18,291,352
4	Vijay Singh, Fiji	16,038,822
5	David Duval	15,540,294
6	Nick Price, Zimbabwe	15,035,115
7	Scott Hoch	15,033,960
8	Hal Sutton	14,021,810
9	Mark Calcavecchia	13,728,300
10	Ernie Els, South Africa	13,249,083

* All US unless otherwise stated

\# As of April 14, 2002

Conquering King

Betsy King was the first player in LPGA history to cross the $5 million barrier, and is the foremost US female golfer in career winnings.

TOP 10 MONEY WINNERS ON THE US SENIORS TOUR

	GOLFER*	WINNINGS# ($)
1	Hale Irwin	20,839,005
2	Gil Morgan	15,305,733
3	Tom Kite	14,205,081
4	Ray Floyd	13,627,680
5	Lee Trevino	12,990,570
6	Tom Watson	12,499,422
7	Jim Colbert	12,220,910
8	Larry Nelson	12,176,478
9	Dave Stockton	10,757,267
10	George Archer	10,030,825

* All US

\# As at April 28, 2002

Hale Irwin joined the Seniors Tour in 1995 after 20 career victories on the regular Tour stretching from 1971 to 1994. Since joining the Seniors he won an additional 32 tournaments to the end of the 2001 season. He has won the PGA Seniors Championships 3 times and the US Seniors Open twice.

TOP 10 MONEY-WINNING GOLFERS (FEMALE)

	GOLFER*	YEARS	WINNINGS# ($)
1	Annika Sorenstam, Sweden	1992–2002	8,869,794
2	Karrie Webb, Australia	1995–2002	7,698,299
3	Betsy King	1977–2002	7,206,744
4	Dottie Pepper	1987–2001	6,658,613
5	Juli Inkster	1983–2002	6,638,337
6	Beth Daniel	1979–2002	6,483,278
7	Meg Mallon	1987–2002	5,992,648
8	Rosie Jones	1982–2002	5,809,080
9	Laura Davies, Great Britain	1988–2002	5,755,405
10	Pat Bradley	1974–2000	5,743,605

* All US unless otherwise stated

\# As of April 8, 2002

Born in 1970, Swedish golfer Annika Sorenstam was College Player of the Year and NCAA champion in 1991, and won more tournaments on the US LPGA Tour in the 1990s than any other woman – a total of 18 – including two US Opens (1995 and 1996). In addition to being the all-time highest-earner, she is 1 of only 2 women to win $1,000,000 in a season on 3 occasions (Karrie Webb is the other).

TOP 10 LOWEST FOUR ROUND TOTALS IN MAJOR CHAMPIONSHIPS

	PLAYER/COUNTRY	VENUE	YEAR	TOTAL
1	David Toms, US	Atlanta, Georgia*	2001	265
2	Phil Mickelson, US	Atlanta, Georgia*	2001	266
3	=Greg Norman, Australia	Royal St. George's, Sandwich#	1993	267
	=Steve Elkington, Australia	Riviera, California*	1995	267
	=Colin Montgomerie, UK	Riviera, California*	1995	267
6	=Tom Watson, US	Turnberry#	1977	268
	=Nick Price, Zimbabwe	Turnberry#	1994	268
	=Steve Lowery, US	Atlanta, Georgia*	2001	268
9	=Jack Nicklaus, US	Turnberry#	1977	269
	=Nick Faldo, UK	Royal St. George's, Sandwich#	1993	269
	=Tiger Woods, US	St Andrews#	1999	269
	=Jesper Parnevik, Sweden	Turnberry#	1994	269
	=Nick Price, Zimbabwe	Southern Hills, Tulsa*	1994	269
	=Davis Love III, US	Winged Foot, New York*	1997	269
	=Tiger Woods, US	St. Andrews#	2000	269

* US PGA Championship

\# British Open Championship

PLAYERS WITH THE MOST RYDER CUP WINS

	PLAYER	WINS
1	Nick Faldo, UK	23
2	Arnold Palmer, US	22
3	=Severiano Ballesteros, Spain	20
	=Billy Casper, US	20
	=Lanny Wadkins, US	20
6	Bernhard Langer, Germany	18
7	=Jack Nicklaus, US	17
	=Lee Trevino, US	17
9	=Tom Kite, US	15
	=José Maria Olazabal, Spain	15

The Ryder Cup was launched in 1927 by British seed merchant and golf enthusiast Samuel Ryder (1858–1936). Held every 2 years (with a break between 1939 and 1945 due to World War II), the venues alternate between the US and the UK. The US originally competed against the UK and Ireland, but, since 1979, it has competed against Europe.

PLAYERS TO WIN THE MOST MAJORS IN A CAREER

	PLAYER*	TOTAL#
1	Jack Nicklaus	18
2	Walter Hagen	11
3	=Ben Hogan	9
	=Gary Player, South Africa	9
5	Tom Watson	8
6	=Bobby Jones	7
	=Arnold Palmer	7
	=Gene Sarazen	7
	=Sam Snead	7
	=Harry Vardon, UK	7
	=Tiger Woods	7

* All US unless otherwise indicated

As of April 15, 2002, includes British Open, US Open, US Masters, and US PGA

Easy Ryder
Since his first victory in 1977, Nick Faldo has become the most successful Ryder Cup player of all time.

Water Sports

TOP 10 OLYMPIC CANOEING COUNTRIES

COUNTRY	GOLD	SILVER	BRONZE	TOTAL
1 Hungary	14	25	21	60
2 =Germany*	22	16	15	53
=Soviet Union#	30	14	9	53
4 Romania	10	10	14	34
5 East Germany	14	7	9	30
6 Sweden	14	11	4	29
7 France	3	7	16	26
8 Bulgaria	4	5	8	17
9 Canada	3	8	5	16
10 =Poland	0	5	10	15
=US	5	4	6	15

The header "MEDALS" spans GOLD, SILVER, BRONZE, TOTAL.

* *Not including West/East Germany 1968–88*

\# *Includes Unified Team of 1992; excludes Russia since then*

Paddling her own Canoe
Mandy Planert of Germany competes in the kayak slalom at the Sydney 2000 Olympic Games. The event was first introduced in the 1972 Olympic Games.

TOP 10 COLLEGES IN THE INTERCOLLEGIATE ROWING ASSOCIATION REGATTA*

COLLEGE	WINNING YEARS (FIRST/LAST)	WINS
1 Cornell	1896–1982	24
2 =California	1928–2001	13
=Navy	1921–84	13
4 Washington	1923–97	11
5 Pennsylvania	1898–1989	9
6 =Brown	1979–95	7
=Wisconsin	1951–90	7
8 Syracuse	1904–78	6
9 Columbia	1895–1929	4
10 Princeton	1985–98	3

* *Men's varsity 8-oared shells event*

The Intercollegiate Rowing Association Regatta has been held since 1895, after Harvard and Yale left the Rowing Association to establish their own annual race. The regatta highlight, the varsity eights event, first took place in Poughkeepsie, New York, but since 1995 has been contested in Camden, New Jersey.

TOP 10 OLYMPIC YACHTING COUNTRIES

COUNTRY	GOLD	SILVER	BRONZE	TOTAL
1 US	17	21	17	55
2 Great Britain	17	14	9	40
3 Sweden	9	12	10	31
4 Norway	16	11	3	30
5 France	12	6	9	27
6 Denmark	11	8	4	23
7 =Australia	5	3	8	16
=Netherlands	4	6	6	16
9 New Zealand	6	4	5	15
10 Spain	9	3	1	13

The header "MEDALS" spans GOLD, SILVER, BRONZE, TOTAL.

Paul Elvström of Denmark became the first person to win gold medals at 4 consecutive Games (1948–60), and went on to compete in a further 4 Games in 1968, 1972, 1984, and 1988. During the last 2 Games, he was partnered by his daughter Trine in the Tornado class.

TOP 10 OLYMPIC SWIMMING COUNTRIES

COUNTRY	GOLD	SILVER	BRONZE	TOTAL
1 US	192	138	104	434
2 Australia	45	46	51	142
3 East Germany	38	32	22	92
4 Soviet Union#	18	24	27	69
5 Germany†	12	23	30	65
6 Great Britain	14	22	26	62
7 Hungary	24	20	16	60
8 Japan	15	20	14	49
9 Netherlands	14	14	16	44
10 Canada	7	13	19	39

The header "MEDALS*" spans GOLD, SILVER, BRONZE, TOTAL.

* *Excluding diving, water polo, and synchronized swimming*

\# *Includes Unified Team of 1992; excludes Russia since then*

† *Not including West/East Germany from 1968 88*

TOP 10 MEN'S 100M FREESTYLE TIMES IN THE SUMMER OLYMPICS

SWIMMER/COUNTRY	YEAR	TIME (SECONDS)
1 Pieter van den Hoogenband, Netherlands	2000	47.84
2 Pieter van den Hoogenband	2000	48.30
3 Matt Biondi, US	1988	48.63
4 Pieter van den Hoogenband	2000	48.64
5 Alexander Popov, Russia	2000	48.69
6 Gary Hall Jr., US	2000	48.73
7 =Alexander Popov	1996	48.74
=Michael Klim, US	2000	48.74
9 Michael Klim	2000	48.80
10 Gary Hall Jr., US	1996	48.81

TOP 10 OLYMPIC WATER POLO COUNTRIES

	COUNTRY	GOLD	MEDALS SILVER	BRONZE	TOTAL
1	Hungary	7	3	3	13
2	US	1	5	3	9
3	=Soviet Union*	2	2	4	8
	=Yugoslavia	3	4	1	8
5	=Belgium	-	4	2	6
	=Italy	3	1	2	6
7	=France	1	-	3	4
	=Great Britain	4	-	-	4
9	=Germany#	1	2	-	3
	=Sweden	-	1	2	3

* Includes Unified Team of 1992; excludes Russia
   since then

\# Excluding West/East Germany 1968–88

TOP 10 OLYMPIC ROWING COUNTRIES

	COUNTRY	GOLD	MEDALS SILVER	BRONZE	TOTAL
1	US	29	29	21	79
2	=East Germany	33	7	8	48
	=Germany*	21	13	14	48
4	Great Britain	21	16	7	44
5	Soviet Union#	12	20	11	43
6	Italy	14	13	10	37
7	=Canada	8	12	13	33
	=France	6	14	13	33
9	Romania	15	10	7	32
10	Australia	7	8	10	25

* Not including West/East Germany 1968–88

\# Includes Unified Team of 1992; excludes Russia
   since then

TOP 10 MONEY-WINNING SURFERS*

	SURFER/COUNTRY	CAREER EARNINGS ($)
1	Sunny Garcia, US	861,580
2	Kelly Slater, US	827,055
3	Mark Occhilupo, Australia	682,263
4	Rob Machado, US	539,947
5	Fabio Gouveia, Brazil	525,353
6	Luke Egan, Australia	517,295
7	Shane Powell, Australia	466,157
8	Flavio Padaratz, Brazil	425,875
9	Peterson Rosa, Brazil	418,372
10	Shane Beschen, US	417,525

* As of February 2002

Source: Association of Surfing Professionals

Surf's Up
Australian champion Mark Occhilupo
(born 1966), previously ranked the world
no. 1 surfer, is the highest non-American
money winner in the sport.

Combat Sports

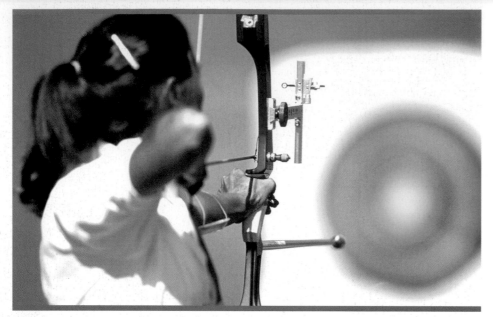

Going for Gold

Introduced as an Olympic event in 1904, archery has its roots in ancient combat. It became only the second sport, after tennis, in which women competed at the Olympic Games.

TOP 10 OLYMPIC FREESTYLE WRESTLING COUNTRIES

	COUNTRY	MEDALS			
		GOLD	SILVER	BRONZE	TOTAL
1	US	44	35	24	103
2	Soviet Union*	31	17	15	63
3	=Bulgaria	7	17	9	33
	=Japan	16	9	8	33
	=Turkey	16	11	6	33
6	=Iran	5	9	12	26
	=Sweden	8	10	8	26
8	Finland	8	7	10	25
9	Korea	4	7	8	19
10	Great Britain	3	4	10	17

* *Includes United Team of 1992; excludes Russia since then*

Great Britain's 3 gold medals in the freestyle event all date from the 1908 Games.

TOP 10 OLYMPIC ARCHERY COUNTRIES

	COUNTRY	MEDALS			
		GOLD	SILVER	BRONZE	TOTAL
1	US	13	8	8	29
2	France	7	9	6	22
3	South Korea	11	6	4	21
4	Belgium	9	6	3	18
5	Soviet Union	1	3	5	9
6	Great Britain	2	2	4	8
7	=Finland	1	1	2	4
	=Italy	0	1	3	4
9	China	0	3	0	3
10	=Germany	0	1	1	2
	=Japan	0	1	1	2
	=Netherlands	1	0	1	2
	=Poland	0	1	1	2
	=Sweden	0	2	0	2
	=Ukraine	0	1	1	2

Archery was introduced as an Olympic sport at the second modern Olympics, held in Paris in 1900. Target shooting replaced shooting live birds.

TOP 10 OLYMPIC JUDO COUNTRIES

	COUNTRY	MEDALS			
		GOLD	SILVER	BRONZE	TOTAL
1	Japan	23	12	13	48
2	France	10	5	17	32
3	Korea	7	10	13	30
4	Soviet Union*	7	5	15	27
5	Cuba	5	7	8	20
6	Great Britain	–	7	9	16
7	Netherlands	4	–	7	11
8	=Brazil	2	3	5	10
	=China	4	1	5	10
	=Germany#	1	1	8	10
	=Italy	2	3	5	10

* *Includes Unified Team of 1992; excludes Russia since then*

Not including West/East Germany from 1968–88

Judo made its debut at the 1964 Tokyo Olympics, but for men only. Women's judo was not introduced until the 1992 Barcelona Games. Judo was not included in the 1968 Mexico City Games.

TOP 10 OLYMPIC FENCING COUNTRIES

	COUNTRY	MEDALS			
		GOLD	SILVER	BRONZE	TOTAL
1	France	39	38	33	110
2	Italy	40	36	26	102
3	Hungary	33	20	26	79
4	Soviet Union*	19	17	18	54
5	Germany#	6	8	9	23
6	Poland	4	8	8	20
7	US	2	6	11	19
8	West Germany	7	8	1	16
9	Belgium	5	3	5	13
10	Romania	3	3	6	12

* *Includes Unified Team of 1992; excludes Russia since then*

Not including West Germany or East Germany 1968–88

Fencing was introduced at the first modern Olympics in 1896. Hungarian competitor Aladár Gerevich (1910–91) achieved the unique feat of winning 7 gold medals at 6 consecutive Games, spanning the 28 years from 1932 to 1960.

LATEST UNDISPUTED WORLD HEAVYWEIGHT CHAMPIONS

YEAR	BOXER/COUNTRY*
2001	Hasim Rahman
1999	Lennox Lewis (UK)
1992	Riddick Bowe
1990	Evander Holyfield
1990	James Buster Douglas
1987	Mike Tyson
1978	Leon Spinks
1974	Muhammed Ali
1973	George Foreman
1970	Joe Frazier

All US unless otherwise stated

"Undisputed" champions are those recognized by the World Boxing Council (WBC), World Boxing Association (WBA), International Boxing Federation (IBF), and World Boxing Organization (WBO).

HEAVIEST WORLD BOXING CHAMPIONS

	BOXER/COUNTRY*	YEAR	WEIGHT (LB)	WEIGHT (KG)
1	Primo Carnera (Italy)	1934	270	122.5
2	Lennox Lewis (UK)	1999	251	113.8
3	=George Foreman	1994	250	113.3
	=Hasim Rahman	2000	250	113.3
5	Frank Bruno (UK)	1995	247	112.0
6	=Riddick Bowe	1993	246	111.5
	=James Douglas	1990	246	111.5
8	=Greg Page	1985	240	108.6
	=John Tate	1979	240	108.6
10	Tony Tubbs	1986	238	107.9

All US unless otherwise stated

Weighing In

British boxer Lennox Lewis is the heaviest heavyweight champion since Primo Carnera in 1934. At the time of his defense of his title against Michael Grant in 2000, their combined weight of 497 lb (225.4 kg) was the heaviest of all time.

Horsing Around

MONEY-WINNING NORTH AMERICAN JOCKEYS

	JOCKEY	EARNINGS ($)
1	Chris McCarron	260,239,073
2	Pat Day	256,418,663
3	Laffit Pincay Jr.	226,071,563
4	Jerry Bailey	218,820,137
5	Gary Stevens	202,224,804
6	Eddie Delahoussaye	190,427,188
7	Angel Corder Jr.	164,561,227
8	Kent Desormeaux	148,784,542
9	Jose Santos	143,494,382
10	Alexis Solis	143,394,762

Source: *NTRA Communications*

Horse Racing
It is estimated that there are 725,000 racehorses in the US. This business and the equestrian industry (including rodeo, recreation, and working horses) supports some 340,000 jobs.

DRIVERS WITH THE MOST WINS

	DRIVER	WINS
1	Herve Filion	14,783
2	Walter Case Jr.	10,124
3	Cat Manzi	9,236
4	Mike Lachance	9,043
5	Dave Magee	8,940
6	John Campbell	8,824
7	Dave Palone	8,234
8	Jack Moiseyev	8,090
9	Eddie Davis	7,977
10	Bill Parker Jr.	7,698

Source: *US Trotting Association*

TOP 10 MONEY-WINNING HORSES

	HORSE	WINS	WINNINGS ($)
1	Cigar	19	9,999,815
2	Skip Away	18	9,616,360
3	Hokuto Vega	16	8,337,603
4	Silver Charm	12	6,944,369
5	Alysheba	11	6,679,242
6	John Henry	39	6,597,947
7	Tiznow	9	6,427,830
8	Stay Gold	5	5,990,209
9	Singspiel	9	5,950,217
10	Sakura Laurel	9	5,763,926

Source: *National Thoroughbred Racing Association (NTRA)*

List-leading horse *Cigar* achieved a total of 19 wins out of 33 starts – 2 in 1993 and 1994, 10 in 1995, and 5 in 1996 – to gain his all-time North American record money total. Bred and owned by Allen Paulson, he retired as a 6-year-old on October 31, 1996 at the end of a 16-race winning streak, tying a record set 46 years earlier by racing legend *Citation*. In 2002, he was elected to the Racing Hall of Fame.

TOP 10 WINNING TIMES OF THE KENTUCKY DERBY

	HORSE	YEAR	TIME (MINS:SECS)
1	Secretariat	1973	1:59.2
2	Monarchos	2001	1:59.4
3	Northern Dancer	1964	2:00.0
4	Spend A Buck	1985	2:00.2
5	Decidedly	1962	2:00.4
6	Proud Clarion	1967	2:00.6
7	Grindstone	1996	2:01.0
8	=Affirmed	1978	2:01.2
	=Fusaichi Pegasus	2000	2:01.2
	=Lucky Debonair	1965	2:01.2
	=Thunder Gulch	1995	2:01.2

Source: *The Jockey Club*

The Kentucky Derby is held on the first Saturday in May at Churchill Downs, Louisville, Kentucky. The first leg of the Triple Crown, it was first raced in 1875, over a distance of 1 mile 4 furlongs, but after 1896 was reduced to 1 mile 2 furlongs. It is said that the hat (known in England as a "bowler"), manufactured in the US by James H. Knapp of South Norwalk, Connecticut, became popular attire at the first Kentucky Derby, thereby acquiring the name "derby."

TOP 10 ALL-AROUND CHAMPION COWBOYS

	COWBOY	YEARS	WINS
1	Ty Murray	1989–98	7
2	=Tom Ferguson	1974–79	6
	=Larry Mahan	1966–73	6
4	Jim Shoulders	1949–59	5
5	=Joe A. Beaver	1995–2000	3
	=Lewis Feild	1985–87	3
	=Dean Oliver	1963–65	3
8	=Everett Bowman	1935–37	2
	=Louis Brooks	1943–44	2
	=Clay Carr	1930–33	2
	=Bill Linderman	1950–53	2
	=Phil Lyne	1971–72	2
	=Gerald Roberts	1942–48	2
	=Casey Tibbs	1951–55	2
	=Harry Tompkins	1952–60	2

The Professional Rodeo Cowboys Association's greatest accolade goes to the PRCA cowboy who wins the most prize money in a year, competing in at least 2 events, and earning at least $3,000 in each.

TOP 10 OLYMPIC EQUESTRIAN COUNTRIES

	COUNTRY	GOLD	SILVER	MEDALS BRONZE	TOTAL
1	Germany*	22	13	12	47
2	US	9	17	15	41
3	Sweden	17	8	14	39
4	France	11	12	11	34
5	West Germany	11	5	9	25
6	Italy	6	10	7	23
7	Great Britain	5	8	9	22
8	Switzerland	4	10	7	21
9	Netherlands	8	9	2	19
10	Soviet Union#	6	5	4	15

* *Not including West Germany or East Germany 1968–88*

\# *Includes United Team of 1992; excludes Russia since then*

These figures include the medal totals for both individual and team disciplines: Show Jumping, Three-Day Event, and Dressage.

TOP 10 JOCKEYS IN THE US TRIPLE CROWN RACES

	JOCKEY	KENTUCKY	PREAKNESS	BELMONT	TOTAL
1	Eddie Arcaro	5	6	6	17
2	Bill Shoemaker	4	2	5	11
3	=Pat Day	1	5	3	9
	=Bill Hartack	5	3	1	9
	=Earle Sande	3	1	5	9
6	=Jimmy McLaughlin	1	1	6	8
	=Gary Stevens	3	2	3	8
8	=Angel Cordero Jr.	3	2	1	6
	=Chas Kurtsinger	2	2	2	6
	=Ron Turcotte	2	2	2	6

The US Triple Crown consists of the Kentucky Derby, Preakness Stakes (held at Pimlico, Maryland, since 1873), and Belmont Stakes (at Belmont, New York, since 1867). The only jockey to complete the Triple Crown twice is Eddie Arcaro on *Whirlaway* in 1941 and on *Citation* in 1948.

On Two Wheels

 ## CROSS-COUNTRY RIDERS IN THE UCI* MOUNTAIN BIKE WORLD CUP, 2001 (WOMEN)

	RIDER/COUNTRY	POINTS#
1	Barbara Blatter, Switzerland	1,485
2	Caroline Alexander, UK	1,015
3	Marga Fullana, Spain	950
4	Annabella Stropparo, Italy	893
5	=Alison Dunlap, US	890
	=Sabine Spitz, Germany	890
7	Chrissy Redden, Canada	788
8	Alison Sydor, Canada	660
9	Mary Grigson, Australia	545
10	Laurence Leboucher, France	475

* Union Cycliste Internationale

Total points scored over a series of 8 competitions

 ## CROSS-COUNTRY RIDERS IN THE UCI* MOUNTAIN BIKE WORLD CUP, 2001 (MEN)

	RIDER/COUNTRY	POINTS#
1	Roland Green, Canada	1,101
2	Jose Antonio Hermida, Spain	1,065
3	Miguel Martinez, France	987
4	Cadel Evans, Australia	811
5	Christophe Sauser, Switzerland	793
6	Julien Absalon, France	759
7	Bart Brenjens, Netherlands	705
8	Kashi Leuchs, New Zealand	693
9	Roel Paulissen, Belgium	680
10	Bas Van Dooren, Netherlands	655

* Union Cycliste Internationale

Total points scored over a series of 8 competitions

 ## COUNTRIES WITH THE MOST TOUR DE FRANCE WINNERS

	COUNTRY	WINNERS
1	France	36
2	Belgium	18
3	Italy	9
4	Spain	8
5	US	6
6	Luxembourg	4
7	=Netherlands	2
	=Switzerland	2
9	=Denmark	1
	=Germany	1
	=Ireland	1

Although French riders won every year from 1903–08, Belgians achieved the most consecutive wins – 7 from 1912 to 1922 (the race was not held in 1915–18).

 ## WINNING SPEEDS OF THE DAYTONA 200

	RIDER*/COUNTRY/BIKE	YEAR	AVERAGE SPEED (MPH)	(KM/H)
1	Matt Mladin, Australia, Suzuki	2000	113.63	182.87
2	Miguel Duhamel, Canada, Honda	1999	113.47	182.61
3	Kenny Roberts, Yamaha	1984	113.14	182.08
4	Scott Russell, Yamaha	1998	111.78	179.89
5	Kenny Roberts, Yamaha	1983	110.93	178.52
6	Scott Russell, Kawasaki	1992	110.67	178.11
7	Graeme Crosby, New Zealand, Yamaha	1982	109.10	175.58
8	Steve Baker, Yamaha	1977	108.85	175.18
9	Miguel Duhamel, Canada, Honda	1996	108.82	175.13
10	Johnny Cecotto, Venezuela, Yamaha	1976	108.77	175.05

* From the US unless otherwise stated

Source: American Motorcyclist Association

The Daytona 200, which was first held in 1937, forms a round in the AMA (American Motorcyclist Association) Grand National Dirt Track series. It is raced over 57 laps of the 3.56-mile (5.73-km) Daytona International Speedway. In addition to those riders named above, the only other non-US winners have been: Billy Matthews (Canada) 1941, 1950; Jaarno Saarinen (Finland) 1973; Giacomo Agostini (Italy) 1974; and Patrick Pons (France) 1980.

 ## MOTORCYCLE WORLD CHAMPIONSHIP RIDERS

	RIDER/COUNTRY	CLASSES (CC)	WINS
1	Giacomo Agostini, Italy	350, 500	15
2	Angel Nieto, Spain	50, 125	13
3	=Mike Hailwood, GB	250, 350, 500	9
	=Carlo Ubbiali, Italy	125, 250	9
5	=Phil Read, GB	125, 250, 500	7
	=John Surtees, GB	350, 500	7
7	=Geoff Duke, GB	350, 500	6
	=Jim Redman, Rhodesia	250, 350	6
9	=Mick Doohan, Australia	500	5
	=Anton Mang, Germany	250, 350	5

The motorcycle World Championship had its inaugural season in 1949, when it was won by British rider Leslie Graham on an AJS. British riders Geoff Duke and John Surtees dominated the event during the 1950s and Mike Hailwood in the 1960s, when Italian bikes won every championship. In the 1980s, the title was won on 6 occasions by 2 American riders, Freddie Spencer and Eddie Lawson. Australia's Mick Doohan dominated the 1990s, riding a Honda.

TOP 10 OLYMPIC CYCLING COUNTRIES

COUNTRY	GOLD	MEDALS SILVER	BRONZE	TOTAL
1 France	37	21	23	81
2 Italy	34	15	7	56
3 Great Britain	10	22	18	50
4 US	12	14	17	43
5 Germany*	11	13	12	36
6 Netherlands	13	15	7	35
7 Australia	7	13	11	31
8 =Belgium	6	8	10	24
=Soviet Union#	11	4	9	24
10 Denmark	6	7	8	21

* Not including West Germany or East Germany 1968–88

 # Includes United Team of 1992; excludes Russia since then

TOP 10 MOTOCROSS COUNTRIES

COUNTRY	WORLD CHAMPIONSHIP WINS 125CC	250CC	500CC	TOTAL
1 Belgium	9	13	21	43
2 Sweden	0	6	8	14
3 =Great Britain	0	1	6	7
=Italy	5	1	1	7
=US	3	3	1	7
6 France	2	4	0	6
7 Finland	1	1	3	5
8 =Netherlands	3	1	0	4
=Russia	0	4	0	4
=South Africa	2	2	0	4

World Motocross Championships have been held since 1947. The first individual championship was in 1957, when the 500cc class was launched, and since then 250cc (1962), 125cc (1975), and sidecar (1980) have been introduced.

French Gold

Having won gold at the 1996 Olympics, record-breaking French cyclist Felicia Ballanger gained a further two golds at the 2000 Sydney Games.

Auto Racing

CART MONEY-WINNERS

	DRIVER	TOTAL PRIZES* ($)
1	Al Unser Jr.	18,828,406
2	Michael Andretti	17,409,368
3	Bobby Rahal	16,344,008
4	Emerson Fittipaldi	14,293,625
5	Mario Andretti	11,552,154
6	Rick Mears	11,050,807
7	Jimmy Vasser	10,124,994
8	Danny Sullivan	8,884,126
9	Paul Tracy	8,331,520
10	Arie Luyendyk	7,732,188

* As of January 1, 2002

Source: *Championship Auto Racing Teams*

CART Success
Michael Andretti, one of the most successful CART riders of all time, races toward the finish at the Milwaukee Mile in 1999.

CART DRIVERS WITH THE MOST RACE WINS

	DRIVER	YEARS	WINS
1	A. J. Foyt Jr.	1960–81	67
2	Mario Andretti	1965–93	52
3	Michael Andretti	1986–2001	41
4	Al Unser	1965–87	39
5	Bobby Unser	1966–81	35
6	Al Unser Jr.	1984–95	31
7	Rick Mears	1978–91	29
8	Johnny Rutherford	1965–86	27
9	Rodger Ward	1953–66	26
10	Gordon Johncock	1965–83	25

Source: *Championship Auto Racing Teams*

Two generations of the Unser family dominate the CART scene: Al and Bobby, both of whom figure in this list, are brothers, while Al's son, Al Jr., also makes a showing here, and as the all-time money winner. In 1998, after pursuing other auto sports, Bobby's son Robby also entered Indy car racing. Michael Andretti, who started his CART career in 1983, is the only current driver in this list. Youngest-ever champion and 2000 Indianapolis 500 winner Juan Montoya also seemed destined for inclusion, but recently transferred to Formula One.

FASTEST GRAND PRIX RACES, 2001

	GRAND PRIX	CIRCUIT	WINNER'S SPEED (MPH)	(KM/H)
1	Italy	Monza	148.571	239.103
2	Germany	Hockenheim	146.240	235.351
3	Belgium	Spa-Francorchamps	137.354	221.050
4	Great Britain	Silverstone	134.359	216.231
5	Japan	Suzuka	132.143	212.665
6	Austria	A1-Ring	130.473	209.977
7	Europe	Nurburgring, Germany	126.848	204.143
8	Spain	Catalunya	125.832	202.508
9	San Marino	Enzo e Dino Ferrari	125.555	202.062
10	US-Indianapolis	Indianapolis	123.055	198.039

Grand Prix racing is European in origin. Since the late 19th century, car races took place on public roads, which is reflected in the construction of today's circuits, which incorporate chicanes and bends that test drivers' skill to the limit. Formula One began after World War II, when a distinction was made between these and less powerful Formula Two cars. Built in 1922, the Monza circuit has always been one of the world's fastest: as early as 1929 it became the first on which drivers broke the 124 mph (200 km/h) barrier.

TOP 10 FASTEST WINNING SPEEDS OF THE INDIANAPOLIS 500

DRIVER	CAR	YEAR	SPEED (MPH)	(KM/H)
1 Arie Luyendyk, Netherlands	Lola-Chevrolet	1990	185.981	299.307
2 Rick Mears, US	Chevrolet-Lumina	1991	176.457	283.980
3 Bobby Rahal, US	March-Cosworth	1986	170.722	274.750
4 Juan Pablo Montoya, Colombia	G Force-Aurora	2000	167.607	269.730
5 Emerson Fittipaldi, Brazil	Penske-Chevrolet	1989	167.581	269.695
6 Rick Mears, US	March-Cosworth	1984	163.612	263.308
7 Mark Donohue, US	McLaren-Offenhauser	1972	162.962	262.619
8 Al Unser, US	March-Cosworth	1987	162.175	260.995
9 Tom Sneva, US	March-Cosworth	1983	162.117	260.902
10 Gordon Johncock, US	Wildcat-Cosworth	1982	162.029	260.760

Car racing in the US on purpose-built circuits dates back to 1909, when Indianapolis Speedway opened and from which year Indy Car racing can be dated. CART (Championship Auto Racing Teams, Inc.) was formed in 1978, and in 1996 the Indy Racing League was established due to disputes over regulations of the Indy 500. Indy 500 races have counted for CART points in 1979, 1980, and 1983–1995. The most fundamental difference between cars used in these races and Formula One cars is that Formula One cars begin from a standing start and race on complex road tracks, with straights and turns, whereas Indy drivers start on the run and race around oval circuits. This produces higher average lap speeds.

TOP 10 FORMULA ONE DRIVERS WITH THE MOST GRAND PRIX WINS

DRIVER/COUNTRY	CAREER	WINS*
1 Michael Schumacher, Germany	1991–	53
2 Alain Prost, France	1980–93	51
3 Ayrton Senna, Brazil	1984–94	41
4 Nigel Mansell, UK	1980–95	31
5 Jackie Stewart, UK	1965–73	27
6 =Jim Clark, UK	1960–68	25
=Niki Lauda, Austria	1971–85	25
8 Juan Manuel Fangio, Argentina	1950–58	24
9 Nelson Piquet, Brazil	1978–91	23
10 Damon Hill, UK	1992–99	22

As of January 2002

The first Formula One race was held at Silverstone, England, on May 13, 1950. In this inaugural year the Championship consisted of only 7 Grands Prix, 6 European plus Indianapolis in the US. The total number of races steadily increased, peaking in 1977 at 17. It was then limited to 16, but a maximum of 17 events was reintroduced in 1996. The 2002 season comprises 17 races, from the Australian Grand Prix on March 3 to the Japanese on October 13, the completion of which raises the total number of Grands Prix races in the sport's 52-year history to 697.

"The Maestro"
The king of the race track during the 1950s, Juan Manuel Fangio (1911–95) won 21 Grand Prix races and secured a record five World titles.

Leisure Pursuits

 ## COUNTRIES SPENDING THE MOST ON CONSOLE AND COMPUTER GAMES

COUNTRY	SALES IN 2000 ($) TOTAL	PER CAPITA
1 Canada	1,732,000,000	56.1
2 US	14,348,000,000	52.1
3 UK	2,648,000,000	44.6
4 Japan	4,155,000,000	32.7
5 Germany	2,648,000,000	21.1
6 South Korea	1,724,000,000	20.9
7 Italy	990,000,000	16.5
8 Sweden	113,000,000	12.7
9 Australia	219,000,000	11.4
10 France	639,000,000	9.7

Source: *Euromonitor*

On a per capita basis, Canada, the US, and the UK have eclipsed video former No. 1 Japan where consumers have increasingly transferred their leisure expenditure to cellular phones, internet subscriptions, and DVDs. In 2000, the US accounted for $14.3 billion out of a total global value of game sales amounting to $48.2 billion.

BOARD GAMES IN THE US, 2001

	GAME*	MANUFACTURER
1	Cranium	Cranium
2	Scrabble (standard)	Hasbro Games
3	Monopoly	Hasbro Games
4	Twister	Hasbro Games
5	Connect Four	Hasbro Games
6	The Game of Life	Hasbro Games
7	Trouble	Hasbro Games
8	Operation	Hasbro Games
9	Guess Who	Hasbro Games
10	Sorry	Hasbro Games

* *Including children's, family, and adult board games*

Source: *NPD TRSTS Standard Service*

Making a Splash
Swimming as a leisure pursuit dates back little more than a century, but it figures prominently among the most popular as a pleasurable route to all-around fitness.

FAVORITE SPORTS ON TV (WOMEN)

SPORT	PERCENTAGE OF WOMEN WITH A PREFERENCE
1 Soccer	13
2 =Baseball	8
=Basketball	8
=Figure skating	8
5 Football	6
6 =Gymnastics	5
=Tennis	5
8 Track and Field	4
9 =Swimming	3
=Volleyball	3

Source: *Ipsos-Reid/Screen Digest*

This list, and the male equivalent, is based on a global survey carried out by the North American market research firm Ipsos-Reid.

FAVORITE SPORTS ON TV (MEN)

SPORT	PERCENTAGE OF MEN WITH A PREFERENCE
1 Soccer	32
2 =Football	9
=Baseball	9
4 Basketball	8
5 Car racing	5
6 Boxing	4
7 =Track and Field	2
=Golf	2
=Tennis	2
10 =Figure skating	1
=Gymnastics	1
=Volleyball	1

Source: *Ipsos-Reid/Screen Digest*

COLLEGE SPORTS IN THE US*

SPORT	PARTICIPANTS IN 1999–2000 WOMEN	MEN	TOTAL
1 Football	–	57,593	57,593
2 Outdoor track	17,788	20,123	37,911
3 Soccer	18,188	18,221	36,409
4 Indoor track	15,701	17,028	32,729
5 Basketball	14,445	15,874	30,319
6 Baseball	-	25,938	25,938
7 Cross-country	11,725	10,786	22,511
8 Swimming/diving	10,033	7,435	17,468
9 Tennis	8,314	7,549	15,863
10 Softball	15,157	-	15,157

* *Based on participation in National Collegiate Athletic Association (NCAA) sports*

Source: *NCAA*

TOP10 INCREASINGLY POPULAR PARTICIPATION ACTIVITIES IN THE US

	ACTIVITY	NUMBER PARTICIPATING* IN 2000	PERCENTAGE INCREASE FROM 1995–2000
1	Skateboarding	9,100,000	101.3
2	Snowshoeing	1,000,000	69.0
3	Snowboarding	4,300,000	55.3
4	Backpacking/wilderness camping	15,200,000	50.5
5	Calisthenics	13,500,000	48.9
6	Mountain biking (on road)	14,300,000	36.2
7	Aerobic exercising	27,200,000	23.9
8	Exercise walking	81,300,000	22.7
9	Martial arts	5,400,000	20.8
10	Camping	49,900,000	16.5

* People of 7 years of age and older, who participated more than once during the year

Source: National Sporting Goods Association

TOP10 PARTICIPATION ACTIVITIES IN THE US

	ACTIVITY	PERCENTAGE CHANGE SINCE PREVIOUS YEAR	NUMBER PARTICIPATING* IN 2000
1	Exercise walking	+0.6	81,300,000
2	Swimming	+2.3	59,300,000
3	Camping	-2.3	49,900,000
4	Fishing	+4.5	48,800,000
5	Exercising with equipment	-4.4	43,200,000
6	Bicycle riding	+0.3	42,500,000
7	Bowling	+1.6	42,300,000
8	Billiards/pool	+0.1	32,200,000
9	=Aerobic exercising	+3.5	27,200,000
	=Basketball	-8.1	27,200,000

* People of 7 years of age and older, who participated more than once during the year

Source: National Sporting Goods Association

Index

Index

Index

Acknowledgments

Special US research: Dafydd Rees

Caroline Ash; Richard Braddish; Thomas Brinkoff; Pete Compton; Luke Crampton; Sidney S. Culbert; François Curiel; Alain P. Dornic; Philip Eden; Bonnie Fantasia; Christopher Forbes; Cullen Geiselman; Russell E. Gough; Monica Grady; Stan Greenberg; Duncan Hislop; Andreas Hörstemeier; Alan Jeffreys; Tessa Kale; Larry Kilman; Robert Lamb; Jo LaVerde; John Malam; Dr. Gregg Marland; Chris Mead; Ian Morrison; Roberto Ortiz de Zarate; Robert Palfry; Tony Pattison; Christiaan Rees; Linda Rees; Adrian Room; Bill Rudman; Robert Senior; Lisa E. Smith; Eric Syddique; Mitchell Symons; Thomas Tranter; Alexis Tregenza; Lucy T. Verma; Tony Waltham.

Absolut Elephant; Academy of Motion Picture Arts and Sciences; *Ad Age Global;* adherents.com; AdRelevance; *Advertising Age; Airline Business;* Air Transport Intelligence; American Association of Botanical Gardens and Arboreta; American Association of Port Authorities; American Film Institute (AFI); American Forests; *American Jewish Yearbook*; American Library Association; American Motorcyclist Association; American Museum of Natural History; American Pet Products Manufacturers Association; American Theatre Wing (Tony Awards); *Amusement Business;* Arbitron Inc; *The Art Newspaper;* Art Sales Index; Associated Press; Association for Library Service to Children (John Newbery Medal), Association of Surfing Professionals; Association of Tennis Professionals (ATP); Audit Bureau of Circulations; Bat Conservation International, *Billboard*; Bonham Group; Booker Prize; *BP Statistical Review of World Energy 2001;* British Antarctic Survey; British Cave Research Association (BCRA); Bureau of Labor Statistics; Cameron Mackintosh Ltd; Canada Geological Survey; Continental Geoscience Division; Cannes Film Festival; Carbon Dioxide Information Analysis Center; Center for Disease Control (CDC); Central Intelligence Agency (CIA); Centre for Environmental Initiatives, UK; Championship Auto Racing Teams (CART); Channel Swimming Association; Christian Research, UK; Christie's; *Classical Music*; *The Columbia Granger's Index to Poetry in Anthologies*; Columbia University (Pulitzer Prizes); Competitive Media Reporting; Computer Industry Almanac, Inc.; Crain Communications, Inc; Death Penalty Information Center; De Beers; Directors' Guild of America (DGA); Drama Desk; Duncan's American Radio; eCountries; Electoral Reform Society; EM-DAT, CRED, University of Louvain, Belgium; Energy Information Administration; Environmental Technology Center; Euromonitor; *FBI Uniform Crime Reports;* The Financial Times Ltd;

Fleetwood-Owen; *Flight International*; Florida Museum of Natural History; Food and Agriculture Organization of the United Nations (FAO); *Forbes*; Formula One Results and Information eXplorer (FORIX); *Fortune;* Global Reach; Golden Raspberry Award Foundation; Gold Fields Mineral Services Ltd; Hockey Database; Hollywood Foreign Press Association (Golden Globe Awards); Home Office, UK; Iditarod Trail Committee; Indianapolis Motor Speedway; Information Resources, Inc; InsideHoops.com; Interbrand; Intercollegiate Rowing Association; International Agency for Research on Cancer; International Association of Athletics Federations (IAAF); International Atomic Energy Agency; International Badminton Federation; International Cycling Union (UCI); International Federation of Red Cross and Red Cross Societies; International Game Fish Association (IGFA); International Labor Organization (ILO); International Olympic Committee (IOC); International Organization of Motor Vehicle Manufacturers (OICA); International Skating Union (ISU); International Ski Federation (FIS); International Snowboard Federation (ISF); International Table Tennis Federation (ITTF); International Tea Committee Ltd; International Telecommunication Union (ITU); International Union for the Conservation of Nature (IUCN); Internet Industry Almanac, Inc.; Ipsos-Reid; Jockey Club; Jupiter Media Metrix; League of American Theatres and Producers, Library of Congress; Lloyds Register-Fairplay Ltd; London Theatre Record; Lycos; Magazine Publishers of America; Major League Baseball, MediaForce, Metropolitan Museum of Art; *Mobile Beat; M Street;* MTV; Museum of Fine Arts, Boston; *Music & Media;* Music Information Database; Mystery Writers of America; National Academy of Popular Music; National Academy of Recording Arts and Sciences (NARAS); National Academy of Television Arts and Sciences (Emmy Awards); National Aeronautics and Space Administration (NASA); National Association for the Advancement of Colored People (NAACP) Legal Defense Fund; National Association of Broadcasters (NAB); National Association of Stock Car Auto Racing, Inc (NASCAR); National Basketball Association (NBA); National Book Critics Circle; National Book Foundation; National Center for Education Statistics; National Center for Health Statistics; National Center for Injury Prevention and Control; National Collegiate Athletic Association (NCAA); *National Directory of Magazines;* National Electronic Injury Surveillance System (NEISS); National Fire Incidence Reporting System (NFIRS); National Fire Protection Association (NFPA); National Football League (NFL); National Fraud Information Center,

National Consumers League; National Gallery, Washington, DC; National Hockey League (NHL); National Hockey League Players' Association; National Opinion Poll (NOP), UK; National Sporting Goods Association; National Steel Bridge Alliance; National Thoroughbred Racing Association (NTRA); Natural History Museum, UK; NetRatings Audience Measurement Service; New York Drama Critics Circle; New York Drama League; Niagara Falls Museum; Nielsen Media Research; NK Lawn & Garden Co; Nobel Foundation; *NonProfit Times;* North American Breeding Bird Survey; Peabody Awards; Phobics Society; The Poetry Poll; Poets, Playwrights, Editors, Essayists, and Novelists (PEN); Produktschap voor Gedistilleerde Dranken; Professional Golfers' Association (PGA); Professional Rodeo Cowboys Association (PRCA); Professional Squash Association; Public Library Association; *Publishers Weekly;* The Recording Academy; Recording Industry Association of America (RIAA); Russell Reynolds Associates; Ryder Cup; Scott Polar Research Institute; *Screen Digest;* Siemens AG; The Silver Institute; Sotheby's; Soundscan; Stanford Institute for the Quantatitive Study of Society; *Statistical Abstract of the United States*; *Stores;* Sundance Film Festival; Taylor Nelson Sofres; TeleGeography; Tour de France; Tourism Industries, International Trade Administration; Transparency International; United Nations (UN); United Nations Centre for Human Settlements (HABITAT); United Nations Children's Fund (UNICEF); United Nations Educational, Scientific and Cultural Organization (UNESCO); United Nations Environment Programme (UNEP); United Nations High Commission for Refugees (UNHCR); United Nations Population Division; United Nations System-wide Earthwatch; Universal Postal Union; US Census Bureau; US Committee for Refugees; US Consumer Product Safety Commission; US Department of Labor; US Department of the Interior; US Geological Survey; US Immigration and Naturalization Service; US National Park Service; US Patent and Trademark Office; *Variety;* Verifone; VideoScan; *Video Store;* Ward's AutoInfoBank; WebElements; Wedding Zone; Westminster Kennel Club; Wildseed Farms; Women's International Squash Players Association (WISPA); World Association of Girl Guides and Girl Scouts (WAGG); World Association of Newspapers (WAN); *World Atlas of Coral Reefs;* World Bank; *World Christian Encyclopedia;* World Conservation Monitoring Centre (WCMC); World Health Organization (WHO); World Intellectual Property Organization (WIPO); World Motocross Championships; World Organization of the Scout Movement; World Science Fiction Society (WSFS); World Tourism Organization (WTO).

Picture Credits

The publisher would like to thank the following for their kind permission to reproduce their photographs: (Abbreviations key: t=top, b=bottom, r=right, l=left, c=centre)

1: Getty Images/David Madison (b), Getty Images/Yang China Tourism Press.Liu (t); 2-3: Photodisc (b), Getty Images/Kauko Helavuo (t); 4: AP/Reed Saxon (b), Alistair Duncan (t); 5: AP/Alessandro Trovati (br); 6-7: Getty Images/Telegraph Colour Library, Corbis/Brandon D Cole (bc); 8-9: Getty Images/Kauko Helavuo; 13: AP/Terry Renna; 14: N.A.S.A; 15: Corbis; 16-17: Corbis/Brandon D Cole; 18-19: Corbis/Galen Rowell; 20: Corbis/David Muench; 21: Getty Images/Jon Arnold; 23: SPL/ArSciMed; 24: Corbis/Dean Conger; 25: Getty Images/Grant V Faint; 26: Dover Publications, Inc. New York; 27: AP/Greg Baker; 28-29: Getty Images/Peter & Stef Lamberti; 30: Corbis/Bettmann; 31: Corbis/FLPA;. 32: Bruce Coleman Ltd/Gordon Langsbury; 33: Corbis/Ecoscene; 35: Bruce Coleman Ltd; 36-37: Bruce Coleman Ltd/Rinie Van Meurs; 38: Corbis/Michael S. Yamashita; 39: Bruce Coleman Ltd/Jorg & Petra Wegner; 41: Corbis/Joe McDonald; 44-45: Corbis/Gunter Marx; 47: Photodisc; 48: Photodisc; 49: Photodisc; 50-51: Getty Images/Yang China Tourism Press.Liu; 53: Getty Images/Charles Nes; 55: Getty Images/Stuart Dee; 56: Corbis/Wolfgang Kaehler; 57: Corbis/Lindsay Hebberd; 58-59: Corbis/Robert van der Hilst, Corbis/Alison Wright (tr); 60-61: Hulton Archive; 62-63: Corbis/David Katzenstein; 64: Corbis/Bettmann; 65: Popperfoto/Reuters; 66: Corbis/Hulton-Deutsch Collection; 67: Corbis/Bettmann; 68: PA/EPA; 69: PA/EPA; 70: Corbis/Michael S. Yamashita; 72: MEPL; 73: Getty Images/Nicholas Veasey; 74-75: Corbis; 76-77: Hulton Archive/U.S. Army Archive Photos; 78: Corbis/Steve Kaufman; 79: Corbis/Galen Rowell; 80: Corbis/John Slater; 82-83: Photodisc; 85: Corbis/Kevin R. Morris; 86-87: Hutchison Library/Crispin Hughes; 88-89: Corbis/Baci; 93: Corbis/Richard Bickel; 95: Art Archive/Museum of Modern Art Mexico/Dagli Orti; 96: PA/EPA; 97: Corbis/Bettmann; 98-99: Getty Images/Andy Sacks; 100-101: Getty Images/Keren Su; 102: Hutchison Library/Wateraid/Liba Taylor; 103: Panos/Giacomo Pirozzi; 104-105: Getty Images/Bob Handelman; 109: PA/Matthew Fearn; 111: PA/Stefan Rousseau; 112: Hulton Archive; 113: Hulton Archive; 115 Getty Images/Derek P. Redfearn; 116: Bridgeman Art Library/Private Collection; 117: Camera Press/Karsh of Ottowa; 119: Bridgeman Art Library/Private Collection; 120-121: Alistair Duncan; 123: Sotheby's Picture Library, London; 125: Jerry Young; 126-127: Photodisc; 128: AP/Reed Saxon; 129: Redferns/Val Wilmer; 130: Redferns; 132: Corbis/Rufus F Folkks; 133: Rex Features; 134: Rex Features; 135: Redferns; 136: Redferns; 137: Rex Features; 138: Corbis/Lynn Goldsmith; 139: Redferns; 140-141: Redferns/Grant Davis; 142-143: Corbis/Norman Parkinson Limited/Fiona Cowan; 144: Redferns/Nicky J Sims; 145: PA; 147: Redferns/John Gumon; 149: Corbis/Vittoriano Rastelli; 150: Redferns/Sue Schneider; 151: Rex Features; 152-153: Kobal Collection/Universal, 1980; 154-155: Pictor International/Gari Wyn Williams; 156-157: Corbis/Gail Mooney; 158: Performing Arts Library; 159: Performing Arts Library; 160: Kobal Collection/Lucas Films Ltd/Paramount, 1981; 161: Corbis/Bettmann; 163: Ronald Grant Archive/Dreamworks LLC, 2001; 164: Ronald Grant Archive/Columbia, 1997; 165: Aquarius Library/New Line, 2001; 166: Kobal Collection/20th Century Fox, 1998; 167: Ronald Grant Archive/United Artists, 1978; 168: Michael Dudok de Wit/Cloudrunner

Ltd/CinéTé, 2000; 169: Ronald Grant Archive/Dreamworks LLC, 2000; 170-171: Kobal Collection/Dreamworks LLC/ Universal, 2001; 172: Ronald Grant Archive/Columbia, 2000; 173: Kobal Collection/20th Century Fox/Sue Adler, 2001; 174: Kobal Collection/United Artists, 1959; 175: Rex Features/Paramount, 1960; 176: Kobal Collection/ Universal/Ron Batzdorf, 2000; 177: Kobal Collection/MGM Universal/ De Laurentis/Phil Bray, 2001; 178: Kobal Collection/Dreamworks LLC/David James, 1998; 179: Kobal Collection/ Fat Free Ltd/ Miramax/ David Appleby, 2000; 180: Kobal Collection/MGM, 1959 (t); 180-181: Kobal Collection/USA Films/Mark Tillie; 182: Kobal Collection/Warner Bros/Robert Zuckerman, 2001; 183: Kobal Collection/ Lions Gate/Jeanne Louise Bulliard, 2001; 184: Kobal Collection/ Dreamworks LLC/Jinks/ Cohen/Lorey Sebastian, 1999; 185: AP/Lionel Cironneau; 187: Ronald Grant Archive/Alphaville/Mohotep Prod, 2001; 188: Kobal Collection/ Universal/Phillip Caruso, 2000; 189: Kobal Collection/Universal, Vivian Zink, 1999; 190-191: Magnus Rew; 193: PA/EPA; 194-195: Getty Images/Sergio Sade; 196-197 Corbis/ Roger Antrobus; 198: Corbis/ David Turnley; 199: Corbis/Nazima Kowall; 200: Getty Images/Bruce Hands; 202-203: Corbis/David Samuel Robbins; 205: PA/EPA; 206: Corbis/Ted Spiegel; 207 Corbis/Nik Wheeler; 208: Corbis/Mark E. Gibson; 209: Corbis/Francesc Muntada; 210: Corbis/Charles O'Rear; 212-213: Getty Images/Shahn Rowe; 214: Corbis/Liu Liqun; 216-217: Getty Images/Richard H Johnston; 218: Panos/Mark McEvoy; 219: Photodisc; 220: Hutchison Library/Nigel Smith; 224-225: Getty Images/VCL; 226-227: Corbis/Roger Ressmeyer; 227: Getty Images/ VCL (tr); 229: Getty Images/VCL(tr); 230-231: QA Photos Ltd; 231: Getty Images/VCL(tr); 232: Getty Images/Jim Corwin; 233: Getty Images/VCL(tr); Getty Images/Samuel Ashfield (br); 235: Getty Images/VCL(tr); 236-237: Alamy.com/Charlie Newham; 237: Getty Images/VCL(tr); 239: AP/Itsuo Inouye; 239: Getty Images/ VCL(tr); 240-241: Getty Images/David Madison; 242-243: Corbis/Duomo; 243: Empics Ltd/Tony Marshall; 244: Empics Ltd/Tony Marshall; 245: Empics Ltd/Tony Marshall; 246: AP/Alessandro Trovati; 247: Empics Ltd/Tony Marshall; 249: Empics Ltd/Andy Heading; 250: PA/Toby Melville; 251: Empics Ltd/Neal Simpson; 252: Corbis/Bettmann; 253: AP/Wade Payne; 255: Empics Ltd/Aubrey Washington; 260-261: Allsport; 265: Empics Ltd/Tony Marshall; 266: Empics Ltd/Jon Buckle; 267: Empics Ltd/Ross Kinnaird; 268: Empics Ltd/Tony Marshall; 269: Popperfoto/Reuters; 270: Getty Images/David Madison; 271: Empics Ltd/Nick Potts; 272: Getty Images/ David Noton; 275: Empics Ltd/Jon Buckle; 276: Empics Ltd/John Marsh; 277: Empics Ltd/Steve Etherington; 279: Photodisc.

All other images © Dorling Kindersley.
For further information see: www.dkimages.com

Publisher's acknowledgments
Dorling Kindersley would like to thank the following for their contributions: Picture Librarian Hayley Smith, Jacket Editor Caroline Reed, Jacket Designer Dean Price.

Index
Patricia Coward

Packager's acknowledgments
Cooling Brown would like to thank Fiona Wild for editorial assistance, Tish Mills and Corinne Manches for their design work, and Peter Cooling for technical support.